Esther in America
The Scroll's Interpretation in and Impact on the United States

Yeshiva University
**THE ZAHAVA AND MOSHAEL STRAUS
CENTER FOR TORAH AND WESTERN THOUGHT**

ESTHER
IN
AMERICA

THE SCROLL'S INTERPRETATION IN
AND IMPACT ON THE UNITED STATES

Edited by
Rabbi Dr. Stuart W. Halpern

Straus Center for Torah and Western Thought
Maggid Books

Esther in America
The Scroll's Interpretation in and Impact on the United States

First Edition, 2020

Maggid Books
An imprint of Koren Publishers Jerusalem Ltd.

POB 8531, New Milford, CT 06776-8531, USA
& POB 4044, Jerusalem 9104001, Israel
www.maggidbooks.com

Koren Tanakh Font © 1962, 2020 Koren Publishers Jerusalem Ltd.
Koren Siddur Font and text design © 1981, 2020 Koren Publishers Jerusalem Ltd.
Megillat Esther text: *The Magerman Edition of the Koren Tanakh*,
© 2020 Koren Publishers Jerusalem Ltd.

ISBN 978-1-59264-561-9, *hardcover*

A CIP catalogue record for this title is
available from the British Library

Printed and bound in the United States

Contents

POP CULTURE PURIM

PRESIDENTIAL POLITICS AND PURIM

THE *MEGILLA* AND MODERN MORALITY

Editor's Introduction

On September 7, 1853, the escaped slave born Isabella Baumfree, now calling herself Sojourner Truth, addressed the crowd assembled in New York City for the Women's Rights Convention, despite the hisses and howls. So rowdy and disruptive were the young males protesting against those assembled that the event became known as the "Mob Convention." Truth, who could neither read nor write, chose, in this fraught moment, to remind those in attendance of an ancient scroll that told the tale of the Jewish queen in Persia and the holiday of Purim. "There was a king in the Scriptures," she said, "and then it was the kings of the earth would kill a woman if she come into their presence; but Queen Esther come forth, for she was oppressed, and felt there was a great wrong, and she said I will die or I will bring my complaint before the king. Should the king of the United States be greater, or more crueler, or more harder?"

Sojourner Truth's usage of Purim as a prism through which to view her fight for equal rights was no anomaly. Throughout our history, Americans have turned to the Scroll of Esther, the *megilla*, as they navigated their liberties, morals, passions, and politics. These recurring references are no accident. Rather, they reflect an appreciation of a story whose themes – freedom, power, fraught sexual dynamics, ethnicity, and peoplehood – continue to define American identity to this day.

Esther in America traces the story's interpretation in and impact on the United States. The first section, "Esther in Early America," opens with my analysis of the depiction of its eponymous heroine in a Puritan manual for women's behavior that was strikingly progressive for its time. Israel Ben-Porat details the scroll's surprising role in the development of the quintessentially American principle of religious freedom. During the American Revolution, as Eran Shalev describes in his chapter, it was Britain's King George III whom the rebels perceived to be embodying the role of King Ahasuerus, manipulated by the Haman-like prime minister, Lord North. The mark of Esther's cousin Mordecai is felt, as I argue, in the account of another diaspora-minded Jewish leader by the same name, Mordecai Manuel Noah. And, as Tzvi Sinensky suggests, Esther's heroic persona finds a literary echo in that beloved heroine of American letters, Nathaniel Hawthorne's Hester Prynne.

In "Emancipation and Proclamations," Ariel Clark Silver, Erica Brown, and Meir Soloveichik examine how Esther shaped the fight against racism and slavery, from the Persian capital Shushan to the American South to Abraham Lincoln's White House. As Silver writes, abolitionist leaders Angelina Grimké, Harriet Beecher Stowe, Frances Ellen Watkins Harper, and Sojourner Truth "elicited Esther to address the immediate existential threat: the sale, suffering, and slaughter of slaves in America prior to the Civil War."

The following section, "Feminist Esther," features Sinensky's tracing of the unexpected revival of Vashti as a model to be emulated despite her downfall in the story's opening verses. Zev Eleff details the attention paid to Esther between 1870 and 1900, including Annie Jonas Moses' publishing of a Purim play in Mobile, Alabama, that, as he notes, "aimed to disabuse erstwhile Esther detractors and disseminate the virtues of the protagonist's femininity." Shaina Trapedo analyzes Queen Esther pageants and perceptions of Jewish, and American, beauty in the early twentieth century and today. And Malka Fleischmann examines the trauma of silenced women in the *megilla* alongside the contemporary #MeToo movement.

In "Diaspora Life and Dual Identities," Emily Colbert Cairns examines the "sainthood" of Esther, particularly beloved by Latin American *conversos*, living outwardly as Christians and inwardly as Jews. In light of the scroll's Jewish heroine and hero having pagan-inspired names, Dara Horn reexamines the traditionally held belief that the names of immigrants were changed at Ellis Island. Alex Maged documents the work of New York's first Jewish orphanage in view of the themes of adoption and parenthood in the Bible, and Shmuel Hain examines the practice of reading the scroll twice on Purim as reflective of the story's "diasporic duality."

From children's literature (Emily Schneider) to art (Samantha Baskind) to the *megilla* in movies (Yosef Lindell), "Pop Culture Purim" offers critical analyses of Esther in the American popular imagination.

Tevi Troy and Philip Getz, in their contributions to "Presidential Politics and Purim," write of First Ladies and fraught governmental crises, with characters and machinations that mirror those of ancient Shushan.

In the book's concluding section, "The *Megilla* and Modern Morality," Mishael Zion ruminates on Hitler and Haman in American memory. Shalom Carmy and Jason Weiner each offers an analysis of the scroll's lessons based on the teachings of the renowned Rabbi Joseph Soloveitchik, examining the book's philosophy and the concept of self-endangerment as it pertains to medical decision-making, respectively. Continuing the examination of major twentieth-century rabbinic leaders, Yosef Bronstein offers a close reading of the Purim lectures of the Lubavitcher Rebbe and Ari Lamm mines the sermons of Rabbi Norman Lamm. The book concludes with Liel Leibovitz's call to action against "America's Hamanite Moment" and Dov Lerner's learned reflection on the "textual ethics" of the *megilla* and the United States Constitution.

As these scholars, rabbis, communal leaders, and writers demonstrate, the Book of Esther has inspired and impacted the American project since its very inception. Rabbis and ethicists, abolitionists and artists, preachers and presidents, have understood the text to speak to their moment. It has offered solace to immigrants, forged solidarity, impacted politics, and, in the spirit of Esther 4:14, roused individuals to realize that deliverance was not to come from some other place, but from their own heroic actions on behalf of their people. As we Americans once again find ourselves navigating antisemitism and bigotry, questioning the limits and purposes of power, reassessing gender dynamics, and grappling with how to keep an ethnically diverse empire from imploding, it is once again to Esther we must turn, to the timeless scroll that continues to urge us to find strength and redemptive possibility in the least expected of places.

Acknowledgments

At the Zahava and Moshael Straus Center for Torah and Western Thought of Yeshiva University, students, faculty, and staff bring into conversation the works of the Jewish tradition and Western art, literature, philosophy, political science, and social thought. I would like to thank Zahava and Moshael Straus for their generous support of the Center, and their continuous encouragement of, and commitment to, our work. I am deeply grateful for the mentorship and friendship of the Center's director, Rabbi Dr. Meir Y. Soloveichik, and express my gratitude to the entire Straus Center staff, in particular Sam Gelman and Rabbi Marc Eichenbaum, as well as Straus Scholar Michael Weiner. I also wish to thank YU's president, Rabbi Dr. Ari Berman, and its provost, Dr. Selma Botman, for their constant wisdom, leadership, and guidance.

Gratitude is extended as well to the incredible Maggid Books team, led by the visionary Matthew Miller and Rabbi Reuven Ziegler, as well as Caryn Meltz and the dedicated and talented copy editor Nechama Unterman. The loving support of Ahuva Warburg Halpern and our wonderful children, Erez, Ayal, and Mayim, made this project possible.

A different version of my "Puritan Purim" appeared in *The Lehrhaus* at thelehrhaus.com and a different version of "Mordecai's Ark" originally appeared in *Tablet Magazine* at tabletmag.com, and both are reprinted with permission. A version of Dr. Emily Schneider's chapter,

"Hidden Heroine," appeared in *Paper Brigade Daily* at the Jewish Book Council. "Lincoln, Esther, and the Rav" is based on remarks originally delivered by Rabbi Dr. Meir Y. Soloveichik in celebration of the publication of the *Mesorat HaRav* commentary on *Megillat Esther* by OU Press. "Esther in the White House" includes revised material from Dr. Tevi Troy's *Fight House* (Washington, DC, 2020). The text and translation of Esther that appear in the back of this book are taken from *The Magerman Edition of the Koren Tanakh*. This translation differs in places from translations appearing elsewhere in the book. Thank you to all of these partners and publications.

Stuart W. Halpern
September 2020/Elul 5780

Dedicated to the memory of Rabbi Dr. Norman Lamm and Mrs. Mindella Lamm, *z"l*, whose decades of work on behalf of Yeshiva University and world Jewry aimed to ensure that "the Jews had light and gladness, and joy and honor" (Est. 8:16). May the merit of their efforts, like the book of Esther itself, continue to inspire.

Esther in Early America

Puritan Purim: Cotton Mather and His Proto-Feminist Esther

Rabbi Dr. Stuart W. Halpern

Cotton Mather had much to say on how women should behave. In fact, he had much to say on many topics, writing 469 books over his sixty-five years. As historian Mark Noll has quipped, Mather, the first colonial to call himself an "American," "never had a thought he felt was unworthy of publication." Mather's fittingly titled *Ornaments for the Daughters of Zion, or, The Character and Happiness of a Vertuous Woman: in a Discourse Which Directs the Female-Sex how to Express, The Fear of God, in Every Age and State of their Life; and Obtain both Temporal and Eternal Blessedness* was published in Boston in 1692. In it, the popular Puritan minister, accomplished scientist, prolific author, owner of the largest private library in the colonies, grandson of Massachusetts Bay Colony spiritual leaders Richard Mather and John Cotton, and son of Harvard President Increase Mather, laid out his vision for womanhood.[1]

---

1. Never one to spare words (in his *Diary* he admits, "I am exceedingly sensible that

3

In his usage of biblical archetypes to describe the proper behavior of the ideal female (the very phrase "Daughters of Zion" is used in the Bible to connote Jerusalem and its inhabitants),[2] including maids,[3] wives,[4] mothers,[5] and widows,[6] Mather demonstrated a surprising affinity for a particular biblical character. While in his later *Magnalia Christi Americana* (1702) Mather used the precedent of Nehemiah, the Persian Jew who rebuilt the walls of Jerusalem in the time of the Second Temple, to describe Massachusetts Bay Colony governor John Winthrop's building the walls of New England ("our American Jerusalem"), here Mather found his prototype in the form of another Persian Jew, the beautiful and wise Queen Esther.[7] Despite his characteristic verbal gymnastics, however, Mather's attempt to fully appreciate Esther's heroism falls short.

---

the Grace of Meekness is very defective in me"), Mather later published additional works on women, including *Elizabeth in Her Holy Retirement* (1710) and *Bethiah: The Glory which Adorns the Daughters of God* (1722), a sequel to *Ornaments*. Mather's visage, like his pen, was prolific. He was the first American whose portrait others bought and hung in their homes. See Rick Kennedy, *The First American Evangelical: A Short Life of Cotton Mather* (Grand Rapids, 2015), vi. Noll's remark about Mather appears in his *A History of Christianity in the United States and Canada* (Grand Rapids, 1992), 86.

2. E.g., Zechariah 9:9, "Rejoice greatly, O daughter of Zion; shout, O daughter of Jerusalem."

3. "She prudently avoids the reading of *Romances*, which do no less naturally than generally inspire the minds of young people."

4. "She will therefore not be too much from home, upon concerns that perhaps to him are *unaccountable*; but if the angels do inquire, where she is, her Husband may reply, as once *Abraham* did, *my wife is in the tent.*"

5. "'Tis possible, her *Children* may *Sin*; but this causes her presently to reflect upon the Errors of her own *Heart* and *Life.*"

6. "The *Kindred* of her Expired Husband are also still Welcome and Grateful to her, upon *his account.*"

7. While composing *Magnalia Christi*, a history of the founding of Massachusetts Bay Colony written in biblical style that described New England as a redemptive society, Mather took to wearing a skullcap and calling himself "rabbi." At the same time, he was composing a textbook geared toward converting Jews to Christianity. See Arthur Hertzberg, *The Jews in America: Four Centuries of an Uneasy Encounter: A History* (New York, 1989), 39–41. Louis H. Feldman argues that Josephus' *Jewish War* was a particularly impactful influence on both Mather and his father in their historical writings and that Cotton took "an extraordinary interest" in Josephus, considering him "a kindred personality, full of soul-searching and very defensive

In *Ornaments for the Daughters of Zion*, a conduct and virtue manual, Mather, New England's most "intellectually and spiritually dynamic pastor" and the greatest North American scholar of his era,[8] brings up Esther multiple times. The first is in praise of the women of his era, whose "beautiful countenance" does not preclude their "good understanding." Such individuals follow in the ancient footsteps of biblical women including Sarah, Rebecca, Rachel, and Esther, who possessed the same "benefits" of good looks and good insight and who simultaneously "feared God." Mather then invokes Esther (juxtaposed to a reference to the *Sota* ritual) as paradigmatic for women, who should demonstrate resolve and integrity in the face of suspicious husbands, refusing to upset the patriarchal order:[9]

> She will even Abstain from all appearance of Evil; and as 'tis abominable unto her to Entertain the least groundless and causeless *Jealousie* of her Husband.... She affects to be an *Esther*, that is, *A hidden One.* But if a foolish and forward Husband will wrong her, with unjust suspicions of her *Honesty*, she will thence make a Devout Reflexion upon her *Disloyalty* to God; but at the same time very patiently vindicate her *Innocency* to man; and the more *patiently* because the *Water of Jealousie* procures greater Blessings to those that have it Unrighteously and Abusively imposed upon them.

---

about his actions, very similar to Paul, whose friend, Mather claims, interestingly without evidence, Josephus was." See Feldman, "The Influence of Josephus on Cotton Mather's *Biblia Americana*: A Study in Ambiguity," in Shalom Goldman, ed., *Hebrew and the Bible in America: The First Two Centuries* (Hanover, 1993). Feldman describes Cotton Mather's desire to convert Jews to Christianity as "very nearly an obsession for him."

8. Kennedy, 86; Hertzberg, 27.
9. In the colonial era, obedience to one's husband was both a religious and legal requirement and the husband represented the household to the outside world, though on occasions wives acted as "deputy husbands," giving instructions to workers, negotiating with Native Americans, and settling accounts. See Laurel Thatcher Ulrich, *Good Wives: Image and Reality in the Lives of Women in Northern New England 1650–1750* (New York, 1991).

Rabbi Dr. Stuart W. Halpern

In a similar vein, in the same section, Mather again invokes Esther by taking the prototype one step further. Not only, as described above, does an "Esther" patiently and respectfully (as she is, after all, "a hidden one") disabuse suspecting husbands of any suspicions they might have regarding her behavior, Esther also models for women their ability to inspire proper behavior in, and even provide salvation for, their husbands.

> Opportunities are those that a Woman *has* to bring over her Husband unto Real and Serious Godliness, and a Good Woman, will *use* those Opportunities. An *Esther*, a Witty *Esther*, what can't she do with the most haughty Husband in the World? ... If her Husband be a Carnal, Prayerless, Graceless man, she will not leave off her Ingenious Perswasions, till it may be said of him, *Behold, he Prayes!* ... If her Husband be under the Power of any Temptation, she will do what she can to prevent his *Destruction*.

Mather, of course, was much concerned with preventing societal destruction (after his death he was hailed as an "American Elijah," a reference to the biblical prophet zealous for God's ways). He played an active role in the hysteria that emerged in and around Salem, Massachusetts, after local women were accused by young girls of witchcraft. The fallout from these accusations, an episode that became known as the Salem Witch Trials, resulted in the executions of fourteen women and five men in the same year *Ornaments for the Daughters of Zion* was published.[10] Mather was

---

10. The degree of his involvement has been subject to much scholarly debate stemming from the work of Robert Calef, a contemporary of Mather's whose decade-long negative portrayal of the latter, eventually published in a book, colors the modern popular perception (inspiring, for example, Mather appearing in Marvel Comics as a scowling villain wearing a green cape). Mather's recent biographer Kennedy notes how Cotton did not support the push to swiftly execute the accused witches, and was a kindly figure who often visited prisons, hosted countless visitors, including a young Benjamin Franklin, in his vast study, and even housed some of the young women who claimed to be possessed by demons in his own home in an effort to cure them. Per Kennedy, Cotton never attended the trials, though he did preach at one of the executions, and wished to err on the side of leniency with the "witches." "If Cotton's advice had been followed [during the trials], it is safe to assume that matters in Salem would have turned out better" (63). Though, as Jan Stievermann writes

6

a pillar of Puritan patriarchy. In *Ornaments* he cites Ahasuerus' decree in Esther 1:20 that "all the Wives give to their Husbands Honour both to Great and Small" as properly demonstrating the "reverence" a wife should have for her husband. As Harvard historian and scholar of early America Laurel Thatcher Ulrich notes, women were thought to play an invisible role in history, "because their bodies impel them to nurture. Their job is to bind the wounds, stir the soup, and bear the children of those whose mission it is to fight wars, rule nations, and define the cosmos." A contemporary of Mather put it, in a 1650 description of the unobtrusive, home-centered role women were expected to play, "Woman's the center & lines are men."[11]

Yet, Mather saw in the biblical Esther a woman of independent action to admire. As scholar of religion Ariel Clark Silver notes, Mather's Esther is obedient while at the same time proactive. She is a "good conqueror" who obeys rules but is spiritually independent of her husband, providing him with salvation. Overlooking female figures in the Christian tradition such as Mary, Mather offered his fellow Puritans a heroine from the Hebrew Bible who modeled a willingness to stay faithful unto death, overcome challenges and adversity, and provide salvation for others. For his era, this emphasis on Esther – a figure from a story largely marginal to Christians – coupled with his very interest in and concern for the inner spiritual lives of women, made Mather rather unique – one might say he was progressive in positioning Esther as a proto-feminist.[12]

(in the General Introduction of *Cotton Mather and Biblia Americana: America's First Bible Commentary – Essays in Reappraisal,* ed. Reiner Smolinski and Jan Stievermann [Grand Rapids, 2011]), in the popular imagination Mather "remains *the* psychopathic witch-doctor and a main culprit for the tragic events in Salem," he agrees with Feldman that "Cotton Mather has had a bad press."

11. Ulrich, *Well-Behaved Women Seldom Make History* (New York, 2007), xxi. The title of Ulrich's book stems from a phrase she coined in an article in a 1976 edition of *American Quarterly* that surveyed the literature about women in Mather's era. The phrase was then tweaked (with "seldom" replaced by "rarely") and popularized by journalist Kay Mills, who used it as an epigraph in her history of women in America *From Pocahontas to Power Suits.*

12. See Ariel Clark Silver, *The Book of Esther and the Typology of Female Transfiguration in American Literature* (Lanham, 2018), 32–36. For Silver's analysis of Esther as "American abolitionist," see her chapter in this volume. As Helen K. Gelinas notes,

Ornaments was not the last time Mather meditated on Esther. His magnum opus, *Biblia Americana*, America's first Bible commentary, which ran a very Matherian 4,500 pages and which he worked on from 1693 until his death in 1728, recapped the story and provided the scholarly interpretations current in Mather's time.[13] In it, Mather cites a wide variety of sources, including the Babylonian and Jerusalem Talmuds, *Mekhilta*, *Pirkei DeRabbi Eliezer*, Zohar, Onkelos, *Seder Olam Rabba*, Saadia Gaon, Rashi, Ibn Ezra, Radak, Nahmanides, Moses of Coucy, Gersonides, Bahya ben Asher, Abravanel, and Seforno, remarking that "the writings of the rabbins [sic] are often very helpful to us."[14] In comments ranging from why Mordecai did not bow down to Haman,[15] to how the myrrh was utilized by the virgins in Ahasuerus' harem,[16] to how Esther could ask the Jews to fast for three days straight,[17] to the "miraculous" timing of Haman's arriving before Ahasuerus when the king was unable to sleep,[18] to the custom of reacting to the mention of Haman's name during the

---

Mather was "an unusually outspoken champion of spiritual equality between the sexes [and]…nurtured and educated his own daughters in a surprisingly egalitarian manner for his time." See her "Regaining Paradise: Cotton Mather's 'Biblia Americana' and the Daughters of Eve," in Smolinski and Stievermann, 463. I thank Israel Ben-Porat for this reference.

13. This commentary has recently been published by a team of scholars through Baker Academic Press. For contextual background and additional analysis of Mather and his work, see Smolinski and Stievermann.

14. Feldman, 143–144.

15. "It is not easy to find reason for *Mordecai's* refusing to pay unto *Haman* the Respect which he required & exposing his whole Nation to an Extirpation…. Probably it was because *Haman* was the race of the *Amalekites*, and under the Curse denounced by God upon that Nation; and therefore, he thought it not proper to give that Honour unto him."

16. "*Myrrhe*, from whence not only a Noble Oyl [oil] was drawn, but being beat unto a Powder, such a Fumigation was made with it."

17. "*Josephus* understands it as only an Abstinence from Delicacies, and a Contentment with Hard & Coarse Fare." For an analysis of Mather's extensive usage of Josephus, see Feldman, 122–155.

18. "Haman should come in at the very Nick of Time, & so determine the Honour, and be made the Instrument of it [ch. 6]; This was from the *Keeper of Israel*, who *never slumbers nor sleeps!* [Ps. 121:4]."

reading of the *megilla* on Purim,[19] Mather, as always, had much to say. Strikingly, however, very little commentary centered on Esther herself. While Mordecai and Ahasuerus' actions and intentions are elaborated upon in Mather's retelling (Mordecai "exhorted [the Jews] unto Fasting, and Humiliation, and Repentance, & to follow the Example of the Ninivites," and Ahasuerus, upon seeing Haman fall upon Esther's bed, "turned every thing to the worst Sense, and made the Posture of his Petition but the Aggravation of his Crime"), Esther as an actor in her eponymous tale is *a hidden one*, meriting only the mention that "Her Beauty was extraordinary."[20]

This interpretation of Esther and the legacy of her actions, however, misses the true significance of her story. When Esther was called upon by Mordecai, it was not, as Mather offers in his *Ornaments of the Daughters of Zion*, to prevent the destruction of her husband, but rather, as the Jewish tradition makes clear, it was to risk everything to provide salvation for her nation. And she does so despite the danger approaching her husband, to whom she is subject, presents.[21] As Mordecai states in his only recorded words in the entire *megilla*:

> Do not imagine that you, of all the Jews, will escape with your life by being in the king's palace. On the contrary, if you keep silent in this crisis, relief and deliverance will come to the Jews from another quarter, while you and your father's house will perish. And who knows, perhaps you have attained to royal position for just such a crisis. (4:13–14)

---

19. "The Book of *Esther* is read in all their Synagogues: & when the Name of *Haman* occurs, they clap their Hands, and cry out, *Let his memory perish.*"
20. Citations from Harry C. Maddux and Reiner Smolinski, eds., *Biblia Americana: America's First Bible Commentary. A Synoptic Commentary on the Old and New Testaments*, Volume 4: *Ezra-Psalms* (Heidelberg, 2013), 139–166. For an extensive discussion of the sources Mather drew upon, particularly in his discussion of Mordecai's refusal to bow, see Introduction, 3–7. As Gelinas notes, "For Mather the very Hebrew word *Almah*, meaning virgin or young woman, connotes a covering, or an aspect of being hidden" (486).
21. For an elaboration of the evolution of Esther's identity, see Joshua A. Berman, "*Hadassah Bat Abihail*: The Evolution of Object to Subject in the Character of Esther," *Journal of Biblical Literature* 120, no. 4 (2001): 647–669.

Esther the Persian, who until this point hid her Jewish identity as Hadassah, is called upon to save her people as they stand on the precipice of destruction. She is to be Hadassah once more. As *New York Times* ethicist Kwame Anthony Appiah writes, "Identities work only because, once they get their grip on us, they command us, speaking to us as an inner voice; and because others, seeing who they think we are, call on us, too."[22] It is Mordecai's beseeching Esther to plead on behalf of her people (4:8), and the courage demonstrated by Esther in entering the king's throne room unannounced and revealing her identity to Ahasuerus at her party, that lead to the salvation of the entire nation.[23] Contra Cotton Mather's reading, it is the destruction of Mordecai and the Jewish people that Esther prevents, not that of her husband.[24]

In 1912, 220 years after Cotton Mather published *Ornaments for the Daughters of Zion*, thirty-eight Jewish women, led by fifty-two-year-old Henrietta Szold, gathered in Harlem, New York, on Purim day.[25] These women, sensing they were living in a historical era of Jewish national significance, gathered to found a new organization dedicated to promoting Zionism in America and improving the health and welfare of

22. *The Lies that Bind – Rethinking Identity* (New York, 2018), 218.
23. See Linda Day, *Three Faces of a Queen: Characterization in the Books of Esther* (Sheffield, 1995), for a discussion of how the Greek translations of Esther emphasize God's historical relationship with the Jewish people in their telling of the story.
24. Since Mather, numerous Americans throughout the ages have invoked Esther as a model of female behavior. The twenty-first century alone has produced works including Dianna Booher's *The Esther Effect: The Seven Secrets of Self-Confidence and Influence* (Nashville, 2001), and Barbara Smalley and Connie Glaser's *What Queen Esther Knew: Business Strategies from a Biblical Sage* (Emmaus, 2003), a management guide blurbed by numerous CEOs, including those of Office Depot and Deloitte and Touche, which offers readers guidance from an "ideal role model for women today." Johnny E. Miles, in his *Superheroes and their Ancient Jewish Parallels* (Jefferson, 2018), compares Esther to Wonder Woman, in a chapter titled "The Diasporic Woman as Hero," and observes that "heroes, like Wonder Woman and Esther, indeed supersede the expectations of the everyday. But that does not make them any less human.... Heroes like Esther mirror something of or about their culture while inspiring nobler acts of selflessness and providing a model for success" (145).
25. For more on Szold's story, see Pamela S. Nadell, *America's Jewish Women: A History from Colonial Times to Today* (New York, 2019); Mishael Zion, *Esther: A New Israeli Commentary* (Jerusalem, 2019), 67.

their brethren in Palestine. As political scientist Samuel Goldman has documented, staking a position rather unique among Christians of the time, Cotton Mather's father, Increase Mather, "never wavered in his conviction that God's promise to restore the Jews to their ancient home-land would one day be fulfilled."[26] With the flowering of the eventual State of Israel in sight, these women evoked the biblical figure whose dedication to her people inspired their own efforts in ensuring Jewish national survival. They, after some time, decided to name their organization Hadassah. In what can best be described as historical coincidence with a sprinkling of divine humor not unlike the events of the Book of Esther itself, the women had changed the organization's name from what they had agreed upon that Purim day. The original name for Hadassah, the charitable women's organization now 330,000 US members strong? Daughters of Zion.

---

26. *God's Country: Christian Zionism in America* (Philadelphia, 2018), 14. Goldman notes that Cotton "initially echoed his father's arguments about the salvation of all Israel, but eventually concluded that the Jews had no further part to play in God's design" (41).

American Artaxerxes: Esther in Early Modern Political Hebraism

Israel Ben-Porat

T he Book of Esther served as a surprisingly significant touchstone in the political thought of early colonial America. In order to properly understand this phenomenon, we must also consider intellectual developments on the other side of the Atlantic. In the sixteenth and seventeenth centuries, after the Protestant Reformation rejected the Catholic tradition in favor of reverting to the word of Scripture alone, "political Hebraism" emerged as a scholarly effort to mine the Hebrew Bible as a foundation for political theory.[1] While the New Testament remained influential, the Old Testament permeated the culture of Reformation England and colonial New England; in particular, Puritans on both sides of the Atlantic

---

1. See Gordon Schochet, Fania Oz-Salzberger, and Meirav Jones, eds., *Political Hebraism: Judaic Sources in Early Modern Political Thought* (Jerusalem, 2008); Eric Nelson, *The Hebrew Republic: Jewish Sources and the Transformation of European Political Thought* (Cambridge, 2010); and Kevin Killeen, *The Political Bible in Early Modern England* (Cambridge, 2017).

sought to reform society in accordance with biblical ideals.[2] Early modern commentators, who largely assumed the historicity of the Esther narrative, grappled with the political implications of this period in Persian history.[3] Early American thinkers participated in debates about the Esther story in European biblical scholarship. The unique nature of the colonial enterprise contributed to new interpretations and applications of Esther. Alongside Walter Raleigh and other English scholars, important colonial figures such as John Cotton, Roger Williams, Anne Bradstreet, and Cotton Mather offered new perspectives on the Book of Esther.[4]

The reception history of Esther in America began in the writings of English explorer Walter Raleigh (1552–1618), who played a significant role in the colonial enterprise in Ireland and Virginia. While on death row in the Tower of London, Raleigh wrote his *History of the World* (1614) in an effort to gain favor with King James I (1603–1625). Raleigh's *History* identified Ahasuerus as the Artaxerxes of Ezra 7, who supported the rebuilding of the Temple, exempted the clergy from taxes, and granted an autonomous Jewish legal system: "His favour was exceeding great to the *Iewes*, as appeareth by the Histories of *Esdras* and *Nehemias*, which fell in his time…. This was likewise that King *Ahashuerosh* who married *Hester*." Raleigh proceeded to offer several pieces of evidence for his position. Firstly, "Whereof if it be needful to give proofe, it may suffice; That *Ahashuerosh* lived in *Susa*, raigning from *India* to *Aethiopia*, and therefore must have been a *Persian*." Secondly, "That hee lived in peace, as appeares by the circumstances of the Historie…. The continuall Warres which exercised King *Darius*…together with the certaintie of his marriages with sundrie wives…doe manifestly prove that *Hester* was

---

2. Theodore D. Bozeman, *To Live Ancient Lives: The Primitivist Dimension in Puritanism* (Chapel Hill, 1988); Achsah Guibbory, *Christian Identity, Jews, and Israel in Seventeenth-Century England* (New York, 2010).

3. See, e.g., Pierre Merlin, *A Most Plaine and Profitable Exposition of the Booke of Esther* (London, 1599), 1–5; William Pemble, *The Period of the Persian Monarchie* (London, 1631). For early modern English interest in ancient Persia, see generally Jane Grogan, *The Persian Empire in English Renaissance Writing, 1549–1622* (London, 2014).

4. For a reception history of Esther, see Jo Carruthers, *Esther through the Centuries* (Malden, 2008); *Encyclopedia of the Bible and Its Reception*, s.v. "Esther (Book and Person)" (Berlin, 2009). Carruthers omits Raleigh, Cotton, Williams, Bradstreet, and Mather's *Biblia Americana*.

not his." Finally, Raleigh drew upon Philo Judaeus (30 BCE–50 CE), a Hellenistic Jewish philosopher: "Whereunto is added by Philo the *Iew*, That … *Ioiachim* [Joiakim] the high Priest the sonne of *Iesua* [Neh. 12:10, 26], caused the feast of *Purim* to bee instituted in memorie of that deliverance. Now the time of *Ioiachim* was in the raigne of *Artaxerxes*."[5] While the conflation of Ahasuerus and Artaxerxes may have stemmed from a perceived fidelity to historical truth, the emphasis on the monarch's affinity for Jews paralleled Raleigh's tolerant attitude toward other religions.[6]

Raleigh's positive perspective adumbrated a general effort in seventeenth-century England to rehabilitate Ahasuerus by deemphasizing the purported tyranny of his early life. Despite his initial encouragement of Haman's plot to annihilate the Jews, Ahasuerus' subsequent reversal of the decree attracted commentators' praise. Evidently, Ahasuerus' earlier actions stemmed from Haman's corrupt manipulation rather than the king's anti-Jewish attitude. Tellingly, in 1626, English clergyman George Hakewill (1578–1648) drew an analogy between Haman's decree and the Gunpowder Plot of 1605, a failed assassination attempt against King James I by English Catholics.[7] This analogy conveniently ignored Ahasuerus' complicity in the intended massacre and unabashedly equated the Persian king with James. That same year, Bishop Joseph Hall (1574–1656) dedicated his *Contemplations upon*

5. Walter Raleigh, *The History of the World* (London, 1614), part 1, book 3, ch. 7 §7 (85–86). For the Darius theory, see, e.g., Merlin, 5–7. On the revival of Philo studies in the sixteenth century, see Eric J. DeMeuse, "*Nostre Philon*: Philo after Trent," *The Studia Philonica Annual: Studies in Hellenistic Judaism* 29 (Atlanta, 2017): 87–110. Raleigh did not invoke Josephus, who identified Ahasuerus as Artaxerxes and Ezra's Artaxerxes as Xerxes the son of Darius; see Flavius Josephus, *The Famous and Memorable Workes of Iosephus*, trans. Thomas Lodge (1602), *Antiquities* book XI, chs. 5–6.

6. Alan Gallay, *Walter Ralegh: Architect of Empire* (New York, 2019), 449. On the political implications of Raleigh's *History*, see Anna R. Beer, *Sir Walter Ralegh and His Readers in the Seventeenth Century* (London, 1997), 22–59; Nicholas Popper, *Walter Ralegh's "History of the World" and the Historical Culture of the Late Renaissance* (Chicago, 2012), 209–253.

7. George Hakewill, *A Comparison between the Dayes of Purim and that of the Powder Treason* (Oxford, 1626); see also Henry Care, *A Word in Season: Being a Parallel between the Intended Bloody Massacre of the People of the Jews, in the Reign of King Ahasuerus; and the Hellish Powder-Plot against the Protestants, in the Reign of King James* (London, 1679).

the Historicall Part of the Old Testament to James' successor Charles I
(r. 1625–1649), "For what doth it else but comment upon that, which
God hath thought good to say of Kings[?]"[8] For these thinkers, the
Book of Esther served as a royalist text.[9]

In the 1630s and '40s, the political reality of Puritan Massachusetts generated new usages of the Book of Esther. Lion Gardin-
er's "Relation of the Pequot Warres" between the colonists and the
Pequot Indians (1636–1638) compared a native diplomat to Mordecai. This biblical invocation "implied a shared – albeit fraught – Judeo-
Anglo-Algonquian historical trajectory" that allusively commented
on the colony's political relations with the indigenous population.[10]
Additionally, the fusion of church and state in Puritan Massachusetts
prompted the usage of Artaxerxes in Ezra 7 as a precedent. Massachusetts, founded by the Puritans in 1630, drew substantially on Mosaic
law. Under the *Body of Liberties* (1641) and subsequent law codes, Massachusetts strictly enforced its biblicist regime, banishing or executing
religious dissidents.[11] Whereas Raleigh had emphasized Artaxerxes'
benevolence to the Jews, Puritans argued that Artaxerxes' involvement
with Jewish affairs indicated that the state should intersect with the
church and advance the cause of religion.

---

8. Joseph Hall, *Contemplations upon the Historicall Part of the Old Testament*, vol. 8
   (London, 1626), "Epistle Dedicatory." Hall identified Ahasuerus as "Xerxes, the
   sonne of Darius" (p. 429).
9. For another royalist treatment of Esther, see Francis Quarles, *Hadassa: or The History of Queene Ester with Meditations thereupon, Diuine and Morall* (London, 1621).
   For more on early modern treatments of Esther herself, see Saralyn Ellen Summer,
   "'Like Another Esther': Literary Representations of Queen Esther in Early Modern
   England" (PhD diss., Georgia State University, 2006).
10. Michael Householder, "American Mordecai: Scriptural Allusion and the Work of
    Remembering in Lion Gardiner's 'Relation of the Pequot Warres,'" *Early American
    Studies* 9, no. 2 (Spring 2011): 412–434 (quotation p. 424).
11. See, e.g., George L. Haskins, *Law and Authority in Early Massachusetts: A Study
    in Tradition and Design* (Lanham, 1960), 141–162; Bozeman, *To Live Ancient Lives*,
    168–192; Edgar J. McManus, *Law and Liberty in Early New England: Criminal
    Justice and Due Process, 1620–1692* (Amherst, 1993), 21–37; Mark A. Noll, *In the
    Beginning Was the Word: The Bible in American Public Life, 1492–1783* (Oxford,
    2015), 98–124.

This argument had first appeared implicitly in the Geneva Bible translation of 1560, which included a marginal comment that Artaxerxes "gave Ezra full authority to restore all things according to the word of God, and to punish them who resisted and would not obey." Ezra's enforcement of Jewish law surely resonated in Calvinist Geneva, which conducted one of the strictest applications of reformed thought.[12] Later, in the 1640s, during the English Civil War between parliamentarians and royalists, the argument resurfaced in the works of dissenting authors. English writer Henry Robinson (1604–1664) condemned the "false lustre of a Nationall Church" advocated by the "Mahumetans in *Turkie*, Papists in *Spaine*, and Lutherans in *Germany*" as "the worke of man and not of God…. And they allege also the great reformations wrought by *Ataxerxes, Ezra* 7. 23." Robinson characterized this notion "as though the Prophet *Ezra* had purposely recorded it, not so much that God might be glorified in *Artaxerxes* great carefulnesse, and just commands for beautifying of his Temple, as to countenance their owne wil-worship and inventions."[13] Similarly, Puritan dissident Roger Williams (1603–1683) excerpted the "Modell of Church and Civill power" (1644), a document written by several New England ministers, which also appropriated Artaxerxes in this way: "The Law of *Artaxerxes, Ezra* 7.23. was not usurpation over the church's liberty, but a Royall and just confirmation of them."[14] The comments of Robinson and Williams reveal the mainstream Puritan perspective, which invoked Artaxerxes as a model for the fusion of church and state.

In contrast, Williams preserved the latter position in order to record his objections to the idea of a religious establishment. Williams

12. Geneva Bible (1560), Ezra 7:25; Philip Benedict, *Christ's Churches Purely Reformed: A Social History of Calvinism* (New Haven, 2002). The Geneva Bible noted regarding Artaxerxes, "The Hebrews write that many of the kings of Persia were called by this name, as Pharaoh was a common name to the kings of Egypt and Caesar to the Romans emperors" (Ezra 7:1), but it did not identify Ahasuerus as Artaxerxes (Est. 1:1).
13. Henry Robinson, *Liberty of Conscience: or The Sole Means to Obtaine Peace and Truth* (London, 1643), 27–28.
14. Roger Williams, *The Bloudy Tenent of Persecution, for Cause of Conscience, Discussed in a Conference between Truth and Peace* (London, 1644), 145. The "Modell" has only survived in excerpts in Williams' work.

marked a key development in Anglo-American political Hebraism on Esther, offering a nuanced reinterpretation of Artaxerxes as a model for religious liberty. Williams largely rejected the Puritans' emphasis on the contemporary relevance of the Old Testament, which he regarded as merely a typology of spiritual ideas rather than a practical guidebook for political theory.[15] Unlike his fellow Puritans in Massachusetts, Williams opposed state compulsion of religious practice, which led to his banishment from the colony in 1636,[16] whereupon Williams founded Rhode Island in accordance with his views on church and state. However, Artaxerxes' status as a pagan monarch – unlike the Israelite kings – established a historical precedent rather than merely a biblical typology. Thus, Williams did not simply dismiss Artaxerxes' political relevance, but rather reinterpreted the character to argue for religious freedom.[17]

Williams began his treatment of Artaxerxes by first acknowledging the Jews' precarious political position in ancient Persia: "[The Jews] were as *Lambes* and *Sheep* in the jawes of the *Lyon*...under the devouring *Tyrants* of the World, both the *Babylonian* and the *Persian*, farre from their owne *Nation*, and the *Government* of their own anointed *Kings*." Artaxerxes ruled as a *"Gentile Idolater,* an oppressing *Tyrant*.... A hand of bloody *Conquest* set the Crown upon [his] head." Accordingly, Artaxerxes' enforcement of religion lacked authority. Secondly, Artaxerxes' "acts of Favour... [did] not amount to a positive Command, that any of the *Iewes* should goe up to build the *Temple*, nor that any of them should practice his own *worship*." Rather, Artaxerxes "freely permits them, and exerciseth a bounteous *assistance* to them."[18] These two arguments

---

15. Perry Miller, *Roger Willams: His Contribution to the American Tradition* (Indianapolis, 1953); Edmund S. Morgan, *Roger Williams: The Church and the State* (1967; New York, 2006); Timothy L. Hall, *Separating Church and State: Roger Williams and Religious Liberty* (Urbana, 1998); Lisa M. Gordis, *Opening Scripture: Bible Reading and Interpretive Authority in Puritan New England* (Chicago, 2003).
16. Roger Williams, *Mr. Cottons Letter Lately Printed, Examined and Answered* (London, 1644), 5.
17. James P. Byrd, *The Challenges of Roger Williams: Religious Liberty, Violent Persecution, and the Bible* (Macon, 2002), 53–86.
18. Williams, *Bloudy Tenent*, 147–148. For reformed views on tyranny, see Robert M. Kingdon, "Calvinism and resistance theory, 1550–1580," in *The Cambridge History of*

undermined Puritan appropriations of Artaxerxes by both delegitimizing the king's power and emphasizing the lack of religious compulsion.

Why, then, did Artaxerxes act so kindly to the Jews? Williams reconciled the coexistence of tyrannical and benevolent tendencies by arguing "that sometimes it pleaseth *God* to open the hearts of *Tyrants* greatly to favour and further his people." Echoing the Geneva Bible, which insisted that Artaxerxes' "fear of God's judgment causes him to use this liberality, and not the love that he bore for God's glory or affection for his people,"[19] Williams pointed to "the common *terrours* and *convictions* of an affrighted Conscience." A variety of biblical examples attested to this phenomenon: "In such fits and *pangs*, what have not *Pharaohs, Sauls, Ahabs, Herods, Agrippas* spoken? and what wonderfull decrees have *Nabuchadnezzar, Cyrus, Darius, Artaxerxes* put forth concerning the *God of Israel*[?], Dan. 3. & 6 & Ezra 1 & 7." Williams highlighted his rejection of religious coercion with a rhetorical question: "But did God put such a thing as this into the heart of the King, viz. to restraine upon paine of Death all the millions of men under his Dominion from the idolatries of their several and respective Countries? to constraine them all upon the like penaltie to conforme to the Worship of the God of Israel[?]"[20] Interestingly, Williams did not suggest that Esther influenced Artaxerxes' favorable attitude toward the Jews. Since he never commented directly on the Book of Esther,[21] it remains indeterminable whether Williams would have conflated Ahasuerus with Artaxerxes as Raleigh did, though the possibility certainly exists. In any case, readers of Williams would

---

Political Thought 1450–1700, ed. J. H. Burns (Cambridge, 1991), 193–218; John Witte, Jr., "Rights, Resistance, and Revolution in the Western Tradition: Early Protestant Foundations," *Law and History Review* 26, no. 3 (Fall 2008): 545–570.

19. Geneva Bible (1560), Ezra 7:23. "In his own biblical study, Williams probably used both the Authorized [King James] Version and the popular Geneva Bible, although he, like most Puritans, apparently preferred the latter" (Byrd, 3 n. 3).

20. Williams, *Bloudy Tenent*, 148–149; cf. [Roger Williams,] *A Paraenetick, or, Humble Address to the Parliament and Assembly for (not loose, but) Christian Libertie* (London, 1644), 4.

21. For a comprehensive index of Williams' scriptural citations, see Byrd, 205–275. Note that Byrd's data suggests that Williams focused much more on the New Testament than on the Old. See also Robert L. Wilken, *Liberty in the Things of God: The Christian Origins of Religious Freedom* (New Haven, 2019), 144–154.

likely have made that association given the general confusion about Persian history and the complexities of biblical chronology.[22]

A few years after Williams' publication, Arthur Jackson (1593–1666) similarly focused on Ahasuerus' favorable attitude toward the Jews. Seeking to historicize Esther, Jackson rejected the opinion that identified Ahasuerus as "Cambyses the sonne of Cyrus…for he all his days was a bitter enemy to the Jews, and hindred the building of the Temple, and therefore surely was not the husband of Esther." Rather, Jackson turned to other biblical kings whose lives seemed more consistent with the Esther story: "The most probable opinion therefore is, that either it was Darius the sonne of Hystaspes, because by other Historians it is said, that his wife was called Atossa, which sounds in part some what like Hadassah…and because he greatly favoured the Jews, as we see, Ezra 6. 1." Alternatively, Jackson pointed to "Xerxes the sonne of Darius Hystaspes, whose wife other Historians call Amestris, not much unlike Esther; or else Artaxerxes Longimanus[,] Xerxes sonne."[23] Jackson's final theory implicitly acknowledged the consistency between Ahasuerus' and Artaxerxes' favorable treatment of the Jews.

A year later, John Mayer (1583–1664) rejected Jackson's conflation on historical grounds: "Which of the *Persian* Kings *Ahashuerosh* was, is not agreed amongst Expositours…some hold him to have been *Artaxerxes*, as *Josephus*, but neither will the time permit this." However, Mayer praised Artaxerxes' exemption of the clergy from taxes: "Heathen Kings being guided only by the light of Nature thought it fit to free the servants of God, who attended continually upon his worship, from taxes, which were imposed upon others, and somewhat like unto this did *Pharaoh* to his Priests in the time of famine [Gen. 47:22, 26]." Mayer's connection to the example of Pharaoh elaborated on an example to which Williams had obliquely alluded in passing. Mayer concluded,

---

22. For other political invocations of Esther in the 1640s, see Obadiah Sedgwick, *Haman's Vanity* (London, 1643); Herbert Palmer, *The Necessity and Encouragement, of Utmost Venturing for the Churches Help* (London, 1643); Samuel Kem, *The Messengers Preparation for an Addresse to the King for a Well-Grounded Peace* (London, 1644).

23. Arthur Jackson, *Annotations upon the Remaining Historicall Part of the Old Testament, to wit, the Books of Joshua, Judges, the two Books of Samuel, Kings and Chronicles, and the Books of Ezra, Nehemiah, and Esther* (Cambridge, 1646), 792.

"Therefore Christian Kings should much more make the Church free ... and to take away any priviledges of the Clergy cannot but be counted a sin against the light of nature."[24] Like Williams, Mayer explicitly articulated the political dimensions of his reading.

Williams' reinterpretation of Artaxerxes unsurprisingly sparked controversy in Puritan New England. Preeminent theologian John Cotton (1585–1652) provided the orthodox response to Williams. Cotton, who served as a leading minister in Massachusetts, declared a natural cohesion between civil and church enforcement, because "there be sundry civil offences, which are also transgressions of the Rule of the word.... There be also offences to the Order and peace of the Church, which tend likewise to provoke wrath against a Civil State." In support, Cotton cited the familiar proof text by "the King of *Persia*" in Ezra 7:23, concluding, "If offences to the Church do provoke wrath against the Civil State, it is no confusion in the Civil State to punish such."[25] Williams replied by reiterating Artaxerxes' pagan status: "This reason indeed Master *Cotton* often inculcates and beates upon it, that the *Pagan kings* of *Persia* were of his mind: I believe Master *Cotton* out of a *zeal* to *God*, but the *Pagan kings* out of a slavish *terror*, which never prevailed so far (that I know of) as to bring them to a kindly *repentance* of their own idolatries, or a true *love* to the *God* of *Israel* or his *people*."[26] This comment highlighted the prevalence of the Artaxerxes argument among Puritan theologians.

The final round of the debate about Artaxerxes and religious liberty appeared in the anonymous series of *Examiner* tracts in the early 1650s. The pro-religious liberty text *Zeal Examined*, probably written by Williams' political ally Sir Henry Vane the Younger (1613–1662),[27]

---

24. John Mayer, *Many Commentaries in One upon Joshua, Judges, Ruth, 1 and 2 of Samuel, 1 and 2 of Kings, 1 and 2 of Chronicles, Ezra, Nehemiah, Esther* (London, 1647), Esther ch. I p. 53, Ezra ch. VII p. 25. Mayer dismissively remarked that Josephus "in many places of his History erreth so much, as that his relation touching this is but of uncertain credit" (Esther ch. I p. 54).

25. John Cotton, *The Bloudy Tenent, Washed, and Made White in the Bloud of the Lambe: Being Discussed and Discharged of Bloud-Guiltinesse by Just Defence* (London, 1647), 70.

26. Roger Williams, *The Bloody Tenent Yet More Bloody* (London, 1652), 105.

27. [Henry Vane,] *Zeal Examined: or, A Discourse for Liberty of Conscience in Matters of Religion* (London, 1652); for the attribution, see David Parnham, "Reconfiguring

prompted an anonymous response entitled *The Examiner Examined,*
which presented twenty-two questions challenging the author of *Zeal
Examined.* The seventh and final questions both invoked Artaxerxes
as a precedent for coercion of religion.[28] Subsequently, *The Examiner
Defended,* probably written by Williams, summarized the arguments in
Bloudy Tenent as a response. Shockingly, *Examiner Defended* followed
the argument to its logical conclusion, condoning religious freedom
for everyone, "whether *Popish* or *Protestant,* or to any particular sect,"
including even idolaters, blasphemers, and heretics.[29] Undeterred, the
opposing side published *Anti-Cotton Answered,* which replied to each
of the twenty-two responses.[30] The intensity of this debate reflected
the political significance of the Esther story in early modern thought.

However, it remains important to acknowledge the limitations
to Williams' notion of religious liberty. Rather than being a modern
liberal prophet, Williams very much reflected the influences of his
seventeenth-century context. Belief in not persecuting religious minorities did not imply a respect for religious difference. Williams did not
accept the relativistic view of multiple legitimate paths toward God;
he firmly believed in his own faith and castigated those who disagreed
with him.[31] Moreover, separation of church and state did not necessitate

Mercy and Justice: Sir Henry Vane on Adam, the 'Natural Man,' and the Politics of
the Conscience," *The Journal of Religion* 79, no. 1 (January 1999): 54–85 (p. 57 n. 9);
for connections to Williams, see *Dictionary of National Biography,* s.v. "Vane, Henry."
28. *The Examiner Examined. Certaine Questions proposed to the Author of Zeale examined
concerning his Principles* (London, 1652), 4, 9.
29. [Roger Williams,] *The Examiner Defended, in a Fair and Sober Answer to the Two
and Twenty Questions Which Lately Examined the Author of Zeal Examined* (London,
1652), 30–31, 89–95. For Williams' views on Islam, see Denise Spellberg, "Muslims,
Toleration, and Civil Rights from Roger Williams to Thomas Jefferson," in *The Lively
Experiment: Religious Toleration in America from Roger Williams to the Present,* ed.
Chris Beneke and Christopher S. Grenda (Lanham, 2015), 85–100 (pp. 85–93). On
the omission of slaves' religions, see the editors' introduction to the latter volume,
p. 17 n. 4.
30. *Anti-Cotton Answered* (London, 1653), 14–15, 34–35.
31. Reiner Smolinski, "'The Way to Lost Zion': The Cotton-Williams Debate on the
Separation of Church and State in Millenarian Perspective," in *Millenial Thought in
America: Historical and Intellectual Contexts, 1630–1860,* ed. Bernd Engler, Joerg O.
Fichte, and Oliver Scheiding (Triet, 2002), 61–96; Feisal G. Mohamed, "A Feminism

the latter's secular nature. Williams' notion of a "wall of separation" between church and state aimed to protect religious purity rather than create a secular disestablishment.[32] Rhode Island struggled to maintain order with its religious diversity, and it perpetuated the pro-Protestant attitude prevalent in other colonies.[33] Despite their deep interest in the Old Testament, Puritans generally looked unfavorably toward real-life Jews, who remained unwelcome throughout colonial New England.[34] Nevertheless, Williams' derivation of religious liberty from Artaxerxes went further than contemporary ideas.[35]

While learned men such as Cotton and Williams debated the political lessons of ancient Persia, a famous Puritan woman offered a literary intervention. Anne Bradstreet (1612–1672), the first published poet in America, addressed the Persian monarchy in her versified retelling of ancient history. Bradstreet's poetry collection *The Tenth Muse Lately Sprung up in America* (1650) contained a section on "Artaxerxes

---

of Convenience: Roger Williams, Egyptian Salafists and Liberty of Conscience for Women," in *Religious Tolerance in the Atlantic World*, ed. Eliane Glaser (London, 2014), 235–252.

32. Daniel L. Dreisbach, *Thomas Jefferson and the Wall of Separation between Church and State* (New York, 2002), 76–79. For arguments denying Williams' influence on disestablishment in the early republic, see Thomas J. Curry, *The First Freedoms: Church and State in America to the Passage of the First Amendment* (New York, 1986), 15; Steven K. Green, *Inventing a Christian America: The Myth of the Religious Founding* (New York, 2015), 39–41.

33. Theodore Dwight Bozeman, "Religious Liberty and the Problem of Order in Early Rhode Island," *The New England Quarterly* 45, no. 1 (March 1972): 44–64; James S. Kabala, "Church and State in Rhode Island," in *Disestablishment and Religious Dissent: Church-State Relations in the New American States, 1776–1833*, ed. Carl H. Esbeck and Jonathan J. Den Hartog (Columbia, 2019), 55–70.

34. Michael Hoberman, *New Israel/New England: Jews and Puritans in Early America* (Amherst, 2011), 86–120; Holly Snyder, "Roger Williams, English Law and Religious Tolerance: The Jewish Experience in the Southern New England Colonies, 1677–1798," in *Religion and the State: Europe and North America in the Seventeenth and Eighteenth Centuries*, ed. Josh B. Stein and Sargon G. Donabed (Blue Ridge Summit, 2012), 107–126.

35. For a contextual approach, see the essays in part one of Beneke and Grenda, eds., *Lively Experiment*. For early modern England, see John Coffey, *Persecution and Toleration in Protestant England 1588–1689* (New York, 2013); Alexandra Walsham, *Charitable Hatred: Tolerance and Intolerance in England, 1500–1700* (Manchester, 2006).

Longimanus." In a series of rhyming couplets, Bradstreet provided the historical context behind the beginning of the Esther story: "Greeks and Egyptians both he overthrows, / And payes them both according as he owes, / Which done, a sumptuous feast makes like a king / Where ninescore dayes are spent in banqueting." Bradstreet's description of the feast explicitly drew upon details from the biblical account: "His Princes, Nobles, and his Captains calls, / To be partakers of these Festivals: / His hangings white and green, and purple dye, / With gold and silver beds most gorgeously." After dispensing with the character of Vashti – "Queen Vasthi also feasts, but 'fore tis ended, / She's from her Royalty (alas) suspended, / And one more worthy placed in her room, / By Memucans advice so was the doom" – Bradstreet turned her attention to the rise of Jewish power under Esther's queenship: "What Esther was and did, the story read, / And how her Country men from spoyle she freed, / Of Hamans fall, and Mordicaes great Rise. / The might of the prince, the tribute of the Isles." Finally, Bradstreet's inclusion of Ezra reflected the influence of Walter Raleigh's *History*, which had conflated Ahasuerus with Artaxerxes: "Good Ezra in the seventh year of his reign, / Did for the Jews commission large obtain, / With gold and silver, and what ere they need: / His bounty did Darius far exceed."[36] Bradstreet's extended engagement with ancient monarchies undoubtedly spoke to contemporary anxieties about the English Civil War, which had resulted in the execution of Charles I in 1649; additionally, her emphasis on Esther's agency paralleled the role of women as "deputy husbands" in Puritan New England.[37]

From Charles I's execution until the Restoration of the monarchy in 1660 under Charles II (d. 1685), Puritans dominated English politics and created a biblicist regime much like the one in Massachusetts.[38] During this Interregnum period, when Oliver Cromwell (1599–1658) ruled England as Lord Protector, Anglican Bible commentator

36. Anne Bradstreet, *The Tenth Muse Lately Sprung up in America* (London, 1650), 106–108.
37. Jane D. Eberwein, "Civil War and Bradstreet's 'Monarchies,'" *Early American Literature* 26, no. 2 (1991): 119–144; Laurel Thatcher Ulrich, *Good Wives: Image and Reality in the Lives of Women in Northern New England, 1650–1750* (New York, 1980).
38. See, e.g., Keith Thomas, "The Puritans and Adultery: The Act of 1650 Reconsidered,"

John Trapp (1601–1669) illustrated how the ideas of both America and Puritanism influenced interpretations of Esther. Firstly, Trapp insisted that Ahasuerus "must needs be *Xerxes*; for he subdued *Ethiopia*, and thereupon made this great feast. He was Lord, we see, of a very great part of the habitable world.... No part of the world is left untouched by him but *America* onely." The exclusion of America from the domain of Xerxes' empire reflected an important development in biblical scholarship, which had to account for the omission of the New World in biblical geography.[39] Additionally, Trapp proceeded to describe how Puritans offered an esoteric reading of Esther: "Those that seek a mysterie in this history tell us, that *Ahashuerosh* typically representeth God the Father soveraigning over all Kingdomes and creatures on earth; chusing some to be heires of heaven, and purifying them for that purpose."[40] Despite his status as a pagan king, Ahasuerus served as a metaphor for the Puritan theology of predestination, that God predetermined only a portion of the population for His grace. Although he did not offer political commentary here, Trapp further demonstrated the adaptability of Anglo-American perspectives on Esther.

During the Restoration, political treatments of Esther reflected opposition to the religious hegemony of the Church of England. In 1661, an anonymous editor published an adaptation of a chapter in Roman-Jewish historian Flavius Josephus' (37–100 CE) *Antiquities* entitled *The Folly and Wisdom of the Ancients*. The subtitle alluded to the text's contemporary significance: "Recommended to the Judicious, to Consider how far the Case therein Exprest, may concern our Present Times, either Prophetically or Parallel." The document contained a literary retelling of "Two Letters of Artaxerxes that Great King, as they are Recorded by Josephus." The initial decree castigated the Jews for "differing in the strange manner of their laws," whereas the reversal acknowledged that

---

in *Puritans and Revolutionaries: Essays in Seventeenth-Century History Presented to Christopher Hill*, ed. Donald H. Pennington and Keith Thomas (Oxford, 1978), 257–282.

39. Hence the origins of the Jewish Indian theory; see Elizabeth Fenton, *Old Canaan in a New World: Native Americans and the Lost Tribes of Israel* (New York, 2020).

40. John Trapp, *A Commentary or Exposition upon the Books of Ezra, Nehemiah, Esther, Job and Psalms* (London, 1657), 24, 104.

the Jews "are *no evil doers*, but live by most *Just Laws*."[41] Similarly, three years later, a pamphlet analogized the political status of Quakers to Haman's description of Jews, citing Esther 3:8–9 on the title page.[42] In the political context of the Restoration, these writers presumably hoped that Ahasuerus/Artaxerxes' respect for Jewish law would inspire favorable Anglican treatment of dissenters in England.

The Esther story continued to engage political thinkers throughout the Restoration period and into the early eighteenth century. After the Glorious Revolution of 1688 deposed Charles II's successor James II, the biblicist regime in Puritan Massachusetts ended under William III's new charter in 1692.[43] Subsequently, theologian Cotton Mather (1663–1728), a prolific author and bastion of Massachusetts' orthodoxy, synthesized Esther scholarship in his mammoth *Biblia Americana* commentary (1693–1728), which grappled with the problem of biblical historicity.[44] After extensive discussion, Mather concluded that Ahasuerus and Artaxerxes referred to the same monarch. Mather approvingly cited the opinion of Humphrey Prideaux (1648–1724),[45] who "determined the Ahasuerus in this Book, to be Artaxerxes…. [Prideaux] brings many unanswerable reasons against those two Pretenders, *Darius* and

41. Anonymous, *The Folly and Wisdom of the Ancients* (London, 1661), title page, 2, 5. For a seventeenth-century treatment of Esther that also used Josephus for source material, see Russell E. Martin, "Muscovite Esther: Bride Shows, Queenship, and Power in *The Comedy of Artaxerxes*," in *The New Muscovite Cultural History: A Collection in Honor of Daniel B. Rowland*, ed. Valerie Kivelson et al. (Bloomington, 2009), 21–42.
42. John Crook, *A True Information to the Nation, from the People Called Quakers* (London, 1664), title page.
43. Michael Winship, *Hot Protestants: A History of Puritanism in England and America* (New Haven, 2018).
44. For more on Mather's interpretation of Esther, see Ariel Clark Silver, *The Book of Esther and the Typology of Female Transfiguration in American Literature* (Lanham, 2018), 27–49; and Stuart Halpern's chapter, "Puritan Purim," in this volume. On Mather and biblical historicity, see Jan Stievermann, *Prophecy, Piety, and the Problem of Historicity: Interpreting the Hebrew Scriptures in Cotton Mather's 'Biblia Americana'* (Tübingen, 2016).
45. Humphrey Prideaux, *Old and New Testament Connected*, 7th ed. (London, 1720), pt. 1, bk. 4, pp. 197–200. The marginalia of the Great Bible (1539) and Bishop's Bible (1568) both cited Prideaux approvingly (Est. 1:1), and both identified the counselors in Ezra 7:14 with the ones in Esther 1:14.

Xerxes." After rejecting the latter two theories of Ahasuerus' identity, Mather invoked a variety of ancient sources, including Josephus, in support of Prideaux's position: "But now, *Josephus* positively tells us, That *Ahasuerus* was this *Artaxerxes* whom we are now claiming for. And the Septuagint, throughout the whole Book, where the Text ha's *Ahasuerus*, reads *Artaxerxes*. And *Severus Sulpicius* [363–425 CE], with many other Ancients as well as Moderns, come into this Opinion." Finally, Mather saw a natural cohesion between the Esther and Ezra narratives: "And the extraordinary Favours, done by *Artaxerxes Longimanus*, unto the Jews, beyond any former Kings of *Persia*, sending first *Ezra*, and afterwards *Nehemiah*, for the restoring of their ancient Prosperity, agree well in their having in his Bosom, such a powerful Advocate as Q. *Esther* for them."[46] In this view, Ahasuerus/Artaxerxes emerged as a benevolent ally of the Jews.

However, Mather's perspective on the favorable status of ancient Persian Jewry also reflected the ambivalent conceptions of Judaism in Puritan thought. Regarding Ezra 7, Mather acknowledged that Artaxerxes granted the Jews a "Liberty to live by their own Lawes, and to judge all Causes according to them. And … a Power to sentence Men according to their own Lawes." Yet Mather's anti-Jewish attitude colored his praise of Artaxerxes: "This *Persian* King, is Evidently possessed with a greater Dread of the Displeasure of God, than the Kings of *Judah* themselves generally were, before the Captivity."[47] Unlike Williams, Mather presumably agreed with the argument of his namesake John Cotton that Artaxerxes served as a model for the fusion of church and state. Furthermore, Mather's opprobrium toward Jewry manifested in his analysis of Ahasuerus' treatment of Vashti: "As the great King of Persia dealt with his proud Queen *Vasti*, so dealt the King of Heaven, with the insolent *Jewes*; Hee hath Repudiated them…. A *Type*, which perhaps, the *Jewes* then little thought of!"[48] Thus, Artaxerxes' benevolence to the Jews did

---

46. Cotton Mather, *Biblia Americana, Volume 4: Ezra-Psalms*, ed. Harry C. Maddux (Tübingen, 2013), 163–164 (see also pp. 139, 791).
47. Mather, 104. The editor refers to Simon Patrick, *A Commentary upon the Historical Books of the Old Testament*, 3rd corrected ed., 2 vols. (London, 1727), 2:663–664.
48. Mather, 143. The editor refers to Trapp, 116.

not lead Puritans to a favorable attitude toward latter-day Israelites or religious dissenters.

As a final note to this reception history of Esther in early colonial America,[49] let us briefly consider how the early modern debates over the politics of Esther might intersect with traditional Jewish thought. Although the Talmud did not conflate Ahasuerus with Artaxerxes,[50] a midrash on Esther did record such an opinion.[51] Additionally, at least two medieval Jewish scholars maintained this position.[52] While rabbinic literature generally offers a negative viewpoint on Ahasuerus,[53] the minority opinion that identified the latter as Artaxerxes undoubtedly viewed him more positively in light of his support of the Jews in Ezra 7. Fittingly, as Jewish tradition connects the reacceptance of the Oral Law to the Purim story,[54] the contrast between Haman's enmity and Artaxerxes' affinity – whatever the latter's motivations or influences – stands out prominently. Beyond merely celebrating the prevention of their annihilation, Jews can fondly remember an eminently favorable Persian monarchy under which they experienced a degree of freedom to pursue their faith unparalleled until the modern State of Israel.[55]

49. For Esther in revolutionary America, see Eran Shalev, "Evil Counselors, Corrupt Traitors, and Bad Kings: The Hebrew Bible and Political Critique in Revolutionary America and Beyond," in *Resistance to Tyrants, Obedience to God: Reason, Religion, and Republicanism at the American Founding*, ed. Dustin Gish and Daniel Klinghard (Lanham, 2013), 105–124; idem, *American Zion: The Old Testament as a Political Text from the Revolution to the Civil War* (New Haven, 2013) 27–34; and Shalev's chapter in this volume.

50. Rosh HaShana 3b conflates Cyrus, Darius, and Artaxerxes. Cf. *Baal HaMaor* ad loc., who distinguished between the three kings.

51. R. Levi in Esther Rabba 1:3. However, *Etz Yosef* there argues that R. Levi referred to the Artaxerxes of Ezra 4, rather than Ezra 7, which have different spellings in the original Hebrew.

52. Ibn Ezra to Esther 1:1, Ezra 4:6 (commentary on Ezra attributed to Rabbi Moshe Kimhi); Ralbag to Ezra 4:7.

53. *Jewish Encyclopedia*, s.v. "Ahasuerus," http://jewishencyclopedia.com/articles/967-ahasuerus; *Encyclopedia of the Bible and its Reception*, s.v. "Ahasuerus" (Berlin, 2009). For rabbinic views on Esther generally, see Aaron Koller, *Esther in Ancient Jewish Thought* (New York, 2014).

54. Shabbat 88a.

55. Cf. David Biale, *Power & Powerlessness in Jewish History* (New York, 1986).

Haman in the American Revolution

Dr. Eran Shalev

Revolutionary Americans who fought for their independence enlisted a vivid biblical imagination to make sense of the political turmoil they faced. A seventeenth-century Calvinist ethos that was inclined toward the Old Testament and singled out New England as a "chosen nation" now resurged throughout the embattled colonies.[1] Armed with the old-new image of an "American Israel" and "Second Israel," late eighteenth-century American revolutionaries operated within

---

1. Mark Noll, *God and Race in American Politics* (Princeton, 2010), 24–25. For explorations of the concept of chosenness and modern nationalism, see Anthony D. Smith, *Chosen Peoples: Sacred Sources of National Identity* (Oxford, 2003); Adrian Hastings, *The Construction of Nationhood: Ethnicity, Religion, and Nationalism* (Cambridge, 1977); William R. Hutchison and Hartmut Lehmann, eds., *Many Are Chosen: Divine Election and Western Nationalism* (Minneapolis, 1994). The Puritans were disciples of a Protestant theology that stemmed with Jean Calvin (1509–1564) and held a harsh deterministic worldview upon which ruled a mighty God that was closer to the Old Testament's Lord of Hosts rather than to the Jesus of the New Testament.

a political culture in which, in the words of Perry Miller, the Hebrew Bible was as "omnipresent ... as ... the air that people breathed."[2]

During the decade of resistance and rebellion (1765–1776) the American public produced and consumed an unprecedented outpouring of speeches, polemical newspaper articles, and sermons on issues pertaining to their political predicament. Much of that outpouring was filtered through the prism of the Old Testament; its themes may indeed have "suffused the minds" of the citizens of the young United States.[3] The participants in the discourse of this Old Testament biblicism were Christians who treated "the American Israel" in terms that were not metaphorical but rather demonstrative of their conviction of a God still operative in history. This Old Testament biblicism provided them with a language to conciliate a modern republican experiment with the desire for biblical sanction, as well as a means to discuss the matters of the hour in a well-known and respected language and imagery. Engaged for the first time with an encroaching administration that threatened their customary liberties, these colonists were thus naturally drawn to narratives that on the one hand underscored their republican sensibilities (particularly the fear of amassed political power and corruption) and on the other hand could make sense to the American public in narratives and archetypes that were well known. One of the popular and meaningful tropes public speakers and commentators made use of was that of the malicious and scheming Haman.

The repeal of the Stamp Act of 1765 in the following year was celebrated in the British American colonies. Colonials who were scared by the attempt to directly tax them for the first time in their history were relieved that the British administration seemed to have come to its senses. Americans wished to assure their monarch that the man ("whoever he be, and whatever is his Station") that had been "the instrument of conveying to his Majesty such Sentiments of his faithful [American] and

---

2. Perry Miller, "The Garden of Eden and the Deacon's Meadow," *American Heritage Magazine* 7, issue 1 (December 1955), http://www.americanheritage.com/articles/magazine/ah/1955/1/1955_1_54.shtml (viewed August 9, 2020).

3. Philip L. Barlow, *Mormons and the Bible: The Place of the Latter-Day Saints in American Religion* (New York, 1991), 5.

loving Subjects...is a vile Slanderer and Accuser of the People, and a Traitor to his Prince." In short, such a man was "as great an Enemy...as was wicked Haman to the Jews."[4] As this quotation hints, the appeal to the story told in the biblical Book of Esther, while emphasizing the king's villainous counselor Haman, became a popular mode of interpreting imperial politics. Emphasizing Haman (who acted as an allegory for George III's ministers and advisers) allowed colonials to protect a seemingly duped king while severely criticizing his policies. It also further underscores the attraction and benefits that Patriots found in the years and months preceding Independence in using the Bible as a guide and manual on oppositional politics in a still monarchical political culture.

The story of the Persian king's pious Jewish wife Esther and her virtuous cousin Mordecai, who together foiled Haman's planned genocidal massacre of the realm's Jews, thus provided British North American colonials with important tropes that would assist them in interpreting court and imperial policy. British North American colonials who, according to Bernard Bailyn, were "generally acquainted" with that particular biblical story, enlisted it frequently from 1765 until the separation from the British monarchy in 1776, after which it became irrelevant when the United States was no longer ruled by a king nor influenced by court politics.[5]

The eighteenth-century tendency to interpret history as a stage on which great men determined single-handedly the fate of nations helped in ascribing political ruin to a single powerful and malevolent enemy of the common good. While a ruthless general such as Julius Caesar was understood to have destroyed the Roman republic for his own selfish purposes, American republicans observed that Persia boasted its own villain: the king's bloodthirsty prime minister, Haman. Demonstrating the classical mindset through which Americans interpreted Haman's character and actions, commentators compared the Persian minister with history's "greatest conquerors, or absolute monarchs," who were never "satisfied with their power." If such juxtapositions were not bold

4. *Boston Gazette*, November 24, 1766.
5. Bernard Bailyn, The *Ideological Origins of the American Revolution* (Cambridge, 1967), 127.

enough, there were those who compared Haman's genocidal ferocity to the psychopathic Roman Caesar Nero, "who wished that all the Romans had one neck, that he might have the pleasure of cutting them all off at one blow."[6] This conflation of biblical and classical corruption enabled revolutionary Americans to identify a history of repeated attacks of power-hungry men, sinking once-virtuous nations and empires, from Persia to Britain, "into the very jaws of slavery, vassalage, and ruin."[7]

The focus on the character and role of that evil minister is deeply instructive for understanding the ways in which authors, commentators, and preachers, and hence presumably their large audiences, made sense of civic corruption (the kind of which they attributed to England) through biblical narratives. This discourse, still monarchical and yet already specked with republicanism, was unmistakably useful: American commentators told their audiences specifically that Haman's friends accused the Jews of being "inclined to republican principles" (which would have been a dangerous accusation in monarchical Persia but a badge of honor in opposition circles in America).[8] This interpretation of court politics and British policy along biblical lines may have eroded the legitimacy of the British monarchy in the long run; more immediately, it helped in articulating commonwealthean modes of thought which were strongly related to notions of civic corruption.

Among "the many wicked men, whose characters are handed down to us in the scripture-history," revolutionary-era Americans seemed to have agreed that Haman was "one of the most remarkable."[9] If earlier generations would probably have interpreted Haman's character in theological terms, revolutionaries represented the scheming minister time and again in a civic language.[10] The story was particularly useful, as we have already noted, for colonial Americans still

---

6. Thomas Reese, "The Character of Haman," in *The American Preacher*, ed. David Austin (4 vols., Elizabethtown, 1791–1793), II, 330, 331.

7. Oliver Noble, *Some Strictures upon the Sacred Story Recorded in the Book of Esther* (Newburyport, 1775), 5.

8. James Murray, *Sermons to the Ministers of State: By the Author of, Sermons to the Asses* (Philadelphia, 1783), 49.

9. Reese, 324.

10. Ibid.

working within a political tradition that exempted monarchs from misdeeds: like George III, the Persian king Ahasuerus "reigned over many distant provinces," and was, "by his prime minister, induced to oppress, and take measures to destroy many of his subjects." The use of the passive voice, underscoring that the king was "*induced*" by his active "prime minister" who "*led* his sovereign to view many of his innocent subjects as rebels" to destroy lawful and law-abiding subjects, is particularly instructive.[11] While ultimately eroding the legitimacy of the king, this language identified modern Hamans as King George's familiars such as Lord Bute and later Lord North, or even military commanders sent to pacify America such as John Burgoyne. Those British Hamans were deemed the main perpetrators in a conspiracy against American liberties, a conspiracy as much against their king as it was against his colonial subjects.[12] It was surely against the king's and the kingdom's best interests to outlaw the Persian Jews, as well as to rob Americans of their British rights, and then, Americans claimed frantically, to "appoint the time of their destruction." But Haman's evil genius, and apparently the English counselors' as well, enabled them to persuade their respective kings to act against their, and their countries', best interests.[13]

This is not to say that American colonials were so naïve as to absolve the king by putting the blame solely on mischievous ministers (though it is unlikely that the talmudic debate in Tractate Megilla [12a] over whether the Persian monarch was a wise king or a foolish king was familiar to them). This interpretation of imperial politics demonstrates, however, the reversion to a traditional mode of political analysis and expression, one in which underlings take the blame for deceiving a monarch against his best own interest. Congress' repeated appeals and petitions to the king in the hope that on learning in person of their sufferings the benevolent George III would immediately return to the policy of Salutary Neglect, demonstrates the persistence of this

---

11. *New York Journal*, September 1774.
12. For the Burgoyne reference see, "Burgoyne's Proclamation," in *Songs and Ballads of the American Revolution*, ed. Frank Moore (New York, 1855), 173.
13. Murray, 52.

mindset.[14] The trope of Haman was thus a perfect fit for criticizing a policy (and its alleged progenitors) while keeping at least nominal respect toward the king.

Yet another characteristic made Haman very useful for American Patriots: Haman, unlike other popular historical villains such as the Roman Catiline and Jugurtha, did not attempt to attack the polity from the outside with military power. Instead he manipulated and duped a monarch to subvert an empire from within. So at least until the beginning of open warfare with the British in April 1775, the courtier Haman was much more relevant for Americans than the enemies of the Roman republic. Nevertheless, Haman's character as portrayed in contemporary polemical literature bore the distinct marks of classical corruption: through his relentless scheming and lying, his ruinous pride and ambition, his political power and consuming hatred for the Jews, the king's advisor was a menace to society, even to a monarchical one that was supposedly more immune than a republic to the harms of corruption. Americans had to speculate on how Haman secured his position in Ahasuerus' court in the first place, as the biblical text gave little evidence on this; they determined that it was not through any distinct merit or ability, but only by being "an adroit courtier, expert in flattery, and by falling in with the king's humours, and ministering to his pleasures, [he] artfully wrought himself into favor."[15]

This view of Haman in light of the imperial scuffing was not confined to the biblically induced colonies of New England, as South Carolinian clergymen also found it convenient to preach the political corruption of Britain's leadership as a story of biblical decadence. Thomas Reese, for example, a southern Presbyterian minister, remarked in a sermon titled "The Character of Haman" that ambition "sticks at nothing to compass its designs. It wades to empire through seas of blood. No principles of religion, virtue or humanity can restrain the

---

14. Salutary Neglect was the pro-American interpretation of the British Empire's apparent indifference toward the development of its American colonies. Advocates of Salutary Neglect believed that the fact that the colonies were left to themselves to develop ("neglected") was beneficial to the colonies and to Britain.

15. Reese, 325.

wretch, whose ruling passion is the lust for power." A conniving courtier such as Haman would sacrifice all to achieve "his beloved object," the destruction of his innocent enemies. He will "stop at no act of cruelty, however horrid, which he thinks may forward his designs. Treachery, poison, daggers, and all the instruments of death are employed without remorse. He cares not how much blood he spills, nor how much misery he causes, if he can only gain his point."[16] Haman, just like other dangerous ambitious men from Julius Caesar to Lord North, "would risk an empire rather than lose this gratification."[17]

Most commentators agreed that the ordeal of the Jews, as told in the Book of Esther, began when Mordecai, depicted by contemporaries as "that great patriot," would pay "no compliments to the ambitious Haman," refusing to bow to the minister and satisfy his limitless pride.[18] Haman, "the second man in the empire, and highly in favour both with the king and the queen," could have been satisfied with his elevated position within the empire, as the king and queen "had every favour shewn [on] him that he could expect." In a language that was still tolerant of monarchy, American colonials depicted the king's aides as British embodiments of Haman, who in republican language was an evil creature whom nothing would please "unless poor Mordecai was brought to his feet." All Haman's honors and riches "were nothing as long as Mordecai the Jew did not cringe to him...his whole heart was set upon this one object, and all his glory could not ease his melancholy while this rub was in his way."[19] So despicable and anti-social was Haman's behavior that he was "ready to tell over all Shusan [biblical Persia's capital city], that this Mordecai was one of the King's enemies, because he did not bow to the nod of his prime minister."[20]

Thus started Haman's egotistical and ferocious campaign against the Jews that would end in his own destruction; the slight to the minister's pride, the fact that Mordecai would not pay him the respect he

---

16. Reese, 331.
17. Murray, 52.
18. *Boston Gazette*, November 4, 1765.
19. Murray, 52–53.
20. Ibid., 49.

thought he deserved, initiated the chain of events that ended with Haman falling "into those very pits" that he had dug for his righteous enemies, and "hang'd on the very gallows ... [he had] erected for others."[21] These gallows, "the tree, which proud Haman for Mordecai rear'd," were a symbol and sign that "virtue endanger'd is spar'd," and that ambitious men "whom no bonds and no laws can restrain" might be "stript of their honors, and humbled" once more.[22] Americans sounded a stark warning to the British Hamans.

Yet Haman's pride was not the most dangerous of the minister's traits. His more fundamental flaw was one well known in the republican idiom, his "insatiate lust for power... and influence." Bernard Bailyn showed long ago how power, the aggressive strive for dominion over other men and its war on liberty, stood at the center of classical republicanism.[23] Patriots repeated this notion time and again when referring to Haman: "The lust of power is a strong passion! It is a sweet thing to ambitious men to see all the world cringing as their humble servants."[24] Had Haman, "whose ruling passion is the lust of power," succeeded in his "bloody purpose... do you think he would have been satisfied?" Obviously he would not; such consuming narcissistic ambition, the complete opposite of virtuous republican disinterestedness, would have continued to propel the "empire through seas of blood."[25] Haman's perceived lust for power was thus repeatedly interpreted in a civic humanist light, as combining "the worst passions of the human heart, and the worst projects of the human mind, in league against the liberties of mankind." While Ahasuerus and George III might have been "naturally of a compassionate and benevolent heart," behind them "court-locusts... designing men, this kind of patriots, always lay their plan with a view, to skulk behind the king's authority." However, if Haman, the "haughty prime-minister – and his junto of court parasites," was able to influence the

---

21. Amicus Republica, *Freeman's Journal*, August 3, 1776.
22. "The Parody Parodized" (1768), in Frank Moore, *Songs and Ballads of the American Revolution* (New York, 1855), 45.
23. Bailyn, 55–60.
24. Murray, 52.
25. Reese, 329, 331.

king and obtain from him "that horrid decree to slaughter the Jews in all the provinces," what did this speak of the king?

As the contest between Britain and the colonies grew more bitter, American Patriots became less forgiving toward the king. As time passed, Americans could see George as "brought into a state of magnificent servitude" by his Haman-like ministers. The Book of Esther told of the danger that "over-grown ministers and courtiers" posed both to kings and states.[26] But now the king too came under censure, as being "too ready to believe evil of his subjects, and to comply with the oppressive measures of his prime minister." Even if not yet a full-blown perpetrator of acts against the colonies himself, George III was still seen through the prism of Ahasuerus, "taken up with his Queen and the luxuries of the court, and committ[ing] the management of his political affairs to a very bad man."[27] The king's status was eroding, and his identification as an Ahasuerus both reflected and propelled his fall from grace.

Once the split between Britain and its colonies became final, and his colonial subjects declared the British king an open enemy, the Book of Esther would become politically irrelevant. Nevertheless, during the decade of American resistance to British attempts to impose taxes on the colonies, the story of the Book of Esther, with its monarchical and courtly contexts, offered Americans an invaluable outlet through which to interpret and contextualize their grievances. Ultimately, it may also have helped them in the process of desecrating and disposing of a king who was time and again presented as a dupe led by a corrupt and murderous minister.

---

26. Noble, 5–6, 11.
27. *New York Journal*, September 1, 1774.

Mordecai's Ark: An American Tale?

Rabbi Dr. Stuart W. Halpern

And Mordecai went forth from the presence of the king in royal apparel of blue and white, and with a great crown of gold, and with a robe of fine linen and purple; and the city of Shushan shouted and was glad. (Est. 8:15)

Bible, square and compass, borne by a master mason, the Judge of Israel in black, wearing the judicial robes of crimson silk, trimmed with ermine, and a richly embossed gold medal suspended from the neck. The procession enters the church... ("Ceremonies at the laying of the corner stone of the city of Ararat on September 2, 1825," *Niles' Register*, Baltimore, Maryland, November 26, 1831)

The bear and the Indians were late. Mordecai Manuel Noah, the Philadelphia-born prominent playwright, journalist, editor, sheriff, lawyer, and diplomat (having briefly served as consul at Tunis, one of the Barbary States in North Africa), had chartered a small boat from

Grand Island in upstate New York to participate in the flotilla celebrating the opening of the Erie Canal in 1825. The boat, which he named *Noah's Ark*, contained, beyond a bear and Native Americans, two eagles, two fawns, and assorted fish, birds, and other animals.[1] The five-ton ship never reached its intended destination of New York City, however, having been damaged attempting to navigate one of the canal's locks, and had to turn back.

Noah's failed *Ark* encapsulated his larger project, attempting to establish a Jewish homeland on Grand Island itself (Noah's maternal grandfather was the Revolutionary War veteran Jonas Phillips, who in 1787 had addressed the Constitutional Convention to advocate for religious liberty). His intention was to improve the condition of the Jews of the world by creating a haven for them, which, through their presence on the island, would develop the island's natural resources for the benefit of all Americans. Additionally, a substantive presence on the island would serve as a bulwark against potential British aggression.[2] Having spent many years advocating, in high-profile public settings[3] and various

<hr />

1. This chapter's account of Noah's story is deeply indebted to Jonathan D. Sarna, *Jacksonian Jew: The Two Worlds of Mordecai Manuel Noah* (New York, 1981), a full-length treatment of Noah's life; Arthur Hertzberg, *The Jews in America: Four Centuries of an Uneasy Encounter: A History* (New York, 1989), 90–98; Adam Rovner, *In the Shadow of Zion: Promised Lands Before Israel* (New York, 2014), 15–43; and Michael Schuldiner and Daniel J. Kleinfeld, eds., *The Selected Writings of Mordecai Noah* (Westport, 1999).
2. Among the Jews that Noah envisioned benefiting from this plan were European Jews who had recently been subjected to the Hep! Hep! Riots in Germany, and Native Americans, whom Noah and others (including, for a time, Thomas Jefferson) believed to have been descendants of the Ten Lost Tribes. In 1837 Noah delivered an address before the Mercantile Library Association in New York titled "Discourse on the Evidences of the American Indians Being the Descendants of the Lost Tribes of Israel." On the imagined history of the tribes subsequent to their dispersal by the Assyrians in 722 BCE, see Cyrus Gordon, "The Ten Lost Tribes," Richard H. Popkin, "The Rise and Fall of the Jewish Indian Theory," and Grant Underwood, "The *Hope of Israel* in Early Modern Ethnography and Eschatology," in Shalom Goldman, ed., *Hebrew and the Bible in America: The First Two Centuries* (Hanover, 1993), 62–101; Zvi Ben-Dor Benite, *The Ten Lost Tribes: A World History* (Oxford, 2009).
3. Including the keynote address at the dedication ceremony of New York's Congregation Shearith Israel's Mill Street Synagogue on April 17, 1818.

media outlets (well beyond the small American Jewish community of his time), for the creation of a state for his brethren in America, Noah believed the "chosen country" for the Chosen People was the United States, that is, at least until the Jews could return to their ancient homeland in Israel. To that end, he wrote to all three living ex-presidents for their thoughts on Jewish American rights, and indeed, John Adams, Thomas Jefferson, and James Madison all wrote back affirming the equality of the Jews of America before the law. Adams' response included his telling the ambitious Noah

> I could find it in my heart to wish that you had been at the head of a hundred thousand Israelites indeed as well disciplin'd as a French army – & marching with them into Judea & making a conquest of that country & restoring your nation to the dominion of it – For I really wish the Jews again in Judea an independent nation.[4]

As historian Jenna Weissman Joselit has noted, the economic and humanitarian components of Noah's plan to purchase the island from New York State, which had bought it from the Seneca Nation, went hand in hand, inspiring the *Christian Intelligencer* to liken Noah to a latter-day Moses or Joshua who would "lead his people through the wilderness to their Canaan in America, flowing with milk and honey."[5] Noah's request to

---

4. "From John Adams to Mordecai M. Noah," 15 March, 1819, available at https://founders.archives.gov/documents/Adams/99-02-02-7097. As Arthur Hertzberg notes, in 1809 Adams wrote that "the Hebrews have done more to civilize men than any other nation. If I were an atheist and believed in blind eternal fate, I should still believe that fate had ordained the Jews to be the most essential instrument for civilizing the nations.... They are the most glorious nation that ever inhabited this earth." However, "while John Adams did not pretend that he loved the Jews, he insisted one had to try, even though 'it is very hard work to love most of them.'" See Hertzberg, 86. John Adams' son, John Quincy Adams, wrote in 1811 that the Jews are "certainly the most extraordinary nation that has ever appeared upon the earth." See John Quincy Adams, *Letters of John Quincy Adams to His Son on the Bible and its Teachings* (Auburn, 1850), 20.
5. "Zion-on-Niagara," *Tablet Magazine* (November 5, 2018), https://www.tabletmag.com/jewish-life-and-religion/273451/zion-on-niagara.

acquire the island was considered by the state assembly in 1820, and the *Albany Daily Advertiser*'s coverage of the story stated that the plan would allow for the Jews to "have their Jerusalem" and "erect their temple" in peace and prosperity on Grand Island. The plan, alas, was rejected as lawmakers didn't want to undervalue the land in advance of the completion of the canal and were hesitant to create a settlement where Jews dwelled apart from their Christian neighbors.

Noah was undaunted, and in 1824, Samuel Leggett, a wealthy friend of Noah's, purchased 2,000 acres for $16,985 (at the time an enormous amount). Newspapers announced that "the foundation stone" of a city to be called Ararat, named for the mountain range upon which the biblical Noah's ark rested after the flood (Gen. 8:4), would be laid close to the time of the canal's official opening (Noah had originally considered naming the site "New Jerusalem"). On September 2, 1825, an elaborate ceremony was planned for Leggett's land on Grand Island and a crowd of locals and a delegation of Indians gathered in anticipation. However, not enough boats could be gathered to bring to the island all those who desired to witness the ceremony, and so the proceedings were quickly shifted to nearby Buffalo's only building large enough to house the day's celebration – St. Paul's Episcopal Church. Thus, soldiers, masons, political leaders, military men, clergy, and musicians proceeded to the church, with Noah, the self-proclaimed "Judge of Israel," at the helm, his ornate costume borrowed from a production of Shakespeare's *Richard III*. Cannons were fired, and a three-hundred-pound sandstone block, upon which was engraved the first verse of the *Shema*, was put on St. Paul's communion table, along with wine, oil, and corn. Noah, in his speech, called upon Jews to settle in this

> "land of milk and honey" [Ex. 3:8] where Israel may repose in peace, under his "vine and fig tree" [Mic. 4:4] and where our people may so familiarize themselves, with the science of government, and the lights of learning and civilation [*sic*], as may qualify them for that great and final restoration to their ancient heritage, which the times so powerfully indicate…. Deprived as our people have been for centuries of a right in the soil, they will learn with particular satisfaction, that here they can till the

land, reap the harvest, and raise the flocks which are unques-
tionably their own; and in the full and unmolested enjoyment of
their religious rights, and of every civil immunity, together with
peace and plenty, they can lift up their voice in gratitude to him,
who sustained our fathers in the wilderness and brought us in
triumph out of the land of Egypt; who assigned to us the safe
keeping of his oracles, who proclaimed us his people, and who
has ever walked before us like a "cloud by day and a pillar of fire
by night" [Ex. 13:21].

In announcing the "re-establish[ment of] the Government of the Jewish Nation...under the auspices and protection of the United States
of America," Noah noted that this "asylum" would be "temporary and
provisionary. The Jews never should and never will relinquish the just
hope of regaining possession of their ancient heritage, and events in the
neighborhood of Palestine indicate an extraordinary change of affairs."

But in the meantime, there would be Ararat. Noah, a devout Jew,[6]
called upon the major rabbinic figures of Europe to lead their flocks to
the island and issued a series of rulings, including granting "equal rights
of privileges" to the "black Jews of India and Africa" as well as to nonrab-
binic sects, including Samaritans and Karaites, and the "Indians of the

---

6. In an 1819 essay titled "The Sabbath," Noah wrote:
    What a noble and illustrious institution is that of *Sabbath*! Millions of beings,
    scattered over the globe, shunning, at the same moment, the allurements of plea-
    sure, the avidity of gain, the habit of labour, and uniting in returning thanks to
    the Disposer of all good, for his manifold blessings, and his paternal protection.
    On this day, man disencumbers himself of care; all temporal concerns are forgot-
    ten, vexatious crosses are no longer remembered, his wearied limbs find repose,
    and all is sunshine around him. He who does not, at proper times, commune
    with his God, loses a great temporal luxury, and hazards his eternal happiness.
    And his Ararat address ended with his appointing
    Roshodes [*sic*] Adar, Feb. 7, 1826, to be observed with suitable demonstrations
    as a day of Thanksgiving to the Lord God of Israel, for the manifold blessings
    and signal protection which he has deigned to extend to his people, and in order
    that on that great occasion our prayers may be offered for the continuance of
    his divine mercy, and the fulfillment of all the promises and pledges made to
    the race of Jacob.

American continent...the descendants of the lost tribes of Israel." The speech appeared in newspapers across America, signed by the "Judge of Israel" and his secretary, Abraham B. Seixas, the nephew of Shearith Israel's first American-born religious leader and a mentor of Noah's, Gershom Mendes Seixas.[7] Noah's rhetoric, coming fifty years after the birth of America, purposely hearkened back to the founding principles of that very nation, and he compared the potential of the "Hebrew nation" of Ararat to enhance the American project through agriculture and industry to the efforts of the original pilgrims who first arrived at Plymouth Bay seeking religious freedom.

Alas, the European rabbis did not heed Noah's call, with one rabbi, Abraham de Cologna, the chief rabbi of Paris, charging Noah with "treason against the Divine Majesty" for attempting to restore Jewish sovereignty before the Messianic Era and suggesting Jews "are too much attached to the countries where they dwell, and devoted to the governments under which they enjoy liberty and protection, not to treat as a mere jest the chimerical consulate of a pseudo restorer."[8] Noah's Ararat plan, despite the theatrics, never got off the ground, just as *Noah's Ark* never made it to its intended destination. Grand Island was sold, relatively cheaply, as timberland in 1833. Noah's boundless energies shifted in subsequent years to other efforts, but his hope was never lost. In 1837 he spoke of how

> the Jewish people must now do something for themselves; they
> must move onward to the accomplishment of that great event
> long foretold – long promised – long expected; and when they

---

7. Seixas, the *ḥazan* and religious leader of Shearith Israel from 1766 until his death in 1816, had, on multiple occasions, envisioned an imminent return of Jews to the Land of Israel. In a 1798 address he remarked, "When we reflect on the situation and circumstances of the present wars, and the depravity and corrupt state of human nature, that prevails almost throughout the world, we must necessarily be led to believe that the glorious period of redemption is near at hand, and that our God will make manifest his intentions of again collecting the scattered remnant of Israel, and establishing them according to his divine promise." See Louis Ruchames, "Mordecai Manuel Noah and Early American Zionism," *American Jewish Historical Quarterly* 64, no. 3 (March 1975): 195–223.
8. Cited in Ruchames, 216.

DO move, that mighty power which has for thousands of years rebuked the proscription and intolerance shown to Jews, by a benign protection of the whole nation, will still cover them with his invincible standard.... Once again unfurl the standard of Judah on Mount Zion, the four corners of the earth will give up the chosen people as the sea will give up its dead, at the sound of the last trumpet. Let the cry be heard in Jerusalem, as it was in the day of the Saracen and the lion-hearted Richard of England, and the rags and wretchedness which have for eighteen centuries enveloped the persons of the Jews, crushed as they were by the persecution and injustice, will fall to the earth.... When taking their rank once more among the nations of the earth, with the good wishes and affectionate regards of the great family of mankind, they may by their tolerance, their good faith, their charity and enlarged liberal views, merit what has been said in their behalf by inspired writers, "Blessed are they who bless Israel."

And so it was, in 1844, at the age of fifty-nine, that Mordecai Manuel Noah, who years earlier had said "if there be any person possessing greater facilities and a more ardent zeal in attempting to restore the Jews to their rights as a sovereign and independent people, to such will I cheerfully surrender the trust," once again launched a plan for Jewish autonomy, this time with a new destination in mind. In front of packed crowds at the New York Tabernacle, Noah, in his "Discourse on the Restoration of the Jews," predicted the Ottoman Empire would fade, and the British Empire would assume control of Palestine, thereby setting the stage for a Jewish return to their biblical homeland. Speaking to his predominantly Christian audience, he proclaimed:

> We have lost all – country, government, kingdom, and power. You have it all – it is yours. It was once ours – it is again to be restored to us. Dismiss, therefore, from your hearts all prejudice which still lurks there against the favoured people of God...and consider their miraculous preservation.... Is it nothing to have had such fathers and founders of their faith as Abraham, Isaac, and Jacob; such mothers as Sarah and Rebecca, Leah and Rachel; such

illustrious women as Miriam and Deborah, Ruth and Esther?...
Is it nothing, my friends, to have outlived all the nations of the
earth, and to have survived all who sought to ruin and destroy us?
Where are those who fought at Marathon, Salamis, and Platea?
Where are the generals of Alexander – the mighty myriads of
Xerxes? Where are the bones of those which once whitened the
plains of Troy? We only hear of them in the pages of history. But
if you ask, Where are the descendants of the million of brave
souls who fell under the triple walls of Jerusalem? Where are
the subjects of David, and Solomon, and the brethren of Jesus?
I answer, Here! Here we are – miraculously preserved – the pure
and unmixed blood of the Hebrews, having the Law for one light,
and God for our Redeemer…. Who can be an infidel when he
looks on the Jews, and sees in them, and the Bible yet firmly in
their grasp, the consummation of all the Divine promises made
to them as a nation? I should think that the very idea, the hope,
the prospect, and, above all, the certainty of restoring Israel to
his own and promised land, would arouse the whole civilized
world to a cordial and happy cooperation. Mankind would spring
from the couch of ease and slumber to see the ensign displayed,
and would exclaim, "The day has come! The promise is fulfilled!"

Calling upon Americans to "pave the way" for a Jewish restoration of
Zion, Noah's speech received a positive review from none other than
the renowned American writer Edgar Allen Poe, who called his thinking
"extraordinary… full of novel and cogent thought." Noah even held a fundraising campaign at Shearith Israel in 1848, one hundred years before
the birth of the modern State of Israel, stating, "It would be the proud-
est day of my life, if I could be present at laying the corner-stone of the
new Temple of Jerusalem." The next year, in an address at the Hebrew
Synagogue in Crosby Street, he envisioned an era in which

> …every country on earth will give up its great men among the Jew-
> ish people, and a combination of talent, wealth, enterprise, learn-
> ing, skill, energy, and bravery will be collected in Palestine, with
> all the lights of science and civilization, and once more elevate

those laws which Moses had consecrated to liberty and the republican form of government. Let us commence the great work, and leave its consummation to our great Shepherd and Redeemer.

Despite support from influential leaders, including many Christians,[9] this attempt too made no progress, and Noah passed away roughly two years later, and, following a fittingly elaborate funeral, was buried in Shearith Israel's Manhattan cemetery. Credited by many, including the late historian Benzion Netanyahu,[10] with anticipating modern Zionism, Noah's story had a particular impact on Israel Zangwill, the playwright most famous for his *The Melting Pot*, a work, set on the holiday of Purim,

---

9. In his earlier Ararat address, Noah, who often argued with Christians who wanted to convert Jews, spoke of how

> We should no more censure the Christians at this day for the cruelties practiced towards the Jews in the early ages, than the Jews should now be made answerable for the factious policies of our ancestors, 500 generations ago. Times have undergone an important change; we all began to feel that we are formed of the same materials, subject to the same frailties, destined to the same death, and hoping for the same immortality. Here then, in this free and happy country, distinctions in religion are unknown; here we enjoy liberty without licentiousness, and land without oppression.

In his 1844 discourse he evoked the belief in God that Jews and Christians share, contra the Jewish people's historical antagonists:

> Egypt, the worshippers of an ox or crocodile, could not love a people who acknowledged only the true God. The Greeks, who murdered Socrates because he taught the existence of that God, equally detested the Jews, who openly proclaimed his unity and omnipotence. The idolatrous Canaanites, the conquered and defeated race, abhorred the Jews for their religious opinions. The Romans, who believed in oracles, soothsayers, and auguries, were always their fierce and reconcilable enemies.

Samuel Goldman, *God's Country: Christian Zionism in America* (Philadelphia, 2018), documents the Christian community's support for Jewish restoration in Noah's time, including by an NYU professor of Hebrew named George Bush, the ancestor of the American presidents. Goldman coins the phrase "doctrine of double Israel" to describe the Christian Zionist belief in the divine role God wishes them to play in their homeland of America, alongside their potential role in assisting Jewish restoration in Israel. See, in particular, 75–82.

10. Rovner, 42.

that wrestled with Jewish identity, persecution, and assimilation.[11] Zangwill, in turn, was an early supporter of Theodor Herzl and the Zionist cause, and chaired the 1895 meeting in which Herzl first presented his plan for the Jewish state.[12]

At its essence, Mordecai Manuel Noah's story, one explicitly connected by Noah himself to the biblical Noah in the naming of both his *Ark* and *Ararat*, a timeless American Jewish story if there ever was one, actually recalls a different biblical predecessor, Mordecai in the Book of Esther. As Adam Kirsch notes in his discussion of the *megilla*,

> To secular, assimilated Jews, in particular, the Esther story has an uncanny familiarity, like an old nightmare that has never been entirely forgotten. After all, Mordecai and Esther, like American Jews today, live in a cosmopolitan, pluralist society where Jews seem defined less by their religious beliefs than by their ethnic loyalties. Just as it is common for American Jews to have first names drawn from Christian or Greco-Roman sources, so these characters are named after Babylonian deities: Mordecai from Marduk, the chief god of Babylon's mythology, and Esther from Ishtar, the goddess of love…. In some essential ways, Jewish life in twenty-first-century America may resemble the Persia of twenty-five hundred years ago more closely than the Poland of three hundred years ago.[13]

Mordecai Manuel Noah's being removed as diplomat to Tunis, as then Secretary of State James Monroe himself wrote in 1815, was due to the perception that Noah's religion would hinder his functioning in the position.[14] The perceived liability of the Jews to the kingdom of Shushan,

---

11. Jo Carruthers, *Esther Through the Centuries* (Malden, 2008), 20.
12. Michael Weingrad, "Messiah, American Style: Mordecai Manuel Noah and the American Refuge," *AJS Review* 31, no. 1 (2007): 75–108. In 1899, Zangwill published a story about Noah, titled "Noah's Ark," which imagined the fate of a German Jew who heeded Noah's call to settle in Ararat.
13. Adam Kirsch, *The People and the Books: 18 Classics of Jewish Literature* (New York, 2016), 33–34.
14. In her analysis of the story of the biblical Joseph, which contains many thematic

despite the positive governmental role Mordecai played in saving the king's life (2:21–23), serves as the core of Haman's accusations against the Jews to Ahasuerus.[15] And of course, questions at the nexus of Jewish loyalty and liability have long plagued America's Jewish community (Noah was often referred to as "Noah the Jew" and "Shylock" throughout his lifetime).[16] The lesson that Noah learned the hard way, that "beneath the veneer of American tolerance lay a considerable layer of anti-Jewish prejudice," despite political involvement and advocacy, has been relearned in subsequent generations.[17] The first Jew to openly confront the challenges and opportunities of American freedom,[18] Mordecai Manuel Noah, like the biblical Mordecai, through his actions, attempted to make the case that Jews could be robed in the clothing of leaders,

and literary parallels to the story of Mordecai and Esther, Carolyn J. Sharp, in her *Irony and Meaning in the Hebrew Bible* (Bloomington, 2009), notes "a keen interest in insider/outsider boundaries and assimilation, the investiture and divestiture of political power, and the masking and unmasking of identity as it relates to power" (55). The same can describe the tensions in Mordecai Manuel Noah's political career.

15. "Haman then said to King Ahasuerus, 'There is a certain people, scattered and dispersed among the other peoples in all the provinces of your realm, whose laws are different from those of any other people and who do not obey the king's laws; and it is not in Your Majesty's interest to tolerate them'" (3:8). See also Kirsch, 43.

16. Schuldiner and Kleinfeld, 8. As Hertzberg wrote in the context of early America and its Jews, "Jews, no matter how intriguing they might be as individuals, remained outsiders. They could become part of America only if they ceased being Jewish" (45).

17. Sarna, 46. For recently published examples documenting this phenomenon, see Rafael Medoff, *The Jews Should Keep Quiet: Franklin D. Roosevelt, Rabbi Stephen S. Wise, and the Holocaust* (Philadelphia, 2019). Medoff recounts that Wise, the Reform rabbi and prominent American Zionist leader, refused, in 1933, to cancel a "Stop Hitler Now" protest rally at Madison Square Garden and compared his stance to Mordecai refusing to back down to "Haman, the Hitler of an earlier Persian day." Encapsulating the challenge of Jews of Wise's era is the remark of First Lady Eleanor Roosevelt, a close friend of Wise's, that "the difficulty is that the country is still full of immigrant Jews, very unlike ourselves. I don't blame them for being as they are. I know what they've been through in other lands, and I'm glad they have freedom at last, and I hope they'll have the chance, among us, to develop all there is in them. But it takes a little time for Americans to be made." See also Bari Weiss, "Donald Trump and the 'Disloyal' Jews," *New York Times*, August 21, 2019, https://www.nytimes.com/2019/08/21/opinion/trump-jews.html.

18. See Sarna, 159–160.

spokespeople, and guardians of their country – for the benefit of their Jewish brethren, and the benefit of all citizens of the realm. Whether that case was a convincing one, in the eyes of their respective Jewish communities or in the minds of the citizenry of their respective home countries, remains open to debate.

Judah Jeitteles, an Austrian leader of the *Haskala* (Jewish Enlightenment) whom some credit with coining the very term *"haskala,"* wrote in 1826 in the Hebrew journal *Bikkurei HaIttim* of the efforts of the American Noah. Echoing the language of Esther 2:5, Jeitteles informed his readers that there was an *"ish Yehudi* (a Jewish man) who dwelled in the *medina* (nation) of North America, and his name was Mordecai Manuel Noah." This Mordecai, who "was sending letters to all the families of the Jews," was, in Jeitteles' opinion, a charlatan to be ignored. Drawing explicitly on the talmudic critique of Mordecai (Megilla 16b) that Mordecai's leadership was only accepted by *most* Jews and not by *all* the Jews, based on the final verse of Esther stating that Mordecai was "popular with the multitude of his brethren (*rov eḥav*)," Jeitteles wrote that "if this was said about Mordecai in those days, how much more so in our days, with regards to Mordecai who dwells in America who is prophesying dreams and nothingness … it should be said that he is not accepted by *all* his brethren, nor *most* of his brethren, nor *few* of his brethren!"

As Michael Eisenberg, a contemporary venture capitalist and American émigré to Israel noted in his polemic commentary on Esther,[19] beyond the possible questioning of Mordecai as a leader, the ending of the *megilla* is further tinged with pessimism and even tragedy, an assimilationist tale of Jews barely retaining their national identity. Unlike the Book of Ruth and its ending genealogy leading to the birth of King David, Esther ends with no look toward a viable future for the Jews of Shushan. Mordecai doesn't leverage his political power to pave the way for a return of the Jews to Israel, where the Second Temple was already standing, but rather is absorbed into the economic and political machine that is the Persian empire. In fact, in his introduction to Eisenberg's book, the Religious Zionist Rabbi Benjamin Lau suggests that contemporary Jews should consider reading, during the *Minḥa* prayers on Purim, the

---

19. *Thus Shall be Done to the Jew* (Ashkelon, 2016) [Hebrew edition].

first two chapters of the biblical Book of Nehemiah, which describe
Nehemiah receiving permission from the Persian king to return to Israel
and rebuild the walls of Jerusalem, as a way to properly end the holiday.[20]
Mordecai Manuel Noah sharpens the question raised by the biblical
Mordecai: Can there be viable Jewish continuity in the diaspora, even
in a country with the freedoms and protections of America? (In a tragic
turn, two of Noah's sons married Christians and one of his grandchildren,
Florence Elizabeth Noah, married Junius Brutus Booth, nephew of Abraham Lincoln's assassin, John Wilkes Booth.[21]) According to Eisenberg
and Israeli Bible scholars including Rabbi Dr. Jonathan Grossman[22] and
Rabbi Menachem Leibtag,[23] the very purpose of the scroll is a satirical
one – to demonstrate that efforts to build vibrant Jewish life outside of
Israel are quixotic. Whether it is the notorious absence of God's name
in the *megilla* as reflective of the hiddenness of His presence outside

---

20. In Lau's words, "If the story of the Megillah is the story of chance and 'the lottery,'
then the story of Nehemiah is the transition from chance to destiny. Rebuilding
Jerusalem and returning the Jewish people to their homeland remains the only
viable solution for the nation that craves an eternal role" (Ibid., 15).

21. "Dream of Jewish State Near Buffalo is Recalled," *New York Times*, September 15,
1975, https://www.nytimes.com/1975/09/15/archives/dream-of-jewish-state-near-
buffalo-is-recalled.html. I thank Dr. Jonathan Sarna for pointing out, in personal
correspondence, the connection to the Booth family. The Noah family tree is available at http://americanjewisharchives.org/publications/fajf/pdfs/stern_p232.pdf.

22. See *Esther: The Outer Narrative and the Hidden Reading* (Winona Lake, 2011) and
his chapter in the festschrift to his father, Prof. Avraham Grossman, who was born
on Shushan Purim, "The Relationship of Megillat Esther to the Diaspora," in *Bless-
ings to Avraham* (Jerusalem, 2018), 1–22. This chapter contains helpful citations of
relevant works on the relationship between *Esther* and the diaspora. See also Elsie
R. Stern, "Esther and the Politics of Diaspora," *The Jewish Quarterly Review* 100, no. 1
(Winter 2010): 25–53, who argues that "Esther's 'message' is not a defense of life
in Diaspora but is, instead, a comic critique of it" and that the book "employ[s] a
barrage of comic techniques to demonstrate that Persian imperial culture and the
forms of Jewishness that develop and flourish within it are meticulous reversals
of…life in the land of Israel" and "the instability of the Diaspora world ensures that
it cannot be paradigmatic and therefore cannot supply any long-term comfort or
confidence." See also the discussion of Carruthers, 39, who cites Jon D. Levenson's
contention that Esther is a "story of the transformation of the *exile* into the *Diaspora*."

23. "Megillat Esther and Its Hidden Message," available at https://tanach.org/special/
purim/purims1.htm.

of Israel, Esther 10:1's description of Ahasuerus' levying of a tax (*mas*) that evokes the mention of Pharaoh placing taskmasters over the Israelites after the death of Joseph (*sarei misim*) in Exodus 1:11, or the story's description of the repeated efforts of Mordecai and Esther to establish the observance of the holiday (9:29–31) reflecting a hesitancy of the wider Jewish community to formally establish a diaspora-focused new holiday, all signs in this reading of Esther point to there being as much of a promising future for Shushan's Jews as there was the chance that a ceremony in St. Paul's Episcopal Church in upstate New York would lead to the first Jewish homeland in 1,800 years. According to other scholars, however, Esther argues not against Jewish diaspora life but for it, albeit reliant upon sound strategic political maneuvering by the Jews of Persia, who, this theory goes, couldn't realistically pack up and move to Israel, nor should they feel compelled to attempt to do so.[24]

On March 21, 2016, the Town Board of Grand Island, alongside a delegation of Jews, Christians, and Muslims, announced plans to celebrate "Mordecai Manuel Noah Day" on July 19, Noah's birthday, with a dinner at Byblos Niagara Resort and Spa. The plan was the brainchild of Michael Barsoum, pastor and founder of the Community of St. Paul on the island, and of many who continue to be inspired by Noah's tale.[25]

---

24. See the relevant discussions in Kirsch; Aaron Koller, *Esther in Ancient Jewish Thought* (Cambridge, 2014); Yoram Hazony, *God and Politics in Esther* (Cambridge, 2015); Jonathan Silver, "The Book of Esther as a Manual for Jewish Survival," *Mosaic*, March 22, 2016, https://mosaicmagazine.com/observation/uncategorized/2016/03/the-book-of-esther-as-a-manual-for-jewish-survival/.

25. Others inspired by Noah's tale include Melissa Shiff, a research associate at the Centre for Digital Arts and Technology at York University, and Louis Kaplan, a professor of History and Theory of Photography and New Media at the University of Toronto, who created a digital map of what Ararat would look like today, complete with an augmented reality app, http://www.mappingararat.com/, and the late award-winning Israeli novelist and journalist Nava Semel's *IsraIsle* (Simsbury, 2016), which imagines Noah's plan as having succeeded, merging Native American and Jewish customs and providing a haven for the Jews during the Holocaust, with characters reciting "Hear O' provoker of the Spirit, Wakan Tanka our spirit, Wakan Tanka is one," a "Jewish chief" envisioning "milking the forests, rolling barrels of resin down the Niagara. A land of buffalo milk and maple honey," and a character noting, "How fortunate that IsraIsle existed by the time the Nazis rose to power in the last century, so that your grandmother could be swiftly granted 'persecuted' status and sail to America

Born in Egypt into a Coptic Christian family, Barsoum was taught to hate Jewish people during his childhood. Forced to flee due to religious persecution in the 1980s, he reexamined his feelings toward Jews, and came to admire their survival despite countless persecutions, including the Holocaust. "I am a refugee myself," he told a reporter for the *Buffalo News*. "My heart is always for people who are persecuted and people who are deprived of their religious liberties."[26] After designing and leading hate prevention seminars in Toronto, Barsoum moved to Grand Island, where he continues his interfaith efforts. "Mordecai Manuel Noah Day," he and the town hoped, would send a message of tolerance and freedom throughout the world. In fact, the *Buffalo News* reported, Barsoum created two books for people to sign for the occasion, "one for religious people, and the other for nonbelievers." He planned to deliver the books to the office of Israeli Prime Minister Benjamin Netanyahu in Jerusalem.

Alas, like so many efforts to bridge Grand Island and Jerusalem, so many efforts to have feet planted in the "land of the free" and eyes raised toward the Promised Land, Barsoum missed the proverbial boat. When I reached out to the reporter who wrote the story for the *News* to find out if Barsoum ever made it to Israel with the signed books, he graciously wrote back, "I spoke to Nate McMurray, Grand Island's Town Supervisor, and it sounds like Michael had good intentions, but got burned out, and didn't follow through on some stuff." Like Mordecai Manuel Noah and his biblical namesake, he never made it to Jerusalem.

---

on board one of the rescue boats. Think what could have happened if the Jews hadn't had a ready-made island shelter." For more examples, see Rovner, 225–226. Weingrad surveys how various retellings of Noah's story, including Yiddish plays (in which Mordecai Manuel Noah's wife is changed from Rebecca to Esther), and Ben Katchor's 1998 graphic novel *The Jew of New York* (with a sample panel depicting a prospective Ararat settler looking for a kosher dining room being invited in by a local fur trader and discussing New York City theater productions), have "used the figure of Noah to try to reconcile Jewish national identity with the possibilities of American life" while navigating between "desperate hopefulness" and "optimistic despair."

26. Michael Canfield, "Two hundred years later, Grand Island proclaims Mordecai Noah Day," *Buffalo News*, April 6, 2016, https://buffalonews.com/2016/04/06/two-hundred-years-later-grand-island-proclaims-mordecai-noah-day/.

Esther the Queen, Hester Prynne, and *The Scarlet Letter* as Biblical Commentary

Rabbi Tzvi Sinensky

T he Book of Esther tells us precious little about Esther's inner world. We know about her early life: the death of her parents, her maturation in Mordecai's house, and how she is taken first to the harem and then to the palace. We know of her accomplishments: how she found favor in the eyes of those who saw her, approached Ahasuerus, and became savior of the Jews. And the text does drop a few hints as to her emotions and development: she shifted from passivity to proactivity, as Mordecai's challenge compelled her to make a fateful decision to throw in her lot with the Jewish people. Yet we wonder: How did her orphaned childhood impact her? What was it like growing up in Mordecai's household? How did she process – if at all – the traumatic experience of being coercively taken into Ahasuerus' harem, raped, and forced to marry the king? Did she experience her rise to the throne with pride, shame, or ambivalence? The *megilla* responds to our inquiries into Esther's emotional life with deafening silence.

This omission, of course, is to be expected from biblical narrative. As Erich Auerbach develops in his magisterial essay "Odysseus' Scar," the protagonists' internal experience is conspicuously absent in the "biblical epic." He offers the example of the binding of Isaac:

> God gives his command in direct discourse, but he leaves his motives and his purpose unexpressed; Abraham, receiving the command, says nothing and does what he has been told to do. The conversation between Abraham and Isaac on the way to the place of sacrifice is only an interruption of the heavy silence and makes it all the more burdensome. The two of them, Isaac carrying the wood and Abraham with fire and a knife, "went together." Hesitantly, Isaac ventures to ask about the ram, and Abraham gives the well-known answer. Then the text repeats: "So they went both of them together." Everything remains unexpressed.[1]

As is equally typical of biblical personalities, midrashim fill in some of these lacunae. In one place, the Rabbis offer a graphic depiction of Esther's anxiety upon hearing of Haman's decree against the Jews:

> "Then the queen was exceedingly distressed" (*vatithalhal*) (Est. 4:4). What is the meaning of *vatithalhal*? Rav said: She began to menstruate. And R. Yirmeya said: Her bowels were loosened. (Megilla 15a)

Then, following the midrashic viewpoint that Esther and Mordecai were married, the Talmud offers an alternative interpretation of the phrase "If I perish, I perish":

> "Go, gather together all the Jews not according to the custom" (Est. 4:16). R. Abba said: It will not be according to custom, for

---

1. Erich Auerbach, *Mimesis: The Representation of Reality in Western Literature* (Princeton, 2013), 11.

every day until now it was under compulsion, but now it will be of my own free will. "And if I perish, I perish" (Est. 4:16): Just as I was lost to my father's house ever since I was brought here, so too, shall I be lost to you [for after voluntarily having relations with Ahasuerus, I shall be halakhically forbidden to you]. (Megilla 15a)

On this reading, Esther is profoundly anxious about not only her survival but also about the eventual prohibition against her return to intimacy with Mordecai.

Finally, the Talmud teaches that upon deciding to enter the king's throne room, Esther was nearly seized by an internal paralysis precipitated by the departure of the Divine Presence:

"And she stood in the inner court of the king's house" (Est. 5:1). R. Levi said: Once she reached the chamber of the idols, which was in the inner court, the Divine Presence left her. She immediately said: "My God, my God, why have You forsaken me?" (Ps. 22:2). Perhaps it is because You judge an unintentional sin as one performed intentionally, and an action done due to circumstances beyond one's control as one done willingly. Or perhaps You have left me because in my prayers I called Haman a dog, as it is stated, "Deliver my soul from the sword; my only one from the hand of the dog" (Ps. 22:21). She at once retracted and called him in her prayers a lion, as it is stated in the following verse: "Save me from the lion's mouth" (Ps. 22:22). (Megilla 15b)

Yet, even taking these aggadic statements together, we are left with a decidedly piecemeal portrait of our protagonist's state of mind.

And so, in seeking to account for Esther's inner experience, we turn to an unexpected source: Hester Prynne, the central character in Nathaniel Hawthorne's nineteenth-century classic *The Scarlet Letter*. Let us begin by briefly reviewing the novel's plot.

Set in mid-seventeenth-century Puritan Massachusetts Bay Colony (today Boston), *The Scarlet Letter* tells the tale of Hester Prynne, whose much older husband Roger Prynne has sent her ahead to the New World. He disappears and is assumed to have died at sea. Having lost hope of his survival, Hester falls into a secret relationship with the minister Arthur Dimmesdale, and ultimately gives birth to a girl, whom she names Pearl. As punishment for her illicit relationship she is compelled by the magistrates to wear a scarlet letter "A," standing for adulterer, across her chest. All but excommunicated, she lives with Pearl on the margins of society, supporting herself through her work as a seamstress. Despite her marginalization, Hester's inherent goodness and acts of kindness ultimately win over the hearts of the community members.

Meanwhile, her husband, who had in fact survived a shipwreck, takes on a new identity as Roger Chillingworth, and comes to suspect that Dimmesdale may be the child's father. Seeking revenge, he becomes the pastor's personal physician, eventually becoming his live-in caretaker. Dimmesdale deteriorates, repeatedly harming himself in seeking to atone for his sins. He and Hester finally decide to flee on a ship to Europe, but are forced to abandon the plan upon learning that Chillingworth has intentionally booked passage on the same vessel. Dimmesdale confesses publicly and dies on the town scaffold from self-flagellation. Pearl and Hester travel to Europe. Pearl marries an aristocrat and remains in Paris. After some time, Hester returns to Boston, living out the remainder of her life performing good deeds in the colony.

A handful of scholars have noted the biblical precedents for Hawthorne's characters.[2] Pearl's name is borrowed from multiple passages in the book of Matthew (13:45–46). Chillingworth, whose all-consuming hatred for Dimmesdale ultimately led to the former's destruction, has much in common with Haman, who was hanged on a gallows of his own making. Dimmesdale might be a stand-in for Mordecai, another religious leader with whom Esther may have had an intimate relation.

Most obvious is Hester, whose name is nearly identical to that of Esther, and whose life experience shares numerous parallels with that of her biblical namesake. Both are beautiful, strong women who are compelled to live in lonely environments, distanced from their communities. They are unhappily married to older men, clinging to secrets whose revelation is essential to the unfolding of their narratives. Both

---

2. For a list, see Matthew Gartner, "'The Scarlet Letter' and the Book of Esther: Scriptural Letter and Narrative Life," *Studies in American Fiction* 23, no. 2 (Autumn 1995).

overcome profound adversity, retain an abiding commitment to their core values in the face of hostile societal opposition, and come to be deeply respected by the people of their communities.

Ariel Clark Silver has further noted the parallels between Esther standing before Ahasuerus to plead for her nation, and Hester's (successful) petition to Governor Bellingham to allow Pearl to continue living with her, as well as Hester's royal bearing as strongly resembling the character of Queen Esther. As Silver puts it, "The more time I spent with Hawthorne, the more I saw the type of Esther in his work. In *The Scarlet Letter*, the type of Esther is a thinly veiled type of redemption through the female."[3]

Why does Hawthorne cast Hester as Esther? One critic concludes that Hawthorne simply sought to destabilize the meaning of the biblical text. Just as the scarlet letter "A" carries multiple and shifting meanings, so too does the biblical text, which is subject to regular reinterpretation, leading Hawthorne to "reread" Esther as Hester. Another possibility is that Hawthorne suggests that while the Puritans saw Hester as an embodiment of sin, in fact she was as pure as the biblical heroine Esther.

But these interpretations fall well short of the mark. In reading Hester as Esther, Hawthorne sheds light not only on the character of Hester, as well as the Puritans' hypocrisy, but also on the Book of Esther. For we may identify four outstanding aspects of Hester's inner world. First, due to events not entirely in her control, Hester suffers immensely. Second, relatedly, she experiences an extended period of communal censure. Third, her kindness is an essential part of her personality, and ultimately wins over the members of her community. Fourth and above all, she draws her resilience from remaining true to her own internal ethical compass, refusing the temptation to assimilate the values of the society around her.

In drawing such a strong parallel to Esther, Hawthorne suggests that we should see Esther in the same light. Esther too experiences tremendous suffering, from the death of her parents, to her traumatic experiences in the harem and palace, to living at the margins of her community. Second, the comparison to Esther suggests that Esther too was

---

3. Ariel Clark Silver, *The Book of Esther and the Typology of Female Transfiguration in American Literature* (Lanham, 2018), viii.

met with significant criticism by members of her community – or, at the very least, was wracked by internal doubts as to what others thought of her. Third, in winning others over with her goodwill and deeds, Esther distinguished herself with kindness. Fourth and most important, Esther, like Hester, was driven by immense internal conviction. While it was Mordecai who urged her to approach the king, Esther made the decision on her own. It was at her initiative that the Jewish community fasted, and she independently hatched the ingenious plot of Haman and Ahasuerus' feasts. And she, along with Mordecai, established Purim as a holiday.

Historical context clinches this reading of Hawthorne's Esther. Hawthorne read Cotton Mather's *Ornaments for the Daughters of Zion*, a conduct manual in which Esther is one of the biblical heroines adduced as a model of proper behavior.[4] Mather's guide was highly influential, and was widely read throughout the nineteenth century. Yet for Mather, Esther was the ideal woman inasmuch as she supported her husband Ahasuerus (!) even as she urged him to improve his character. Hawthorne, alongside other nineteenth-century authors, broke from *Ornaments*, transforming Esther-as-Hester into an independent-minded, strong-willed, creative, elegant woman who was willing to break convention in order to do what was right. In so doing, Hawthorne offers us a three-dimensional view of Esther's rich inner world.

---

4. Jacob Mason Spencer, "Hawthorne's Magnalia: Retelling Cotton Mather in the Provincial Tales," unpublished Harvard dissertation, 2015. See Stuart Halpern's chapter, "Puritan Purim" in this volume.

Emancipation and Proclamations

From the Palace of Shushan to Uncle Tom's Cabin: Esther as American Abolitionist

Dr. Ariel Clark Silver

A few years before Nathaniel Hawthorne claimed Esther for the American literary canon in *Legends of the Province House* (1838–39), Angelina Grimké invoked Esther in her important rhetorical pamphlet, "An Appeal to the Christian Women of the South" (1836). Grimké was the first American woman writer to appreciate the value of the Persian queen on the page and apply her figurative social power to the central economic, cultural, and political issue of antebellum America: abolition. Hawthorne continued to wrestle with this complex female type of redemption and salvation throughout his career in fiction as he sought to fulfill the divine destiny of the American woman through his protagonists – Esther Dudley, Hester Prynne, Zenobia, and Miriam.[1]

---

1. For more on Hawthorne and Esther, see my chapters "'A' is for Atonement:

Hawthorne discovered, however, that female redemption is often followed by reversal and revenge, as Esther turns from saving her people to ensuring an end to their oppression. But it was Grimké and other female authors and activists, including Harriet Beecher Stowe, Frances Ellen Watkins Harper, and Sojourner Truth who elicited Esther to address the immediate existential threat: the sale, suffering, and slaughter of slaves in America prior to the Civil War.

Grimké summoned the figure of Esther at the apex of her appeal to her fellow southern white Christian women, drawing on their devotion to the Old as well as New Testament. After calling forth other Jewish female figures from the Hebrew Bible – the midwives Shiphrah and Puah, Moses' sister Miriam, and Huldah the prophetess from II Kings – who could serve as instructive models of holy intervention in the face of destruction, captivity, and deception, she concentrated her energy on Esther, who stepped in to stave off the religious genocide of her people in the Persian Empire, a slaughter that could have claimed her own life as well. Grimké, a daughter of the South Carolina planter class turned abolitionist protester, viewed her own anti-slavery efforts in precisely these terms: she was seeking to eradicate a practice lest it consume both the slaves and their Christian masters. In her "Appeal," she cast Esther in the role of the southern Christian woman, who does not advocate for the oppressed until she sees that her fate is inextricably bound to those held in bondage:

> Is there no Esther among you, who will plead for the poor devoted slave? Read the history of this Persian queen, it is full of instruction; she at first refused to plead for the Jews; but, hear the words of Mordecai, "Think not within thyself, that *thou* shalt escape in the king's house more than all the Jews, for if *thou altogether holdest thy peace at this time,* then shalt there enlargement and deliverance arise to the Jews from another place: but *thou and thy*

Hawthorne and Hester" and "Beyond Redemption: Queen Esther, Zenobia, and Miriam" in *The Book of Esther and the Typology of Female Transfiguration in American Literature* (Lanham, 2018) as well as the chapter by Tzvi Sinensky, "Esther the Queen, Hester Prynne, and *The Scarlet Letter* as Biblical Commentary," in this volume.

father's house shall be destroyed." Listen, too, to her magnanimous reply to this powerful appeal: "I will go in unto the king, which is *not* according to law, and if I perish, I perish."[2]

Grimké urged her female readers to move, like Esther, from the role of a submissive female to one motivated by sacred conviction. She exhorted them to speak, for the price of their continued silence would have led to shared destruction. They were not to count the cost, as they, like Esther, contravened the current law. Rather, they were to act boldly for their own benefit and that of their enslaved sisters, no longer subjecting "*woman* to the scourge and the chain, to mental darkness and moral degradation."[3]

The figure of Esther held great emotional and rhetorical power for Grimké because of the biblical heroine's capacity to evolve. Unlike some other female types deployed to direct the conduct of women in theological or political discourse throughout the ages, Esther demonstrated a remarkable and unpredictable development over the course of her own story, arriving at moments of profound discernment, independence, and engagement. Angelina Grimké had made such a journey herself, which she recorded in her remarkable journal, first refusing communion with the Episcopalians,[4] then leaving the material comforts of her southern home and way of life and following her sister Sarah to the more austere Quakers, committing both to their faith and to their brand of social justice, which revolved principally around the abolition of slavery. When widespread attacks on the abolition movement emerged during the "Abolition Summer" of 1835, Angelina Grimké and her sister Sarah rose to the occasion, responding with the power of the pen. Educated in the ravages of slavery, they embarked on a two-pronged appeal to a very

---

2. A. E. Grimké, "An Appeal to the Christian Women of the South," *The Anti-Slavery Examiner* 1 (1836): 25.
3. Ibid.
4. Grimké's departure from the Episcopal Church was the first of several protests conveying her skepticism over clerics standing in the way of radical cultural change. Her search for spiritual fulfillment and social justice eventually led her away from organized religion altogether. For further discussion of Grimké's development as an ethical thinker and writer, see Stephen Howard Browne's *Angelina Grimké: Rhetoric, Identity, and the Radical Imagination* (East Lansing, 1999).

specific audience: white Christian southerners. Angelina wrote to the women and Sarah wrote to the clergy. Through their letters and essays, the Grimkés argued that southern white women must speak up in solidarity with their slaves, both because their lives were intertwined with those they held in bondage and because they too lacked agency, and therefore must be on the side of liberation.

In her "Letters on the Equality of the Sexes," Sarah Grimké suggested that the virtue of white as well as black women was severely compromised by complicity in the system of slavery. Exposure to or encouragement of such abusive immorality corrupted white women as well. Enslaved black women were physically violated not just for the labor their bodies could produce, but for the sexual gratification their bodies could provide, and the capital those bodies could generate, children who were routinely sold for profit or set to labor before their very eyes. Esther, in the mind of the Grimké sisters, was therefore a contemporary white Christian southern woman, mired in a system of female abuse that took advantage of her many virtues and involved her in the wholesale deprivation of women – black and white – caught in slavery's dark web. But biblical Esther had changed, as Angelina Grimké exhorted her fellow southern females to do:

> If there were but *one* Esther at the South, she *might save* her country from ruin…let them embody themselves in societies, and send petitions up to their different legislatures, entreating their husbands, fathers, brothers and sons, to abolish the institution of slavery… [and] no longer to barter the *image of God* in human shambles for corruptible things such as silver and gold.[5]

Here in her "Appeal," Grimké drew less on the demure qualities of the Jewish handmaid who found favor with the king and more on the fearless qualities of a queen who discovered the peril of her people, and by rising to their defense, found herself. Esther had decided to act. She fasted, approached the king without an invitation, convened banquets, unmasked deception, and sought the right to self-defense against the

---

5. Grimké, 25–26.

decreed attacks. Angelina Grimké pleaded with her fellow southern females to likewise make common cause with those in bondage, to "no longer reduce *American citizens* to the abject condition of *slaves*"[6] by acting to end the social and economic practice which was chaining them all.

Shortly after Grimké composed her appeal to southern white women, she planned a public tour to encourage northern women to join local abolitionist societies. In *An Essay on Slavery and Abolitionism* (1837), Catharine Esther Beecher confronted Angelina publicly, arguing that whatever "throws a woman into the attitude of a combatant, either for herself or others," throws her out of her "appropriate sphere."[7] Angelina wrote back, refuting the idea that she must stay out of politics because she was a woman. For the Grimké sisters, abolition concerned both race and gender. Informed advocates such as the Reverend Samuel May acknowledged, with wry understatement, that more than half of those held in bondage were women "whose condition in some respects was more horrible than that of the males."[8] Some ministers, such as May, invited the Grimkés to "testify of the correctness of our allegations against slavery, and tell more of the horrors than we knew."[9] The Grimkés demonstrated that women could and should speak in public, even when it led them into the "arena of political collision."[10] They recognized that slavery was both a moral and political issue, and that women had everything to do with its endurance or eradication. Implicit in their argument for abolition was a plea for female equality, but it was "as strenuously opposed and as harshly denounced as was our demand for the immediate emancipation of the enslaved."[11]

Even as Angelina debated with Catharine Beecher about the public role of women in the contest over slavery, she provided the inspiration needed by Catharine's sister Harriet Beecher Stowe to combat the practice. In 1838, Angelina married the prominent abolitionist Theodore Dwight Weld and together they published the highly influential expose,

6. Ibid.
7. Catharine Esther Beecher, *An Essay on Slavery and Abolitionism* (Philadelphia, 1837), 102.
8. Samuel J. May, *Some Recollections of Our Anti-Slavery Conflict* (Boston, 1869), 234.
9. Ibid.
10. Beecher, 103.
11. May, 237.

Slavery As It Is (1839), from which Harriet Beecher Stowe drew much material for the composition of *Uncle Tom's Cabin* (1852). This connection is particularly significant given the use Stowe made of the Esther trope, both for characters in the novel and for herself as the author of a work that inspired the action needed to save her country from the slow genocide of bondage and subjugation. Like Angelina Grimké, she appealed to religious ideals in *Uncle Tom's Cabin*, fusing sentimental and political concerns into a literary form. She drew on the cultural and theological sympathies of her readers, causing them to feel the scourge of slavery and imagine the possibility of a society more responsive to the principles of humility, justice, and mercy.[12]

But in the hands of Stowe, Esther evolved again. Now she was cast not as a southern Christian woman, but as a northern abolitionist, someone like Angelina Grimké or herself, who summoned her courage and spoke up to redeem her nation. This development was due, in great measure, to the passage of the Compromise of 1850, which included the Fugitive Slave Act. Where the Grimké sisters, native southerners turned northern abolitionists, could focus their energy primarily on a southern audience in the decade before such a deal was brokered, Stowe needed to address northern citizens who were now involved in the enforcement of a practice once outside their purview. The Fugitive Slave Act challenged the position of northerners opposed to slavery. Neutrality was no longer possible. One was either complicit or defiant. In the face of such a legal act, the figure of Esther as a northerner also had to change. Here was Esther on the other side of Haman's decree. She could no longer remain at ease and watch her fellow citizens suffer. In penning *Uncle Tom's Cabin*, Stowe "compared herself to the Carthaginian women who 'had cut off their hair for bow-strings to give to the defenders of their country' and declared her willingness to do likewise."[13]

As a northerner sympathetic to the cause of abolition, Esther also could no longer be moved by or appeal to religious sensibilities alone. She could no longer remain in the realm of the female who was

---

12. See Micah 6:8.
13. Jeanne Boydston, Mary Kelley, and Anne Margolis, *The Limits of Sisterhood: The Beecher Sisters on Women's Rights and Woman's Sphere* (Chapel Hill, 1988), 157.

protected by, or derived her force from, others. Rather, she had to "leave her sphere in order to defend it against the violations of a world that treats human beings as property."[14] Such was the role of Mary Bird, the wife of an Ohio legislator in *Uncle Tom's Cabin*. Like Esther, she stepped across a threshold without having a scepter extended to her, advancing cautiously and cleverly. A model of female entreaty and influence, she uses both rhetoric and logic to persuade her husband of the moral shortcomings of the Fugitive Slave Act,[15] much as Esther convinces Ahasuerus of the suspect motivations behind the decree he has issued. In a deft turn, Mary also exposes his appeal to public interests above private feelings as a further move to denigrate the oppressed. Her use of agency is primarily indirect in the novel, but her commitments are clear: she will break the fugitive slave law the first time she has the chance.

In Stowe's work, Esther not only moved figuratively from the South to the North, she also migrated across the color line. Cast initially as a southern white woman who needed to recognize her complicity in the horror before her, then as a northern white woman forced to engage with the institution of slavery, Esther was now also asked to play the role of a slave woman, particularly that of a slave mother. When Stowe lost a child to cholera in the years before writing *Uncle Tom's Cabin*, she came to identify with those who routinely had their children taken from them. Though biblical Esther is not described as having had children, she, in a sense, became a mother to the Persian Jews when she used her position in court to protect them. Eliza Harris, the most prominent slave mother in *Uncle Tom's Cabin*, echoed the determination of Esther when she declared, "They have sold you! but your mother will save you yet!"[16] Both Esther and Eliza recognized their existential predicament – "If I perish, I perish" (Est. 4:16) – but still resolved to fight. This determination was furthered detailed by the writer Frances Ellen Watkins Harper, a black woman born to free parents in a slave state, when she composed the poems "Eliza Harris" (1853) and "The Slave

---

14. Ibid, 160.
15. See John Gatta, *American Madonna: Images of the Divine Woman in Literary Culture* (New York, 1997), 58.
16. Harriet Beecher Stowe, *Uncle Tom's Cabin; Or, Life Among the Lowly* (Boston, 1852), 60.

Mother" (1854), which describe a figure who "was nerv'd by despair and strengthened by woe" even as a "storm of agony"[17] swept through her brain. Though Harper did not grow up as a slave, she invested her entire life in the redemption and advancement of her people, writing volumes of protest poetry, serving the anti-slavery cause as a traveling lecturer and agent, and educating freed men and women in the South.

The character of Eliza Harris is an important female contrast to Mary Bird and other women who are sympathetic to the cause of abolition: she is black rather than white, slave rather than free, and she cannot use rhetoric and persuasion alone to achieve her aims. Unlike those on the other side of the color line who protest the abuse, she must challenge the system directly. Her defiance against authority is a stronger form of the civil disobedience displayed by her white colleagues. Like Esther, she must transgress the law in order to triumph. After escaping from slavery in the South with the help of white women including Rachel Halliday and Mary Bird, she makes her way to Canada, France, and then Liberia. Her own journey to freedom projects the possibility of liberation at last for those held in bondage, even as it hearkens back to the figure of Esther, who saved herself and her people from destruction.

The black Esther figure embodied in fiction by Eliza Harris bears some similarity in fact to Sojourner Truth, a slave mother who also escaped to freedom with one of her children.[18] Possessed, like Esther, of multiple names and identities, Isabella Baumfree fought for her own liberation and that of others. Separated from her parents as a child and sold to other slave owners, she later successfully sued for the return of her enslaved son, Peter, the first black woman to win such a case. Isabella worked in New York until 1843, when she felt called to become an itinerant preacher, taking upon herself the name of Sojourner Truth. Drawing on both orthodox and unorthodox spiritual understanding, she evolved into an ardent abolitionist and feminist. She collaborated with black men and white women in the anti-slavery and suffrage movements, but also developed her own brand of communitarian civil rights activism which

---

17. Henry Louis Gates Jr. and Nellie Y. McKay, eds., *The Norton Anthology of African American Literature* (New York, 1997), 413–414.
18. For more on Truth, see the chapter by Erica Brown in this volume.

included recruiting black troops for the conflict, relief efforts for freed men and women, and campaigns for desegregation. Truth became, in the words of Harriet Beecher Stowe, a "Libyan Sibyl,"[19] renowned for her declarations on freedom and her devotion to its realization.

Sojourner Truth is best known for her speech "Ar'n't I a Woman?" (1851) which she delivered with "the air of a queen," according to Frances Gage, who recorded and perhaps rhetorically altered her remarks when she wrote them down in 1878.[20] Two years later, Truth invoked Esther directly in a speech in New York (1853) to address the oppression of black females and to underscore the need for them to come forth and speak. Through her words, Truth was determined to command respect despite her compromised status even as she demonstrated the power of articulating ideas and having them inscribed by others. Esther modeled this value when she "wrote with all authority" (Est. 9:29) the decrees pertaining to Purim, an annual festival that would commemorate the end of the conceived annihilation. Indeed, Purim imagines a world where the social order is upended: the high are made low, the low are made high, and the poor are showered with gifts. Black Esther figures such as Frances Ellen Watkins Harper and Sojourner Truth also envisioned a world of racial reconstruction through their written and verbal work. For them, the call to abolition was above all a call to action. As Esther well knew, the threat of annihilation cannot always be answered with only a threat in return. These women would need to speak, write, and act in order to save their people and redeem the nation from the transgression of its stated ideals.

In the process, these female abolitionists sought to challenge the status quo without allowing themselves to be sacrificed to the cause. Esther had presumably learned from Vashti's sad fate, as Grimké, Stowe, and Truth learned from figures like Little Eva in *Uncle Tom's Cabin*, who were consumed in the process of seeking to surmount injustice. In order to save but not succumb, they had to move from being loving but spent figures like Uncle Tom to figures like Aunt Chloe in *Sketches of Southern Life* by Frances Ellen Watkins Harper. Aunt Chloe educates herself, engages in politics, and extends her standing in the world through her

19. Harriet Beecher Stowe, "Sojourner Truth: Libyan Sibyl," *Atlantic Monthly* (April 1863).
20. See "The Narrative of Sojourner Truth" (1878) in Gates and McKay, 199.

instinct to survive. Her speeches and articles remind her audience that "we are all bound up together in one great bundle of humanity,"[21] a theme that underscores cooperation over altruism. In the novel for which she is most remembered, *Iola LeRoy* (1892), the female protagonist, Iola, will not allow herself to become a "suffering victim"[22] like Vashti or Little Eva.

As female abolitionists continued to invoke Esther, male opponents treated them more like Vashti, beginning with slave women. Distressed over the loss of their power and privilege, they commanded, abused, and punished women like Harris and Truth at whim. Frances Harper, the free black abolitionist, responded to such humiliation when she wrote the poem "Vashti" (1857), describing a woman who "would rather die" than suffer such degradation, a woman "who could bend to grief, but would not bow to shame."[23] When slave women actually challenged the authority of their masters, they were threatened with death. Soon white abolitionists who advocated for change discovered the meaning of such disrespect. Angelina Grimké and her sister were branded by ministers as "dangerous persons, disorganizers, [and] infidels."[24] When Stowe published *Uncle Tom's Cabin*, the *Southern Literary Messenger* accused her of stepping outside the "hallowed precinct" of her prescribed domestic role and the *Southern Quarterly Review* charged her with "malignant bitterness" and a "foul imagination."[25] Esther still had to surmount the decrees meant to suppress any woman who would act like Vashti.

More than two decades after the publication of *Uncle Tom's Cabin*, Stowe reconsidered the role of Esther in *Woman in Sacred History* (1873) by first reckoning with Vashti, illuminating the challenge that male power posed to female efforts aimed at achieving social and political justice. In this book of commentary on female figures in the Jewish and Christian canon, written in the midst of Reconstruction, Stowe engaged sacred texts to confront the social, religious, and political restrictions placed on women even after the emancipation of the slaves. *Woman in Sacred*

---

21. Gates and McKay, 410.
22. Ibid, 411.
23. Ibid, 416–417.
24. Ibid.
25. Boydston, 159.

History advanced the acceptance of such an approach to scripture, treating characters in the canon with the "same freedom of inquiry"[26] as those in any other text. Her exploratory text on biblical women also reflects the pilgrimage Stowe had made from her fervent Protestant abolitionism before the Civil War to a more ecumenical engagement with the unresolved "woman question" in the wake of the conflict.[27] Stowe sought not only to scrutinize, but to correct imbalance and overcome prejudice by portraying women like Deborah and Esther who were a "moving power"[28] for others. Her argument for "the equality of the sexes in their spiritual nature"[29] was also a desire to demonstrate the divine nature of women and claim for them their "half of the kingdom" (Est. 5:3, 7:2). The project of Esther was not only to save her people and end their oppression but to end her own by asserting her true nature as the female face of the divine.

At its heart, *Woman in Sacred History* functions not only as a commentary on biblical women but on the female fight for freedom, bringing into crescendo the tireless efforts made by Stowe and so many other women to eradicate slavery and its consequences. Her treatment of Esther in this text is preceded by a discussion of "The Dirge of Rachel" and followed by an exposition on "Judith the Deliverer," moving the reader from the plight of women, particularly slave women, who weep for their lost children to the campaigns of uncompromising women who succeed in emancipating those held in bondage. The same biblical book that records the cries of Rachel later bears witness to the worship of the "Queen of Heaven in the streets of Jerusalem and the cities of Judah" (Jer. 44:17). That movement, from slave mother to

---

26. Harriet Beecher Stowe, *Woman in Sacred History: A Series of Sketches Drawn from Scriptural, Historical, and Legendary Sources* (New York, 1873), 18.
27. Stowe was raised as an evangelical Protestant, and her early work, including *Uncle Tom's Cabin*, comes out of that tradition, but her own exploration of religious history and scripture led to an intense interest in the female divine in her later work, including *Woman in Sacred History*. For further discussion of Stowe's religious trajectory, see Nancy Koester's *Harriet Beecher Stowe: A Spiritual Life* (Grand Rapids, 2014) and "Calvinism Feminized: Divine Matriarchy in Harriet Beecher Stowe" in John Gatta's *American Madonna* (New York, 1997).
28. Stowe, *Woman in Sacred History*, 195.
29. Ibid, 87.

venerated woman, mirrors the progressive thesis of her work, that as women become more aware of their divine nature and their capacity to liberate themselves as well as others, the more power they have to understand and act. Her perfect example of such progress is Hagar, an enslaved handmaid who later becomes the mother of a "great nation."[30] Stowe's challenge to the country after the war is to imagine men and women who had been held in bondage emerging as esteemed and engaged citizens, valued for their contributions across many spheres. The ardent antebellum Esther, having achieved tremendous anti-slavery success, now prepares for the arrival of the Hagar of reconstruction.[31]

---

30. Stowe, *Woman in Sacred History*, 44.
31. For a more complete discussion of the figure of Hagar in American literature and culture, see Janet Gabler-Hover, *Dreaming Black/Writing White: The Hagar Myth in American Cultural History* (Lexington, 2000).

Finding Her Voice: Black Female Empowerment and the Book of Esther

Dr. Erica Brown

In *The Bible in Politics*, Richard Baukham advises readers "to listen to anyone who claims that the Bible has been misused against them…"[1] The Hebrew Bible has, throughout its long exegetical history, been read not only as a source of law and inspiration but also as a political weapon to both create and reinforce unjust political structures. Such hermeneutics of marginalization can do more than impact the reader. When the Bible is the foundational text of a society, such readings can shape a culture of exclusion. Baukham asks us to be conscious of these aspects of interpretation and to be mindful of their implications: "The peril of blindness to the influence of our interests on interpretation can also be countered by attention to the work of interpreters whose political and

---

1.   Richard Baukham, *The Bible in Politics: How to Read the Bible Politically* (Louisville, 2011), 18.

economic circumstance are different than our own. American black slaves read the Bible very differently from the way their masters read it."[2]

The Bible has also been used in political contexts to provide strength to the very minority voices who have often been stung by its interpretation. Thus, we turn to the Book of Esther. While some have read the book as confirming class and gender hierarchies,[3] others saw in the character of Esther a model of quiet, determined, and transformational leadership that challenged conventional royal and patriarchal norms.[4] Black scholars in South Africa after its Apartheid years, for example, tried to reinterpret some of the complexities of the story to question class and colonialism, while over a century earlier, black female abolitionists turned to Esther, seeking justification for their public activism.

"...Oppressed communities must liberate the Bible so that the Bible can liberate them," writes Itumeleng J. Mosala, contemporary scholar of religious studies at the University of Cape Town. "An oppressed Bible oppresses and a liberated Bible liberates."[5] Because the

---

2. Ibid.
3. There is a history of Christian condemnation of the Book of Esther, which charges that the book is overly sexual, violent, or lacking in spiritual import. While not the same as class and gender analyses, theses readings all see this biblical book as a locus for criticism. See, for example, L. B. Paton, *International Critical Commentary: Esther* (London, 1908), 101; C. H. Cornill, *Introduction to the Canonical Books of the Old Testament*, trans. G. Box (New York, 1907), 257; D. J. A. Clines, "Review of W. Hermann, *"Esther im Streit der Meinungen,"* in *Society for Old Testament Study Book List* (1988), 78; Bernard W. Anderson, "The Place of the Book of Esther in the Christian Bible," *Journal of Religion* 30 (1950): 32–43; Robert Pfeiffer, *Introduction to the Old Testament* (New York, 1941), 747; and L. E. Browne, "Esther," in *Peake's Commentary on the Bible* (London, 1962), 383. For a broad review of negative Christian readings of Esther, see Frederic W. Bush, "The Book of Esther: *Opus non gratum* in the Christian Canon," *Bulletin for Biblical Research* 8 (1998): 39–54.
4. See Esther Fuchs, "Status and Role of Female Heroines in the Biblical Narrative," in *Women in the Hebrew Bible: A Reader*, ed. Alica Bach (London, 2013); Timothy K. Beal, *The Book of Hiding: Gender, Ethnicity, Annihilation and Esther* (London, 1997); Timothy Laniak, *Shame and Honor in the Book of Esther* (Atlanta, 1998); Solomon Talmon, "'Wisdom' and the Book of Esther," *Vetus Testamentum* 13, no. 4 (1963): 419–455.
5. Itumeleng J. Mosala, *Biblical Hermeneutics and Black Theology in South Africa* (Grand Rapids, 1989), 189. The unpublished dissertation can be accessed at https://open.uct.ac.za/bitstream/handle/11427/8395/thesis_hum_1987_mosala_ij.pdf?sequence=1.

Bible was used as a text to suppress black independence during South Africa's Apartheid years, Mosala and other black South African scholars have tried to reread and repurpose the Bible as a text of liberation rather than a text of exclusion and oppression. "No other political or ideological system in the modern world that I know of derives itself so directly from the Bible as the ideology of Apartheid," he writes. "The superiority of white people over black people, for example, is premised on the divine privileging of the Israelites over the Canaanites in the conquest texts of the Old Testament."[6] If the Bible was used as a foundational text to defend structural racism in South Africa, Mosala's more contemporary reading would chip away at that notion since, for those who read the Bible with serious political implications, the liberation of a people is also dependent on the liberation of the book.

Specifically readjusting the lens of Esther to reflect a story of survival under colonial manacles, Mosala writes: "The book of Esther builds its story around the memory of very difficult times under colonial exile. The specific lesson it seeks to draw attention to revolves around the struggle for survival. In particular, two forms of survival are accented in this story: cultural and national survival. Needless to say, these two types of survival are inseparable, though not identical."[7] Esther, in his view, needed reinterpretation in light of the double shackling women

---

See also Randall C. Bailey, "'That's Why They Didn't Call the Book Hadassah!': The Interse(ct)/(x)ionality of Race/Ethnicity, Gender, and Sexuality in the Book of Esther," in *They Were All Together in One Place? Toward Minority Biblical Criticism*, ed. R. C. Bailey, T. B. Liew, and F. F. Segovia, *Society of Biblical Literature Semeia Studies* 57 (Atlanta, 2009): 227–250. For more on African readings of the Bible, see Hugh R. Page, *The Africana Bible: Reading Israel's Scriptures from Africa and the African Diaspora* (Minneapolis, 2009).

6. Itumeleng J. Mosala, "The Implications of the Text of Esther for African Women's Struggle for Liberation in South Africa," in *The Postcolonial Biblical Reader*, ed. R. S. Sugirtharajah (Malden, 2006), 135. First published in *Semia* 59 (1992): 129–137.

7. Mosala, "Implications," 139. That Esther was read as a survival manual in exile for the Jews is supported by scholars like Jonathan Magonet, who argues that it depicts "not a world of ethics or morality, but of relative ethics and values of survival"; see "The Liberal and the Lady: Esther Revisited," *Judaism* 29 (1980): 174; and Yoram Hazony, who reads the entire book with political eyes. Unable to have "cohesiveness, direction, and strength," Hazony argues, the Jews of ancient Persia lacked the "possibility of freely seeking and implementing any Jewish ideal ..." (*The Dawn: Political Teachings*

experienced during Apartheid. They not only fought against dominant and punitive white rule, they also tried to resist black patriarchal norms. African women were asked, like Esther, to "sacrifice gender struggles to national struggles."[8] Mosala attempts to liberate African women by rereading biblical texts free of the ideology and agenda that suppresses marginalized people with the hope that "engaging Esther in this way will contribute to efforts to move beyond a unitary, male-dominated history of rhetorical theory through the recovery and recognition of a work that does not announce itself as rhetorical theory, but has operated as such."[9] Mosala regards his reclamation project as adding a multi-valenced way of looking at a story; at the same time, he paradoxically sees the text as a confirmation of the double bind he describes: "Mordecai reaps the fruit of the struggle. African women who work within liberation movements and other groups will be very familiar with these kinds of dynamics."[10] Mosala, in suggesting that it is only Esther who puts her life in danger, while Mordecai benefits, twists the text, ignoring Mordecai's stubborn resistance to bowing to his enemy in chapter 3 and imperiling himself with a public display of protest in chapter 4. By suggesting that black women see themselves in this power dynamic – fighting for national recognition while remaining themselves unrecognized and underappreciated by the men around them – Mosala may be just as guilty of misreading the Bible as those he criticizes.

Madipoane Masenya, professor of Old Testament studies at the University of South Africa, is less convinced of Esther's worth to the

---

on the Book of Esther [Jerusalem, 1995], 3–4). In the absence of political autonomy, Esther and Mordecai's chief leadership responsibility was ensuring survival rather than influence. That they achieved both in the end made the story worth repeating.

8. Ibid. For more on the role of gender in the Book of Esther, see Esther K. Fuchs, "Status and Role of Female Heroines in the Biblical Narrative," *Mankind Quarterly* 23 (1982); Timothy K. Beal, *The Book of Hiding: Gender, Ethnicity, Annihilation and Esther* (London, 1997); and Timothy Laniak, *Shame and Honor in the Book of Esther* (Atlanta, 1998).

9. Mosala, *Biblical Hermeneutics,* 194.

10. Mosala, "Implications," 140. Some scholars believe that Esther intentionally used her feminine wiles to gain power rather than remain vulnerable. See Sidnie Ann White, "Esther: A Feminine Model for the Jewish Diaspora," in *Gender and Difference in Ancient Israel,* ed. Peggy L. Day (Minneapolis, 1989), 167.

cause of both female and black national liberation. Masenya is troubled by class issues in the book, where a royal elite lived in excess at the expense of the poor: "The class portrayed in this document cannot be helpful to many African women whose socioeconomic conditions render them largely invisible."[11] Though she admits that some readers will relate to elements in Esther that may make an

> African-South African [*sic*] female reader identify with the story, as a whole she [the female reader] finds the story of Esther offering no liberative possibilities for oppressed women. It does not enhance them in their own right. Instead, it perpetuates stereotyped ideas that women cannot act on their own (cf. Mordecai's influence on Esther's life), that they are evil (cf. Esther's request for a second day of murder), and that they are tricksters (cf. Esther's humility before the king on two occasions).[12]

Upon investigation, these claims of Esther's docility do not stand. Esther acted on her own without Mordecai's prompting with her command to Mordecai and the nation to fast (Est. 4:16-17), as mentioned earlier. It was she who invited the king and Haman to two wine parties of her own making to reveal Haman as a villain and to save her people (5:4, 5:8). It was she who was given Haman's property to designate as she willed (8:6). It was she who declared Purim a day to be celebrated for the ages (9:29–32). While the text pauses to recognize Mordecai's promotion and his new royal attire (8:15), the reader assumes that Esther was similarly garbed all along.

---

11. Madipoane J. Masenya, "Esther and Northern Soho Stories: An African-South African Woman's Commentary," *University of South Africa Institutional Repository* (2001), 35. http://uir.unisa.ac.za/handle/10500/5343. Accessed May 12, 2020.
12. Madipoane J. Masenya, "Reading the Book of Esther through the Lenses of an African-South African Woman," conference paper (Johannesburg, 1998), 9. See her essay, "Their Hermeneutics Was Strange! Ours Is a Necessity! Rereading Vashti as African-South African Women," in *Her Master's Tools? Feminist and Postcolonial Engagements of Historical-Critical Discourse*, ed. Caroline Vander Stichele and Todd Penner (Atlanta, 2005), 179–194.

Masenya additionally criticizes Esther for the self-defense of her people, claiming that Esther displayed "cruelty against many innocent Persians" as revenge against Haman. Despite the fact that Haman's plans were never carried out, Esther "had the courage to request a second day of murder," again against innocent people. In contrast to Masenya's reading of prolonged murder, however, Esther asked for a second day only so that the Jews of Shushan could defend themselves against attack. The only person in the scroll who is actually a trickster is Haman, who decreed annihilation for the Jews without even mentioning their nationality to Ahasuerus (3:8).[13] Although Masenya compares her interpretation directly to her own personal experience of the white Christian political leadership of South Africa who exploited blacks, she seems to manipulate the actual text of the book:

> Given my South African history, this story cannot help but remind us of how native inhabitants were plundered also in the name of God. The "chosen" race came in and found the "heathen" indigenous people, took their land, and colonized their minds and cultures in the name of the God of the Bible. The text of Esther is thus problematic for such factors as class perspectives, its ethnic biases, and its ideology of colonization.[14]

Masenya does not "liberate" Esther, as Mosala attempts to, but instead regards her as a symbol of the worst kind of colonizer, ignoring aspects of the biblical text to do so. It was Ahasuerus who, rather than reverse Haman's decree, forced the Jews to defend themselves, though only against the Persian neighbors who sought to kill them first: "The king has permitted the Jews of every city to assemble and fight for their lives; *if any people or province attacks them*, they may destroy, massacre, and exterminate its armed force together with women and children, and plunder their

---

13. For more on biblical tricksters, see Susan Niditch, *A Prelude to Biblical Folklore: Underdogs and Tricksters* (Chicago, 2000). There are those who contend that Esther was a trickster but do so in the context of assuming leadership from a powerlessness. See Ann W. Engar, "Old Testament Women as Tricksters," *The Bucknell Review* 33, no. 2 (1990): 143.

14. Masenya, "Esther and Northern Soho Stories," 31.

possessions" (8:11). The same king who permitted this also allowed the Jews to plunder the Persians they killed but, as the text emphasizes, the Jews refused to do so: "They disposed of their enemies…but they did *not* lay hands on the spoil" (9:16). This ancient demonstration of intentional restraint is a far cry from Masenya's plundering, making us wonder, yet again, at how carefully these scholars read the biblical text itself in their desire to reinterpret it.

Such was not the case over a hundred years earlier and thousands of miles away. The Book of Esther was read carefully by a number of black women fighting for emancipation in the United States in the 1800s. These early abolitionists saw in Esther a model of outspoken female leadership, while seemingly ignoring the fact that Esther fought for the freedom of her people from death, not slavery. In fact, Esther contended that had her people only been sold into slavery, she would not have approached the king in protest – "Had we only been sold as bondmen and bond-women, I would have kept silent" (7:4). These women, nevertheless, regarded Esther as a female leader with courage and conviction who spoke up despite prevailing norms.

Maria Stewart, a black freedwoman and abolitionist, struggled not only against a white society that enslaved blacks but against black men who kept black women silent. Stewart hoped that other black women would soon join her in her sweeping, salvific mission. In one of her four public speeches in Boston, in Boston's Franklin Hall on September 21, 1832, Stewart tried to stir black women to recognize their double bind in "Why Sit Ye Here and Die?"

> …such is the powerful force of prejudice. Let our girls possess what amiable qualities of soul they may; let their characters be fair and spotless as innocence itself; let their natural taste and ingenuity be what they may; it is impossible for scarce an individual of them to rise above the condition of servants. Ah! why is this cruel and unfeeling distinction? Is it merely because God has made our complexion to vary? If it be, O shame to soft, relenting humanity![15]

---

15. "A Lecture at the Franklin Hall, Boston, September 21, 1832" (*Productions of Mrs.*

Society, Stewart pointed out, rejected the ingenuity of black women and kept them enslaved, a condition whereby their contributions would never be made apparent to society. By creating a public role on the speaking circuit, Stewart was actively seeking to eliminate the invisibility of the black woman.

To that end, Stewart cited Esther directly in her "Farewell Address to Her Friends in the City of Boston" (September 21, 1832). Esther was an exemplar of the political platform she herself sought. "What if I am a woman?" she charged. "Is not the God of ancient times the God of these modern days? Did he not raise up Deborah, to be a mother, and a judge in Israel? Did not Queen Esther save the lives of the Jews?" Stewart was one of the first black women to speak openly about both black and women's rights and to do so to a mixed audience.[16] Here, Stewart claimed her voice using both Deborah and Queen Esther as biblical precedents, citing two female leaders who brought redemption to the Israelites. Through them, Stewart was able to exert the rights of her own demoralized people for liberation and to assert her own right to speak out against injustice.[17]

The choice of Deborah and Esther from among other biblical heroines was likely intentional for an audience familiar with their narratives. Stewart referenced biblical women who assumed leadership roles in narratives where men were essentially helpless without female intervention. Together, the hero and the heroine achieved national salvation in times of crisis. Deborah, in the Book of Judges, sat beneath a palm tree between Ramah and Bethel, and "the Israelites would come to her for decisions" (4:5). Yet, upon charging her chief general Barak to fight the Philistines – summoning a male to take command – he issued his own demand, "If you will go with me, I will go; if not, I will

---

Maria W. Stewart, 51–56), in Dorothy Porter, ed., *Early Negro Writing, 1760–1837* (Baltimore, 1995), 136–140.

16. Maria Stewart, "An Address Delivered at the African Masonic Hall, Boston, February 27, 1833," in Marilyn Richardson, *Maria W. Stewart, America's First Black Woman Political Writer: Essays and Speeches* (Bloomington, 1987), 68.

17. For the full text of the speech, see https://search-alexanderstreet-com.libproxy. mit.edu/view/work/bibliographic_entity%7Cdocument%7C2666125#page/24/ mode/1/chapter/bibliographic_entity%7Cdocument%7C2666121.

not go" (4:8). Deborah was charged with leaving the shade of her tree to accompany Barak to the frontlines, enhancing her visibility and expanding her leadership role. Deborah even articulated the stakes for Barak in male shame, but he was secure enough to forgo possible defeat in order to have Deborah at his side in battle. "'Very well, I will go with you,' she answered. 'However, there will be no glory for you in the course you are taking, for then the Lord will deliver Sisera into the hands of a woman.' So Deborah went with Barak to Kedesh" (4:9).

Stewart's reference to Esther may be even more telling. While Stewart positions Deborah as mother and judge, true to the text, Esther's maternal role is inconsequential. As Michael V. Fox notes, "Esther becomes a hero, not by bearing children, but because of her words and actions."[18]

Esther went from being an object to having subjects, from a vulnerable orphan and exile to a position of prestige in Ahasuerus' vast empire, a position that materially elevated her life but one that initially accorded her little power. Although Mordecai told her to stay quiet on two occasions (2:10 and 2:20), he did, in the very same chapter, tell her to speak out to foil a conspiracy plot against Ahasuerus. He asked her once again in chapter 4 to approach the king to save her people. Mordecai depended upon Esther in order to exercise his own leadership, much the way Barak was dependent on Deborah to exercise his.

While Deborah summoned Barak, Esther must wait to be summoned, and this agonizing wait became her excuse for not defending her people when Mordecai insisted she do so. As Susan Zaeske notes, "A central feature of the exilic rhetoric of Esther is the risky nature of the act of speaking."[19] Significantly, Esther's first words were actually a defense of her silence. While Esther may not have understood the reason for her enforced reticence, she was frightfully aware of the costs of speech. Approaching the king without official sanction was a death sentence. Esther had been silenced and then self-silenced, unwilling to place herself where she was not wanted.

---

18. Michael V. Fox, *Character and Ideology in the Book of Esther* (Columbia, 1991), 209–210.
19. Susan Zaeske, "Unveiling Esther as a Pragmatic Radical Reader," *Philosophy and Rhetoric* 33, no. 3 (2000): 199.

> All the king's courtiers and the people of the king's provinces know that if any person, man or woman, enters the king's presence in the inner court without having been summoned, there is but one law for him – that he be put to death. Only if the king extends the golden scepter to him may he live. Now I have not been summoned to visit the king for the last thirty days. (Est. 4:11)

Esther's first "speaking part" in 4:11, a full two chapters after she is introduced, mentions her fear as an unwanted presence, a barrier she quickly overcame. She then charged her maidens and the Jews of the empire to fast with her as she prepared to protest Haman's decree.

That Stewart should station herself in the tradition of Esther is no surprise, for as her "Farewell" makes clear, Stewart may have believed herself to have been sent by God on a mission to save her people, a mission like that of Esther, that endangered her. Mordecai, who emphatically told Esther to be passive and quiet, suddenly made a grandiloquent case for her leadership, as if prying open the young beauty's mouth. Demonstrating the transformation Esther underwent, the chapter closes with a reversal of command: "Mordecai ... did just as Esther had commanded him" (4:17). Positioning herself as a spiritual descendant of Esther, Stewart, too, found a sudden, divinely inspired voice. Stewart wanted to claim that a woman's voice, her voice, could speak to the troubles of the day with moral authority, just like the biblical women before her, joining black men in their fight for emancipation. Stewart had an "urgent, divinely inspired mission to the black community," writes Marilyn Richardson, that "allowed Stewart to quickly find her true voice, one full of assurance, spirit, energy, creative imagination, and fervor."[20]

Stewart was not the first black woman to see in Esther divine permission to speak out for the sake of her people. Sojourner Truth (born Isabella Baumfree, 1797–1883) was born into slavery but escaped with her infant daughter in 1826. At the Ohio Women's Rights Convention in 1851, she gave a rousing talk, "Ar'n't I a Woman?" that was first documented and published a month later by Marius Robinson, editor of the Ohio newspaper *The Anti-Slavery Bugle*, who had attended the convention. Seven years

---

20. Richardson, 14.

before Stewart, Sojourner articulated the double bind of black women. It was not anguish enough that white men shackled their bodies. Black men shackled their right to protest: "Then that little man in black there, he says women can't have as much rights as men, 'cause Christ wasn't a woman! Where did your Christ come from? Where did your Christ come from? From God and a woman! Man had nothing to do with Him." Like Stewart, Sojourner questioned the dominant religious paradigm using religious idioms. If Jesus was born of a woman, then women had every right to speak in God's name. She took the figure of Eve, regarded in Christianity as the temptress responsible for the fall of mankind, and reworked her story to support the power women had: "If the first woman God ever made was strong enough to turn the world upside down all alone, these women together ought to be able to turn it back, and get it right side up again! And now they is asking to do it, the men better let them."

Sojourner's speech on this occasion was notably short and ended abruptly: "Obliged to you for hearing me, and now old Sojourner ain't got nothing more to say."[21] It was only two years later, at the New York City Convention, that Sojourner, perhaps more accustomed to public speaking by this time, referenced Esther: "There was a king in the Scriptures; and then it was the kings of the earth would kill a woman if she come into their presence; but Queen Esther come forth, for she was oppressed, and felt there was a great wrong, and she said I will die or I will bring my complaint before the king." Sojourner did not suggest that the Israelites were oppressed and, therefore, Esther spoke out in support for their cause, but that "she was oppressed," manipulating the biblical narrative to give herself a platform. Her comparison of the ancient story to the present day continued: "Should the king of the United States be greater, or more crueler, or more harder" than the king of the Scriptures whom Esther approached, despite the fact that he might easily kill a woman who came into his presence?[22]

---

21. "Compare the speeches," *The Sojourner Truth Project*, https://www.thesojourner-truthproject.com/compare-the-speeches/.
22. "Sojourner Truth: Speech at New York City Convention," ed. Heidi Jacobs, *Society for the Study of American Women Writers* (December 5, 2004), https://www.lehigh.edu/~dek7/SSAWW/writTruthSpeech2.htm.

Sojourner was unable to read. Her unusual way of learning Scripture may, in fact, have contributed to her creative reinterpretations. According to Drema R. Lipscomb, Sojourner liked to have the Bible read to her without commentary. Sojourner was so irritated by the adults who read to her with their own interpretations of the text that she replaced them with children, who usually did not comment and did not mind repeating the verses enough times that Sojourner could commit them to memory. "She did not want the explication of others; she wanted to interpret the scriptures as she saw them."[23] Memorizing verses enabled her to offer her own novel readings when delivering speeches.

Stewart and Sojourner may also have understood the irony in the Esther story that not only did Ahasuerus tolerate Esther's visible breach of court protocol, he actually rewarded her for speaking:

> On the third day, Esther put on royal apparel and stood in the inner court of the king's palace, facing the king's palace, while the king was sitting on his royal throne in the throne room facing the entrance of the palace. As soon as the king saw Queen Esther standing in the court, she won his favor. The king extended to Esther the golden scepter which he had in his hand, and Esther approached and touched the tip of the scepter. "What troubles you, Queen Esther?" the king asked her. "And what is your request? Even to half the kingdom, it shall be granted you." (5:1–3)

In the end, Esther's speech did not endanger her in these verses. It empowered her.[24] Such was the case with these early black female abolitionists. For these courageous women, the fear of speaking out was soon eclipsed by the act of speaking out, which further demonstrated the necessity and power of their words.

---

23. Drema R. Lipscomb, "Sojourner Truth: A Practical Public Discourse," in *Reclaiming Rhetorica: Women in the Rhetorical Tradition*, ed. Andrea A. Lunsford (Pittsburgh, 1995), 232.
24. For more on the role of silence and speech in Esther, see my "Keeping Silent," in *Esther: Power, Fate, and Fragility in Exile* (New Milford/Jerusalem, 2020), 349–358.

Stewart, however, became increasingly unsure of her success. Like Esther in the text above, she worried that her leadership would go unrecognized. In her farewell address, Stewart recalled her arrival in Boston and her fruitless search to find allies, others who, like her, were willing to publicly call attention to the injustice done to her people. Stewart describes her shame after first speaking her mind:

> When going home, reflecting on what I had said, I felt ashamed, and knew not where I should hide myself. Something said within my breast, "Press forward, I will be with thee." And my heart made this reply, Lord, if thou wilt be with me, then I will speak for thee as long as I live. And thus far I have every reason to believe that it is the divine influence of the Holy Spirit operating upon my heart that could possibly induce me to make the feeble and unworthy efforts that I have.

Aligning herself with Deborah and Esther may even have hinted, as suggested by scholar Susan Zaeske, that Stewart thought God had invested her with special powers of speech in a white and male-dominated society. It was her belief that channeling God enabled Stewart to oppose and override Paul's muzzling of women in the Book of Corinthians:[25]

> As in all the congregations of the Lord's people, women should remain silent in the churches. They are not allowed to speak, but must be in submission, as the law says. If they want to inquire about something, they should ask their own husbands at home; for it is disgraceful for a woman to speak in the church.[26]

Stewart preempted her audience, who likely knew and supported Paul's constraints on a woman's public presence, by mentioning this problem directly, essentially using what she would have regarded as Old Testament verses to subvert a New Testament sentiment. In a brash rhetorical move akin to those of Sojourner Truth, Stewart assured her audience

---

25. Ibid.
26. I Corinthians 14:33–35 (NIV).

that had Paul lived to see the plight of her people, he would not have refused her the right to protest.

> Did St. Paul but know of our wrongs and deprivations, I presume he would make no objections to our pleading in public for our rights. Again; holy women ministered unto Christ and the apostles; and women of refinement in all ages, more or less, have had a voice in moral, religious, and political subjects. Again; why the Almighty hath imparted unto me the power of speaking thus, I cannot tell.

Stewart confessed ignorance as to why God selected her as a conduit for these messages of redemption. In this admission, we might see another possible connection to the Book of Esther. While Esther had been selected queen in a competition, she did not see herself as selected to lead the Jews in this national moment of crisis until Mordecai persuaded her. Stewart indicates that she, too, had to be convinced. God, she presumed, persuaded her to assume the mantle of leadership and would subsequently protect her from the criticisms waged against her:

> I believe, that for wise and holy purposes, best known to himself, he hath unloosed my tongue, and put his word into my mouth, in order to confound and put all those to shame that have rose up against me. For he hath clothed my face with steel, and lined my forehead with brass. He hath put his testimony within me, and engraven his seal on my forehead.[27]

Despite explaining who gave her the authority to speak out and why, Stewart conceded that she had failed in her mission in Boston. Unlike Esther, Stewart, unable in the present moment to command anything,

---

27. Stewart's audience would have been familiar with the New Testament story Stewart obliquely references of a deaf man with a speech impediment who was brought to Jesus. Jesus put his fingers in the man's ears, spit and touched the man's tongue and commanded the ill man's mouth to open. "The man's ears were opened and his tongue was loosed; he could hear clearly and speak plainly" (Mark 7:31–35). By using such an image, she subtly suggests that God pried open her shut mouth.

took leave of the city, hoping, at least, for heavenly recognition: "I believe that a rich award awaits me, if not in this world, in the world to come." That Stewart regarded herself as unsuccessful in the moment is not how history will remember her. Richardson describes Stewart as a "bold and militant orator" who called on "black women to develop their highest intellectual capacities into all spheres of the life of the mind." She regards Stewart as at the forefront of black female activism.[28]

As evident from these examples, Esther has been and will likely still be read with a political agenda. Some black scholars saw in Esther stereotypes that merely reinforced the hierarchical structures that further entrapped them. Baukham cautions against this kind of reading: "There is no word of God to sanction anything in this book. So here, as in many modern political instances, we must beware of supposing that we cannot welcome an obviously good political result without approving all of the means which produced it."[29] In the absence of God's overt appearance, it may be best not to draw definitive conclusions about gender politics from Esther's pages, where surely expediency and survival were more pressing concerns.

These critics, nevertheless, still took the Book of Esther seriously, much in the spirit of Toni Morrison's observation of the role of Scriptures in her life, "The Bible wasn't part of my reading, it was part of my life."[30] But there were early abolitionists who saw and heard in Esther a female voice of heroism worthy of emulation. Unlike Esther, these women would not live to see their battles won, but, in speaking out, they added important and critical voices to the American annals of emancipation. Inspired by a woman they never met, these abolitionists paradoxically influenced generations of women they never met, reminding us that "history is not of such a black and white character."[31]

---

28. Richardson, xv.
29. Baukham, 126.
30. Charles Ruas, *Conversations with American Writers* (New York, 1985), 97.
31. Baukham, 126.

Lincoln, Esther, and the Rav: A Study in Statesmanship

Rabbi Dr. Meir Y. Soloveichik

On September 13, 1862, the Rev. W. W. Patton, an American pastor in Chicago and prominent abolitionist, took a contingent of clergymen to the White House and presented Abraham Lincoln with a memorandum containing one central message: that the president should utilize his authority as wartime commander-in-chief to issue a proclamation freeing the slaves in the South.

> We urge you, therefore, as the head of this Christian nation, from considerations of moral principle, and, as the only means of preserving the Union, to proclaim, without delay, National Emancipation. However void of authority in this respect you might have been in time of peace, you are well aware, as a statesman, that the exigencies of war are the only limits of its powers, especially in a war to preserve the very life of the nation. And these exigencies are not to be restricted to what may avail at

the last gasp prior to national death, but are to be interpreted to include all measures that may most readily and thoroughly subdue the enemy. The rebels have brought slavery under your control by their desperate attack upon the life of the republic. They have created a moral, political, and military necessity, which warrants the deed, and now God and a waiting world demand that the opportunity be used. And surely the fact that they have placed in our power a system which, while it exposes them, is itself the grossest wickedness, adds infinitely to the obligation to strike the blow.[1]

This memorandum, remarkably, founded its demands on a *dvar Torah*, citing the turning point in the *megilla*, where Mordecai galvanizes Esther into action:

At the time of the national peril of the Jews, under Ahasuerus, Mordecai spoke in their name to Queen Esther, who hesitated to take the step necessary to their preservation, in these solemn words: "Think not with thyself that thou shalt escape in the king's house, more than all the Jews. For if thou altogether holdest thy peace at this time, then shall there enlargement and deliverance arise to the Jews from another place; but thou and thy father's house shall be destroyed; and who knoweth whether thou art come to the kingdom for such a time as this?" And your memorialists believe that in Divine Providence you have been called to the Presidency to speak the word of justice and authority which shall free the bondman and save the nation. Our prayer to God is, that by such an act the name of Abraham Lincoln may go down to posterity with that of George Washington, as the second savior of our country.[2]

---

1. *Pilgrim's Letters: Bits of Current History Picked Up in the West and the South, During the Last Thirty Years, for the Independent, the Congregationalist, and the Advance* (Boston/Chicago, 1888), 27.

2. Ibid., 28.

We must appreciate the moral power of the scripture they are citing. As soon as Mordecai hears of the decree, he acts dramatically, defiantly, and publicly, donning sackcloth and wailing in the streets. Suddenly the courtier with a profoundly Persian name – linked to the pagan god Marduk – publicly identifies as a Jew, and he asks Esther to do likewise, before the royal presence of the king himself. Esther hesitates, provoking the response that the ministers later cite to Lincoln: "Think not with thyself that thou shalt escape in the king's house, more than all the Jews."[3] As Rabbi Aharon Lichtenstein once put it, Mordecai's assault on Esther is one that appeals "to the deepest recesses of the Jewish soul."[4]

The ministers, in 1862, thus adopt this tale for their own allegory, a makeshift *mashal,* an accusation sourced in scripture. They are identifying themselves with Mordecai: it is they who have been protesting slavery in the streets. Lincoln, like Esther, has suddenly and miraculously risen to power; as they understand it, he has the power to end slavery, but he has not acted. By citing Mordecai, they are subtly suggesting that his anti-slavery position was a posture, that deep down he was apathetic, that he did not really care.

This was the message delivered to Lincoln on September 13. It was only several days later, on September 22, that Lincoln issued his proclamation that slaves in rebel states would be henceforth forever free. And so it would seem that the ministers' message hit home, and their scriptural citation, their *dvar Torah,* had its desired effect.

The truth, however, is that the Emancipation Proclamation had already been sitting in a drawer for many weeks; but Lincoln knew that short of a battlefield victory it would have no effect. It was only after the battle of Antietam, which occurred four days after this meeting, only after the union achieved some form of victory, that Lincoln remarked that "I think the time has come now – the action of the army against the rebels has not been quite what I should have best liked. But they have been driven out of Maryland, and Pennsylvania is no longer in danger

---

3. Ibid., 28.
4. Aharon Lichtenstein, *By His Light: Character and Values in the Service of God,* adapted by Reuven Ziegler (New Milford/Jerusalem, 2016), 152.

of invasion."[5] Lincoln, no less than these ministers, wanted slavery destroyed; but he understood that just boldly embracing a moral ideal would not actually end slavery. He understood that this goal could only be achieved with wisdom, even if that meant that he would not outwardly embrace the full range of his abolitionist cause. It was these complexities that made Lincoln who he was; he combined great moral goals with the political craftiness necessary to achieve them.

This is easy to miss. The legend of Lincoln, all too often, lies in depictions of his sainthood. Tolstoy once described touring the Caucasus, and coming upon a nomadic tribe that knew little of the outside world. After he told them of the heroes of European history, the chieftain replied that there was an even more extraordinary man of whom they wished to hear:

> But you have not told us a syllable about the greatest general and greatest ruler of the world. We want to know something about him. He was a hero. He spoke with a voice of thunder; he laughed like the sunrise and his deeds were strong as the rock and as sweet as the fragrance of roses. The angels appeared to his mother and predicted that the son whom she would conceive would become the greatest the stars had ever seen. He was so great that he even forgave the crimes of his greatest enemies and shook brotherly hands with those who had plotted against his life. His name was Lincoln and the country in which he lived is called America, which is so far away that if a youth should journey to reach it he would be an old man when he arrived. Tell us of that man.[6]

This is the legend of Lincoln, Lincoln as angel and saint. Even Tolstoy himself, who may have understood human beings better than any other writer in the history of literature, reflected that

---

5.   John Niven, ed., *The Salmon P. Chase Papers* (Kent, 1993), 394.
6.   Leo Tolstoy, "Tolstoy on Lincoln," *New York World,* February 7, 1909, https://en.wikisource.org/wiki/Tolstoy_on_Lincoln.

Of all the great national heroes and statesmen of history Lincoln is the only real giant. Alexander, Frederick the Great, Caesar, Napoleon, Gladstone and even Washington stand in greatness of character, in depth of feeling and in a certain moral power far behind Lincoln. Lincoln was a man of whom a nation has a right to be proud; he was a Christ in miniature, a saint of humanity, whose name will live thousands of years in the legends of future generations. We are still too near to his greatness, and so can hardly appreciate his divine power; but after a few centuries more our posterity will find him considerably bigger than we do. His genius is still too strong and too powerful for the common understanding, just as the sun is too hot when its light beams directly on us.[7]

Yet to speak this way is to fundamentally misunderstand Lincoln's genius, and the essence of a truly successful political leader. Had Lincoln been a saint, who enthusiastically demanded abolition at every moment and in every context, he would have been a great American moral figure but he would not have been elected president. As the Lincoln scholar Harold Holzer has noted, Lincoln's gradualism was the source of his ability to achieve the presidency, and thereby lead the country to abolition. The lesson of Lincoln's life is that for great leaders a sweeping moral vision is necessary but not sufficient; what is also required is the ability to proceed in a way that those goals can be attained.

Rightly understood, in a very different context, that is ultimately the lesson of the Book of Esther as well. Mordecai galvanized Esther into action, but she did not follow his plan, which was to storm immediately into her husband's throne room and demand that the Jews be spared. That would have ended with Esther's certain death. Instead she laid an elaborate strategy over several days, played on the insecurities of a paranoid king, and then, at the right moment, at her Antietam, she seized the opportunity, and her political play resulted in the death and downfall of Haman and the salvation of the Jews. Mordecai inspired Esther, but the statecraft was entirely of her own conception. Rabbi Soloveitchik put it this way:

---

7. Ibid.

Mordecai held the view that immediate, spontaneous action on the part of Esther is inevitable. Esther should appear before the king, taking the risk of being rejected and executed, and plead with him hysterically to spare her people. Esther did not concur with Mordecai. Esther, with her incisive intelligence, understood that no plea addressed to the king would produce any results. Hysterical crying, supplication, begging, would at best be ineffectual. At worst, they may cause the infliction of more harm. Since Haman had succeeded in brainwashing Ahasuerus and in arousing in him paranoid, mortal fear of assassins and rebels, there was no power in the world that would be capable of dissuading Ahasuerus from destroying all his imaginary enemies. Could anyone sway Stalin from his mad designs.... Esther could avail herself of one method only, namely, to turn the tables on Haman, to accuse him of plotting against the king and the empire, to arouse doubts in the sick king's mind concerning Haman's loyalty and devotion...yes, Mordecai was the initiator, the teacher, the first messenger; he awakened her, he fired her imagination and sensitized her heart. Through him came the inspired word to her. Yet the strategy was hers, the critical decisions how and when to do it were hers. She could not consult Mordecai, and even if she could, she would not have accepted advice from him.[8]

Esther, like American history, contains lessons for leaders today. In Spielberg's extraordinary movie about Lincoln, Daniel Day Lewis, playing Lincoln, attempts to convey to a member of his own political party why having moral ideals – including an understanding of the evil of slavery – is essential, but not enough. He reflects how he discovered when working as a surveyor that in the wilderness, "a compass will point you true north from where you're standing, but it's got no advice about the swamps and deserts and chasms that you'll encounter along the way. If in pursuit of your destination, you plunge ahead, heedless of obstacles, and achieve nothing more than to sink in a swamp.... What's

---

8. Joseph B. Soloveitchik, *Days of Deliverance: Essays on Purim and Hanukkah* (Jersey City, 2007), 81.

the use of knowing true north?"[9] In the Esther story, Mordecai is the one who first stresses "true north"; but once Esther is pointed in that direction, she is the only one who knows, politically, how to get there, without falling into pits and political pitfalls along the way.

This explanation, however, provokes a very basic question. Did Mordecai not understand this? How could he not see that what he was proposing to Esther – storming into the throne room and protesting Haman's decree – was folly? Here, Rabbi Soloveitchik's commentary on Esther allows us to suggest something new. Rabbi Soloveitchik has stressed Esther is one of the very few books of the Bible that was written as the age of prophecy drew to a close:

> ...the Megillah contains the story of events that occurred in the twilight hour of Jewish history. It marks the passing of a bright, beautiful, summer day, full of sun, color and joy, a day on which God's word was on many tongues and His spirit in many hearts. It ushers in a dark, dreary autumnal night of silence and fear, a night in the course of which God stopped speaking to His people. At that time, the covenantal community was losing, slowly but surely, the most precious of all gifts: prophecy. The great covenantal dialogue between man and God that had commenced with Abraham was about to be terminated, and the prophetic community faced a stark, ruthless reality – a non-prophetic existence. With the transition from a prophetic to a non-prophetic community, the Jewish historical experience changed completely.[10]

We are now able to analyze Mordecai's actions. In earlier books of the Tanakh, aside from the kings themselves, the central actors on the political stage are prophets. At times they are themselves the leaders: Joshua, Samuel; and at times, more often, they are taking on the leaders: Elijah, Elisha, Isaiah, Jeremiah. The prophet knows none of statecraft's Lincolnian complexities: they are there to deliver a moral message, come what may. If Ahab murders and steals an Israelite's land, it may not be

---

9. *Lincoln*, directed by Stephen Spielberg (Touchstone Pictures, 2012).
10. Soloveitchik, 70.

politically prudent for a subject of this king to storm into the throne room and tell him that what he did was wrong. But that does not stop Elijah, who has no compunctions, and does exactly what Mordecai had asked of Esther: he storms into the throne room, declaiming in outrage, "Shalt thou murder and also inherit?" To paraphrase the script of the Lincoln film, the obligation of the prophet is to proclaim true north, and to always seek it without compromise.

This is, of course, the approach that Mordecai adopts, and when we ponder the text we are able to understand why. The Land of Israel is mentioned in Esther only in the context of Mordecai's biography: he is the son of Kish, whom Nebuchadnezzar exiled from Jerusalem with King Jeconiah of Judah. This means that Mordecai's father experienced the end of the kingdom of Judea, of the First Temple, of the age of Jeremiah, and Huldah, and of other prophets. The prophetic model of leadership was part of his patrimony. Mordecai's father was almost certainly an intimate of prophets in the Holy Land; he would also have known Ezekiel, who fearlessly and publicly proclaimed his prophecies in the streets of Babylon.

But what of Esther? We are told that Esther was an orphan, Unlike Mordecai, Esther knew no one from the generation of Judea, of the age when prophets stormed royal courts with the words "Thus saith the Lord." Esther's experience is not that of Mordecai; and perhaps the *megilla* informs us of their respective biographies in order to lend a deeper dimension to their perspectives. Mordecai seeks to act as a prophetic figure; he storms the streets of Shushan, and he tells Esther to act as Elijah would have, to storm the court of the king. Esther, however, understands that the political and religious reality has changed. As Rabbi Soloveitchik notes, the Torah tells us the story of the prophetic community at the hour of triumph, at the hour of revelation and direct contact with God. But Esther, he argues, faced a new question: "How can the Jew triumph over his adversaries and enemies if God has stopped speaking to him, if the cryptic messages he receives remain unintelligible and incomprehensible?"[11]

---

11. Ibid., 72.

Esther, in other words, understands that the age of prophecy is coming to an end. A new approach to politics, to safeguarding the Jewish people in a hostile environment, needs to be adopted, while retaining the faith and loyalty of the past. Esther still asks of all Israelites to gather in fasting and prayer. She still seeks divine salvation, but her actions are performed with intuition, with intrigue, playing on the king's emotions, balancing the power structures at court. The characters in Esther provide the first example in the Bible in which a statesman struggles with the mysterious, inscrutable, will of God, believing that he or she is an instrument in the hands of providence itself. Esther, to paraphrase Spielberg's film, must grope her way forward toward true north while avoiding political pitfalls along the way.

It is striking, then, that precisely in September 1862, when the ministers met with Lincoln, and cited, of all books, the story of Esther, Lincoln was pondering the inscrutability of the divine will while still reflecting the earnest faith that God had placed him in his position in order to act. Thanks to his secretary John Hay, we know that Lincoln had that September scribbled some thoughts, not meant for publication, about providence:

> The will of God prevails. In great contests each party claims to act in accordance with the will of God. Both *may* be, and one *must* be, wrong. God cannot be *for* and *against* the same thing at the same time. In the present civil war it is quite possible that God's purpose is something different from the purpose of either party – and yet the human instrumentalities, working just as they do, are of the best adaptation to effect His purpose. I am almost ready to say that this is probably true – that God wills this contest, and wills that it shall not end yet. By His mere great power, on the minds of the now contestants, He could have either *saved* or *destroyed* the Union without a human contest. Yet the contest began. And, having begun He could give the final victory to either side any day. Yet the contest proceeds.[12]

---

12. *The Collected Works of Abraham Lincoln* (New Brunswick, 1953).

The historian Mark Noll once reflected that "Lincoln is clearly a believer in God and providence, yet it's a more mysterious God than his contemporaries worshiped."[13] His God, in other words, was not the miraculous Being encountered in Exodus but rather the inscrutable, but still providential, divine presence of Esther. Lincoln's secretary notes that in his words Lincoln

> admits us into the most secret recesses of his soul…. Perplexed and afflicted beyond the power of human help, by the disasters of war, the wrangling of parties, and the inexorable and constraining logic of his own mind, he shut out the world one day, and tried to put into form his double sense of responsibility to human duty and Divine Power; and this was the result. It shows – as has been said in another place – the awful sincerity of a perfectly honest soul, trying to bring itself into closer communion with its Maker.[14]

Lincoln, a man once known as an agnostic, found God precisely in His inscrutability; as the writer Dan Gilgoff put it, "Though he attended a Christian church, Lincoln's God hewed closer to the Old Testament's ruler of nations." To celebrate Esther, and to celebrate Lincoln, is to reflect not only on moral heroism but also on statesmanship, on the ability to achieve moral goals, at times through means that are less than ideal. This is why Lincoln waited for the victory at Antietam before declaring emancipation. Yet once the opportunity was ripe, issue it he did, resulting in what Frederick Douglass called "the first step on the part of the nation in its departure from the thraldom of the ages."[15]

Rabbi Soloveitchik's insight, that Esther presents us with the first biblical tale in a post-prophetic period, allows us to reflect more deeply on the essence of statesmanship. It was Sherman who said of Lincoln

13. Dan Gilgoff, "Abraham Lincoln's Religious Uncertainty," *USA Today,* February 12, 2009, https://www.usnews.com/news/history/articles/2009/02/12/abraham-lincolns-religious-uncertainty.
14. "Meditation on the Divine Will," *Abraham Lincoln Online: Speeches & Writings,* http://www.abrahamlincolnonline.org/lincoln/speeches/meditat.htm.
15. *Life and Times of Frederick Douglass* (Hartford, 1881), 30.

that "of all the men I have ever met, he seemed to possess more of the elements of greatness, combined with goodness, than any other."[16] This is perfectly put; Lincoln's refusal to lose sight of true north while combining hard-headed calculating statesmanship and brutal war-waging is a rare example of goodness and greatness enhancing each other. It is this Esther-based encounter with the ministers in 1862, over a year before the Gettysburg address and several before the second inaugural, where we first find this manifest. Herein we discover why there was no one like Lincoln; and why we will very probably not see his like again.

---

16. *Memoirs of General William T. Sherman* (New York, 2000).

Feminist Esther

Vashti Comes to America

Rabbi Tzvi Sinensky

Vashti, Ahasuerus' first queen, is among the most enigmatic characters in the Book of Esther. While the king revels with his subjects for some six months, he commands Vashti to appear before him "to display her beauty to the peoples and the officials" (Est. 1:11). For unstated reasons, Vashti refuses to attend. The king, infuriated, consults with his advisors, one of whom recommends "that Vashti never [again] enter the presence of King Ahasuerus," and that the king "bestow her royal status upon another who is more worthy than she" (1:19). This leads Ahasuerus to launch an international search for a new queen, setting the stage for the selection of the Jewess Esther and the remainder of the book's narrative.

What are we to make of Vashti's refusal? Is she a villainess who deserved her fate, heroic conscientious objector, or simply a literary non-entity who paves the way for Queen Esther's rise? To set the stage for the reception of Vashti in the New World, it is worth beginning with an overview of classical Jewish and Christian readings of this cryptic character.

For the Jewish community, of course, the Book of Esther has played a central role for millennia. The story is traditionally viewed as a paradigmatic case of God's hidden hand in history, and Esther and Mordecai are valorized as heroes. Vashti's character, in contrast, has been interpreted in an overwhelmingly negative light. The Midrash identifies her as the granddaughter of Nebuchadnezzar, who had destroyed the First Temple,[1] and credits her with convincing Ahasuerus to abrogate the Second Temple rebuilding project referenced in Ezra 4:6.[2] In recompense for having brutally forced her Jewish servants to work naked on Shabbat, she is bidden to appear unclothed on the seventh day of the party.[3] Hardly a pawn of the hedonic king, Vashti too seeks promiscuity – after all, the verses state explicitly that just like her husband, she had been holding a parallel party in the palace – and would have happily appeared naked (aside from her crown), which is precisely how the Rabbis imagine that she is bidden to appear.[4] She refuses her husband's request not out of modesty or principle but vanity, only because she grows a tail or contracts leprosy.[5] As a result of her wickedness, while the text leaves her ultimate fate unclear, according to the ancient Rabbis she is executed.[6] Put simply, the rabbinic tradition depicts Vashti as a vile scoundrel, the wicked counterpart to the righteous Queen Esther.[7]

Unlike early rabbinic interpretation, however, the Book of Esther received relatively little attention in the Church.[8] While Esther was incorporated into the New Testament, this inclusion was largely begrudging. It is no coincidence that the first Christian commentary on Esther, by Rabanus (Hrabanus) Maurus, did not appear until the ninth century.[9] Martin

---

1. Esther Rabba, *Petiḥta* 12.
2. Esther Rabba 1 to Est. 2:1.
3. Megilla 12b.
4. Megilla 12a–b.
5. Ibid.
6. See Leviticus Rabba, *Shemini*, 12.
7. See my "Vashti: Feminist or Foe?" *The Lehrhaus* (March 6, 2019), https://thelehrhaus.com/scholarship/vashti-feminist-or-foe/, and for an excellent summary of the rabbinic portrayal of Vashti, see Malka Z. Simkovich, Zev Farber, and David Steinberg, "Ahasuerus and Vashti: The Story *Megillat Esther* Does Not Tell You," https://www.thetorah.com/article/ahasuerus-and-vashti-the-story-megillat-esther-does-not-tell-you, March 6, 2017.
8. See, for example, Jo Carruthers, *Esther Through the Centuries* (Malden, 2008), 7, 12–13.
9. Laurence A. Turner, "Finding Christ in a Godless Text: The Book of Esther and Christian Typology," in *No One Better: Essays in Honour of Dr. Norman H. Young*,

Luther went so far as to write, "I am so hostile to this book [2 Maccabees] and Esther that I wish that they did not come to us at all, for they have too many heathen unnaturalities."[10] In 1837, the Reverend W. Niblock, Headmaster of London High School, offered a catalog of Christian concerns with Esther: "It contains no promise to the Church, makes no mention of the Gospel, has no type or prophecy of the Messiah, does not once introduce the name of God or recognize his providence, reveals none of 'those precious and fundamental doctrines' found elsewhere in the Old Testament and is not quoted in the New Testament."[11] Lewis Bayles Paton (1864–1932), an American biblical scholar, archaeologist, and historian, later asserted: "The book is so conspicuously lacking in religion that it should never have been included in the Canon of the OT, but should have been left with Judith and Tobit among the apocryphal writings."[12]

Noting this long history of dismissal by Christian thinkers, the contemporary Christian scholar Frederic Bush, while advocating that Christians pay closer attention to the Book of Esther, acknowledges that he faces a steep uphill climb, titling one of his articles, "The Book of Esther: Opus non gratum (underappreciated work) in the Christian Canon."[13]

Christian neglect notwithstanding, the Middle Ages saw a resurgence of interest in the character of Esther herself, albeit not on a popular level. Christian medieval discussions[14] focused on Esther as a

---

ed. Kayle B. de Waal and Robert K. McIver (Oxford, 2016).

10. "Of God's Word: xxiv," in *The Table-Talk of Martin Luther,* trans. William Hazlitt (Philadelphia, 1893).

11. Carruthers, 13.

12. Louis Bayles Paton, *The Book of Esther: International Critical Commentary* (Edinburgh, 1908), 97.

13. *Bulletin for Biblical Research* 8 (1998): 39–54.

14. Susan Zaeske, "Unveiling Esther as Pragmatic Radical Rhetoric," *Philosophy and Rhetoric* 33, no. 3 (2000): 206, summarizes the medieval literature:

Churchmen found the Esther story useful in their efforts to influence the rhetorical behavior of noblewomen because it provided a model of a pious queen that seemed particularly appropriate for Christian queens. In his ninth-century "Expositio in librum Esther," Hrabanus Maurus urged the empress Judith (second wife of Louis the Pious) to "[a]lways place Esther, a queen

model for contemporary queens. Additionally, Christian writers relied on the Greek version of the story, in which the name of God appears frequently, making it a more comfortable religious text on which to rely.[15] Still, these recommendations for royals notwithstanding – it remains unclear whether any female sovereigns in fact utilized the book in this way – Esther remained a closed book for the masses.

Esther was finally popularized in Christian circles during the Puritan period, thanks to Cotton Mather's classic *Ornaments for the Daughters of Zion*, a conduct manual in which Esther appears as one of the biblical heroines adduced as a model of proper behavior.[16] For Mather, Esther was the ideal woman inasmuch as she supported her husband Ahasuerus even as she urged him to improve his character. Mather's guide was highly influential and was widely read through the nineteenth century.[17]

But even as Mather wrote extensively about Esther, he paid scant attention to Vashti. This usage differential remained the norm through much of the eighteenth century. Here is an n-gram graph, representing the percentage of total published books[18] that include at least one usage of the word Esther over the last five hundred years:

---

like you, before the eyes of your heart, as someone to be imitated in every act of piety and sanctity" (qtd. in Lois L. Honeycutt, "Intercession and the High-Medieval Queen: The Esther Topos," in *Power and the Weak: Studies on Medieval Women*, ed. Jennifer Carpenter and Sally-Beth MacLean [Urbana, 1995], 129). In a letter to the wife of Charles the Bald, Pope John VIII urged her to advocate on behalf of the church in the same way Esther pleaded for the people of Israel. Likewise, a prayer written for the coronation in 876 of Charles the Bald's daughter Judith praises Esther as so blessed by God as an intercessor that "by means of her prayers" she was able to incline "the savage heart of the king toward mercy and salvation" (ibid.). Indeed, from the ninth century to the twelfth century, concludes Honeycutt, "at least a passing reference to Esther became nearly formulaic in the literature addressed to medieval queens" (ibid., 133).

15. Zaeske, 193–220.
16. For more on Cotton Mather, see Stuart Halpern's chapter, "Puritan Purim," in this volume.
17. Jacob Mason Spencer, "Hawthorne's Magnalia: Retelling Cotton Mather in the Provincial Tales," unpublished Harvard University dissertation, 2015.
18. At least those in Google's extensive database.

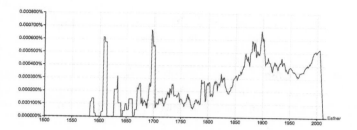

And here is Vashti:

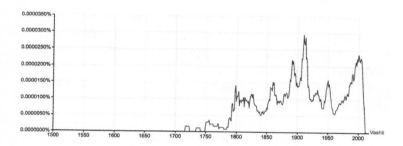

The contrast speaks volumes. Note the glaring absence of Vashti's name in published books before the eighteenth century. Even afterward, a close reading of the graphs indicates the dramatic gap between usages of the two throughout. And so, as the close of the eighteenth century approached, while Esther was invoked by Mather, a highly popular and influential author, as a model wife, Vashti was effectively ignored.

As a result of this lacuna, as the first wave of feminists began to rise in the nineteenth century, Vashti still remained "unclaimed" in the Christian West. This vacuum created an opening for "a remarkable number of nineteenth-century women poets" and authors to begin turning to Vashti as a role model.[19]

As early as 1820, in her *Judith, Esther and Other Poems*, American poet Maria Gowen Brooks (1794–1845) offered a vigorous defense of Vashti's refusal to appear before the king. It was amid this shifting

---

19. Shira Wolosky, "Women's Bibles: Biblical Interpretation in Nineteenth-Century American Women's Poetry," *Feminist Studies* 28, no. 1 (Spring 2002): 202.

environment that, in 1847, Great Britain's Poet Laureate Lord Alfred Tennyson issued a paean to the deposed queen:

> O Vashti, noble Vashti! Summon'd out
> She kept her state, and left the drunken king
> To brawl at Shushan underneath the palms. (*The Princess,* Part 3)

While writing from the other side of the pond, Tennyson's depiction of Vashti was to prove highly influential among leading American thinkers and activists.

The year 1857, just four years prior to the American Civil War, saw another key development, with outspoken abolitionist Frances Harper joining the ranks of fellow feminists in penning a poem simply titled "Vashti" – a title that would have been unheard of in the eighteenth century. Harper depicts Vashti's defiant, emotional response to the king:

> "Go back!" she cried, and waved her hand,
>   And grief was in her eye:
> "Go, tell the King," she sadly said,
>   "That I would rather die…"
>
> She heard again the King's command,
>   And left her high estate;
> Strong in her earnest womanhood,
>   She calmly met her fate,
>
> And left the palace of the King,
>   Proud of her spotless name –
> A woman who could bend to grief,
>   But would not bow to shame.

Harper's vivid depiction reflects the larger alliance between feminists and abolitionists in the nineteenth century. Both groups sought to rectify the immoral exclusion of a significant segment of society, and many were active in both feminist and anti-slavery circles.

In 1878, another famed abolitionist and feminist, Harriet Beecher Stowe, weighed in regarding Vashti's fate:

> Now, if we consider the abject condition of all men in that day before the king, we shall stand amazed that there was a woman found at the head of the Persian empire that dared to disobey the command even of a drunken monarch.... Vashti was reduced to the place where a woman deliberately chooses death before dishonor.[20]

For Harper and Beecher Stowe, Vashti became the great exemplar of the disenfranchised individual – woman, slave, or both – who refuses to consent to her master's advances.[21]

Later, Anglo-American poet, lawyer, and politician John Brayshaw Kaye named his 1984 poem "Vashti." Kaye portrays Vashti as a wise and virtuous woman who finds herself exiled because of court politics; she adopts an orphan girl, Meta, and takes care of her, and lives out her life after the palace in solitude, but also close to nature and beauty, and loved by her adopted daughter. Such a description of Vashti would have been unthinkable some two hundred years prior. The integration of Vashti into non-polemical literature is perhaps the greatest testimony to the way in which she had deeply penetrated popular culture.

Perhaps most influential was Elizabeth Cady Stanton's 1895 *Women's Bible*. Comparing Vashti favorably with numerous female biblical heroines, Stanton declares:

> We have some grand types of women presented for our admiration in the Bible. Deborah for her courage and military prowess; Huldah for her learning, prophetic insight and statesmanship, seated in the college in Jerusalem, where Josiah the king sent

---

20. Harriet Beecher Stowe, *Bible Heroines: Narrative Biographies of Prominent Hebrew Women* (New York, 1878), 125, https://babel.hathitrust.org/cgi/pt?id=hvd.rsm3x2&view=1up&seq=10.

21. As Wolosky (202) notes, in 1891, suffragette Anna Howard Shaw similarly praised Vashti in an article entitled "God's Women," published in *The Woman's Journal* (March 7, 1891).

his cabinet ministers to consult her as to the policy of his government; Esther, who ruled as well as reigned, and Vashti, who scorned the Apostle's command, "Wives, obey your husbands." She refused the king's orders to grace with her presence his revelling court. Tennyson pays this tribute to her virtue and dignity:

"Oh, Vashti! noble Vashti! Summoned forth, she kept her state, And left the drunken king to brawl in Shushan underneath his palms."[22]

As Lucinda Chandler, fellow feminist and co-author of the *The Women's Bible* with Cady Stanton, writes on the very next page: "Vashti is conspicuous as the first woman recorded whose self-respect and courage enabled her to act contrary to the will of her husband. She was the first woman who dared."[23] *The Women's Bible* has been cited countless times in contemporary treatments of Vashti's heroism.

Despite the initial congruity among feminists and black activists, in time Vashti began to take on a life of her own in the black community. For instance, "Vashti" became a relatively common first name that black people gave to their children. Perhaps the most prominent example is Vashti Murphy McKenzie (b. May 28, 1947), a bishop of the African Methodist Episcopal Church, and the first female elected bishop in the denomination's history. Peter H. Reynolds' 2003 classic children's book *The Dot*[24] follows a young lady named Vashti; Reynolds reports that he came up with her name after a chance encounter at a Massachusetts coffee house with a young lady named Vashti.[25]

---

22. Elizabeth Cady Stanton, *The Women's Bible* (New York, 1895), 85–86.
23. Ibid., 87. An even more assertive, self-empowered Vashti appears in Ella Wheeler Wilcox's "The Revolt of Vashti," composed in 1909. In 1917, Helen Hunt Jackson struck a similar note in her poem "Vashti," which appeared in *Sonnets and Lyrics* (Boston, 1887), 16–17.
24. Somerville, 2003.
25. In a Q&A published on his website (http://www.peterhreynolds.com/dot/Dot_QandA.html), Reynolds explains:
    Q: Where did the name of the main character come from?
    A: Vashti is the name of the main character in *The Dot*. This was inspired by a young girl who I met at a coffee shop in Dedham Square, Massachusetts. She

Individuals named Vashti are also featured as major characters in numerous twentieth-century works of black literature. To take just a few illustrative examples: In Toni Morrison's novel *Beloved*, Vashti is the name of Stamp Paid's wife. A woman named Vashti plays a prominent role in the theatrical production of "For Your Soul's Sake – A Soul Opera" (2007); like her biblical namesake, she speaks about making independent, principled decisions, irrespective of how they will be received by others. The black actress Butterfly McQueen portrays a servant girl named Vashti in the 1946 film *Duel in the Sun*. The simple fact that Vashti appears so prominently in twentieth-century black literature suggests just how mainstream her name has become among members of the community.

There is even an organization named Vashti, whose mission statement reads in part: "VASHTI is a value-driven, faith-based communication and leadership enhancement initiative. VASHTI was conceived to strengthen the presence and voices of black women and girls as progressive facilitators, teachers, trainers and advocates."[26]

What can help to account for the unique staying power of Vashti in the black community in particular? In his groundbreaking work on the relationship between fiction and jazz music, *The Hero and the Blues*, black literary critic Albert Murray (1916–2013) explains: "What must be remembered is that people live in terms of images which represent the fundamental conceptions embodied in their rituals and myths. In the absence of adequate images they live in terms of such compelling images (and hence rituals and myths) as are abroad at the time."[27] Black people before and after emancipation often turned to the Bible for personal examples as to how to ensure freedom and live a whole and meaningful

---

was selling flowers to raise money for her school. After I bought a carnation, she asked what I was doing. I said, "Painting. Here…you can have this one. I'll sign it to you – what's your name?"
"Vashti."
I smiled. "Vashti? You're the very first Vashti I've met! Can I use your name in my next book?"
Her big brown eyes lit up. "YES!"
She disappeared with the drawing I had made for her. I have not seen her since. Perhaps one day she will discover *The Dot* and make the connection!

26. https://www.pfaw.org/vashti-for-african-american-women-and-girls/.
27. Albert Murray, *The Hero and the Blues* (New York, 1995), 13–14.

life. As Anthony Pinn, a contemporary black theologian, has contended, black religion can be seen as "the quest for complex subjectivity, a desire or feeling for more life meaning. In other words, black religion's basic structure entails a push or desire for fullness."[28] This desire to not just revere but to embody their role models gave Vashti a far more interpretively integrated role in the black community.

With the passage of the 19th amendment in 1920 granting women the right to vote, the Vashti rhetoric settled down. But, owing to her already extensive interpretive history, Vashti rose once again to feminist fame in the 1980s. It was "during that decade that Alice Laffey, an expert on women in the Old Testament, noted that it was not surprising that Vashti appealed to modern feminists more than Esther did, as 'buried in Esther's character is also full compliance with the patriarchy.'"[29] As Laffey put it succinctly, "Vashti never speaks yet her actions speak loud and clear: NO! She will not become the sexual object of drunken men!"[30] Similarly, Valerie Freireich's 1996 short story "Vashti and God" explores the queen's inner world in great depth, even imagining that Vashti had a hand in assisting Esther's transition to the throne. And, moving into the new millenium, in *Vashti's Victory and Other Biblical Women Resisting Injustice,*[31] Reverend Laverne McCain Gill presents Vashti as the paragon of anti-patriarchal resistance, in whose footsteps other biblical women walked.

Given the embrace Vashti has received on American shores over the past two hundred years, it comes as no surprise that as the #MeToo movement began to develop in October 2017, Jewish activists began underscoring the importance of "reclaiming the Purim narrative for Queen Vashti and Queen Esther."[32] One headline in a Jewish newspaper

---

28. Anthony Pinn, *Terror and Triumph: The Nature of Black Religion. The 2002 Edward Cadbury Lectures* (Minneapolis, 2003), 173.
29. Ashley Ross, "The Feminist History of the Jewish Holiday of Purim," *Time* (March 23, 2016), https://time.com/4269357/queen-vashti-feminist-history/.
30. Alice Laffey, *An Introduction to the Old Testament: A Feminist Perspective* (Philadelphia, 1988), 216.
31. Cleveland, 2003.
32. Sheila Katz, "Reclaiming the Purim Narrative for Queen Vashti and Queen Esther, *JWI,* https://www.jwi.org/articles/reclaiming-the-purim-narrative-for-queen-vashti-and-queen-esther.

declared, "Vashti Was the First #MeToo Survivor."[33] Erica Brown, in an *Atlantic* article titled "Having an Esther Moment," noted that the only argument against championing Vashti as a hero is the tragic fact that "she didn't change court culture; she was its victim."[34]

A 2019 novel, Anna Solomon's *The Book of V.*, goes so far as to reimagine Vashti as Vivian Barr, a Watergate-era woman who refuses her husband's demand that she perform a humiliating favor, suggesting that the stories of Vashti and contemporary women are deeply intertwined in ways that the reader might not have recognized. As Solomon put it in an op-ed about the book, "If anything was clear during the Purim celebrations of my childhood – and I'll be honest, between the costumes and groggers and carnival vibe, not much was clear – it was this: No one wanted to be Vashti." But further exploration led Solomon to recognize that there was another side to the queen. Perhaps she wasn't a "leprous prostitute" but a woman who "turns out to be virtuous ... maybe even good and beautiful and brave."[35]

In sum, ever since "coming to America," Vashti's status as a feminist and black hero has been secure, rising in prominence whenever the subjects of slavery and mistreatment of women have risen on the communal agenda. Yet while Vashti's legacy as feminist icon in wider American culture seems secure, one chapter has yet to be fully written. What will happen in the Modern Orthodox Jewish community, for whom Vashti is not a blank canvas, but one drawn with sharply contrasting images? Will Modern Orthodox Jewish day schools continue portraying Vashti as a villain? Will she be celebrated instead? Or will the complex question of her character simply be sidestepped by rank-and-file classroom educators? Time will tell, though I suspect that in many schools, a transformation is already well underway. Either way, one thing is certain: ever since she arrived on these shores in the nineteenth century, the American view of Vashti has never been the same.

33. David Charles Pollack, "Vashti Was the First #MeToo Survivor," *Forward*, February 26, 2018, https://forward.com/opinion/395071/vashti-was-the-first-metoo-survivor/.
34. Erica Brown, "Having an Esther Moment," *The Atlantic* (March 8, 2020), https://www.theatlantic.com/ideas/archive/2020/03/esther-sex-and-power/607534/. See also Malka Fleischmann's chapter in this volume.
35. Anna Solomon, "The Other Queen of Purim," *Tablet Magazine* (March 9, 2020), https://www.tabletmag.com/jewish-life-and-religion/299486/the-other-queen-of-purim.

An "Essentially Feminine" Hero: The Rise of Esther in American Jewish Life, 1870–1900

Rabbi Dr. Zev Eleff

In June 1850, a Jew from Savannah, Georgia, wrote in support of the biblical Esther. The pseudonymous "Judaea" was aware that Esther suffered from several severe implications of her narrative: she married a non-Jewish king and then sanctioned Jewish violence against their Persian enemies. Despite this, the Georgian Jew contended that "Esther is entitled to stand in the foremost rank among the Jewish women." She "may be called heroine" because, the writer alleged, Esther acted appropriately in her moment, vindicated by the fact that her actions activated the return of the Jewish people to the Holy Land and the construction of the Temple.[1] The English novelist Grace Aguilar deployed a similar strategy in her 1845 work on "Women of Israel." Aguilar downplayed

---

1.   Judaea, "Mordecai Esther," *Asmonean*, June 23, 1850, 5.

Esther's and Mordecai's gory vengeance heaped upon Haman and his sons and instead highlighted Esther's "woman's work," namely, her "strength of prayer."[2] Aguilar tried her very best to portray Esther as Victorian, not at all "in a vindictive and unfeminine light," gaining the approval of Solomon da Silva Solis, an American Jewish intellectual who had a hand in bringing Aguilar's publications to the United States.[3]

These defenses of Esther betoken the challenging reception of this biblical figure in America during the nineteenth century. It wasn't just Esther's intermarriage and role as the leader of a "bloodthirsty" band of Hebrews in Shushan that unnerved Victorian-era Jews. The total absence of God from the narrative did much to push the Book of Esther down in the biblical power rankings. But in due time, the Book of Esther made a comeback. In the 1870s, Jews in the United States started to refurbish Esther's legacy. They were convinced that Esther's biblical biography was very useful to address major concerns: the rise of antisemitism and in their campaign to revive an increasingly disenchanted lot of Jewish women to restore religious identity to their homes and enliven the spiritual energies of their husbands, fathers, and sons.

American Jews possessed a surfeit of Jewish heroines. In addition to the classical matriarchs of Genesis, they touted Ruth and Deborah. Ruth was the "outsider" who observed the best of Judaism and converted her way into "insider" status.[4] Along with Rebecca, Deborah was the inspiration for several Jewish periodicals in the United States and Europe.[5] Esther, freighted with complicated baggage, was therefore expendable. Some Jews did not bother to defend Esther, even as Purim reemerged as a popular Jewish holiday. In 1862,

---

2. See Grace Aguilar, *The Women of Israel*, vol. I (London, 1845), 146–147.

3. Ibid., 151; and S. Solis, "Remarks on Miss Aguilar's 'Women of Israel,'" *Occident* (May 1846): 88.

4. See my "For Insiders or Outsiders? The Book of Ruth's American Jewish Reception," in *Gleanings: Reflections on Ruth*, ed. Stuart W. Halpern (New Milford/Jerusalem, 2019), 195–209.

5. See Maria T. Baader, "From 'the Priestess of the Home' to 'the Rabbi's Brilliant Daughter': Concepts of Jewish Womanhood and Progressive Germanness in *Die Deborah* and the *American Israelite*, 1854–1900," *Leo Baeck Institute Year Book* 43 (January 1998): 50–52. My thanks to Dr. Jonathan Sarna for alerting me to this important article.

Myer S. Isaacs and other Jewish socialites established the Purim Association of New York. Its purpose was to hold festive masquerades on Purim and some other occasions, not unlike the classy soirees held by high-class groups. The proceeds were distributed to the local Jewish hospital, benevolent societies, and orphan asylum.[6] Yet, a report of the inaugural Purim Ball reveals that women and men preferred to dress up as familiar Shakespearean figures, French monarchs, and characters from the pages of the Brothers Grimm rather than Esther, Mordecai, or other Jewish personalities.[7] Subsequent iterations of the grand affair included more Purim-themed pageantries but still maintained a cool embrace of Esther and the Purim account.[8]

When discussed, commentators described Esther with apologetic overtones. For example, several mid-nineteenth-century rabbinic writers in the United States published essays around Purim time which called into question the historical accuracy of the Book of Esther, pointing out the tale's absence from Persian texts.[9] Christians also paid little attention to Esther. Besides the vengeful aspects of the tale, Protestant and Catholic theologians struggled to make meaning out of the Book of Esther since the text possesses not a single reference to God.[10] Some Jews lobbied, to no avail, for Esther to enter the public ranks of Joan of Arc, Madame Roland, Maria Theresa, or even Cleopatra.[11] Other Jews, still beholden to the sacred book, preferred to focus on the self-assured

---

6. On the Purim Association, see Philip Goodman, "The Purim Association of the City of New York (1862–1902)," *Publications of the American Jewish Historical Society* 40 (December 1950): 135–172.

7. See J.S.R. "The Purim Ball," *Jewish Messenger*, March 21, 1862, 88–89.

8. The exception proves the rule. In 1866, a journalist reported about the Purim Ball that the "essentially Hebrew character of the affair, was in itself a pleasant surprise." See "Purim Suggestions," *Jewish Messenger*, March 9, 1866, 1.

9. See, for example, Isidore Kalish, "Prefatory Remarks to the Book of Esther," *Israelite*, February 23, 1855, 261; M.E.M., "Remarks on the Book of Esther," *Israelite*, March 28, 1862, 310; and "Authenticity of the Book of Esther," *Jewish Messenger*, September 9, 1864, 73.

10. See Jo Carruthers, *Esther Through the Centuries* (Malden, 2008), 21–49. I am grateful to Dr. Stuart Halpern for alerting me to this excellent work.

11. See "Esther," *Jewish Messenger*, March 14, 1862, 78.

Mordecai than the timid Esther; the former admonished the latter to do the right thing on behalf of her people.[12]

Esther became more useful as her narrative seemed to fit better into the exigencies of American Jewish life. First, Jews in postbellum America looked to the Book of Esther for inspiration to grapple with an increasing awareness of indigenous antisemitism, what one historian has described as the "emergence of a full-fledged anti-Semitic society."[13] To be sure, Jews since the colonial era had been cognizant of their "outsider" status in some realms of American life.[14] Yet, events during and after the Civil War focused their consciousness and elevated the stakes. Foremost, this situation was amplified by public instances of anti-Jewish action like Ulysses S. Grant's General Orders No. 11 that expelled "Jews as a class" from his military territory in December 1862 and Abraham Lincoln's countermanding of that directive about two weeks later.[15]

Eventually, American Jews found the Purim tale useful to cope with this sad reality. Situated in Persian exile, Esther's story, as Scott Langston has argued, simultaneously contains warnings of bigotry in a host nation and the support that American Jews might experience in a "foreign" land.[16] Fittingly, Jews cast General Grant as a Haman figure immediately after General Orders No. 11 and six years later when he ran for president.[17] In 1872, Rabbi Leopold Wintner of St. Paul, Minnesota, wrote about growing bigotry toward Jews that conceived them as a "class" apart from other Americans. Wintner also alluded to Lincoln as he praised the modern spirits that checked Grant-like personalities and the rising instances of antisemitism. This way, offered Wintner, "like the first Haman, who found

---

12. See "Our Old Hero," *Jewish Messenger*, March 6, 1868, 1.
13. Leonard Dinnerstein, *Anti-Semitism in America* (New York, 1994), 35.
14. For a survey of American Jewry's encounter with intolerance and openness, see my "The Jewish Encounter with Discrimination, Tolerance and Pluralism in the United States," in *Interpreting American Jewish History at Museums and Historic Sites*, ed. Avi Decter (Lanham, 2016), 161–178.
15. See Jonathan D. Sarna, *When General Grant Expelled the Jews* (New York, 2012), 3–23.
16. See Scott M. Langston, "Reading a Text Backward: The Book of Esther and Nineteenth-Century Jewish American Interpretations," in *The Book of Esther in Modern Research*, ed. Leonard Greenspoon and Sidnie White Crawford (London, 2003), 200–216.
17. See Sarna, 49.

his doom through the agency of Queen Esther, so will also the Hamans of our days fall before that beautiful and illustrious Queen – Civilization!"[18] Another Jewish writer allegorized Esther to the Jews in the United States, like the diplomat Oscar Straus who worked alongside benevolent rulers and governments that halted hatred. Jews could take a lesson from Esther and "help perpetuate the republic."[19] Others envisioned Esther as the orphaned and immigrant Jew of Shushan on New York's Lower East Side who required ennobling support from her government.[20]

The second reason for Esther's revival in American Jewish life concerned religious declension. In the 1870s, American Judaism was in sorry shape. To help remedy this, Jewish elites looked to women to inspire themselves and their husbands and fathers to return into the religious fold. During the prior decades, the Civil War had an unusual impact on Jews. On the one hand, Jews had been in a very good position in the garment industry to leverage their social networks to profit from the need for soldier uniforms and, later on, a desire among home-ward-bound and cash-carrying Union veterans to reenter civilian life well dressed in the latest suits and styles.[21] The influx of wealth in the American Jewish community had resulted in a synagogue boom. In addition, the war's lesson in moral authority and the powerful image of Abraham Lincoln had combined to impress the need for strong top-down leadership structures. Both items – what I have called elsewhere "determinants of change" – had increased the stature of the American rabbinate.[22] Yet, the rise in rabbinic authority and the appearance of cavernous and unfamiliar synagogue buildings had also tended to alienate the rank-and-file from religious life.

---

18. "The Hamans of History and of Our Days," *Israelite*, April 12, 1872, 8. See also "In the King's House," *American Hebrew*, March 3, 1893, 576.
19. Judaeus, "What Would You Do if You Were a Rabbi?" *Jewish Messenger*, April 18, 1890, 3. On Straus and antisemitism, see Naomi W. Cohen, *A Dual Heritage: The Public Career of Oscar S. Straus* (Philadelphia, 1969), 67–73.
20. "Merry Purim," *Jewish Messenger*, March 14, 1884, 3.
21. See Adam Mendelsohn, "Beyond the Battlefield: Reevaluating the Legacy of the Civil War for American Jews," *American Jewish Archives Journal* 64 (2012): 83–111.
22. See my *Who Rules the Synagogue? Religious Authority and the Formation of American Judaism* (New York, 2016), 129–158.

This was particularly true among the rising generation of American Jews in the 1870s.[23] For example, a pundit in New York feared that "young Israelites do not manifest that love for the synagogue which their fathers and forefathers showed."[24] Another in Philadelphia noted that among the local synagogues he frequented it was evident that a "large proportion of the children of congregants is not present."[25] In Baltimore, a journalist opined much of the same, adding that synagogue-goers were better off without the younger crowd. "There are a great many young persons whose behavior during services is really scandalous," complained David Binswanger. "Talking, giggling, and a general want of attention are not only very annoying to the worshippers and disrespectful to the officiating ministers, but they are positively sacrilegious in violating the properties of the House of God."[26] Binswanger claimed that he was in receipt of "several communications calling attention to the want of decorum," testimonies that supported his grim report of Jewish religious life.[27] Binswanger's brother in St. Louis similarly lamented that Jews in his community disregarded the Sabbath and other features of Jewish law in the synagogue and in the home. His coreligionists "believe in Saturday as the day of rest," bemoaned Augustus Binswanger, "but not as a holy day."[28] All this amounted to a religious downturn and a collective search for ways to rescue Jewish life from this nadir.

One popular prospective savior was the Jewish woman. Rabbi Kaufmann Kohler – in this period, his "face looked rather paler than usual," according to one report – suffered through terrible synagogue attrition in Chicago.[29] He struggled to bring "business men, and chiefly the young people," to religious services. He therefore called on the "Jewish woman, who best represents the heart of the household" to support his cause.[30]

---

23. Ibid., 167–174.
24. "Hebrew Rabbinical Education," *New York Herald*, June 11, 1872, 5.
25. "Why Are They Absent?" *Jewish Record*, February 14, 1879, 4.
26. "Behavior in the Synagogue," *Jewish Chronicle*, February 9, 1875, 5.
27. Ibid.
28. See Augustus Binswanger, *An Address before Shaare Emeth Congregation, St. Louis, MO* (Chicago, 1887), 7.
29. "Too Many Rabbis," *Daily Inter-Ocean*, June 20, 1879, 3.
30. Kaufmann Kohler, *The Origin of the Sabbath* (Chicago, 1876), 19–20.

To be sure, women were also affected by the far-reaching religious malaise. One Jewess in Gotham put her rabbis on notice that unless they improved their craft, she and her friends would continue to quench their intellectual curiosities at the Sunday lectures of the Ethical Culturalist and self-proclaimed heretic Felix Adler:

> We like to be instructed on subjects with which we sympathize. We prefer to listen to all sermons on Saturdays; but if our rabbis decline to leave the beaten track and cull flowers for us in the open fields, do not blame us for figuring among the Sunday audiences. Besides, many of us young ladies are not long from school – a foreign accent, and occasional breaches of grammar grate upon our ears.[31]

This case notwithstanding, Kohler and rabbis of all kinds looked to women to persuade their husbands and brothers to return to Judaism. In almost all ways, Kohler was nevertheless a staunch advocate of a traditional view of the "delicate" woman as leader of her household, cultivating those domestic virtues that produced a "robust man" and ensured Jewish life within and without the home.[32] In Kohler's words, "women's responsibility stands uppermost in fashioning the character of men. Not only at home, but also in society at large."[33]

Much of his evidence was borne out of biblical interpretation. He pointed to Miriam and Deborah who, as Kohler interpreted it, exercised leadership by inspiring Moses and Barak to act.[34] Yet, both examples

---

31. Sylvia, "A Hint to Our Preachers," *Jewish Messenger*, March 28, 1877, 5.
32. Kaufmann Kohler, *Esther or the Jewish Woman* (New York, 1888), 2. On Kohler's view of Jewish womanhood, see Karla Goldman, "The Ambivalence of Reform Judaism: Kaufmann Kohler and the Ideal Jewish Woman," *American Jewish History* 79 (Summer 1990): 477–499. Kohler argued that his view of women's roles was different than earlier perspectives. The Old World, maintained Kohler, "dresses the young woman for the marriage market ... building a golden cage around her to make her look upon her life as a mere pleasure ground and play, until life's solemn duties take her by surprise and disappoint her in her false and foolish expectations." See Kohler, *Esther or the Jewish Woman*, 7.
33. Ibid., 6.
34. See Karla Goldman, *Beyond the Synagogue Gallery: Finding a Place for Women in American Judaism* (Cambridge, 2000), 164.

appeared as sidelights in a published sermon that focused on Esther. Kohler approved of Esther's integrity, accepting Mordecai's guidance and urging Ahasuerus to exercise his monarchical powers to vanquish Haman and support Jewish interests. These were lessons that ought to have resonated in Kohler's time. "Women's idealism may redeem the commonest of men from his coarseness and lift him to purer and nobler views and habits," preached Kohler. "She can by her finer tact elevate the tone of conversation, and by her glow of enthusiasm and sympathy charm the silliest man into reverence of the truly good and pure and perfect; and again, by levity and flippancy drag the loftiest aims of men down into the mire of selfishness and vulgarity."[35]

Obedience and compromise were familiar tropes for Reform Jewish leaders deploying Esther as their scriptural loadstar. Kohler's colleague, the journalist Moritz Ellinger, wrote in 1881 of contemporary Esthers who secured "family life" with doses of "gentleness." Appearing in the pages of the New York Purim Association's popular annual magazine, the attitude reflected this organization's newfound embrace of Esther, as well.[36] Ellinger traced the "Esthers" of Jewish history. He drew a straight line of Esther's spiritual heirs, plotting Gracia Mendes Nasi of the Spanish-Portuguese exile in the sixteenth century and Rebecca Gratz in the United States of the mid-1800s as coordinates that led to the major task before American Jewish women later on in that century.[37] Rabbi Julius Goldammer of Cincinnati praised Esther as that "noble and generous woman" who risked her life, not to mention royal luxury, for her people.[38] Also in the Queen City, Rabbi Isaac Mayer Wise praised Esther's willingness to obey the sagacious Mordecai.[39] On a different

35. Kohler, *Esther or the Jewish Woman*, 6.
36. On the reception of the Purim Association's *Purim Gazette*, see, for example, "The Purim Festivities," *Jewish Messenger*, March 17, 1865, 91.
37. "A Few Jewish Women," *Purim Gazette*, 1881, 9–10. I am grateful to Elisa Ho of the Jacob Rader Marcus Center of the American Jewish Archives for supplying me with a digital copy of this rare publication. Ellinger's essay was apparently well received and republished in a New York Jewish newspaper as "A Few Jewish Women," *American Hebrew*, April 1, 1881, 78.
38. "The Story of Esther," *Israelite*, March 18, 1870, 8.
39. See "Mordecai Richly Rewarded," *American Israelite*, November 29, 1878, 4.

occasion, the pragmatic Wise compared himself to Mordecai and his progressive rabbinical school's much-needed benefactors to Esther who gave pause to her "busy life of plenty" and "cast a glance at the misery of [her] poor brethren who are being inhumanly maltreated and outraged."[40]

Orthodox Jews also celebrated "our Esthers [who] do good for the cause of our faith when some of the sterner sex are careless."[41] The New York tradition-touting journalist Myer Isaacs preferred Esther over Vashti. In one case, suggested Isaacs, "we may perhaps regard her as the forerunner of the present advocates of women's rights."[42] Likewise, Isaacs – perhaps owing to his role in starting the New York Purim Association during the prior decade – preferred the "essentially feminine" Esther over more independent women of the Torah like Abigail and Deborah. In kind, Isaacs deflected some of the challenges to Esther's biblical biography, like her marriage to the non-Jewish Ahasuerus, by claiming that these marked Esther's willingness to make sacrifices, a credible quality for a devout American Jewish woman.[43]

Rabbi Henry Pereira Mendes of Shearith Israel in New York produced a Purim play that took certain liberties with the tale of Esther to admonish the women in the audience to look after their husbands' spiritual well-being. In archaic prose, Mendes imagined Mordecai upbraiding the Jewish maidens of Shushan. Mendes blamed them for the miscreant behaviors of the young men and the "irreligion" spreading throughout their land:

> Oh, ye young women! Ye have much
> To do with irreligion such
> As now has seized on our young men!
> You countenance their folly when
> They mock what's holy, just to please

---

40. "The Good and Wise Mordecai," *American Israelite*, January 27, 1882, 244.
41. "Purim," *Jewish Messenger*, March 19, 1875, 4.
42. The subject of Vashti's proto-feminism was taken up in Walter Besant's novel, *The Rebel Queen*. See Joseph Silverman, "The Rebel Queen," *American Hebrew*, March 23, 1894, 624–626.
43. "Esther," *Jewish Messenger*, March 10, 1876, 2. Isaacs also distanced Esther from the Bible's female "warriors" in "The Book of Esther," *Jewish Messenger*, March 15, 1879, 5.

Their fancies. If you'd only seize
Each opportunity to say
You scorn the man who throws away
Respect and duty, quickly he
To his religion true would be![44]

Mendes did not hold back, peppering Mordecai's rebuke with contemporaneous religious infractions. Like Kohler's sermon, Mendes pointed out the low regard that American Hebrews held of the Sabbath. More concerned with traditional Jewish practice than his Reform colleagues, Mendes added to his script transgressions against the kosher dietary laws:

For shame ye maidens! Yours the fault,
Whose echoes reach high heaven's vault!
Refuse to smile upon the man
Whose coward, dastard spirit can
Incite him thus to sin, and ye
Will find our faith will honored be!
Ye join them when on Sabbath nights,
They seek unsanctified delights!
Ye join them when, in faithless mood,
They sit and eat forbidden food.
Ye join them when they dare refuse
To own that they by birth are Jews![45]

Mendes' remedy, issued through his Mordecai character, was clear: "Set good example, you, the maids, and never shall portentous shades."[46] Like his rabbinic counterparts, Mendes was convinced that women played a role in reviving Jewish life by awakening their languishing menfolk. More than any other biblical heroine, Esther was the figure who played this part. After some convincing, she accepted Mordecai's direction and initiated a plot to convince her husband to save the Jewish

---

44. H. Pereira Mendes, *Esther: A Purim Play* (New York, 1899), 14.
45. Ibid., 15.
46. Ibid.

people. Deborah and other female Torah personalities could be fitted to subordinate position. Yet, none fit so comfortably as Esther. All this helped elevate Esther in American Jewish discourse. By June 1880, a rabbi in Evansville, Indiana, could confidently sermonize before his listeners that the "history of Esther is undoubtedly familiar to every one of you."[47]

What is more, Esther's rebound took place in religious and lay circles. In fact, there is some evidence that Jewish women embraced this presentation of Esther and advised other Jewesses to apply that wisdom to their lives. In Mobile, Alabama, Annie Jonas Moses published a Purim play in the 1870s that aimed to disabuse erstwhile Esther detractors and disseminate the virtues of the protagonist's femininity. In Moses' rendering, Esther resisted intermarrying but, in the end, deferred to the far-thinking Mordecai: "It is thy faith, Esther, that bids me urge thee still. Think of thy people, their sufferings and their degradation." To further assuage Esther's doubts, Mordecai begs her to "seek then this power that may be granted thee! Endeavor to relieve or assist your brethren in affliction."[48] Similarly, the southern playwright downplayed Jewish vengeance. Ahasuerus applauds the Jews, citing that "they have acted wisely and generously! They fought only when necessitated and have spared the homes and substance of those made desolate."[49] What is more, in response to Jewish military ethics and Esther's sacrifice of her own Jewish identity, a Persian messenger relays that "many of the people of the land became Jews."[50] Esther is gladdened and reports to Ahasuerus that "thy Queen is but a humble representative of the virtues of her people."[51] Likewise, a Jewish woman in Chicago concluded her own Purim poem in a similar vein:

---

47. "Mordecai a Type of Israel," *American Israelite*, June 4, 1880, 5. Not everyone was converted into an Esther proponent. For instance, see Emil G. Hirsch, "The Story of Esther," *Reform Advocate*, March 9, 1895, 39–40. Hirsch much preferred the Hanukka story over Esther's.

48. Annie Jonas Moses, *Esther: A Drama in Five Acts* (Mobile, 1871), 10.

49. Ibid., 22.

50. Ibid., 21.

51. Ibid., 22.

> Esther knelt once more
> To save her people through her eloquence.
> Then, with a pure devotion, meekly turned
> And lifted up her heart and hands to God.[52]

These sentiments trickled down to America's Jewish children. For instance, Jennie Morris of the New York Hebrew Free School won an essay prize for her "Esther" composition. After rehearsing the broad themes of the Book of Esther, the young lady beseeched "every girl" to "bear in mind that she has the power of influencing those around her by her sincere, religious and modest conduct." For Jewish males – "every boy and man" – the Free School's star student advised them to remain open to the "elevating and refining influence of those who follow the faithful and sincere conduct of women, who also go in the way of women such as Ruth and Queen Esther."[53]

These portrayals of a feminine Esther resonated best with Jewish women whom the historian Jacob Rader Marcus had in mind when he wrote that "with very few exceptions, the American Jewesses of the postbellum years were apparently satisfied with their lot in life."[54] Then again, Queen Esther was also agreeable to others who recognized that women's roles were in significant flux and therefore desired an Esther who challenged the status quo. During the 1890s, Jewish women – like the individuals who founded the National Council of Jewish Women in 1893 – became more aware of their capacity to shape synagogue life and to promote activism in other causes like suffrage and immigrant care.[55]

One such exemplar was Rosa Sonneschein, the editor of the *American Jewess*. She used her magazine to advocate for women in religious life and in the political sphere. On one occasion, Sonneschein depicted

52. Eve Davieson, "Esther," *Reform Advocate*, March 7, 1896, 55.
53. Jennie Morris, "Esther," *American Hebrew*, February 29, 1884, 40.
54. Jacob Rader Marcus, *The American Jewish Woman, 1654–1980* (New York, 1981), 66.
55. See Goldman, *Beyond the Synagogue Gallery*, 195–196; Melissa R. Klapper, *Ballots, Babies, and Banners of Peace: American Jewish Women's Activism, 1890–1940* (New York, 2013), 1–8; and Pamela S. Nadell, *America's Jewish Women: A History from Colonial Times to Today* (New York, 2019), 101–107.

Esther as a model for the modern Jewish woman. Borrowing from the antisemitism-sensitive trope, Sonneschein admitted "that Israel is still pursued and persecuted by living Hamans," and like in the Purim story, "so also do we believe in the existence of many Esthers." For Sonneschein, Esther was political and bold, daring and, in Sonneschein's rendering, independent. Sonneschein also wrote of an Esther of old and new "who in time of trial and danger would sacrifice life and happiness for God and family, for Israel and its adherents."[56]

In addition, Sonneschein printed Rabbi David Philipson's essay on "The Ideal Jewess" that drew on the Book of Esther to illustrate his charge for Jewish women on the brink of the twentieth century. "The story tells us that the *man* Mordecai could not accomplish the task of deliverance without the aid of the *woman* Esther," wrote Philipson. "Is this not in a sense typical? Is not woman the saving influence in the finer life of man?" He averred that the "time [has] come again when it appears as though the mainstay of our faith is woman."[57] Philipson sympathized with and encouraged increases in women's rights in many sectors but not at the cost of losing her leadership in the home:

> Men are frequently heard to say, my wife, my daughters are the religious members of the family, they represent me. Is salvation again to come to the Jews through woman? Can Esther in this sense be regarded as a type? ... As far as external rights go, let woman have them all as long as they do not endanger her womanliness; let her have all the advantages of education, of developing mind and heart; let her have a directing hand in all the institutions of our modern life, but let her be shielded from all the influences that shall make her merely like man and less than woman.[58]

All told, the reception of Esther in this period reflects how Jews read the Bible in their particular contexts. In fact, Americans of all types

---

56. "Queen Esther," *American Jewess* 6 (March 1898): 296.
57. David Philipson, "The Ideal Jewess," *American Jewess* 4 (March 1897): 257.
58. Ibid., 257–259.

understood their villains as modern Pharaohs and Hamans.[59] Perhaps less intuitive and made clearer through historical sources is how biblical narratives are selected and personalities are summoned at particular moments. The renewed attention paid to Esther in the final decades of the nineteenth century indicates the all-important need to calibrate historical memory and contemporary trends to form meaningful interpretation.

---

59. See, for example, Mark A. Noll, "The Image of the United States as a Biblical Nation, 1776–1865," in *The Bible in America: Essays in Cultural History*, ed. Nathan O. Hatch and Mark A. Noll (New York, 1982), 39–58.

The Esther Aesthetic and Jewish Beauty Queens in Early Twentieth-Century America

Dr. Shaina Trapedo

After a six-month nationwide search, doe-eyed and dark haired nineteen-year-old beauty Katherine Spector was crowned "Prettiest US Jewess" in front of a crowd of 22,000 people in Manhattan's Madison Square Garden on Purim day, March 11, 1933, at the annual "Queen Esther" contest sponsored by the Jewish National Workers' Alliance. As "Queen," Spector won a trip to Palestine and was expected to make several public appearances like her predecessors of former years. However, the New Jersey native's reign was short-lived. A gossip column published in the *Daily News* asserted that Spector was not actually a "girl" as the contest rules stipulated. She was accused of being a fraud who was "secretly married," which resulted in Spector, and the "Queen Esther" contest, being shrouded in scandal for years to follow.[1]

Female beauty contests can be traced back to ancient myths and legendary tales – from Paris' judgment that sparked the Trojan War[2] to Scheherazade in *A Thousand and One Nights* to Cinderella folklore – and seem to have always invited scandal and censure.[3] In addition to hosting a variety of obvious social ills including objectifying women and indulging the male gaze, relegating a woman's worth to looks over intellect or character, and perpetuating unrealistic and non-diverse standards of beauty, pageants also problematize notions of race, ethnicity, and nationhood in claiming that a single female body can represent the ideals of an entire people or community.

The story of Esther, crypto-Jew turned Persian queen, is intricately bound up with questions of appearance versus authenticity, the construction of female subjects, and the formation of national identity. Set during the Babylonian exile when the Jews were living under the control of King Ahasuerus, also identified as Xerxes I, who ruled the

---

1. Spector, who was an accomplished musician and performer pursuing an acting career, sued the News Syndicate Co. Inc. for libel when Ed Sullivan ran a story in the *Daily News* "imputing unchastity to her" (claiming she was the common-law wife of one William Shemin), thus sabotaging the valuable publicity she received from the contest that was widely publicized throughout North America. While the jury found that Spector was "falsely charged with a secret marriage and false abandonment… and leading a dual existence," and awarded her $11,500 in damages to her personal health and for lost earnings from potential endorsements, engagements, and stage and motion picture opportunities, the trial judge, Justice Kenneth O'Brien, overturned the jury's verdict on the grounds that the "verdict was grossly excessive and disturbs the conscience of the court; her damages were purely fictitious" and that the "conclusion reached was the result of matter not in the record and undoubtedly by reason of bias and prejudice." Seven years later, in 1942, Spector won on appeal at the Supreme Court of NY.

2. According to Greek mythology, when the goddesses Hera, Athena, and Aphrodite vie for a golden apple inscribed with the words "fairest one," Zeus directs the case to prince Paris of Troy, a reputedly excellent judge of beauty. Each goddess bribes Paris to find in her favor and ultimately Paris accepts Aphrodite's offering of Helen of Sparta, the most beautiful woman in the world and wife of the Greek king Menelaus. The Greeks' attempt to retrieve Helen leads to the Trojan war.

3. See, for example, Sarah Banet-Weiser, *The Most Beautiful Girl in the World: Beauty Pageants and National Identity* (Berkeley, 1999).

Persian Empire from 486 to 465 BCE,[4] the so-called beauty contest in the second chapter of the *megilla* provides the means for Jewish salvation against the threat of genocide. Following Queen Vashti's dismissal on account of her disobedience, a nationwide search is launched:

> Let there be sought for the King beautiful young maidens; and let the King appoint commissioners in all the provinces of his kingdom, that they may gather together every beautiful young maiden to Shushan the capital to the harem…and let their cosmetics be given them. Then, let the girl who pleases the King be queen instead of Vashti. (2:2–4)

Mordecai is quick to call Esther's attention to pageant politics when he warns her not to reveal "her people or her kindred" (2:10). In order to not arouse prevailing antisemitic sentiments, Esther is advised to conceal her Jewish heritage. While it is possible for Esther to have practiced Judaism in private and make no outward show of observance, what about physical markers of her identity? Did Esther "look Jewish"? To what extent does Jewish identity conform to notions of race and ethnicity? As we come to learn, the success of the heroine – and her people – rested on the verisimilitude of her outward appearance as a Persian (pageant) queen.

And yet, it could not be clearer that Esther was a reluctant contestant. Twice the *megilla* tells us that Esther was "taken" (*vatilakaḥ*, 2:8, 16), implying she was brought to the capital against her will. The Midrash takes this redundancy to signify that Esther initially went into hiding when the edict was first announced and forcibly brought to the harem. During the ensuing twelve-month preparation period, Esther did not indulge in the cosmetics, apparel, and treatments offered like the other women, and was again coerced into appearing before the king when it was her turn to do so. Nevertheless, King Ahasuerus "set the royal crown upon her head" (2:17).

---

4. For more on the historicity of the Esther story and Ahasuerus' identity, see Jo Carruthers, *Esther Through the Centuries* (Malden, 2008), David J. A. Clines, *The Esther Scroll: The Story of the Story* (Sheffield, 1984), and Sidnie White Crawford and Leonard J. Greenspoon, eds., *The Book of Esther in Modern Research* (New York, 2003).

For many scholars and modern readers, Esther's selection is cause for mourning, not celebration – a personal tragedy for a young Jewish woman compelled to martyr her modesty to a pagan despot. Yet Mordecai reads her appointment as divine providence: "And who knows whether it was just for such a time as this that you attained the royal position?" (4:14), prompting biblical commentators to unpack Esther's exceptional allure as a virtue that granted her access and influence she would never have had otherwise.

Being placed on a pedestal feels like the last thing the biblical heroine would have wanted; nevertheless, the deployment of Esther as a paragon of Jewish female beauty became widely popular in Jewish communities around the world in the 1920s and '30s. "Esther pageants" in the early twentieth century grew into a diasporic phenomenon that can be traced from Palestine into Europe and South and North America. During the period historians have called the Age of Mass Migration (1850–1914), America absorbed more than 30 million immigrants, including nearly 2 million European Jews. The estimated number of Jews in New York went from 60,000 in 1880 to 1.3 million by 1914, when World War I impacted US border policy.[5] The *megilla*, which captures the Jews' struggle to preserve tradition within the framework of "modern" life under Persian rule, must have resonated loudly with American Jewry. Like during the time period of the Babylonian exile, Jewish immigrants were confronted with the challenge of ensuring the continued existence of a nation with no territory, appointed leader, or central place of worship. Would ethnic survival be dependent on maintaining insularity or was there a successful way to integrate into civic life and avoid the hazards of assimilation? How does one prioritize familial, religious, and national obligations when they compete with each other?

Such concerns were even more complicated for American Jewish women at the turn of the century as suffragists gained momentum and the influx of women into the workforce granted unprecedented

---

5. See Timothy J. Hatton and Jeffery G. Williamson, *The Age of Mass Migration* (Oxford, 1998); and Gur Alroey, "Jewish Migration, 19th Century to Present," in *The Encyclopedia of Global Human Migration*, ed. Immanuel Ness (Oxford, 2013).

financial independence. As social historian Kathy Peiss argues in *Hope in a Jar*, in the early decades of the twentieth century, the puritanical associations of cosmetics with the "painted faces of actresses and prostitutes" were being replaced by the modern sensibility that makeup was a medium of self-realization and expression while the melting pot of America further destabilized the belief that the ideal face was "defined by pale skin and blushing cheeks."[6] Just like the Italian, Irish, Greek, and Slavic immigrants who arrived in the US between 1880 and the Immigration Act of 1924, Eastern European Jews who came ashore were also not considered white.[7] For Jewish women seeking agency and belonging, the possibility that one's identity could be altered with lipstick, mascara, and powder was as compelling as it was contested.

During this era of Jewish relocation and reinvention, how are we to understand the popularity of "Queen Esther" beauty contests across America? Were they civic displays of Jewish pride honoring Esther's legacy or acts of assimilation designed to parallel icons like the Miss America pageant inaugurated in Atlantic City in 1921?

I suggest that it is precisely at this moment of Jewish national instability in the early twentieth century that the Esther text was perceived to be of critical importance for American Jewry, and I believe it continues to bear relevance in discussions of countenance, character, and American identity today. Unlike any other biblical narrative, the Book of Esther offers a model of a people who do not have the luxury of relying on God's presumed favor and instead shape their own destiny based on merit, ingenuity, and self-reliance consistent with the American dream. In what follows, I offer a brief exploration of how female beauty is defined in the context of the Esther narrative, how the appropriation of Esther's image reveals more about Jewish social anxieties of the time than the biblical narrative itself, and to what extent beauty might be understood as a Jewish virtue.

---

6. Kathy Peiss, *Hope in a Jar: The Making of America's Beauty Culture* (Philadelphia, 2011), 28 and 39.

7. See Karen Brodkin, *How Jews Became White Folks and What That Says About Race in America* (Rutgers, 1998).

Dr. Shaina Trapedo

BIBLICAL BEAUTY AND THE ESTHER AESTHETIC

Esther appears last in a long line of beautiful biblical women who play various roles in shaping the history of the Jewish people from Eden to exile. Among others, Sarah, Rebecca, Rachel, Tamar, Rahab, Abigail, Bathsheba, Job's daughters, and Esther are all described as *yafeh* (beautiful), the Hebrew term used to signify a pleasing or attractive physical appearance.[8] While *yafeh* remains an abstract concept – never assigned a specific shape, skin tone, eye position, or nose structure – most often ascribed to women, it is a unisex adjective also attributed to male figures including Joseph, David, and Absalom. As exotic strangers passing through Egypt, Sarah, Rebecca, and Joseph's beauty arouse the desire of authority figures, implying a connection between beauty and sexuality, but also power, privilege, and possession.[9]

In Esther's case, the perception of beauty, and its function in ranking one human being over another, is activated by her multicultural context. Within Ahasuerus' vast kingdom, spanning 127 provinces from India to Ethiopia wherein "each people [speaks] in its own language" (1:22), the Jews were a displaced minority.[10] Given the volatile political landscape of Ahasuerus' empire, it's not hard to imagine how prejudice and xenophobia might have reared their heads within the harem, and evaluations of phenotypes may have been charged by bias and bigotry.[11]

---

8. On the use of *yafeh* in the Hebrew bible, see Robert L. Hubbard, "The Eyes Have It: Theological Reflections on Human Beauty," *Ex Auditu* 13 (1997): 57–72; Hannah K. Tervanotko, "Gendered Beauty: Observations on Portraying Beautiful Men and Women in the Hebrew Bible," in *'So good, so beautiful': Studies into Psalms, Ethics, Aesthetics, and Hermeneutics brought together in Honour of Dorothea Erbele-Küster* (Gorinchem, 2015), 42–52.

9. See David Penchansky, "Beauty, Power, and Attraction: Aesthetics and the Hebrew Bible," in *Beauty and the Bible: Toward a Hermeneutics of Biblical Aesthetics* (Atlanta, 2013), and Luke Ferretter, "The Power and the Glory: The Aesthetics of the Hebrew Bible," *Literature and Theology* 18, no. 2 (June 2004): 123–138.

10. Esther's "people" are exclusively referred to by the ethnoreligious term *Yehudim* (Jews) rather than *Yisrael* or *benei Yisrael*, which never appear in the *megilla*. On the use of the term "Jew" as a marker of ethnic and religious identity from antiquity to the present, see Cynthia M. Baker, *Jew* (New Brunswick, 2016).

11. According to the *Midrash Rabba*, Esther's selection was, in part, a punishment to the Persian women who "used to speak contemptuously to the Jewish girls, saying that they were so ugly and that no one would look at them" (5:3).

The *Me'am Loez*, an early eighteenth-century anthology of rabbinical commentary, breaks down the logistics of the expansive search, positing that each province conducted a local contest among all of its "beautiful young maidens" (2:3) and sent the regional winner on to the capital as a representative. In this manner, all of the women who were gathered and presented to the king were considered the most beautiful by the conventions of their local communities.

Although Esther ends up receiving the crown, a more fitting title might have been Miss Congeniality, as the Talmud suggests that her character was more lovely than her countenance. While R. Meir says that Esther was given the Hebrew name Hadassah (2:7) "after the designation of the righteous who are called *hadasim*" (myrtles), Ben Azzai argues that Hadassah signifies Esther's stature as neither "tall nor short, but of average height, like a myrtle."[12] R. Neḥemya claims that Hadassah acquired the Persian name *Esther* because it approximates the Aramaic word for moon (*saḥara*), a common expression of beauty; yet R. Yehoshua b. Karḥa infers Hadassah was "of greenish complexion, like a myrtle," quite inconsistent with the fair pallor of the moon. He adds, however, that Esther was "endowed with a touch of grace by God, which made her appear beautiful to the nations and Ahasuerus."[13] While no consensus is reached on Esther's physical attractiveness, the *megilla* affirms that "Esther obtained ḥein (grace) in the eyes of all who beheld her" (2:15). R. Elazar explains that this verse "teaches that [Esther] appeared to each person as a member of his own nation," as it is human nature to "find members of [one's] own nation to be the most appealing."[14]

While Plato and Aristotle's definitions diverge, both theorize beauty as objective, located in the proportions and arrangements of external forms that exist independent of an observer. Although Esther's ability to gain favor in the eye of *every* beholder suggests a universal appeal consistent with classical aesthetics, rabbinic literature affirms the inter-subjective nature of physical beauty, ever informed by social and

12. Megilla 13a.
13. Ibid.
14. Ibid.; *Maharsha* to Megilla 7a.

cultural preferences and biases.[15] Rather than unifying disparate groups in recognition of a singular ideal, Esther's profile becomes a palimpsest upon which viewers narcissistically project their own physiological features. R. Elazar's exegesis, and early Judaic hermeneutics more broadly, anticipates the definition of beauty proposed by eighteenth-century philosopher David Hume in his essay "On the Standard of Taste": "Beauty is no quality in things themselves: It exists merely in the mind which contemplates them; and each mind perceives a different beauty. One person may even perceive deformity, where another is sensible of beauty; and every individual ought to acquiesce in his own sentiment, without pretending to regulate those of others."

Esther's predecessor, Queen Vashti, whose name is derived from the Old Persian word for "beautiful woman," is also described as beautiful (*yafeh*) in the *megilla* (1:11), though commentators spill much ink in painting the two women as foils.[16] In the Midrash, Vashti is cast as an immoral and vain exhibitionist. When an argument breaks out over whether Persian or Medean women are more beautiful, Ahasuerus boasts that his wife is Babylonian, making her the fairest of them all, while also posing the female body as an artisanal domestic product. In objection, the courtiers reply that even the ugliest woman adorned as a queen looks attractive, which inspires Ahasuerus to summon Vashti to appear in nothing but her crown in order to end the debate once and for all. The *megilla* relates that "Queen Vashti refused to come" (1:12), which has led to many scholars reclaiming Vashti as a proto-feminist.[17] Nevertheless, the midrashic view maintains Vashti's beauty was skin-deep; the commentators deliberate on Vashti's apprehension about presenting herself in this exposed manner – either because it feels beneath the

---

15. In his *Daf Yomi* column on Nedarim 66, Adam Kirsch concludes that beauty "meant a long head, fine and smooth hair, wide eyes, small ears, a full nose, thin lips, flat stomach, and narrow legs" for women in the talmudic era ("The Talmud's Guide to Jewish Feminine Beauty," *Tablet Magazine* [2015], https://www.tabletmag.com/sections/belief/articles/daf-yomi-138).

16. On the Persian origin of Vashti's name, see Carey A. Moore, *Esther* (New Haven, 1995), and Karen H. Jobes, *Esther: The NIV Application Commentary* (Grand Rapids, 1999), 66.

17. See Tzvi Sinensky's chapter, "Vashti Comes to America," in this volume.

dignity of a queen or because her confidence wavered – but conclude that the only reason she disobeys the king is a sudden outbreak on her skin causing disfigurement.[18]

Investing in beauty for the sake of self-indulgence, distraction, and shaming others is displayed as antithetical to Jewishness in the Esther narrative, though self-adornment and physical refinement are not rejected wholesale. Esther prepares for her unsolicited visitation to Ahasuerus, an action punishable by death, by praying and fasting for three days. Dramatic irony draws the contrast between the two women into sharper focus: Vashti was executed for refusing a summons and now Esther enters unbidden at her own peril. In addition to spiritual preparation, the *megilla* notes that "Esther put on her royal robes" (5:1) and commentators elaborate on the transformation: "She dressed herself in bejeweled robes and a dress woven of the finest silk bedecked with fine African stones. She placed her golden slippers on her feet and royal crown on her head ... [and] God illuminated her face like the sun."[19] Although Esther initially seems artless in ornamentation, she is keenly aware of the rhetorical efficacy of appearance, particularly an alluring one. Through regal self-fashioning, Esther owns her role as Ahasuerus' chosen queen, the symbolic female representation of the future of the Persian empire. In response, the king grants "up to half the kingdom" to the clandestine Jewess (5:3), ultimately enabling her to shift his favor more positively toward her own people.[20]

While Esther's ethnic ambiguity works to the Jews' collective advantage, others perceive it as a threat. Martin Luther famously refused to offer commentary on Esther's eponymous text, perhaps because he

---

18. *Me'am Lo'ez* (1:9–12).
19. *Me'am Lo'ez* (5:1).
20. Esther has become the prototype for a woman who mobilizes beauty, timing, and proximity to power to influence leaders in support of the Jewish people and/or traditional (biblical) values. Most recently, during her vice-presidential campaign in 2008, former beauty pageant winner Sarah Palin was paralleled with Queen Esther by supporters; see Michael Joseph Gross' *Vanity Fair* article "Is Palin's Rise Part of God's Plan?" (https://www.vanityfair.com/news/2010/10/sarah-palin-as-queen-esther-201010). For more on the Esther paradigm in American politics, see Tevi Troy's chapter in this volume.

saw her as literalizing the antisemitic metaphor of the Jew as a deceptive prostitute, which he articulates in *Against the Jews and Their Lies* (1543): "[L]et us suppose that somewhere a pretty girl came along, adorned with a wreath, and observed all the manners, the duties, the deportment, and discipline of a chaste virgin, but underneath was a vile, shameful whore.... What good would her fine obedience in observing outwardly all the duties and customs of a virgin's station do her?" While Luther's anxiety about the duplicity of external appearances is directed at the Jews, it applied more broadly to ongoing debates about artificial observance and "true believers" in sixteenth-century Reformation Europe.

Luther's hostility was embraced by German Protestants in the late nineteenth century and fed into racial constructions of Jewishness that emerged in the period, such as the best-selling antisemitic text *Les Femmes d'Israël* (1898) which includes a lengthy discussion of French actress Sarah Bernhardt as an example of the mythic Jewess, whose bewitching beauty conceals a degenerate core.[21] The same physiognomic features that contributed to Bernhardt's global celebrity – her thin frame, pale skin, "Hebraic" nose, and frizzy red hair – become markers of the unhealthy and dissimulating body of the Jew which is taken up in the "race science" used to legitimate differences between Aryans and Jews in the twentieth century.[22]

While the *megilla* highlights beauty's capacity for destruction and redemption – as well as the complex relationships between surface, substance, and subjectivity – it also shows that hazards lie not in beauty itself, but in its application.

---

21. Nazi propaganda drew directly from Luther's writings in the 1930s when his 1543 treatise was reprinted and even held up at rallies. See Christopher J. Probst, *Demonizing the Jews: Luther and the Protestant Church in Nazi Germany* (Bloomington, 2012).
22. Negative perceptions of the Jewish female body are still operating in the twenty-first-century film industry, as evidenced by the experiences of actors like Emmy Rossum, who has been vocal about the antisemitism she's experienced as a Jewish celebrity, and Winona Ryder (born Winona Laura Horowitz), who has been encountering Jewish stereotypes in the film industry since the 1990s. Rossum shares that casting agents defensively qualify their disbelief that she "doesn't look Jewish" as if it were a compliment, and Ryder has lost roles for looking "too Jewish," yet has also been told, "Wait, you're Jewish? But you're so pretty!" (https://www.jta.org/quick-reads/winona-ryder-says-mel-gibson-asked-her-is-she-was-an-oven-dodger).

COMPETITION OR CONNECTION? QUEEN ESTHER PAGEANTS IN THE 1920S AND 1930S

In 1872, another kind of "beauty queen" was born into an Orthodox Jewish family in the Polish shtetl of Krakow. By the turn of the century, Chaja Rubinstein had built an empire and earned worldwide renown as Madame Helena Rubinstein, cosmetics entrepreneur, art patron, and philanthropist, credited with creating the modern beauty industry.[23] In contrast to her long-time rival Elizabeth Arden, whose brand hinged on social elitism, Rubinstein's company leveraged her identity as an international connoisseur catering to women of all ages and complexions. In 1915, Rubinstein opened her first New York salon after establishing posts abroad in Australia and throughout Europe. By the 1930s, the Helena Rubinstein Corporation offered hundreds of cosmetic products and a multitude of beauty treatments, from creams, lipsticks, and hair colorization to skin analysis, light therapy, and deportment classes. When Rubinstein relocated her New York salon to a space not far from Arden's famous red door on Fifth Avenue in 1928, she ran an advertisement in *Vogue* that read: "These new Maisons de Beauté are the response to an expanded demand: A demand for a new type of beauty which is not a type at all, but is a perfection aimed in every detail toward the expression of individuality."

As evidenced in the African, Oceanic, and South American art collection Rubinstein amassed, and the marketing campaigns she ran that claimed to provide "secrets of the orient" and featured icons of the Italian Renaissance, Rubinstein "championed a multicultural identity and a nonhierarchical assessment of beauty" that reflected America's diversity in the early twentieth century.[24] Although Rubinstein considered herself a non-practicing Jew, Kathy Peiss argues that Rubinstein's Jewish identity heightened her sensitivity to the "varying beauty needs and skin types of women of different ethnic origins." In *War Paint*, a monograph on the Arden-Rubinstein rivalry, Lindy Woodhead notes that while Rubinstein adopted the name Helena as homage to the

---

23. See Michèle Fitoussi, *Helena Rubinstein: The Woman Who Invented Beauty* (Sydney, 2012).
24. Mason Klein, *Helena Rubinstein: Beauty Is Power* (New Haven, 2014), 20.

legendary Greek beauty, in keeping her Jewish surname, the queen of cosmetics stood in opposition to the antisemitism and racism of her day.[25]

It is against this social and historical backdrop that we must view the rise of national beauty contests in America, and the Queen Esther pageants that gained popularity in the 1920s and '30s, when makeup meant modernity and investing in physical appearance was considered a form of female empowerment and expression. The decade following World War I also saw an increase in protections for minority populations and the rights of all peoples regardless of birth, nationality, language, race, or religion. Under these conditions, modern Jewish culture began to flourish, and even before Esther's reputation was borrowed for beauty contests, the biblical saga of the bold and beautiful diasporic Jew captivated a range of public audiences.

As reported in the *Chicago Tribune* on March 16, 1913, a cast of 350 Jewish schoolchildren were to perform the "Great Pageant of Esther" the following Sunday in honor of the Purim festival to a public crowd of 2,000; the showcase would stage the epic story in pantomime, dance, and song and be directed by Miss E. C. Erlich, a local award-winning writer. In 1915, at the largest open-air event of its kind in Selig (now Luna) Park in Los Angeles, a cast of over 100 presented the "Pageant of the World's Birth," a dramatic spectacle representing six impressive biblical scenes, involving animals from the park's zoo, including "Queen Esther in her glory," organized by the Roosevelt Auxiliary to benefit United Spanish War Veterans.[26] A similarly large-scale "Queen Esther pageant" featuring nearly 200 "children, old men and beautiful women" was announced in the *Washington Post* in August 1923 as a fundraiser for local community playgrounds in the Alexandria/DC area.[27] While the performative afterlives of Esther are difficult to trace in early twentieth-century America, these headlines suggest her famed beauty and character were creatively represented through the arts and channeled in the spirit of public service.

---

25. Lindy Woodhead, *War Paint: Madame Helena Rubinstein and Miss Elizabeth Arden* (Hoboken, 2003), 108.
26. "Pageant of the World's Birth: Spanish War Veterans Plan Brilliant Spectacle," *Los Angeles Times*, September 3, 1915, p. II 1.
27. "Elaborate Preparations for Queen Esther Pageant Next Month for Playground," *Washington Post*, August 5, 1923, p. 15.

The appropriation of Esther's legacy for female beauty competitions, however, would prove a more complicated matter.

In *The Most Beautiful Girl in the World*, Sarah Banet-Weiser shows that the rise of beauty events that crowned an individual body as representative of American national identity was hardly a linear or uncontested development.[28] Miss America, the longest-running beauty contest in the US, can trace its roots back to the 1920s when newspapers selected "Inter-City Beauties" from mailed-in photographs, and those winners went on to various competitions, including the one held in Atlantic City in 1921, organized, in part, to attract tourists at the end of the summer season. Over the next few years, other beauty contests at the local and national levels emerged, including the International Pageant of Pulchritude in Galveston, Texas, which would become the precursor for the Miss Universe contest. As displays of civic pride, prominence, and modernity, organized competitions spread like wildfire throughout Palestine, South America, and Europe.[29]

In 1929, Erzsébet Simon, a blond-haired, blue-eyed Hungarian Jew, won the Miss Hungary competition before going on to win the first annual Miss Europe beauty pageant. Although Simon was invited to compete in the Miss Universe pageant in America later that year, antisemitic responses and messages of moral import from religious figures (including Bishop Christopher Edward Byrne of Galveston where the contest was to be held) led to Simon's withdrawal.[30] However, Lisl Goldarbeiter, who considered herself a practicing Jew, won the title of Miss Austria out of 1,200 contestants that same year and did travel

28. Sarah Banet-Weiser, *The Most Beautiful Girl in the World: Beauty Pageants and National Identity* (Berkeley, 1999). See also Lois Banner, *American Beauty* (Chicago, 1984).
29. On the use of Queen Esther pageants to advance the Zionist agenda abroad in the early twentieth century, see Bat-Sheva Margalit Stern, "Who's the Fairest of Them All? Women, Womanhood, and Ethnicity in Zionist Eretz Israel," *Nashim: A Journal of Jewish Women's Studies & Gender Issues*, no. 11 (Spring 5766/2006): 142–163, and Adrina Brodsky, "Electing 'Miss Sefaradí' and 'Queen Esther': Sephardim, Zionism, and Ethnic and National Identities in Argentina, 1933–1971," in *The New Jewish Argentina* (Leiden, 2012).
30. In his letter to Simon, Roman Catholic clergyman Byrne described the competition as a "vulgar advertising stunt" that jeopardized the modesty and self-respect of the young participants.

to Texas with her mother in 1929, despite the letter she too received from Bishop Byrne. Goldarbeiter, who had the fair complexion of her father and dark hair of her mother, won the title of Miss Universe by a unanimous decision, yet she also faced the ugliness of antisemitism when she returned to Europe and eventually withdrew from public life.[31]

As Sarah Banet-Weiser argues, national beauty contests "offer a glimpse at the constantly changing and always complicated stories about the nation itself: Who counts as part of the nation? What does it mean to be a specifically feminine representative of a nation? How are social concerns – such as racism, multiculturalism, and 'family values' – mediated in and through women's bodies on a public stage?"[32] I believe these questions were just as present and perhaps even more politically charged when Esther was chosen as queen of Persia in the fourth century CE. The establishment of "Queen Esther" beauty contests for young Jewish women abroad and in America at the turn of the century seems contrary to the biblical heroine's ethos; Esther was an unwilling participant who concealed her Jewish identity, while the young women participating in these events donned their Jewishness as well as their evening attire.

In surveying historical records, Philip Goodman finds that the Purim Association of the City of New York organized yearly philanthropic balls that often included the presentation of a "Queen Esther" beginning in the late 1880s.[33] The Jewish Education Association of Indianapolis sponsored its first annual Queen Esther contest in 1912, which continued to run for over twenty years. While records are limited, contests within the Jewish community of the greater New York area scaled up as pageant culture in America steadily grew. Starting in 1929, the Jewish National Workers' Alliance hosted its first Queen Esther Pageant timed to coincide with the festival of Purim, which sought to

---

31. See Ro Oranim, "How Anti-Semitism Robbed the Jewish Miss Europe of her Crown," *The Librarians* (2018), https://blog.nli.org.il/en/miss_europe/. See also Péter Forgács' documentary "Miss Universe 1929" (Mischief Films, 2006).

32. Banet-Weiser, 2.

33. Philip Goodman, "Purim Association of the City of New York (1862–1902)," *American Jewish Historical Society Publications* 40, no. 2 (December 1950).

find "the most beautiful of the Jewish girls of the Country." Photographs were received over a period of several months and popular vote determined which girls would travel to New York to appear before a panel of twelve judges. Fannie Rachel Moses of Brooklyn was chosen as "Queen Esther" and runner-up Esther Manischewitz of Cincinnati received the title "Lady-in-Waiting." The geographical distance represented by the winners contributed to the notion of a dispersed yet unified American Jewish community, while the prize – a free trip to Palestine – further underscored the contest's nationalistic objectives. The following year, the same event was held at Madison Square Garden and featured a performance by star-of-the-Yiddish-stage Stella Adler supported by a company of acclaimed Jewish actors and twenty ballet dancers, much like the pomp and circumstance that had come to embellish contests like the Miss America pageant. In terms of their similar social agendas, the Queen Esther pageants likewise used this platform to show that the Jewish community also produced beautiful, service-oriented citizens, as typified by their chosen "queen."

By the time Katherine Spector was crowned "Queen Esther" in 1933, beauty contests worldwide had become increasingly contested spaces. Once seen as opportunities for women who had recently become consumers of fashion and cosmetics to participate in a new form of physical self-realization and social freedom (in many ways consistent with the ideals of the suffragist movement and the first wave of feminism), this pop culture trend drew outrage from all sides. From within the Jewish community, religious dissenters saw the practice of displaying and judging female bodies as an abomination of Jewish values and a debasement of Esther's character. In January 1930, Rabbi Kook sent a letter to Mayor Dizengoff urging him to cancel the "monster of the selection of a beauty queen from among Eretz Israeli Judaism" which had been part of the annual Tel Aviv Purim festivities since 1926.[34] Feminist critics were less concerned with modesty and more outraged by the commodification of the female body that pageants allowed and the social control men exercised over women by perpetuating restrictive beauty

---

34. See Nina S. Spiegel, *Embodying Hebrew Culture* (Detroit, 2013), 48.

ideals.[35] While a few "Queen Esther" pageant fundraisers unaffiliated with Jewish institutions continued into the late 1930s, opposition from women's groups, combined with the financial difficulties of the Great Depression, impeded all beauty contest organizers throughout America for the next several years.[36]

It is possible to read the short-lived Queen Esther pageants coordinated by American Jews during this period not as acts of assimilation, but as acts of self-preservation and aspiration: like the biblical ingénue who successfully negotiated living in different realms of presentation, perhaps Jewish immigrants could script a similar "ending" for themselves as foreign inhabitants who not only gain protection from their host country, but achieve acceptance and prominence. At the same time, hosting contests designed to parallel an American cultural practice yet restrict participation to Jewish women allowed communities to outwardly validate their claims of national inclusion on the basis of beauty without forfeiting the security of insularity. While the risks and affordances of that representation are constantly shifting, Esther's legacy pushes us to keep asking ourselves where, how, and why we seek belonging.

Bess Myerson's selection as the first and only Jewish Miss America winner in 1945 offers a fraught response to these questions. For Banet-Weiser, Myerson "represented the thousands of people for

35. See Lois Banner, *American Beauty* (Chicago, 1984), and Naomi Wolf, *The Beauty Myth* (New York, 2002). For a recent reflection, see Lauren Collins, "Miss America's History-Makers and Rule-Breakers," *New Yorker* (August 31, 2020), https://www.newyorker.com/magazine/2020/09/07/miss-americas-history-makers-and-rule-breakers.
36. For instance, pastor Rev. B. L. David of Liberty Baptist Church "cordially invited [its] members and friends to witness…'The Coronation of Queen Esther' [in which were] several princesses contesting for the crown" before a panel of community judges formed by "some of Atlanta's best leading citizens," in an announcement printed in the May 15, 1938, *Atlanta Daily World*. The following year, the *Los Angeles Times* announced the "first annual Queen Esther Ball…under the direction of Henry Bellows, writer and producer associated with Cecil B. De Mille," sponsored by the Merchants, Manufacturers and Professionals Club and designed to benefit the Los Angeles Sanitarium; the event, to be held at the Ambassador hotel, would be "climaxed by the crowning of Queen Esther I, who will be selected from among 64 'princesses,' each nominated by separate social, fraternal or philanthropic groups" (*Los Angeles Times*, March 8, 1939, p. A24).

whom American soldiers were fighting. Beautiful, talented, the daughter of immigrants, she was living proof of or testimony for the reliability of the American Dream. Her body, identified publicly as Jewish, situated Myerson as a specific site for displacing a nation's troubles, anxieties, and guilt."[37] Of course, there are many degrees of separation between tolerance and acceptance, and several public figures and industries refused to recognize Myerson's title. When Myerson became the target of open antisemitism, she partnered with the Anti-Defamation League and used her public platform to spread the message "You Can't Be Beautiful and Hate," actively aligning beauty with moral virtue.

To some degree, I see the Miss America pageant's decision to eliminate the swimsuit portion of the century-old contest in 2020 as a symbolic step closer to an "Esther aesthetic" and the biblical heroine's lasting impact toward a definition of beauty that creates unity without dissolving differences. In shifting focus from outward aspects of the female body to voice, poise, and civic purpose, the modern-day pageant moves closer to a leadership competition, advancing a definition of beauty that holds space for women of all backgrounds while operating on the metric of *ḥein* (grace). At a time when Jewish life is more diverse than ever – from Eastern Europe to Ethiopia and beyond – and in an America that is profoundly divided on issues of race, religion, and equality, perhaps Esther has been positioned all along "for such a time as this" – teaching us that beauty, like any privilege, is one that must be used in the service of others.

---

37. Banet-Weiser, 158.

Speaking Away Silence: Esther and the Beginning of the End of Trauma

Malka Fleischmann

At the end of the first chapter of the Book of Esther, the narrative exhibits a peculiar fixation upon speech and language.

In the wake of Queen Vashti's refusal to abandon her women-only feast and appear before King Ahasuerus and his male public, the king's anger induces him to seek counsel, resulting in the decision to send letters "into all the king's provinces, into every province according to the writing thereof, and to every people after their language, that every man should bear rule in his own house, and speak according to the language of his people" (Est. 1:22).

This preoccupation with speech and language is especially strange in light of the fact that the chief concern relating to Vashti's insubordination, as articulated by Memucan, was that the queen's actions would "come abroad unto all women, to make their husbands contemptible in their eyes" (Est. 1:17), and in light of the fact that his advice was to widely publicize Vashti's dismissal and her being disinherited. Yet, after the missive's pithy reference to the safeguarding of male authority, the dramatic first chapter of the *megilla* ends with only the letter's puzzling directive toward each male subject to, when bearing rule in his own house, "speak according to the language of his people."

Expounding in just a few words upon this bizarre final verse, the medieval French exegete Rashi arrests us with his elucidation: "He can compel his wife to learn his language if her native tongue is different."

In other words, amid feelings of fury and fear arising from a woman's refusal to obey and the potential consequences of her fellowship with other women, the men of Shushan issue a gag order of sorts. They silence the women by dictating the terms of their speech. They acknowledge their counterparts' capacity for self-expression, but they render themselves deaf to it by allowing a woman's native tongue to waste inside her while she is compelled to live her life through alien speech – to live with a coerced lexicon and attempt authenticity using turns of phrase given to her by others.

* * *

On October 15, 2017, actress Alyssa Milano tweeted, "If you've been sexually harassed or assaulted write 'me too' as a reply to this tweet." Within a day, Milano's virtual bid elicited millions of responses across Twitter and other social media platforms, and the #MeToo movement, first founded by social activist Tarana Burke in 2006, took mighty root in American life, quickly accruing global popularity as well.

And, while the effects of the movement have been so profound as to rattle workplace policies across multiple industries, uproot high-ranking officials and executives from their positions, and birth new legislation in Congress, it is the element of noise – the cacophonous sum total of these and other effects – generated by this movement that so aptly addresses the needs of victims of abuse. Sound – theirs and their allies' – in place of silence.

The movement's astounding acceleration and agitation were profound enough to earn it a wave of opposition. Among critical voices, there are many that doubt victims' motives, believing that the choice to publicize trauma is a bid for attention and that the movement, at large, is a witch hunt.[1]

But, whether or not the movement grew to the incalculable influence it possesses today and whether or not the force achieved on its digital stage has been, on balance, positive, the simple aims of Burke's original "me too" affirmation would have been and remain critical to the rehabilitation of victims of abuse. For victims, publicity and conquest were never the targets, and, for many, never desired.

What opponents and skeptics of the movement fail to understand is that the motivation for post-trauma confession and confiding, the motivation for ending one's silence, is not revenge – for erasure of trauma is impossible – but is, instead, the overwhelming and evolutionarily adaptive desire to end one's own suffering and prevent the start of others'. At worst, victims are motivated by the noble desire for recovery and for justice producing greater safety for all.

Embedded in the words "me too" are correctives – or, at least, salves – to some of the traumas endured by victims of abuse, most of which persist long after the period of abuse ends. (As founder, Tarana Burke once said, "…the violence doesn't end with the act. The violence is also the trauma that we hold after the act."[2])

Isolation, the critical container for successful abusers, is methodically secured and maintained during the period of abuse and is often sustained by the disoriented victim long after finding safety. Fears about poor reception, as well as feelings of self-reproach and embarrassment, prevent victims from overcoming that isolation and sharing their accounts of abuse. What's more, sowed in the time that they were mistreated and damaged by people meant to love them is a profound lack of trust in themselves and others, painfully felt by victims as they reenter the world with skepticism and timidity. Even long after abuse ends, flashbacks, nightmares, and other symptoms

---

1. Tovia Smith, "On #MeToo, Americans More Divided By Party Than Gender," *NPR*, October 31, 2018, https://www.npr.org/2018/10/31/662178315/on-metoo-americans-more-divided-by-party-than-gender.
2. Tarana Burke, "Me Too is a movement, not a moment," TED talk (January 4, 2019), https://www.youtube.com/watch?v=zP3LaAYzA3Q.

Malka Fleischmann

of PTSD roil yet in the body, like phantom already-removed poison. The resultant accumulation of these feelings is deafening, burdensome, confusing, exhausting, and continually traumatizing.[3]

Thus, the posture and substance of the words "me too" enter as a corrective. First are the implications of listening and acceptance, gently but firmly countering fears of dismissal and incredulity. In order to utter the words at all, one would first have to choose to be present, to hear another person's story, and to affirm it. Second is a sort of witnessing or testimony, helping to reestablish the victim's trust in the wider world's capacity to hold his or her suffering and not deepen or renew it. Third is the suggestion of fraternity and sameness, correctives to the shame and loneliness of the experience – loneliness that began in the abuser's carefully constructed isolation of the victim and that persisted maximally as long as he or she bore the experience in silence. And fourth is the indication of a willing and abundant presence. "Me too" signals to the victim that here – in this counterpart and in this conversation – is a welcome environment in which to unburden oneself of that which is injurious and saddening.

There is safety in "me too." There is community, and there is empathy as well – infinite empathy when stated without caveat or investigation. "Me too" nods in agreement in a way that recalls a person's value, and it beckons forth drained but still desperately yearning reserves of strength. It serves as a mechanism of reunification, drawing the victim toward others, toward the long-forgotten but still familiar, and toward the process of reenergizing that which has been depleted. It softly says, "It is time for you to rejoin the world."

* * *

3. Cesiah Guerra, "Isolation and Domestic Violence," BTSADV, https://breakthe-silencedv.org/isolation-and-domestic-violence/; Anonymous, "What Emotional Abuse Does to Your Brain," *A Voice for the Innocent* (February 3, 2017), https://www.avoicefortheinnocent.org/emotional-abuse-brain/?gclid=EAIaIQobChMI56_9uPrh6QIVFIvIChoxjQ-EEAAYASAAEgIVrPD_BwE; and Ann Pietrangelo, "What are the Short- and Long-Term Effects of Emotional Abuse?" *Healthline* (March 29, 2019), https://www.healthline.com/health/mental-health/effects-of-emotional-abuse#long--term-effects.

In its great wisdom, following the first chapter's understated and terrifyingly crisp reference to the establishment of a movement to subjugate women, the *megilla* finds redemption in Esther's story, demonstrating narrative correctives to silence prefiguring the #MeToo movement's.[4]

When we're first introduced to Esther as she enters an extended pageant for the crown, we are told that she "had not made known her people nor her kindred; for Mordecai had charged her that she should not tell it" (Est. 2:10). Soon thereafter, when it is Esther's turn for presentation before the king, it is said of her that she "requested nothing" (2:15). Five verses later, the text reiterates the fact that Esther remains mum about her lineage, saying, "Esther had not yet made known her kindred nor her people; as Mordecai had charged her; for Esther did the commandment of Mordecai, like as when she was brought up with him" (2:20). Closing the second chapter is Esther's conveying the regicidal plot of Bigthan and Teresh, but doing so "in Mordecai's name" (2:22). Thus, the *megilla*'s introduction of Esther paints her, excepting a brief communication in someone else's name, as silent and deferential.

Soon, though, Esther begins inching toward her own voice.

In the fourth chapter, when Mordecai sends word to Esther to beseech the king to save the Jewish people from Haman's genocidal plan, Esther is, at first, reticent, reminding Mordecai that those who approach the king without being summoned are put to death. In response, Mordecai warns Esther that her aristocratic station will not safeguard her from any harm that befalls the Jewish people, and then, in one of the most empowering and faithful verses in all of Tanakh, he says, "And who knoweth whether thou art not come to royal estate for such a time as this?" (Est. 4:14). The pivot is clear. Having been coaxed into assuming responsibility, an emboldened and steadily more commanding Esther sends word to Mordecai to instruct the Jews of Shushan to fast on her behalf as she undertakes

---

4. For another analysis of Esther through the prism of the #MeToo movement, see Erica Brown, "Having an Esther Moment," *The Atlantic* (March 8, 2020), https://www.theatlantic.com/ideas/archive/2020/03/esther-sex-and-power/607534/.

their salvation. The chapter concludes with the words, "So Mordecai went his way, and did according to all that Esther had commanded him" (4:17), thus inverting the existent dynamic by which Esther consistently obeyed Mordecai's instruction.

In the seventh and eighth chapters of the *megilla*, as Esther has decidedly begun a campaign for her people's deliverance, the text details her character's crescendo.

Not only does she ask for her life and the lives of her people to be spared, but she specifies that they be saved "at my petition" and "at my request" (Est. 7:3), as if her voice, itself, making these appeals, bears weight enough to justify them. Later, in the eighth chapter, no longer hiding her identity but instead carrying quite a bit of cachet, with the inverted dynamic again at play, Esther is said to have been the one to reveal Mordecai's identity to the king (8:1). Other verses deepen our sense of Esther's newfound power, stating, "And Esther spoke yet again before the king" (8:3), as well as depicting her unbridled emotion and audacious claim of identity when she says, "Or how can I endure to see the evil that shall come unto my people? Or how can I endure to see the destruction of my kindred?" (8:6).

But, perhaps the narrative turns most deeply evidencing Esther's empowerment and reclamation of voice surface in the book's last mentioning of its heroine, as if to suggest that her evolution is complete.

First, when it is said that she "wrote down all the acts of power, to confirm this second letter of Purim," Esther is called "Esther the queen, the daughter of Abihail" (Est. 9:29). This is the only time, throughout the *megilla*, that Esther is identified, at once, by her royal station and her lineage. Elsewhere, one or the other, if not just her name, represents the sum total of her identity. But at this moment, when Esther is writing her own story and the story of her people, when she is committing her version of events to the annals of history, she does so as a fully realized person, with a robust identity and in a fully matured and liberated voice. Inhabiting all of her parts – her past and present – she writes the narrative that will determine the Jewish future. Though initially kept silent and made alien to her own identity, she is now returned to herself completely.

Second, commenting on the final verse of the *megilla*'s ninth chapter,[5] Rashi writes, "Esther requested of the sages of the generation to commemorate her and to write this book with the rest of the Scriptures..." And so, finally, not only has Esther come to cherish and esteem her own voice's power for self-narration, but she views its amplification across time as something valuable. She views her life and story as something instructive for her people and humanity at large. Though initially suffering the disorientation and loneliness inherent in a life of secrecy, she is now returned to her people and comfortably and powerfully joined with a wider world.

And so, as the *megilla* concludes, the cultural ills of its first chapter are rectified. Where men once reigned unchecked, fearing the strength of female solidarity and abusing their power to subdue their female counterparts, peoplehood has emerged the victor, and women are now equal players, as Esther and Mordecai share the Purim story's stage. Where women were once manipulated and managed – granted sparing language for the articulation of their inner lives – they are now the storytellers. Without external directives, undisguised and lionhearted, Esther will not remain silent. And neither she nor her people will allow themselves to be controlled.

* * *

In her first memoir[6] American author and civil rights activist Maya Angelou writes, "There is no greater agony than bearing an untold story inside of you." The sentiment calls to mind Simon and Garfunkel's lyric, "Silence, like a cancer, grows."[7] And, whether prose or poetry, both ideas imply a dual call to action – a communal groundswell of care. A person must tell her story, and her people must listen to it. And, when someone is made sick by mounting silence, we must be there to excise that harmful growth.

---

5. Esther 9:32, "And the commandment of Esther confirmed these matters of Purim; and it was written in the book."
6. *I Know Why the Caged Bird Sings* (New York, 1969).
7. "Sounds of Silence," Columbia Records, 1966.

Perhaps the key to one of the *megilla*'s most mystifying features – namely, the absence of any mention of God – lies in humanity's overcoming its own silence.

To unburden ourselves from trauma and keep concealment of it from poisoning our spirits, we must speak to one another and be born anew into community. We must nourish our faith in human voices – our own and our allies'. We must demonstrate to ourselves and our neighbors the dazzling capacities for trust and empathy that we possess. We must recall former versions of weakened and diminished spirits, returning ourselves to them and returning them to the wider world.

And, perhaps, to do all of this noisy work with our own voices – to uproot societal ills, heal wounds, and connect the isolated – we may need to mute some things. Perhaps, to fully express our loudly resounding reliance on ourselves and each other, we must allow our efforts to take the foreground, leaving God's work to the mystery, humility, and subtlety of the background.

As a faithful people, Jews would be quick to identify God in answer to Mordecai's rhetorical question to Esther, "And who knoweth whether thou art not come to royal estate for such a time as this?" But as a faithful people in another sense, Jews must also celebrate the verse's urging our trust in God's best imitation – humankind. The words echo between all other verses of the *megilla*, suffusing every pause with urgency, as if intoning the rallying cry not just of Purim but of all of humanity's ever-unfolding story – *And who knows whether you endured or witnessed the unspeakable things that you did so that, for such a time as this, you might beautifully, empathically, and courageously speak away the silence?*

Diaspora Life and
Dual Identities

Saint Esther in
Latin America

Dr. Emily Colbert Cairns

O f all biblical figures, Esther is the most beloved amongst crypto-Jews, *conversos* who converted to Catholicism but lived privately as Jews. Between the years 1478 and 1834, many Jews throughout the Spanish-speaking world were under threat of death by the Inquisition for practicing the Jewish faith.[1] Many fled Spain in what became known as the Sephardic diaspora and relocated to Northern Europe,

---

1. Although the Inquisition was formally abolished in 1834, by this time most *conversos* were fully assimilated into Christianity in the Iberian Peninsula (which encompasses Spain and Portugal) except for more isolated groups, including the *Chuetas* in the island of Mallorca, Spain, and the Jews of Belmonte, Portugal. The latter lived isolated in the mountains of northern Portugal and believed themselves to be the only surviving Jews, until they were "discovered" by anthropologist Samuel Schwartz in the 1920s. They were fearful and reluctant to reveal their religious identity, which was kept hidden for so many years. To this day, this community has a synagogue, but secret Jews from surrounding towns are only revealed as Jewish upon funerary rites, which occur in the Jewish cemetery.

the Ottoman Empire (especially Turkey and Greece), and Northern Africa.[2] Others made their way to the Americas, as Spain held colonies in this "New World" (from 1492 to 1810). Those who relocated to the Americas still faced persecution by the Spanish Inquisition headed by the *Suprema* (Council of the Supreme and General Inquisition) in Seville, which directed branches in Mexico, Peru, Guatemala, and New Granada.

Converso Jews "were created" in Spain after the first mass pogroms that began in 1391 in a wave of antisemitism led by the preaching of Ferrand Martínez, who sought to convert Jews to Christianity.[3] Anyone with Jewish blood, even with one grandparent who was Jewish, was marked as unclean according to the *limpieza de sangre* (purity of blood) mandates. Between 1391 and 1492, some Jews chose to convert to rid themselves of the unclean or impure background and left Jewish practice in its entirety. Others initially maintained their Jewish identity and then either converted while retaining their Judaism in secret (i.e., became *conversos*) or fled Spain when Judaism was officially outlawed in 1492. Until the expulsion, these groups lived side-by-side. Even within families, historians have documented parents and children separated along religious lines. Amidst this context of death-defying Jewish practice, Esther rose to unique prominence, a veritable "patron saint," even referred to as "Saint Esther" in inquisitorial trials.[4]

Esther, fittingly, serves as a beloved heroine and a model in the writings of *conversos* from Spain and Portugal who were forced to live dual lives and hide their identity in the Iberian Peninsula and in colonial Latin America. After all, in the biblical tale, Esther concealed her identity, utilizing her hidden Jewish identity to save the Jewish people. Her story of triumph in adverse circumstances resonated deeply for Jews facing

---

2. For more on the Sephardic diaspora, see David L. Graizbord, *Souls in Dispute: Converso Identities in Iberia and the Jewish Diaspora, 1580–1700* (Philadelphia, 2004).

3. *Converso* Jews were also referred to as New Christians, which contrasted to those descended from Christians, called Old Christians.

4. David E. Gitlitz, in *Secrecy and Deceit: The Religion of the Crypto-Jews* (Philadelphia, 1996), shows that crypto-Jews throughout Spain and New Spain, including the island community of Mallorca, and Belmonte, Portugal, maintained fasts in honor of *Santa Rainha Esther* (117).

similar circumstances throughout the Sephardic diaspora, particularly women, the central purveyors of home-based hidden Jewish practices.[5] With public displays of Judaism in the synagogue not an option, in the privacy of *converso* homes Esther took on an importance even greater than in that of normative Judaism.[6]

In the *Biblia Ladinada*, the vernacular version of the Old Testament compiled in fourteenth-century Spain utilized by *conversos*, Mordecai instructed Esther not to divulge her Jewish origins when arriving at the court.[7] Seeking freedoms outside of the Iberian Peninsula and following their merchant husbands, crypto-Jewish women in the Americas were similarly displaced from their birthplace. Officially, the Spanish Crown led by the "Catholic Kings" Isabel and Ferdinand (1469–1504) did not allow Jews and their descendants, *conversos*, to relocate to the New World when it was part of the Spanish Kingdom (1492–1810). However, many were able to buy false papers that demonstrated a Christian ancestry. In the case of the Carvajal family that we will study in detail in just a moment, the uncle Luis de Carvajal, the Elder, who was governor of northern New León, managed to bring almost his entire family to the New World. Even though they were *conversos* and crypto-Jews, Luis, the Elder, staunchly upheld his Catholic orthodoxy. Upon relocating to locations like Mexico and Peru, their dual lives delivered them into the hands of inquisitors on multiple occasions. As many *conversos* settled in

---

5. My research supports the scholarship of Renée Levine Melammed in *Heretics or Daughters of Israel? The Crypto-Jewish Women of Castile* (New York, 1999) and *A Question of Identity: Iberian Conversos in Historical Perspective* (Oxford, 2004) and Miriam Bodian in *Dying in the Law of Moses: Crypto-Jewish Martyrdom in the Iberian World* (Bloomington, 2007), who theorize that crypto-Judaism is a matriarchal religion.

6. Gitlitz shows that in the 1593 *auto da fe* in Granada, Spain, the Fast of Esther emerged as the second most important holiday (second to Yom Kippur) (43).

7. All the translations, unless otherwise marked, are my own. This chapter refers to two contemporary Bibles, the *Biblia Ladinada* and the *Ferrara Siddur*. The former is based upon a now-lost fourteenth-century manuscript composed in Spain and I use Moshe Lazar's Escorial I.J.3 edition (Madison, 1995). The latter was composed in Ferrara in 1552 for the use of the *converso* population living there. According to Lazar, the *Biblia Ladinada* is an ancestor of the *Ferrara Siddur*. It stands to reason that the Carvajal family or members of their network of crypto-Jews would have had access to these Castilian Bibles.

urban centers including Mexico City and Lima, the New Spanish (today Mexican) branch of the Inquisition could still closely monitor their daily lives. If a family lapsed in attending church, or a servant reported heterodox practices such as refraining from eating pork, *converso* families were reported to the Inquisition. In fact, the Inquisition published a list of *converso* observances to make citizens aware of heterodox practice and to encourage them to report any misstep. Listed amongst the traditions of the *Law of Moses* (a term used by the Inquisitors in contradistinction to the ruling Catholic *Law of Christ*) these practices included celebrating the Sabbath on Friday and Saturday, using different dishes and cutlery to observe the laws of *kashrut,* and not eating pork.

Crypto-Jewish women in colonial Latin America faced significant disadvantages. While the male members of their households participated in global trade networks, these women, living outwardly as Catholics and within the home space as Jews, were responsible for the continuity of the Jewish faith, but even within the home had to hide their faith so that servants would not be clued in. These women were tasked with starting a life in a totally new context in which they were under threat. If one member of a family or within the social network of crypto-Jews was apprehended by the Inquisition, almost always the person being questioned under torture would reveal details of their entire network of practitioners. These women, therefore, secretly used the inward tools of the home and their bodies, when they could, in order to live on their own terms and within the Jewish faith.[8] They formed a concept of religious piety that was hybridized and rooted in their everyday material world concerning food preparation, washing and cleaning the home, and faith practices concerning the body, including fasting. As the anthropologist James Scott writes, these women used tools, "weapons of the weak," to control what they could and give order to their world while outwardly appearing as Catholics.[9] This unique religious dynamic, what I term the

8. For more on the global trade networks developed in the Sephardic diaspora, see Jonathan Israel, *Diasporas within a Diaspora: Jews, Crypto-Jews and the World of Maritime Empires 1540–1740* (Leiden, 2002).
9. See James Scott, *Weapons of the Weak: Everyday Forms of Peasant Resistance* (New Haven, 1987).

"Sephardic difference," serves as a way to understand crypto-Judaism as female-centered and inscribed upon the body.[10]

To exemplify the relationships that *conversos* had with Esther, let us focus on a prominent crypto-Jewish family in New Spain: the Carvajals. The Carvajal family was the linchpin among a network of crypto-Jews in New Spain. The religious leaders within the family's hidden Jewish practices were women, as many of the men within the Carvajal family and their larger community took part in the transatlantic trade networks common throughout the Sephardic diaspora that took them across the Atlantic to Europe and Africa. The women led crypto-Jewish observance of the *Law of Moses*, including celebrating the Sabbath by having clean clothing and bedsheets, avoiding fish with scales, and upholding the fast of Esther.

The Carvajal family was put to death following their second inquisitorial trial (1595–96) in New Spain for Judaizing. Most historians and scholars have focused on the male members of this family, especially Luis de Carvajal, who wrote his autobiography while in prison.[11] We will instead focus on his two sisters, Leonor and Isabel de Carvajal, and their trial records, as they shed a new understanding on crypto-Judaism.

For the Carvajal women, as seen in both their actions and their writings, Esther was their inspiration. As the passage below from the trial of Leonor and Isabel's mother demonstrates, theirs was a life of outward practice and hidden resistance.

> ...after she turned to the Law of Moses, away from Spaniards' Law of Christ. [The crypto-Jews] had taken the sacraments of the Mother Church but did so without any feeling. And although she didn't make fun of them, and confessed that she took communion, she did so only to obey the rules, because she did not

---

10. I develop this concept of the Sephardic difference in my monograph *Esther in Early Modern Iberia and the Sephardic Diaspora: Queen of the Conversas* (Cham, 2017). I thank Palgrave MacMillan who have granted permission to reproduce ideas from original research in this chapter.

11. For further reading on Luis de Carvajal, see Seymour B. Leibman, *The Enlightened; The Writings of Luis de Carvajal, El Mozo* (Miami, 1967), Martin A. Cohen, *The Martyr: Luis de Carvajal, A Secret Jew in Sixteenth-Century Mexico* (Albuquerque, 1973), and Alonso Toro, *La familia Carvajal* (Mexico City, 1977).

believe that Jesus Christ was their author [of the sacraments], nor did she believe him to be God. (MSS 95/96 v. 4, 334v[12])

We see in this passage the careful and thoughtful negotiation between identities in New Spain. We also see precisely what was at stake in everyday life for crypto-Jews – public participation in the church and a faith that was interior and distinct from the dominant group.

While the veneration of the figure of the Virgin Mary – known as the "Cult of Mary" – held huge sway over Spaniards in Iberia and the colonial world, for the Carvajal women, as for so many *conversos*, Esther was "Saint Esther" in their private letters. In Luis' letters to his sisters he invokes biblical feminine figures as models for them. He wrote to Catalina from prison: "Pray, Pray, as Anna and Esther did in danger; hope as did the blessed Judith and Salome."[13] The sisters also passed notes to each other through the walls of the Inquisition hidden in avocado skins. This Catholicized reverence of a biblical woman developed from the dual context of Catholicism and Judaism in which the sisters lived their everyday lives.

We read in Isabel's trial how the Carvajal women would construct an altar within the house to avoid suspicions and appear as normative practicing Catholics:

---

12. These unpublished trial manuscripts are housed today in the Bancroft Library Special Collections in Berkeley, California. I analyze manuscripts MSS 95/96 v. 3 and MSS 95/96 v. 4 from Leonor and Isabel's second inquisitorial trials (1595–96) after which they were both put to death.

13. Janet Liebman Jacobs, *Hidden Heritage: The Legacy of the Crypto-Jews* (Berkeley, 2002), 107. These four biblical references address and celebrate the strength of female heroines, who, as devout Jewesses, use both prayer and fasting to resist adversity. Judith's tale is told in a work considered canonical by Catholics and apocryphal by Protestants. Anna and Salome appear in the New Testament (the latter is an unnamed daughter of Herod whom Josephus names as Salome). As Yosef Hayim Yerushalmi develops in his text on Jewish historiography, *Zakhor: Jewish History and Jewish Memory* (Seattle, 1996), what we witness between the biblical figures and the Carvajal women is the collapsing of historical and liturgical time. These women stand as key figures that are relevant for the present realities of late sixteenth-century colonial figures. They are recalled and memorialized through religious worship to create personal links and meaningful connections.

There was an altar in the main living room of the house that had some images that she used to trick those who entered. Sometimes, she would kneel in front of the images to make it seem to the household that she was Spanish (i.e., Christian). And my mother had a rosary that she would hold in her hands and bring to Mass although she would never pray with it nor would she entrust herself to Jesus Christ nor his blessed mother, but instead it was used to feign [a Christian identity]. (64r-v)

Despite the presence of Catholic ritual objects in their home, they would teach each other the songs and prayers of their crypto-Jewish faith. As it says in Isabel's trial from her testimony: "We sing with happiness, praises to the lord" (344r).[14]

In addition to prayers, fasting was one of the central practices of crypto-Judaism. It was a way in which women could control their own bodies and through their bodies their religious identity. We read in Isabel de Carvajal's trial: "...doña Isabel contemplated the fast of Queen Esther on all of the three days in which Queen Esther had not eaten" (78r). The way that fasting is represented in the trial closely parallels the biblical version of the Book of Esther in the *Biblia Ladinada*, in which it was written: "And Esther asks them to tell Mordecai: go, bring together all the Jews who live in Shushan, and fast for me; and my maidens and I will fast: and then I will enter to see the king, although it is against the rule of the land; and as I am lost, lost I will be. And Mordecai came, and he did all the Esther commanded" (689). Scholar Martin Cohen demonstrates that the Carvajal women fasted in honor of this heroine – to give them strength to continue their crypto-Jewish practices in the face of their own persecution. Isabel took these fasts further than other members of her family, extending the period of abstinence and fasting even when ill. We read in the trial how Isabel upheld the fast of Esther:

---

14. See Michelle Hamilton's article "La poesía de Leonor de Carvajal y la tradición de los criptojudíos en Nueva España," *Sefarad* 60, no. 1 (2000), 75–94, which discusses these poetic compositions in detail.

The said doña Isabel upheld the fast in contemplation of the fast of Queen Esther, in all of the three days she had not eaten even an egg with ash, and on Saturday doña Isabel only did not fast because it was a holiday, and then she began to fast on Sunday at midday like it is said to continue with her fasting. (229r-v)

This three-day fast in honor of Esther was typical within crypto-Jewish practice throughout Spain and the Americas, particularly since one could not easily celebrate Purim with a feast and a party.[15]

In addition to fasting, Isabel would use a ciliary, or hair shirt, within her religious worship. This ciliary was made of rough bristles and worn underneath the clothing and would scratch and make the wearer bleed. The hair shirt supposed a constant and physical commitment to faith by the practitioner. This type of faith act parallels Catholic penitentiary practice. We read in Isabel's trial:

...doña Isabel brought a discipline (ciliary) and she would hit herself every day and then fast to observe the said Law of Moses. She confessed that she had not done as much penitence as she wanted due to health concerns, and she promised to not do less than she had promised God. (229r-v)

---

15. Crypto-Jews throughout the Sephardic diaspora celebrated the fast of Esther for a three-day period instead of the one-day fast held in normative Judaism. Gitlitz explains that Josephus "who was much read by crypto-Jews talks of a three-day fast" (413). The Mishna says to read the *megilla* on the fourteenth day of Adar, which usually occurs in March. Upon the "Expulsion generation" dying away, "Judaizing conversos had difficulty in fixing the precise date of Purim" (379). Among crypto-Jewish communities throughout the Iberian world, the fast of Esther was celebrated according to the lunar calendar. In Mallorca "in the 1670s Judaizers kept the fast of Esther two days after the new moon in March. Seventeenth-century Portuguese *conversos* observed it on the full moon of February" (379). Irene Silverblatt, in *Modern Inquisitions: Peru and the Colonial Origins of the Civilized World* (Durham, 2004), shows the central role that the fast of Esther had within the crypto-Jewish community of Lima, Peru, in the seventeenth century. Female figures, including prominent figure Mencia de Luna, would observe the fast for three straight days (36). For a contemporary legacy which includes these fasts in places such as New Mexico, see also Liebman Jacobs.

The penitentiary context that includes flagellation and fasting reveals a more Catholic practice than the Carvajals would otherwise have experienced in their daily lives had they been practicing normative Judaism.

Other crypto-Jewish figures in the Americas also looked to Queen Esther as their model. Mencia de Luna was burned at the stake during the Great Jewish Complicity of 1635–1639 in Lima, Peru, in which most of the crypto-Jewish community perished at the hands of the Inquisition. We read in the testimony of her trial about the secret gatherings held in her house, where fellow *conversos* would observe the fast of Queen Esther for three days in September.[16] Like the Carvajal women, Mencia de Luna created a feminine community around her worship. She explained to the inquisitors that she was taught to Judaize in Seville and named her mother and sister as Jewish. Many children of crypto-Jews were only taught Judaizing practices upon reaching an age in which they could keep the secret of their traditions from the dominant Catholic majority. Along with observing the Sabbath by wearing clean shirts and putting clean linens on the beds, and not eating fish with scales or bacon, the fast of Esther is designated in her trial as a central tenet of Mencia de Luna's crypto-Jewish worship.

As we have seen, crypto-Judaism in Latin America and throughout the Sephardic diaspora was a hybrid faith, a mix of constituent Catholic and Jewish influences. Just as the biblical Esther's hidden Jewishness was the key to her survival, crypto-Jewish women like Isabel and Leonor used their bodies to secretly practice Jewish ritual and preserve their faith. For women like the Carvajal sisters, Esther became the head of a new type of Jewish religiosity, a matriarchal, female-led practice within their homes, often manifesting itself on and in their own bodies. They bled for her with hair shirts, they fasted for her, but above all they looked to her for guidance at a time when more and more of their endangered cultural heritage rested in their hands.

---

16. Silverblatt shows that they observed "the fast for Queen Esther, which they celebrated in the month of September for three days straight" (36).

It's Kind of a Funny Story

Dr. Dara Horn

I t's supposed to be a funny story, maybe even a goofy one – so much so that we're even supposed to tell it while drunk. And despite its near-miss genocide – or let's be real, *because of* its near-miss genocide – it manages to be the most lighthearted and entertaining story in the entire Hebrew Bible. The Book of Esther feels weirdly familiar to American Jews accustomed to American entertainment. Saturated with sex, booze, and raunchy jokes, starring a nice Jewish girl and a comic-book villain whose personal defeat comes from the R-rated equivalent of slipping on a banana peel, it's a story that seems tailor-made for American Jews to enjoy – especially in its wildly improbable ending, a Marvel Universe-worthy story of the triumph of good over evil. In short, it's what we as American Jews have long internalized as what's *supposed to* happen. Our lives here, in the land of the free, are supposed to be exactly this: a delightfully frivolous, elaborately decisive refutation of the dour history of diaspora Jewish life.

The American Jewish literary critic Adam Kirsch has pointed out that "in some essential ways, Jewish life in twenty-first-century America may resemble the Persia of twenty-five hundred years ago more closely than the Poland of three hundred years ago." Kirsch isn't only referring to the setting's anything-goes atmosphere, but to its diaspora Jewish community that has access to the highest echelons of non-Jewish power. In the Book of Esther, Persia is an environment, like today's United States, where non-Jews welcome Jews into their boardrooms and their backyards – and it's for this reason that the villain's genocidal decree comes across as a total shock. But long before that decree is signed and sealed, there is the barest, tiniest hint in the text that all is not well for the Jews of Persia. When Esther ascends to the Persian throne, her cousin Mordecai famously warns her to keep her Jewish identity a secret. But the text's hint comes much earlier than that, when we first meet this Persian Jewish family. Then we are told, as briefly as possible, that our heroine's name is Hadassah, a Hebrew name, but that she is known as Esther, a Persian name derived from the goddess Ishtar – the ancient Persian equivalent of naming an American Jewish girl Christine. The text tosses off this detail as nothing. We aren't even provided with a Hebrew name for her cousin Mordecai, whose name is clearly derived from the god Marduk. These Jewish characters' decidedly non-Jewish names simply sit there in the text, unacknowledged, a deeply hidden signal that there was already something painful going on in Persia, a set of compromises that the official story leaves forever buried.

It is here that the Book of Esther suddenly becomes eerily familiar for American Jews, this tidily happy story our ancestors have passed down to us as the thinnest veneer over an enormous and completely buried trauma. I am speaking, specifically, of a very particular and fairly recent historical experience: the almost entirely forgotten trauma, buried under a delightful and convenient legend, of a very specific Jewish experience here in the United States. To see just how deeply buried this trauma is, how completely submerged it is under joyful comedy, we must revisit the legend that has replaced it, the astonishing invention and brilliant twist that our most recent ancestors have passed down to us. The most foundational legend of American Jewish history is a story of name-changing, and it fits right into this pattern. It is a story right out of the Book of Esther, and its happy-go-lucky premise is just as false.

American Jews are a highly educated group of people – and not just educated, but great at asking annoying questions. In the most recent Pew Survey, forty-nine percent of American Jews claimed that a key part of their Jewish identity involved "being intellectually curious." In other words, American Jews see themselves as people who don't merely value their university degrees, but also their skepticism, their critical thinking skills, and their refusal to take anything at face value.

So I didn't think it was a big deal a few years ago when I gave a public lecture at a Jewish institution and casually mentioned a basic historical fact. In my remarks, I pointed out that the story that so many American Jews have heard in their families, that their family's surnames were changed at Ellis Island, is a myth.

I assumed that most educated people knew that. At Ellis Island National Park, which has been up and running for nearly thirty years, this fact is routinely announced on public tours. More recently, we have entered an era where genealogy has become trendy, bolstered by cheap DNA testing that has led tens of thousands of Americans down the rabbit hole of ancestry research, for which they can find ample guidance from online forums, TV documentaries, family tree construction software, and accessible archival databases in their quests to discover their roots. With this public glut of information, which of course includes the journeys of millions of American Jews' forebears through Ellis Island, I hardly thought the fun fact I mentioned was news.

Wow, was I wrong.

After that talk, I was mobbed by people – angry people. It wasn't even a line; it was a scrum. These were well-read, highly educated American Jews who crowded me as I left the podium to correct me on the facts. As each one of them furiously explained to me, maybe *most* people's names weren't changed at Ellis Island, but *their* great-grandfather was the exception. None of these people offered any evidence, other than to assure me that "my great-grandfather wouldn't lie!"

Weird things happen at public talks. I've had people present me with twenty-page confessions of their federal crimes. So I didn't lose any sleep over my Ellis Island mob. But then it happened to me again. I wrote an article for a Jewish publication in which I compared the "My name was changed at Ellis Island" story to similar historical material, such as Washington chopping down the cherry tree, the CIA killing Kennedy, and the lunar landing being faked to impress the Soviets. This did not go over well in the comments section. Hundreds of people felt the need to explain to me – since clearly I had not done my homework – that I was totally wrong, because…well, instead of evidence, they then inserted a five-hundred-word anecdote about their great-grandmother from Ukraine whose name was changed at Ellis Island from Rogarshevsky to Rogers, *so there.* Of course, comments sections are generally not great places for intelligent discourse, but these Jewish commenters were actually all very articulate and thoughtful. Most of the people who explained their family history to me probably have graduate degrees.

There is so much to say about the founding legends of diaspora communities, and about mythmaking and its purpose. But by now I know that I have to get the facts out of the way first. So, for the record: No, your family's name was not changed at Ellis Island, and your ancestors were not the exception. Here is how we know.

First of all, there was no language problem at Ellis Island. Immigration inspectors there were not rent-a-cops. These were highly trained people who were required to be fluent in at least three languages, and additional translators circulated to ensure competency – and in this context, the languages spoken by Jewish immigrants were far from obscure. Second, immigration processing at Ellis Island wasn't like checking ID at today's airports. These were long interviews, twenty minutes or more, because the purpose of this process was to weed out anyone who was likely to become, in the jargon of the time, "a public charge." So this was not a situation where some idiot behind a desk was just moving a line along.

Even if it were, here's another essential fact: *Nobody at Ellis Island ever wrote down immigrants' names.* Immigrants' names were provided by ships' manifests, compiled at the port of origin. Now maybe you're thinking that this whole dumb-guy-changed-my-family's-name thing might have happened on the European end. Wrong again. Ships' manifests in Europe were based on passports and other state-issued documents. Those compiling ships' manifests were very careful to get them right, because errors cost them money and potentially their jobs. This was due to yet another fun fact: any immigrant who was improperly documented on board these vessels had to be sent back to Europe at the shipping company's expense.

Still not convinced? Well, none of the foregoing matters either, because we also have actual legal evidence – specifically, thousands of court records from the 1920s, '30s, '40s, and '50s of Jewish immigrants and their children filing petitions in New York City Civil Court in order to change their own family names.

In her book *A Rosenberg by Any Other Name*, the historian Kirsten Fermaglich tracks these court filings. For legal name changes, petitioners had to provide the court with their reasons for changing their names. And that's where you see the heartbreaking reality behind the funny stories about Ellis Island. In these legal petitions, as Fermaglich unemotionally reports, we meet thousands of American Jews, most of them born in the United States, explaining under oath that they are changing their names because they cannot find a job, or because their children are being humiliated or discriminated against at school, that with their real names, no one will hire them for any white-collar position – that, essentially, American antisemitism has prevented their families' success.

In her analysis of thousands of name-change petitions, Fermaglich notes many clear patterns. One is that those with Jewish-sounding names overwhelmingly predominated such court filings. In 1932, for instance (nearly a decade after the closure of Ellis Island), over sixty-five percent of name-change petitions in New York were filed by people with Jewish-sounding names. For perspective, the next-largest group, those with Italian-sounding names, made up a mere eleven percent of filings. Granted, the Jewish population of New York that year was twice the size of the city's Italian-American population. It was not, however, six times the size of the city's Italian-American population. Another pattern Fermaglich uncovered is that petitioners with Jewish-sounding names often filed name-change petitions *as families*; frequently the motivation cited for the name change involved the educational and professional prospects of the petitioners' children. Yet the most horrifying aspect of these petitions, which Fermaglich rather dispassionately describes, is how they reveal ordinary American Jews in the debasing act of succumbing to discrimination instead of fighting it.

American antisemitism during the decades that followed the mass migration was, as Fermaglich puts it, "private" and therefore "insidious." In the earlier part of the twentieth century, such discrimination was not subtle, appearing in job advertisements with the warning "Christians Only" or at hotels and restaurants posting signs declaring

"No Dogs or Jews Allowed." (My childhood piano teacher, a Juilliard alumnus and retired cocktail pianist, once told me how he was hired as a young man in the late 1940s to play in the lobby of Florida's prestigious Kenilworth Hotel, where performing musicians were named on lobby signs. As he approached the hotel, he saw the dreaded sign reading "No Dogs or Jews Allowed," and wondered how he, Alan Wolfson, would manage to pass. He soon found himself playing a grand piano beside a marquee the hotel had provided, announcing: "Tonight's Performer: Alain de Wolfe.") By midcentury, these explicit markers had morphed into an elaborate glass ceiling that was an open secret, expressed at first through carefully worded advertising for things like employment or public accommodations ("Sabbath observers need not apply"; "Churches nearby") and later through byzantine job and school application forms that, as Fermaglich explains, demanded information not only about the applicant's birthplace and citizenship, but also equally mandatory and entirely irrelevant information about the applicant's parents' and grandparents' birthplaces, parents' professions, mothers' maiden names, and grandparents' surnames. Fermaglich points out the profound, "corrosive" effect of this type of intense and unacknowledged discrimination on the target population: "The unofficial nature of American anti-Semitism encouraged many Jews to resist discrimination by using bureaucratic name-change petitions to reshape their personal identity rather than civil rights activism to change an unfair society."

This is, of course, textbook gaslighting. You can't protest discrimination when it isn't really there, when it's all in your head. There really were churches near that hotel. Sabbath observance really could interfere with the duties of that office job. Those colleges just wanted to get to know their applicants better. What unpatriotic spoilsport would claim otherwise? Fermaglich is careful to note that the vast majority of Jewish name-changers did not actually cast off their Jewish identities; most continued living in predominantly Jewish neighborhoods, contributing to Jewish organizations and participating in Jewish communal life. Fermaglich presents this point optimistically, as a grand refutation of the popular assumption that such people rejected their Jewish identities. But to me, this fact demonstrates just how profoundly oppressive the situation must have been, if even those who valued their Jewish identity felt that a name change was necessary. These people were not "self-hating Jews." They were simply staring down a reality that they could not deny. And as the wording of their petitions reveals, they also could not allow themselves to admit exactly what that reality was.

As I pored through Fermaglich's selections from this ream of archival material, what I found most heartbreaking was witnessing how these Jewish name-changers participated in the very humiliation that they were seeking to escape. They did so not merely by changing their names, but by censoring their own self-expression *during the very act of changing those names* – because in their court filings, as Fermaglich reports, virtually no petitioners identified antisemitism as their motivation.

Instead, the Jewish petitioners almost uniformly referred to how their names were "foreign-sounding," or "difficult to spell and pronounce" – even, Fermaglich notes, "when the name was spelled phonetically." "The name Greenberg is a foreign-sounding name and is not conducive to securing good employment," one very typical petition reads. Rose Lefkowitz declared her last name "difficult to pronounce." (Is there more than one way to pronounce "Lefkowitz"?) Louis Goldstein declared his name "un-American, uneuphonius, and an economic handicap" – a petition that was rejected by the judge, whose name was also Louis Goldstein. (Those who beat the odds in an unfair system, of course, are the ones most invested in maintaining it.) Max Hymowitz described how his son Emmanuel found their shared surname "cumbersome" and "an annoyance"; his father felt that changing their name would "substantiate and promote his son's comfort and interests, socially, educationally, economically, and patriotically." One couple, pleading on behalf of their family, testified that "the name of Tomshinsky is difficult to remember and properly spell, and because of this, petitioners and their children have been subject to embarrassment and your petitioners believe that it would be to the best interests of their children as they mature, to have the family name changed to the proposed name of Thomas." In fact, the only petitioners Fermaglich cites whose filings actually mention antisemitism are non-Jews seeking to change their Jewish-sounding names, so as not to be mistaken for Jews.

Of course, many names circulating in the United States during this period were "difficult to pronounce and spell" – for example, LaGuardia, Roosevelt, Juilliard, Lindbergh, DiMaggio, Vanderbilt, Earhart, Rockefeller, and Eisenhower. Yet as the remarkably low numbers of non-Jewish name-change petitioners in New York City demonstrate, such families and their forebears do not appear to have been "subject to embarrassment" or affected "socially, educationally, economically, and patriotically" by having names that were "difficult to pronounce and spell." Fermaglich interprets these Jewish petitioners' participation in this elaborate gaslighting operation to mean that, as she gently puts it, "Jews were uncomfortable talking about anti-Semitism, and may have even been ashamed of their experiences with anti-Semitism." The difficulty these American Jewish families were facing had nothing to do with spelling or pronunciation, but none of them could admit it. And thus the process of hiding one's name became embedded within the more elaborate process of hiding the reasons why.

This brings us to the reality behind the funny family stories of names that were "changed at Ellis Island." The Ellis Island legend is simply the final step in this multigenerational process of denying, hiding, and burying the reality that American Jews feared most – namely, the possibility that they were not welcome here.

So now we know the myth, and we know the reality. And now we can ask the more interesting questions: Why did so many American Jews' ancestors tell this story about their names being "changed at Ellis Island"? What purpose did it serve then, and why do educated skeptical people still want to believe it now?

Those people who accosted me at my talk and online weren't stupid. They were responding to something enormously powerful and important. This mythological story about the Jews' arrival in America is part of a deep pattern in Jewish history, one that is much bigger than a single generation of immigrants and their children. It goes back centuries, all the way to Esther herself.

Nearly every diaspora Jewish community in world history has at least one founding legend, a story about its origins that members of that community accept as fact, no matter how ridiculous that story might be. According to the medieval Spanish Jewish author Abraham ibn Daud, for example, the Jewish community of Spain rose to prominence when a ship carrying Babylonian Torah scholars was hijacked and the scholars taken captive; the rabbi who wound up in Cordoba became the key figure in transforming the Jewish community there into the center of the Jewish world. The details of this story, like the Ellis Island one, make it utterly impossible that any element of it is true. But that didn't stop generations of Spanish Jews from accepting it as fact. The same can be said of the many legends about the founding of the Polish Jewish community, whose details range from Poland's name being derived from Hebrew roots (spoiler: it's not) to tractates of the Talmud being carved onto the trees of the Polish forest – tales whose obvious ridiculousness did not stop them from being repeated as fact by everyone from the kingmaking nineteenth-century Yiddish author I. L. Peretz to the twentieth-century Israeli Nobel Laureate S. Y. Agnon.

There are endless examples of origin stories like these. Jewish communities in France claimed that Jews had lived there since the time of the First Temple in Jerusalem, 2,500 years ago – it's not true, but it was a great alibi for explaining to their Christian neighbors why they weren't involved in killing Jesus. Jewish communities in parts of Algeria similarly claimed they had been living there since the time of the Second Temple, 2,000 years ago – also not true (though it was true in other parts of North Africa), but it was a great alibi for telling Muslims that they were already there before the Islamic conquest. One of my favorite founding legends is a story about the very first Jewish diaspora community, the Israelites' biblical sojourn in Egypt. Rabbinic tradition claims that one reason the Israelites survived their time in Egypt was that they never changed their Jewish names. But Moses, Aaron, and Phinehas are all of Egyptian etymological origin. And those are nothing compared to the names in the Book of Esther. Jews have been changing their names to non-Jewish ones, whether or not they have admitted it, for a long, long time.

There's a clear pattern to these legends, which are all about living in places where you are utterly vulnerable and cannot admit it. These stories express the Jewish community's two highest hopes and deepest fears. The first hope is that the Jews in this new place will remain part of the chain of Jewish tradition, and the second hope is that the local population will accept them. The fears, of course, are the inverse – of being cut off from that chain going back to Mount Sinai, and of being subject to the whims of the non-Jewish majority. These fears couldn't be more real, because being a diaspora community means being vulnerable. It is a high-wire act of the highest order. There are political strategies for dealing with that vulnerability, but these founding legends are an emotional strategy, and their power is unmatched.

Think about the details of these stories. In ways that made sense to each community, they each created a fantasy of total acceptance in a non-Jewish setting, and of total continuity with Jewish tradition. In the Spanish story, the captive rabbi survives, untraumatized and unscathed, to become the communal leader – and poof, the chain of Torah scholarship is unbroken between Babylonia and Spain. In the Polish story, the non-Jews of Poland love the Jews so much that they named their country after Hebrew words the Jews said, and even their country's natural landscape is inscribed with Jewish texts. These are fantasies that Polish Jews desperately needed to get them through the far less welcoming reality they lived in.

As minorities limited by sheer numbers in their ability to control the majority's determination of their fate, all diaspora Jewish communities are fundamentally vulnerable. One might contort oneself to believe otherwise, but this unforgiving fact also applied to the American Jewish community at the time when two million Jews arrived through Ellis Island, and perhaps even more so, to the American Jewish community at the time when those two million people's children became adults. Surviving and thriving in this reality required far more than bravery and resilience. It demanded creativity, imagination, and above all, an utterly irrational faith in the fantasy of acceptance. Believing in a fantasy takes conscious effort. It requires convincing oneself of the absolute necessity of believing, and then never relenting, ever.

Imagine what it was like for these new Americans and their children, living in what they hoped was the first place in centuries where their families could live full and free lives – until they discovered that when they applied for a job as Rosenberg no one would hire them, but when they applied as Rose, everyone would. Imagine the private humiliation of changing your name, of accepting the unspoken yet undeniable fact that your own name, the intergenerational marker of who you are, is publicly considered revolting. Imagine the trauma of betrayal: the reawakened memories of the places you or your parents fled at enormous risk and expense in order to spare yourself and your children this very same humiliation, and then the slow, seeping, soul-shaking discovery that this new place is in fact no different. Imagine not merely accepting this new and devastating reality, but even lying in court about your motivations for succumbing to it – or, even worse, internalizing that lie to the point where you yourself believe it, because the reality is too painful to acknowledge.

Now imagine telling your children, years later, about what you did.

Telling them the truth wouldn't only implicate you. It would also implicate America. You'd be telling your children that you thought you would be accepted here, but you were fooled, this place is just like everywhere else – only more insidious, because the discrimination isn't written into the law, so you can't even publicly protest it. All you can do is submit to it, publicly agree with it, announce in court of your own free will that your own name is "un-American," that the very essence of who you are is unacceptable, and voluntarily change your name. If you tell that story to your children, you'd be confirming two enormous fears: first, that this country doesn't really accept you, and second, that the best way to survive and thrive is to dump any outward sign of your Jewish identity, and symbolically cut that cord that goes back to Mount Sinai – which in the case of names like Cohen, it actually does.

Now imagine that instead of telling your children these psychologically damaging things, you have another option. You can do what Jews have done for thousands of years, and create an origin story that turns those fears into hopes. You can tell your children that something funny happened at Ellis Island, something completely innocent that didn't hurt you but only helped you. If you tell that story, you've accomplished two things. First, you've made America into a place where people maintain their Jewish identity without any interruption of the line to Sinai, and second, you've made America into a place so welcoming that happy non-Jews greet you at the door, and then make innocent mistakes that coincidentally help you to fit right in, at no cost to you or to the three-thousand-year-old tradition you want to maintain. This is the story that carries us to today.

In the Book of Esther, the Jews of the Persian Empire are stunned when they hear of the genocidal decree, which seems to come from nowhere. Reading this story every year, I was long puzzled by their surprise. After all, weren't these the same people who were too nervous to use their Hebrew names, the ones who are like Mordecai, who told Esther to keep her identity a secret? I finally understood that sudden horror after the 2018 massacre in a Pittsburgh synagogue and other lethal attacks on American Jews in recent years. Those attacks have been so shocking and disorienting not merely because of their sheer violent horror, but because they contradict the story American Jews have told themselves for generations, and which I imagine Persian Jews had told themselves as well – which is that America, or Persia, was never a place where anti-Jewish sentiment affected anyone's life. This is the legend that the ancestors of today's American Jews created for their descendants. We were told that our ancestors were definitely not humiliated people facing the life-limiting reality of American antisemitism even though that is demonstrated by thousands of court records. No, our ancestors were brave and hopeful people whose names were changed by happy accident, by welcoming representatives of America who opened up that golden door. We don't simply prefer this founding legend. We need it. The story is more important than the history, because the story is the device that makes meaning.

For some people, like my angry readers, it's upsetting to learn that the Ellis Island story is "only" a legend. But I find it empowering, because it reveals the enormous emotional resources available to our ancestors and to us. Our ancestors could have dwelled on the sordid facts and passed down that psychological damage. Instead, they created a story that ennobled us, and made us confident in our role in this great country – which means we have that creative power too.

I think of that creativity now when I read the Book of Esther, as an American Jew descended from people who used that creative power to protect me, to make sure I always thought the best of my country, to ensure that I always had faith that I belonged. While no doubt purporting to tell a historical tale, the Book of Esther is also a creative work, one whose story unfolds with a deliberate lightheartedness that reminds me of the Ellis Island story, a story created to bring light and joy to everyone who hears it. Other ancient Jewish stories, likes those of Passover and Ḥanukka, tell a similar story of a triumph over evil, but those stories do not bury their trauma under laughter and joy.

But the Book of Esther does, and that's what makes it so profoundly American. It insists on presenting us only with the fun parts, with the scary parts relegated to sudden moments of suspense, swathed in distracting off-color jokes. How did Hadassah wind up as Esther, in this wonderful Persian Empire where a nice Jewish girl makes it to the top? How did my American Jewish family wind up with such a conveniently non-Jewish name? Well, it's kind of a funny story. There is no darkness here, or if there is, we'd rather not hear about it – not because we're afraid of the truth, but because we need, have always needed, the strength the story gives us. As Jews, we've seen more than our share of darkness. Here in America, like everyone else, we deserve what the Book of Esther tells us the Jews finally got: light and joy, gladness and honor. Or maybe let's call it the pursuit of happiness.

Her name used to be Hadassah, and then it was Esther. It's kind of a funny story, one that ends with light and joy. Everything turns out fine, just the way we always knew it would. I'll drink to that. Won't you?

Mordecai as Foster Father: Exegetical Insights from New York's First Jewish Orphanage

Rabbi Alex Maged

On November 6, 1863, a short column on the second page of the *New York Times* reported on the festive dedication of a new Jewish institution in Manhattan. "The occasion was of more than ordinary interest to the Jewish residents of New-York," exclaimed its authors. "All the wealth and high respectability, all the beauty and the fashion of which the sons and daughters of Israel who have cast their lot in this community possess so largely recognized a share, were represented in immense force, and the number of the general multitude could not be calculated at less than several thousands." Under such circumstances was the Hebrew Orphan Asylum of New York formally inaugurated. As the first Jewish orphanage in New York,[1] it represented, to the editors

---

1. See Hyman Bogen, *The Luckiest Orphans: A History of the Hebrew Orphan Asylum*

of the *Times*, "that strong bond of sympathy which keeps a people of peculiar race and religion specially united in a land of their adoption."[2]

Yet while the establishment of the Hebrew Orphan Asylum may have struck New York's leading journalists as newsworthy in its time, those more closely affiliated with the institution recognized nothing novel about the practice of caring for Jewish orphans in exile. On one occasion, in fact, Rabbi Hermann Baar, the asylum's superintendent, traced such efforts all the way back to the biblical holiday of Purim. Speaking on the eve of that holiday, in a sermon titled "A Model Orphan," Baar drew deliberate parallels between himself, his colleagues, his students, and the heroes of the Purim story:

> My children: As often as I have spoken to you, I have tried to give you short addresses on themes which either may improve your heart or character, or be of benefit to you when you leave this house and enter the great arena of life. I have never ventured, however, to make the peculiar condition under which you are placed here in this Institution – I mean the duties which specially devolve upon you as orphans – a subject of my discourse. It happens today that I can introduce to your particular notice a model orphan, from whom you can learn much that may be conducive to your future welfare and prosperity; I would, therefore, request you listen to me with more than usual attention.
>
> My children, next week we celebrate the Purim festival.... Among the prominent figures who were chosen by God to give this festival a peculiar significance we observe an humble orphan-girl named Esther. Esther, whose original Hebrew name was "Hadassa," that is, the myrtle, was deprived in her earliest childhood of both her parents, and as at that time orphan houses were not known, it was a matter of course that the nearest relatives should take an interest in those children who had lost their dearest ties on earth. Thus it happened that Esther, after the death

---

of New York (Urbana, 1992).

2. "The Hebrew Orphan Asylum," *New York Times*, November 6, 1863, https://www.nytimes.com/1863/11/06/archives/the-hebrew-orphan-asylum.html.

of her parents, found a home in the house of her cousin Mordecai. Here, under the guidance of her excellent guardian, she grew up and perfected herself in every virtue that can embellish body and mind ...

My children, assisted by kind and benevolent friends, I try to impress upon you, hourly, daily and weekly, the highest principles of good conduct and morals. I never miss an opportunity to request you, and really as only a father would request his children, to accustom yourselves to industrious habits, to attend diligently to your studies, never to utter a falsehood, to treat kindly your surviving father or mother, and to evince at least a slight feeling of gratitude for the benefits you receive in this house ...

[The story of Esther] show[s] you, my children, that every orphan has in his own hands the material for rising in life. And you will certainly succeed, if you listen with confidential trust to the counsels of those who are appointed to level for you the road upon which you have to enter when you quit this house. Mind their teachings, hearken to their words, lend your ears to their well-matured reasonings ...

It would, of course, be a rare occurrence if in our days an orphan should be designated to occupy a royal throne, but if such a thing is almost an impossibility, it is by no means out of your power to become royal masters upon the throne of your own soul, that is, if you try to rule your passions with discretion, your temper with moderation, your conduct with propriety, and thus assist us in forming of all of you model orphans, and of this house a model asylum, in honor of God and the sublime principle of sympathetic love and world-embracing humanity. Amen.[3]

In Baar's remarkable rendition, the story of Purim – a story traditionally associated with such themes as providence, exile, assimilation, and

---

3.   Hermann Baar, *Addresses on Homely and Religious Subjects: Delivered Before the Children of the Hebrew Orphan Asylum* (New York, 1880). Many thanks to Dr. Jonathan Sarna for directing me to this collection.

redemption – is cast instead as a story that primarily concerns *adoption*. By framing the story in this way, Baar helped his audience mine from the *megilla* a message that he hoped they would find particularly poignant as Jewish orphans growing up in nineteenth-century New York. But Baar's focus on Purim's "adoption theme" was not only pedagogically clever. It was also exegetically astute – perhaps more so than Baar himself realized. To that end, I would argue that the story of Purim *does*, ultimately, turn upon Mordecai's act of adoption. In fact, it seems that Mordecai and Esther – whom Tanakh identifies as the authors of the *megilla* (Est. 9:26–29)[4] – hinted as much to us, in the text of the *megilla* itself. They did so by employing the very same literary strategy on display in "A Model Orphan." Like Baar, that is, Mordecai and Esther *also* drew upon a prior biblical text that is broadly concerned with the issue of "Jewish adoption" in order to contextualize the meaning of the Purim miracle. In this way, they taught their people that the key to prospering in exile lies principally in the concern we show for the fatherless and motherless among us.

In particular, the biblical text upon which, I would suggest, key parts of the *megilla* may have been fashioned, is the law of levirate marriage – i.e., the law of *"yibbum"* (Deut. 25:5–10). To be sure, the *yibbum* law, as presented in Deuteronomy, never refers directly to "orphanhood," narrowly defined. Yet *yibbum* is perhaps the oldest social welfare practice attested to by the Torah;[5] it reflects biblical civilization's most ancient intuitions about the lengths to which the community must go in order to support survivors of a family who have lost their head of household.[6] In

---

4. See, however, Bava Batra 15a, which attributes authorship of the *megilla* to the "Men of the Great Assembly." Possible reconciliation may lie in the fact that Mordecai was a member of this body (cf. Rashi, ad loc.).
5. For one notable biblical example of pre-Sinaitc *yibbum*, see Genesis 38:8–9. For more on the ancient origins of the *yibbum* practice, see Millar Burrows, "The Ancient Oriental Background of Hebrew Levirate Marriage," *Bulletin of the American Schools of Oriental Research* 77 (1940): 2–15, JSTOR, www.jstor.org/stable/1355235.
6. Although *yibbum* served in its original context to promote the economic and social welfare of the *yevama*, it should be noted that later rabbinic authorities discouraged the practice on a number of grounds. See, e.g., Bekhorot 13a; Yevamot 39b, 109a; *Shulḥan Arukh, Even HaEzer* 165.

this respect, one might rightly read the *yibbum* rite as the Torah's quint-essential "law of adoption":

When brothers reside together, and one of them dies and has no son, the wife of the deceased shall not be married outside the family to another man. Her husband's brother shall consort with her, taking her in marriage, and performing the duty of a husband's brother to her, and the firstborn whom she bears shall succeed to the name of the deceased brother, so that his name may not be blotted out of Israel. But if the man has no desire to marry his brother's widow, then his brother's widow shall go up to the elders at the gate and say, "My husband's brother refuses to perpetuate his brother's name in Israel; he will not perform the duty of a husband's brother to me." Then the elders of his town shall summon him and speak to him. If he persists, say-ing, "I have no desire to marry her," then his brother's wife shall go up to him in the presence of the elders, pull his shoe off his foot, spit in his face, and declare, "Thus shall be done to the man who does not build up his brother's house." And they shall call his [family's] name throughout Israel: "The house of him whose shoe was pulled off." (Deut. 25:5–10)

Under the biblical *yibbum* law, a man whose brother has died without progeny (=the *"yavam"*) is urged to marry his widowed sister-in-law (=the *"yevama"*). Should the *yavam* decline to do so, he is then desig-nated as a *"ḥoletz"* ("one whose shoe was pulled off"): he is stripped of his footwear, his face is spat upon, and the elders of the city publicly decry his refusal to support his needy relatives to the fullest extent mandated by law.

Perhaps the best way to appreciate the relevance that the *yib-bum* passage bears to the Purim *megilla* is to focus first upon the sharp condemnation issued against the *ḥoletz* at the height of his humiliation: "Thus shall be done to the man who does not build up his brother's house." Unsurprisingly, this striking proclamation knows no full equivalent in the annals of biblical history. Yet as astute students of the Purim story may already have realized, there *is* one other instance – and only one such instance – found in Tanakh of its curious opening phrase, "Thus shall be done to the man who…" (…ככה יעשה לאיש אשר). It occurs at the peak of the Purim *megilla*:

> On that night the king could not sleep, and he gave orders to bring the book of records, the annals, and they were read to the king. It was found written how Mordecai had told about Bigthana and Teresh, two of the king's eunuchs, who guarded the threshold, and who had conspired to assassinate King Ahasuerus. Then the king said, "What honor or distinction has been bestowed on Mordecai for this?" The king's servants who attended him said, "Nothing has been done for him." The king said, "Who is in the court?" Now Haman had just entered the outer court of the king's palace to speak to the king about having Mordecai hanged on the gallows that he had prepared for him. So the king's servants told him, "Haman is there, standing in the court." The king said, "Let him come in."
>
> So Haman came in, and the king said to him, "What shall be done for the man whom the king wishes to honor?" Haman said to himself, "Whom would the king wish to honor more than me?" So Haman said to the king, "For the man whom the king wishes to honor, let royal robes be brought, which the king has worn, and a horse that the king has ridden, with a royal crown on its head. Let the robes and the horse be handed over to one of the king's most noble officials; let him robe the man whom the king wishes to honor, and let him conduct the man on horseback through the open square of the city, proclaiming before him: '*Thus shall be done to the man whom the king wishes to honor.*'"
>
> Then the king said to Haman, "Quickly, take the robes and the horse, as you have said, and do so to the Jew Mordecai who sits at the king's gate. Leave out nothing that you have mentioned." So Haman took the robes and the horse and robed Mordecai and led him riding through the open square of the city, proclaiming, "*Thus shall be done to the man whom the king wishes to honor.*"

Then Mordecai returned to the king's gate, but Haman hurried to his house, mourning and with his head covered. When Haman told his wife Zeresh and all his friends everything that had happened to him, his advisers and his wife Zeresh said to him, "If Mordecai, before whom your downfall has begun, is of the Jewish people, you will not prevail against him, but will surely fall before him." (Est. 6:1–13)

In many ways, this scene constitutes the climax of the *megilla*. Literarily, it opens the second half of the scroll's ten chapters; liturgically, it is introduced by the heightened inflection of the cantor's voice; narratively, it represents Mordecai's moment of personal triumph over Haman. Given all of this, one might be tempted to brush off as mere coincidence the fact that Haman's proclamation – delivered at the apex of this very scene – happens to evoke a similar proclamation issued as part of the arcane and apparently unrelated *yibbum* ritual recorded hundreds of chapters earlier in the Bible.

Yet consider that the specific proclamation which the *megilla* attributes to Haman must have been imputed to him by *somebody else*. After all, neither Haman nor the crowds assembled at Mordecai's procession were native Hebrew speakers; they likely spoke Persian, the *lingua franca* of the Achaemenid Empire. Thus, Haman's pronouncement, as recorded in our *megilla*, cannot represent a direct quote. Rather, its exact formulation must have been chosen, purposefully, by the authors of the *megilla* – by Jewish authors, that is; authors who would have been familiar with the *yibbum* law; authors whose composition would enter the same canon that codified this *yibbum* law; and, maximally, authors who – as mentioned above – may even have been Esther and Mordecai themselves.

Might we then entertain the possibility that Haman's proclamation, in the *megilla*, *intentionally* recalls the proclamation of the elders, in the *yibbum* law? Perhaps we should – particularly as there seems to be much more connecting these two texts than the overlap of a similarly stated public pronouncement. Indeed, despite the relative brevity of the *yibbum* law – it spans no more than six verses in total – close analysis reveals multiple literary intersections between it and the *megilla*. Such intersections include the following:[7]

1. In both Mordecai's procession and the *yibbum* law, the term "desire" (ח.פ.ץ) captures the motivation driving the drama of the scene. In the *megilla*, it is Ahasuerus' desire to honor Mordecai that prompts Mordecai's triumphant circuit of Shushan: "Thus shall be done to the man whom the king desires (חפץ) to honor." In the *yibbum* law, conversely, it is the *holetz's* lack of desire to marry the *yevama* which prevents the *yibbum* from taking place: "But if the man has no desire (לא יחפץ) to marry his brother's widow... [and] persists, saying, "I have no desire (לא חפצתי) to marry her..." (Deut. 25:7–8).

2. Incidentally, the term "desire" (ח.פ.ץ) appears at one other critical juncture in the *megilla*, this one also reminiscent of the *yibbum* law: "In the evening she would go, and in the morning she would return to the second house of the women, to the custody of Shaashgaz, the king's chamberlain, the guard of the concubines; she would no longer come to the king unless the king desired (חפץ) her, and she was called by name (ונקראה בשם)" (Est. 2:14). Like the *holetz*, king Ahasuerus is presented – in his case, on a daily basis – with an eligible suitor who ultimately fails to win his "desire." The king even declines to refer to these suitors by their "names" – much like the *holetz* neglects to uphold the "name" of his deceased brother (Deut. 25:6–7), and therefore assumes a diminished name himself: "And they shall call his name (ונקרא שמו) throughout Israel: 'The house of him whose shoe was pulled off'" (Deut. 25:10). Of course, one maiden – Esther – does eventually win over the king; she alone, it would seem, earns his "desire," and the right to be "called by name." Ironically,

---

7. This list catalogs connections between the text of the biblical *yibbum* law and the text of the *megilla* (with particular emphasis upon the text of Mordecai's procession). One also finds intriguing connections between *yibbum* and Purim expressed or implied in the writings of the ancient Rabbis; several such connections are collected in the footnotes.

however, Esther rises to this rank only because she deliberately *conceals* her name, and the name of her family – Mordecai instructs her, at this point in the plot, not to identify the people and place to which she belongs (cf. Est. 2:10). Thus, for the duration of their relationship, Ahasuerus knows his wife not by her true name, Hadassah (Est. 2:7), but as "Esther" – a name which may actually mean "she of hidden identity": "she of *no name*."[8]

3. Another key word describing the motives of the *yavam* is "refuse" (מ.א.ן). Thus, the *yevama* declares: "My husband's brother refuses (מאן) to perpetuate his brother's name in Israel; he will not perform the duty of a husband's brother to me" (Deut. 25:7). In the *megilla*, meanwhile, Esther's and Mordecai's rise to power is facilitated by marital "refusal" of a different sort – the refusal of Ahasuerus' former wife, Vashti, to cater to the whims of her lascivious husband: "But when the attendants delivered the king's command, Queen Vashti refused (ותמאן) to come; so the king became furious and burned with anger" (Est. 1:12). It is this refusal that opens the door for the "desire" (ח.פ.ץ) that Ahasuerus later develops for Esther, as described above.

4. Both Mordecai's procession and the *yibbum* law unfold at prominent gathering places within the "city:" "the city square," in the case of the *megilla* (Est. 6:9, 11); the "gate" where the "elders of the city" sit, in the case of the *yibbum* law (Deut. 25:7–8). Indeed, the "gate" where the city's officials sit features prominently in the *megilla* as well, for it is the site where Mordecai is most commonly found (Est. 2:19; 3:2; 4:2, 6; 5:9, 13; 6:12). More specifically, it is at the "gate" where Mordecai discovers the plot whose foiling his procession recognizes: "In those days, while Mordecai was sitting at the king's gate, Bigthan and Teresh, two of the king's eunuchs, who guarded the threshold, became angry and

---

8. See, in this vein, Megilla 13a: "R. Yehuda says: Hadassah was her name. Why was she called Esther (אסתר)? Because she concealed (מסתרת) the truth about herself, as it is stated: 'Esther had not yet made known her kindred nor her people' (Est. 2:20)." See also Ḥullin 139b: "Where does [an allusion to] Esther (אסתר) appear in the Torah? [From the verse stating]: 'And I shall surely hide (הסתר אסתיר)...' (Deut. 31:18)."

conspired to assassinate King Ahasuerus" (Est. 2:21). It is also at the "gate" where the original confrontation between Mordecai and Haman occurs: " And all the king's servants who were in the king's gate would kneel and prostrate themselves before Haman, for so had the king commanded concerning him, but Mordecai would neither kneel nor prostrate himself" (Est. 3:2).[9]

5.   In both texts, fear looms large over the loss of a particular family line – that is, the loss of a "father's/brother's house." In the *yibbum* law, this is most poignantly articulated through the court's previously cited edict: "Thus shall be done to the man who does not build up his brother's house" (בית אחיו). In the *megilla*, it is invoked by Mordecai as he attempts to persuade Esther to intervene on behalf of her fellow Jews: "For if you keep silent at such a time as this, relief and deliverance will rise for the Jews from another place, but you and your father's house (בית אביך) will perish" (Est. 4:14). Instructive, too, is the focus in both texts on the possibility of finding salvation through an alternative source: "If you keep silent at such a time as this, relief and deliverance will rise to the Jews from another place" (ibid.); "The wife of the deceased shall not be married outside the family to another man" (Deut. 25:5).

6.   Both the *ḥoletz*, in the *yibbum* law, and Mordecai, at his procession, are made to "face" the opinion of an adverse party very publicly, and very directly.[10] At the end of the *ḥalitza* ceremony, the sister-in-law of the *ḥoletz* "spits in his face" (וירקה בפניו) – *"veyarka befanav"* (Deut. 25:9). By contrast, Haman, in the *megilla's* turn of phrase,

---

9.   Notably, one midrash explicitly – if somewhat cryptically – connects the gates of the *megilla* to the gates of *yibbum*: "'And all the king's servants who were in the king's gate' (Est. 3:2): these are the magistrates, as it is written: 'Then his brother's widow shall go up to the gate' (Deut. 25:7)" (*Midrash Panim Aḥerot* 2:3).

10.   Interestingly, the term used by the *megilla* to describe Haman as an adversary is "צרר" – as in the phrase "צרר היהודים, adversary (צרר) of the Jews" (Est. 3:10, 8:1, 9:10). This is a very particular designation: it is the same designation, in slightly different grammatical form (צרה as opposed to צרר), used to refer to wives of the same husband (see I Sam. 1:6), and would, of course, commonly apply to the *yevama* after *yibbum* (as it might before *yibbum*, as well). Indeed, the status of the "צרה" is a major issue in Tractate Yevamot – so much so that it is the issue to which the very

"calls out before the face of Mordecai" (וַיִּקְרָא לְפָנָיו) – "*vayikra lefanav*" – "Thus shall be done to the man whom the king desires to honor" (בִיקָרוֹ) – "*biykaro*" (Est. 6:11). Thus – in another clever turn of phrase – the "spit" (יָרַק) that rains down upon the *holetz* is replaced, in the *megilla*, by "glory" (יְקָר) that is conferred upon Mordecai.[11]

7. Both Mordecai's procession and the *yibbum* law culminate with the disgrace of an individual whose shame finds sartorial expression. At the end of Mordecai's procession, "Mordecai returned to the king's gate, but Haman hurried to his house, mourning and with his head covered (חֲפוּי רֹאשׁ)" (Est. 6:12).[12] At the end of the *yibbum* law, "The wife shall go up to him in the presence of the elders, pull his sandal off his foot, spit in his face, and declare, 'Thus shall be done to the man who does not build up his brother's house.' Throughout Israel his family shall be known as 'The house

---

first chapter is addressed (see, generally, Yevamot 1:1–4). Altogether, in fact, the "צָרָה" is mentioned a remarkable forty times throughout the *mishnayot* in Tractate Yevamot.

11. As I was nearing completion of this chapter, I discovered the recording of a private audio lecture in which Rabbi David Fohrman mentions several of the connections we make here between the *yibbum* law and the *megilla*, including #6, which had not occurred to me independently. Rabbi Fohrman argues at length that the *holetz* is motivated by a complicated form of passive-aggressive "hatred" for his dead brother, and, on that foundation, he suggests that the key point of the Purim connections is to hint that Haman's "hatred" is psychologically similar in kind to that of the *holetz*. In our view, however, the primary goal of the Purim-*yibbum* connections is to provide insight into the nature of Mordecai's heroism, rather than Haman's hatred. To that end, the key connection, on our reading, is the "adoption" connection, which scholars do not appear to have previously discussed; Mordecai bringing Esther under his care after her relatives die is given central importance in the *megilla*, just as the *yavam*'s bringing of the *yevama* into *his* family after *her* relative dies is, of course, the central point of the *yibbum* ceremony. See David Fohrman, "Purim: How Thin Is the Line Between Esther and Haman?" *Aleph Beta*, www.alephbeta.org/playlist/thin-line-between-esther-and-haman.

12. Per the Midrash, this "mourning" was observed in part because Haman's daughter committed suicide upon hearing her father issue his honorary proclamation before Mordecai ("Thus shall be done to the man..."). This legend adds yet another layer to the *yibbum* parallel: Mordecai, like the *yavam*, protects a vulnerable relative (Esther) and comes to honor; his adversary (Haman), like the *holetz*, embarrasses a vulnerable relative (Haman's daughter), and is himself debased as well. See Esther Rabba 10:5.

of him whose sandal was pulled off'" (חליץ הנעל‎) (Deut. 25:9–10).
Interestingly, these are inverse outcomes: the foot of the *ḥoletz* is
uncovered, while the head of Haman is covered.[13]

There are, it turns out, several layers of overlap between the Purim story
and the *yibbum* law, each fascinating to consider in its own right. Most
saliently, though, it seems that the author of the *megilla* planted these
parallels in order to point out the contrast between two protagonists
in particular: the *ḥoletz*, on the one hand, and Mordecai, on the other.
For instance, while the *ḥoletz* is derided with a proclamation of ridicule,
Mordecai is escorted by a proclamation of praise. While the *ḥoletz* is
humbled in the city square, Mordecai is honored at the city gate. While
the *ḥoletz* bears the mark of his indignity in his dress, in the *megilla*, it is
Mordecai's *enemy* who meets this fate. In short, sensitive readers of the
megilla cannot participate in Mordecai's parade of glory without also
re-experiencing, from deep within their memory, the *ḥoletz's* march of
shame. It is almost as though the author of the *megilla* were urging us to
identify Mordecai, in his moment of grandeur, as a sort of "anti-*ḥoletz*";
to realize that his triumph over Haman came about, in no small part,
because he had once acted as a kind of "*yavam*."[14]

    This, of course, is not the paradigm we usually apply to Mordecai.
Most of us celebrate Mordecai as a prophet and a preacher; as a politician and a penman; as a polyglot par excellence. Yet while Mordecai did
serve each of these roles on behalf of his people, the Mordecai whom

---

13. Remarkably, the use of "shoes" to taunt an adverse party – a most unusual practice,
to be sure – is not limited to the *yibbum* context. As pointed out to me by Harry
Glazer, it also crops up in the conflict between Mordecai and Haman. To wit, a
midrash relates that Mordecai had once purchased Haman as a slave, and written
the contract of sale on the sole of his shoe; later, when Haman would command
Mordecai to bow to him, Mordecai would respond by waving his shoe before Haman (see *Aggadat Esther* 5:9; cf. Megilla 15a–b). Perhaps it was in connection with
this legend that the custom arose of writing the name "Amalek" – the nation from
which Haman originates – upon the sole of one's shoe.
14. By extension, of course, the parallels we noted also appear to associate Esther with
the *yevama*, and Ahasuerus/Haman with the *ḥoletz*. These secondary connections
are not the focus of the present study, but one readily recognizes the potential they
offer for yielding further insight into the *megilla*.

the *megilla* presents us with was, first and foremost, a *parent*. More specifically – as Baar noted duly – Mordecai was an *adoptive parent*. He was, in other words, a quasi-*yavam*:

> Now there was a Jew in the capital of Shushan whose name was Mordecai son of Jair son of Shimei son of Kish, a Benjaminite, who had been carried away from Jerusalem among the captives carried away with King Jeconiah of Judah, whom King Nebuchadnezzar of Babylon had carried away. He had adopted Hadassah, that is Esther, his uncle's daughter, for she had neither father nor mother; the girl was fair and beautiful, and when her father and her mother died, Mordecai adopted her as his own daughter... (Est. 2:5–7).

Like the *yavam*, Mordecai welcomed into his home the female survivor of a deceased male relative.[15] Unlike the *ḥoletz*, who "refused" (מ.א.נ) to show magnanimity under such circumstances, Mordecai, in the *megilla's* turn of phrase, quietly "adopted" (א.מ.נ) Esther in her time of need.[16] This, apparently, is critical information: it is among the first significant details about Mordecai included in the text's introduction of him, and it is repeated for emphasis before Esther's momentous audience with Ahasuerus a few verses later (Est. 2:15). Both explicitly and intertextually, then, the *megilla* seems to be positioning Mordecai's adoption of Esther as a pivotal event in the Purim narrative. One even begins to sense that the two stories are interdependent – that Mordecai's emergence as guardian of Israel was made possible *only because* he had previously claimed guardianship of Esther.

---

15. Interestingly, classical *yibbum* concerns the brotherly line, whereas in the *megilla*, it is the *parents* of Mordecai and of Esther who are brothers (Est. 2:7). This distinction gives genealogical expression to the notion that the relationship between Mordecai and Esther represents some sort of "*yibbum* derivative"; as a parent births a child, so too does the expansive ethos of *yibbum* engender, over time, ever-widening conceptions of familial obligation.

16. Per the Talmud, moreover, Mordecai actually ended up marrying Esther (see Megilla 13a). This interpretation both strengthens, and finds support in, the *yibbum* parallel we are proposing.

In fact, that may be precisely what the *yibbum* law predicts. For it turns out that the *yibbum* law, delivered near the end of the Book of Deuteronomy, is followed a few verses later by yet another law relevant to Purim: the law of Amalek. It was an Amalekite, of course – Haman the Amalekite – who instigated the *megilla*'s core conflict, by plotting genocide against the people of Mordecai. And it was due to earlier such attempts that the Torah promised, in Deuteronomy, the abolition of Amalek's legacy: "You shall blot (תמחה) the memory of Amalek" (Deut. 25:19). Yet it was in the law issued just *prior* to this one – the *yibbum* law – that the Torah *first* raised the issue of "blotted" memories: "When a man dies," that law demands, let his brother adopt the family, "so that the name [of the decedent] shall not be blotted out (ימחה) of Israel."

This law, implies the Torah, is the primary imperative – the alpha and omega; the *sine qua non*; the precondition of Jewish continuity. To prevail over those who seek to erase you from history, the Torah teaches, you must – above all else – ensure that you are not tacitly assisting those efforts. Therefore, you must take care of the *yevama* before you take care of Amalek. You must tend to your family before you tend to your foes. You must, in short, do all that you can to support the vulnerable among you – the deceased, the widow, and the orphan – before you call upon God to reciprocate in kind.[17]

All this, Mordecai did. As an official at the "city's gate," he likely exhorted countless *yevamim* who presented themselves before him to protect the welfare of their *yevamot* and to preserve the memory of their brothers. As Esther's adoptive parent, he himself protected the welfare of his cousin, and preserved the memory of his uncle. And it was thanks to this "strong bond of sympathy" that Mordecai managed, in the days of Purim, "to keep a people of peculiar race and religion specially united in the land of their adoption."[18]

17. See, in this regard, *Lekaḥ Tov* Esther 2:7: "'For she had no father or mother' (Est. 2:7): Let the orphan come, who has no father or mother, and serve as the redeemer of Israel, about whom it is said: 'We became orphans, and there is no father' (Lam. 5:3)."
18. "The Hebrew Orphan Asylum," *New York Times*, November 6, 1863, https://www.nytimes.com/1863/11/06/archives/the-hebrew-orphan-asylum.html.

A Tale of Two Readings: Diasporic Duality in the Book of Esther

Rabbi Shmuel Hain

T wo singular features of the halakhic schedule of *megilla* reading inform my teaching and preaching about the Book of Esther, as an educator and synagogue rabbi living in the diaspora. Each of these halakhic phenomena is unique to the Book of Esther and requires explication. Together they underscore the duality of this beloved biblical book, its multifaceted theological messages regarding Jewish life in the diaspora, and its nuanced view of the Israel/diaspora dynamic.[1]

---

1. There are many other aspects of the holiday and of the *megilla* that do not directly emerge from the diasporic nature of Purim and Esther per se, even if they may be impacted by the exilic context of the story. For an exploration of some of these themes, see https://www.yutorah.org/lectures/lecture.cfm/757402/rabbi-shmuel-hain/the-mitzvot-of-purim-more-than-meets-the-eye/.

Rabbi Shmuel Hain

I. NIGHTTIME AND DAYTIME READINGS

One most unusual aspect of the *megilla* reading schedule is the requirement to read Esther twice, first at night and again during the day of Purim. This reading redux has no parallel in Jewish liturgy.[2] It is especially curious given that the original practice was to read the *megilla* only once, by day. The *mishnayot* in Tractate Megilla only make reference to a daytime reading. The nighttime reading is first attested to in the Talmud Bavli (Megilla 4a) in the name of the *amora*, R. Yehoshua b. Levi: "R. Yehoshua b. Levi said: A person is obligated *likrota* (to read it) at night and then *lishnota* (to repeat it) during the day."[3] Indeed, the consensus of medieval decisors is that the daytime reading retains primary status.[4] Why, then, even have a nighttime reading of Esther?

This question becomes even more acute in many Jewish communities where the nighttime reading has become more popularly attended than the daytime reading. Why did the Rabbis institute a nighttime reading and risk overshadowing, and even displacing, the more central obligation of the daytime reading by making it seem redundant?[5]

2. No other book in the biblical canon is read twice in one day. Some sections of the Torah are read twice over the course of a year. For example, the conclusion of *Ki Tetzeh* is read both when its turn comes in the yearly rotation and on the Shabbat before Purim. In these instances, however, the passage is read in two different contexts – once as the standard weekly Torah reading and once as the special reading before Purim of *Parashat Zakhor*. The only other instance when the community reads the same text twice in the same day is the Torah reading on minor fast days (*"Vayeḥal"*), which is read at both *Shaḥarit* and *Minḥa*. Nevertheless, the case of the Book of Esther is still singular, as every individual (and not just the community as a whole) is obligated to repeat the reading (of an entire book!) in the same manner and, ostensibly, for the same purpose within twenty-four hours.

3. Academic scholars and traditional commentators (see, for example, Rabbi Shlomo Hakohen [Vilna], *Responsa Binyan Shlomo*, vol. I, no. 58) alike have noted this historical development of the dual readings.

4. This perspective is most clearly expressed in the Tosafists' view that the daytime reading requires a second *Sheheḥeyanu* blessing because the concepts of publicizing the miracle and the other daytime obligations make it the primary reading (see *Tosafot* Megilla 4a, s.v. *"Ḥayav"*).

5. In fact, the language and logic of R. Yehoshua b. Levi's ruling led some of his students to misinterpret his view and assume the *megilla* was only to be read once, at night. See the continuation of the passage in Megilla 4a: "Some students understood

One explanation for the additional nighttime reading is that it is precisely intended to be preliminary and preparatory to promote a more careful, in-depth daytime reading. Netziv (*Meromei Sadeh, Megilla* 4a) notes the curious verb the Talmud employs in describing the daytime reading. Instead of using the same, more straightforward term for the daytime reading as for the nighttime – *likrot* – to read, R. Yehoshua b. Levi uses the atypical and ambiguous term *lishnot*. Netziv explains that *lishnot* means to study, not merely to repeat. "The daytime reading needs to be done with familiarity and knowledge so as to understand and analyze the text. Like any learning of a passage, one's first pass is done without analyzing its elements. On the second reading, one is able to pay closer attention for deeper analysis." For Netziv, the initial reading familiarizes one with the words and basic storyline while the second reading furnishes the reader with an opportunity for a hermeneutic reading more characteristic of more thorough, in-depth study.[6]

But a more fundamental explanation for the double reading of Esther each Purim may be offered. In Harvard professor Jon D. Levenson's introduction to his commentary of Esther, he writes: "The book of Esther is many things, so many, in fact, that it would be a capital mistake to view it from only one angle." Levenson proceeds to list some of the more familiar readings of Esther: a tale of palace intrigue, a story of lethal danger to the Jews narrowly averted by heroic rescue, a fairy tale of an orphan in exile rising to the rank of the most powerful woman (or person) in the empire, and a story of how a humiliated and endangered minority came to be respected and

---

from this (the term *lishnota*) that one is obligated to read at night and to study its tractate of Mishna by day (as the term *lishnota* can be understood to mean studying Mishna)."

6. This explanation of why we require two readings of Esther aligns with the broader midrashic theme of Purim as a holiday celebrating the renewal of the Sinai covenant, specifically expressed through the willing acceptance of the Torah and a commitment to study it with greater depth. See, for example, Shabbat 88a. What better way to highlight this motif than to take the central text of the holiday and add a preparatory reading, thereby making the primary daytime reading a microcosm of the rededication of the covenant and an opportunity for in-depth study?

feared by the gentiles with one of their own honored by appointment to the second highest post in the empire. Perhaps it is because of all these angles, and many more, as well as the multiple literary layers of the *megilla* including satire, comedy, and tragedy, that two readings of the text were deemed necessary. As Levenson himself notes, "…readers who are satisfied that they know what Esther means would be well advised to examine it again in search of other dimensions."[7] Reading the *megilla* on Purim a second time is not merely about being afforded the opportunity to study the same narrative in greater detail. It is a call to approach the story a second time from a different perspective.

To take this a step further, I encourage students and congregants to embrace the rabbinic obligation to hear the *megilla* twice on Purim by actually reading the Book of Esther twice and to read it each time from opposite vantage points. Indeed, each of the protagonists and their actions may be read from radically different, and even opposite, perspectives. Is Ahasuerus a foolish king or a politically cunning, and wicked, monarch? Is Mordecai a paragon of righteousness and wise political influence or is his story a cautionary tale of a Jewish courtier seeking too much influence? Is Esther merely an object of the men in her life (Mordecai, Ahasuerus) or is she the paradigm of Jewish female agency and heroism? In each of these examples, reading the *megilla* from these opposing perspectives enriches the narrative in significant ways.

But beyond its main characters, the double reading of the *megilla* facilitates deriving dual – and even dueling – messages from the story. These takeaways emerge from central questions of the narrative and a number of dimensions of the story.[8] In teaching about dual readings

---

7. Jon D. Levenson, *Esther: A Commentary*: Old Testament Library (London, 1997), 1.
8. These include political, sociopolitical, particularist, and universalist dimensions. It is also important to note that many modern readers derive opposite messages from Esther. In addition to the commentary by Levenson listed above, a number of recent works on Esther have informed my teaching in general and this chapter in particular: Adele Berlin, *Esther*, JPS Bible Commentary (Philadelphia, 2001); Erica Brown, *Esther: Power, Fate, and Fragility in Exile* (New Milford/Jerusalem, 2020); Michael Eisenberg, *The Vanishing Jew: A Wake Up Call From the Book of Esther* (2017);

of the *megilla*, I often focus on its most essential theological question: What is God's role in the story?

God does not appear in the story of Esther, nor is God mentioned or referred to, not even by circumlocution. Yet, God is not simply absent from the story, because God may very well be the central character in Esther from beginning to end. This silence regarding God's place in the events of the story has yielded two fundamentally opposite readings. Many modern readers, including Bible scholars and theologians, assert that Esther is operating in a world where God is fully absent. As Yeshiva University professor Aaron Koller states: "The author of Esther makes it abundantly clear not only that God is not playing a role in history, but that his place has been usurped by humans...God is not just hidden, but he has been replaced."[9] In this reading, God is not mentioned in the *megilla* because the author has written a story that does not involve God in any sense.

Traditional commentators and many modern Bible scholars reject this reading, marshaling textual and thematic support[10] to prove that the Book of Esther teaches (or at least assumes) that God plays an active, if hidden, role in all its events. As the literary critic Harold Fisch writes: "In the end there is only one ruler whose commands, never officially promulgated, are unchanging and whose will prevails. He lurks behind the costly hangings of the court and whispers in the ear of Ahasuerus in the night. It is of him that the subtext speaks and whose deeds it records."[11] For these readers, Esther's vital message that the divine Being is always controlling events even when God's presence is hidden, emerges from, and is reinforced by, the omission of God's name.[12]

Michael V. Fox, "The Religion of the Book of Esther," *Judaism* 39, no. 2 (Spring 1990): 135–147; idem., *Character and Ideology in the Book of Esther*, 2nd ed. (Grand Rapids, 2001); Yoram Hazony, *God and Politics in Esther* (Cambridge, 2016); Aaron Koller, *Esther in Ancient Jewish Thought* (Cambridge, 2014).

9. Koller, 99–101.

10. See Fox, 137–144, for a thorough overview, with analysis and critique, of these textual allusions, plot elements, and larger motifs.

11. Harold Fisch, *Poetry with a Purpose: Biblical Poetics and Interpretation* (Bloomington, 1988), 14.

12. This is the classic rabbinic approach to Esther, expressed in the oft-cited midrash (see Ḥullin 139b): "*Esther min haTorah minayin? Ve'anokhi haster astir* – What is the

But each of these readings on its own downplays the full significance and impact of the *megilla*'s silence about God's role. The requirement to read Esther twice bids us to fully inhabit that silence by embracing each of these seemingly mutually exclusive readings. Doing so invites the reader to acknowledge the deliberate uncertainty about God's role in the story. As Michael V. Fox describes it: "The religious attitude of the book is like an optical illusion that shifts orientation as you stare at it, but which (to continue the analogy) can temporarily be fixed in a certain orientation by the viewer's decision to see it one way or the other."[13]

To take one important example. One of the *megilla*'s critical turning points, Mordecai's impassioned speech to Esther imploring her to act on behalf of the Jews, captures the epistemological indeterminacy of the book as a whole.[14] Mordecai warns Esther: "For if you keep silent at this time,

---

source of Esther in the Torah? 'And I will surely hide My countenance.'" Yoram Hazony proposes an important modification to this classic reading, taking into account the politics of Esther. He suggests that Esther is a paradigmatic example of the combination of human and divine causation.

> But the fact that Haman's downfall and the ultimate reversal of his decree are every bit the political handiwork of Mordechai and Esther, and the fact that God's name has been erased from this story and from this picture of the world, does not create a picture of the world without God in it. What it creates is, rather, a picture of the world without prophets, without men and women who know how to recognize God's voice and see his hand in the course of events. *But the world is the same world*, whether or not there are any prophets to give God's name to things. *God is still there, as he was before.*" (Hazony, 205; emphasis added)

Hazony's reading argues for the book's continuity with the rest of the Bible and minimizes the actual discontinuity of Esther from the rest of the Bible, especially in its silence about the role of God.

> Even with God's name removed, the *plain meaning* of the Esther narrative is that the young queen and the Jews of Susa petitioned God to strengthen her hand in her approach to the king, and that God answered their cry, granting Esther success in all her efforts. *Another way of saying the very same thing, in the idiom of the prophets*, is that God raised up Mordechai and Esther to save Israel, and that God delivered Haman and his allies into their hands.

The major flaw in Hazony's reading is that the text deliberately does not use the same language as the rest of the prophets.

13. See Fox, 146.
14. Stuart Lasine, in an important review article, identifies the various typologies of indeterminacy in the Bible. See Stuart Lasine, "Indeterminacy and the Bible: A Review

relief and deliverance will come to the Jews from another quarter (lit. place), while you and your father's house will perish. And *who knows*, if it was for a time like this that you reached this royal station" (4:14; emphasis added).

This statement is often cited as the best evidence that the *megilla* recognizes God as an active force in its events. Indeed, many scholars and commentators read Mordecai's conviction in an inevitable salvation as predicated on God's eternal covenant with the Jewish people. But even this statement of Mordecai remains a subtle allusion, a hint. Mordecai professes his faith that the Jews will be saved, but the basis for this confidence remains ambiguous.[15] Even more significantly, Mordecai's phrase, "who knows?" highlights his hesitancy. By proffering it as a "who knows," Mordecai both expresses a possibility, while granting that it is only that.[16]

This pivotal passage, and the *megilla* as a whole, carefully create and maintain uncertainty on the essential question of God's role in the narrative, thereby refusing to foreclose either possible reading. This uncertainty is precisely what the *megilla* seeks to convey. Because in a profound sense, this uncertainty is what defines Esther as a quintessentially diasporic text. The Book of Esther does not just take place in exile; it captures the essence of Jewish life in the diaspora, with all of its uncertainty. In contrast to the biblical books which recount God's manifest presence in the lives of the Israelites during the time of the Temple and prophecy, God's presence is hidden in Esther, as it is throughout the trials and tribulations of *galut*. In the diaspora, God's presence is not visible, audible, or dramatic. The diasporic duality of the Book of Esther teaches us that uncertainty about God's activity is endemic to diasporic existence.

To be clear, the uncertainty of diasporic life does not mean repudiating faith. The theology of exile expressed in the question "who knows?"

Article of Literary and Anthropological Theories and Their Application to Biblical Texts," *Hebrew Studies* 27, no. 1 (1986): 48–80. An epistemological indeterminacy refers to an intended indeterminacy of the text.

15. Is it God or, as Fox suggests, Jewry's inner strength and potential for self-help?

16. Note also that Mordecai does not state unequivocally that Esther might have become queen for this specific moment. Instead, he phrases it as perhaps you have been placed in this position to meet exigencies in a time "like this." This point is also made by Fox, 145. See the critique of Levenson, 15–21. Hazony, chapter 25, has a full analysis of all biblical examples of the phrase "who knows" to support his reading of Esther.

is a theology of possibility. And Mordecai's challenge, a challenge met and exceeded by Esther's heroism, is one of faith and decisive action in the face of uncertainty. As Fox writes, "The author of Esther would have us hold to confidence even when lacking certainty and an understanding of details. To *act* in such circumstances demands special courage … to act on a faith that is more hope than certitude."

This is what it means to be a Jew living in *galut*. To simultaneously embrace those who read Esther, and understand the roughly two thousand years of Jewish exile, as reflecting total divine absence, and those who see clearly the hidden hand of divine providence in Esther and throughout the twists and turns of Jewish history. By identifying fully with the duality of Esther and diasporic life, we may yet achieve the most profound, and realistic, stance of faith – a faith rooted in the possibility of providence, even when events seem to weigh against its likelihood as in the dark days after the issuance of Haman's decree. Ultimately, the *megilla*'s indeterminacy conveys the message that we, too, may hold on to the possibility of faith, even when we are uncertain about where God is in times of crisis and God's role in our deliverance.

The rabbinic requirement to read Esther twice, then, fosters an appreciation for the duality of the book and its theological messages.[17] When our readings of the text fully embrace this duality, we act out and demonstratively fulfill the great theme of Esther – *venahafokh hu* – the reverse (or the opposite) occurred (9:1).[18]

II. PURIM AND SHUSHAN PURIM

A second unique aspect to the scheduling of *megilla* reading involves the observance of Purim as a whole. Strikingly, Purim is celebrated on two different days (the fourteenth and fifteenth of Adar), Purim and

---

17. In addition to the duality of the protagonists and the messages of the *megilla* we have sketched, Levenson summarizes the many structural and stylistic dualities of the book; see Levenson, 5–12.

18. Erica Brown, in her preface to *Esther*, makes an additional note about Esther and exile: "The Book of Esther asks its celebrants to turn the world upside down because that is what can be expected in exile: the unpredictable, the surprise turn, the change in fate. If Purim is a holiday to examine exile, then Esther is its textbook and our guide" (x-xi).

Shushan Purim, depending on one's location. The distinction between the experiences of the walled and unwalled cities at the time of the Purim story is recorded in the *megilla* itself (9:15–28), but it remains most unusual to have different populations celebrating a holiday on different days.[19] It even seems to subvert one of the leitmotifs of Purim, the importance of fostering unity amongst the Jews in order to overcome Haman's plot.[20] Moreover, the normative view that determines which locales are considered walled cities, namely those which were walled at the time of Joshua (see Mishna Megilla 1:1), is exceedingly peculiar.[21] Why establish two different days of Purim in the first place and why consider the walled cities in the time of Joshua as walled cities for the purpose of Shushan Purim?

To answer these questions, we need to examine closely the relationship between Purim and Shushan Purim. By understanding their intricate dynamic we will gain deeper insight into the nature of the split celebration of Purim and its message for diaspora/Israel relations today.

---

19. Nahmanides, in his opening comments on Megilla (2a), strenuously objects to the division of Purim into two separate days. See his commentary there for a lengthy explanation of the phenomenon based on the history of the establishment of the holiday.

    In light of the ambiguity of verse 21, the Rabbis could have interpreted the *megilla* in a way to unify observance; e.g., both locales should celebrate both days. This possible reading, along with another possibility, to have Shushan residents celebrate a second day on the fifteenth after celebrating with everyone on the fourteenth, are raised in Megilla 2b along with others.

    The walled vs. non-walled distinction seems to have unfolded in stages. Initially, the *megilla* contrasts Shushan with all other cities (see verses 15–18). Only beginning with verse 19 does the *megilla* differentiate between walled and unwalled cities and the language it uses – "*osim*" – may imply that this verse is attesting to a practice that had developed years after the events of the narrative.

20. Many others have noted that Esther's call to gather all of the Jews together to fast on her behalf (4:16) may serve as a corrective to Haman's claim that the Jews are a spread out and divided people (3:8). This is further memorialized in the requirement to distribute gifts to fellow Jews on the holiday of Purim (9:19, 22).

21. It is unclear when the status of walled cities was determined to be based on the time of Joshua as opposed to the time of Ahasuerus. The Tosefta (1:1) records a debate on this point while the Mishna records only the view of the time of Joshua. The Jerusalem and Babylonian Talmuds (Talmud Yerushalmi and Talmud Bavli) each have extensive discussions of this debate.

The Bavli makes two suggestive statements about the observance of Purim and Shushan Purim. These formulations, at first glance, appear to be in tension with each other. First, in its discussion of a range of options for the proper celebration of the days of Purim (2b), the Bavli raises the possibility that residents of unwalled towns should celebrate on the fourteenth day of Adar while residents of walled cities should have the option of celebrating on either the fourteenth or the fifteenth. The Gemara rejects this suggestion by citing the language of the verse (9:31), "In their times," which implies mutually exclusive celebrations. "The time when the residents of one place celebrate Purim is specifically not the same time when the residents of another place celebrate Purim." Further on (5b), the Bavli raises the question of working on Purim and Shushan Purim and notes that eulogies and fasting are prohibited on both days of Purim, even on the day which is not observed in the specific locale: "Rava said: It is prohibited for those who observe Purim on this day to eulogize and fast on that day, and those who observe Purim on that day to eulogize on this day."

So which formulation of Purim and Shushan Purim is correct? Are the two observances totally distinct, justifying mutually exclusive celebrations on two different days, or do the two days form a unified whole, as per the prohibition on fasting and eulogizing on both days for all? The most precise answer is that both formulations are correct and the relationship between the two days is nuanced. The *megilla* makes clear that the experience of salvation was markedly different for Shushan (which later became walled cities as a whole) than it was for other cities. The Bavli's initial statement (2b) affirms that Jewish unity does not require uniformity. Hence, the two different experiences of salvation require two distinct days of celebration. At the same time, the *megilla* also makes clear that the Jewish people as a whole faced the existential threat of extinction. Therefore, even when not celebrating Purim in your home locale, the Bavli rules (5b) that one must identify with the experience of Jews in a different place and refrain from eulogizing and fasting.

The Yerushalmi (Megilla 1:1) has an extensive discussion about why the time of Joshua became determinative for the walled cities. The Yerushalmi explains that this time period was chosen in order to afford honor to the Land of Israel (and to Jerusalem in particular) which was in a state of destruction at the time of the Purim story.[22] This remarkable explanation requires unpacking. Logically, the Yerushalmi concedes, the status of walled cities should be determined based upon whether they were walled in the time of Ahasuerus rather than the time of Joshua. However, such a determination would have diminished the standing of Jerusalem and other destroyed walled cities in the Land of Israel. Why is this significant? Why was it so important to include Jerusalem in the designation of walled cities?

It appears that the centrality of Israel as a whole, and Jerusalem in particular, are at stake in the celebration of Purim. Many others have noted that there are only two cities in all of the Bible which are referred to with the moniker "*bira*" – capital city. Those two cities are Jerusalem (specifically the Temple) and Shushan (specifically the King's palace).[23] One layer of the Purim story as a paradigmatic tale of Jews in exile suggests that Shushan had become the new Jerusalem, perhaps even for the Jews residing in Shushan. As an important corrective, the celebration of Shushan Purim cannot be held without celebrating that very day in Jerusalem. To afford honor to Israel, indeed.

Two messages emerge from our overview of Purim and Shushan Purim. First, the celebrations on these days are both distinct and interconnected, teaching us that Jewish unity acknowledges and respects the experience of others, while still maintaining one's own identity. Second, in celebrating Shushan Purim we dare not forget the capital of the Jewish people and the centrality of Jerusalem.

Taken together, the dual lessons of Purim and Shushan Purim provide us with an apt metaphor for engaging questions about Israel/diaspora relations and Jewish peoplehood today. Celebrating Purim on different days while acknowledging the experience of Jews in other locales is a powerful model for the Israel/diaspora relationship. It teaches us that we can identify the independent significance and stature of both

---

22. Like the Bavli, the Yerushalmi notes the verbal analogy (*prazi/prazi*) as support for this view. But the linguistic derivation is not the primary reason in the Yerushalmi, in contrast to the Bavli. Maimonides (Laws of Megilla 1:5) codifies the reason of the Yerushalmi.

23. For one example, see Yehuda Zoldan, "Shushan HaBira ViYerushalayim HaBira," *Maamarei Emunat Itekha* 33 (Shevat-Adar II 5760), http://www.daat.ac.il/daat/kitveyet/emunat/33/03302.htm.

the Israeli and diaspora Jewish communities, even as we recognize that we are both just a part of the Jewish nation as a whole. At the same time, including Jerusalem in the celebration of Shushan Purim reminds us of Israel's centrality as the corporate headquarters of the Jewish people, even and especially for those of us residing in the diaspora.

Pop Culture Purim

Hidden Heroine: Interpretations of Queen Esther in Two Children's Picture Books

Dr. Emily Schneider

American children's books about Queen Esther adopt different perspectives on her singular role in Jewish history, but virtually all invite readers to empathize with her extraordinary situation. Esther's story highlights both the perils of Jewish life throughout history, and the necessity for both men and women to combine subterfuge and courage to survive. Yet one inescapable fact about Purim is the female heroism at the center of the tale, which offers authors a chance to explore the life of a woman defined by contradiction: Esther must first conceal her identity, but later reveals it in an act of selfless bravery. In both Mordicai Gerstein's *Queen Esther the Morning Star*[1] and *Esther's Story*, by Diane

---

1. Mordicai Gerstein, *Queen Esther the Morning Star* (New York, 2000).

Wolkstein and illustrated by Juan Wijngaard,[2] Esther begins as a vulnerable figure, totally dependent on Mordecai, her male guardian. Only her exceptional beauty brings her to the attention of King Ahasuerus, a figure of fickle male authority, and her fidelity to his arbitrary rules is all that keeps her safe. Esther's commitment to saving her people from annihilation leads her to negotiate the possibilities of asserting herself without threatening her own existence. In Gerstein's version, Esther enacts a key role in a colorful morality tale, presented with theatrical excitement and an inevitable happy ending. Wolkstein and Wijngaard present Esther through her own words, as she narrates her progress from orphan to queen with introspection and dramatic tension. Both versions of the queen seek to reconcile the limits of her gender role with her ultimate triumph as a defender of her people.

Mordicai Gerstein (1935–2019) infused his many works for children with a sense of joy and optimism; his interpretation of Esther is no exception. His prefatory "Author's Note" identifies Esther's Persian name (Ishtar) with Venus, the morning star, "the last to fade after all the other stars are gone." Esther embodies, therefore, a paradox of the Jewish people. She is hidden from view, yet she endures past the machinations of Haman and his allies. None of the threats which Esther faces deter her, although Gerstein's descriptions of her position in the capricious world of Ahasuerus' court cast doubt on her eventual fate. The king is foolish, and emotionally dependent on others' deference to his power. As Penny Schine Gold noted in *Making the Bible Modern*,[3] a comprehensive study of twentieth-century children's Bibles as used in supplemental Jewish education, heroines such as Rebecca, Deborah, Ruth, and Esther were popular subjects of this illustrated genre: "The resulting combination of text and picture provides children with a vision of female presence beyond what the text alone could provide."[4]

A potentially troubling element of the Purim narrative, as modern sensibilities encounter it, is that Esther's appearance is predicated on the disappearance of another queen: Vashti. Gerstein is faithful to the biblical

---

2. Diane Wolkstein, *Esther's Story* (New York, 1996).
3. Penny Schine Gold, *Making the Bible Modern* (Ithaca, 2003).
4. Ibid., 159.

account of Vashti's disobedience, in which her insolence is compounded by the fact that she is hosting a women's banquet when she chooses to refuse her husband's command. Seated at a table surrounded by her guests, "all the princesses and wives of the governors and satraps over whom she ruled," Gerstein's Vashti is as imperious as Ahasuerus himself. "Tell the king I will not come," Gerstein has her respond, turning her face to one side and stretching out her hand toward the king's emissary. Gerstein conveys the injustice of Vashti's banishment through this scene and the king's hysterical response. Soon he is seeking a new queen who will obey him unconditionally. The contrast between the two scenes is unavoidable. Vashti is degraded from her position holding court over other women to being dragged through the streets by the king's guards. The biblical account is explicit that Vashti's actions set a dangerous precedent to other wives, who might be tempted to assert their own independence. Since Gerstein omits any reference to rabbinic sources which depict Vashti as morally debased, punished for her immodesty with a disfiguring tail (Megilla 12b), children are left with an unexplained injustice: Esther, a woman exalted in Jewish history for her courage, is only in a position to act because of another woman's rebellion and replacement.

Esther becomes the lucky wife chosen for her beauty. Mordecai warns her not to reveal her Jewish identity because her new husband is impetuous and cruel. Esther has no choice but to participate in this terrifying charade, made even more fraught when the villain, Haman, appears. He poisons the king's mind against Esther's cousin and the Jewish people, asserting they are a danger within the realm as they remain stubbornly loyal to their own laws. Gerstein's pictures are comically exaggerated, lessening the sense of emergency which the details of Haman's nefarious plot provide. When Esther cautiously approaches the king, Gerstein shows him as an obese and scowling tyrant insecurely clutching his sword. When he notices her, he is "overcome with love." The cartoon-like transition from fury to pliant agreement with his wife is the stuff of caricature. Similarly, Haman's overblown arrogance deforms him, "his eyes popping with rage," a verbal image matched by Gerstein's picture of him stamping and fuming. Even the construction of a gallows on which Haman plans to kill the hated Mordecai turns into a family project, his wife looking on as their ten sons struggle to make the structure work.

Dr. Emily Schneider

When Esther finally summons up all her strength to intervene on behalf of her people, confessing that she is a Jew and a target of Haman's murderous plot, her husband's response diminishes the moment's gravity: "I completely forgot! I don't even remember why he wanted to do such a stupid thing…. Guards…take him away!" Gerstein has him proclaim. The book concludes with a transition from narrowly averted tragedy to the delights of holiday observance, as Mordecai, Ahasuerus, and Esther consume a huge plate of *hamantaschen* pastries. Esther is no longer hidden, saved by her own daring, but also by the unpredictable whims of a self-centered male ruler. In the end, her story is a reassuring fable about good triumphing over malice and of the continuation of Jewish existence through history.

Esther's Story offers a different perspective on the heroic queen. Diane Wolkstein (1942–2013) draws on both the Bible and on midrashim from various talmudic and post-talmudic sources. In her complex re-imagining of Esther's life, complemented by Juan Wijngaard's (b. 1951) expressive paintings, the woman who emerges is both object and subject, a victim of exploitation as well as an icon of female valor. *Esther's Story* is for older picture-book readers, who will identify with its premise, that Esther is keeping a diary given to her by her guardian, Mordecai. Esther, an orphan, is aware that her true name is Hadassah, "myrtle," chosen by her mother for its association with the fragrant plant, but soon a series of events related by Mordecai force her to adopt a new identity. Hadassah goes into a form of hiding, to be replaced by Esther, meaning "secret or concealed." From then on, Esther is forced to conceal her true self, and to act as a proxy in a larger plan effected by men. Wolkstein does not conceal the emotional effects of this arrangement on the young girl.

Wolkstein and Wijngaard expose the darker side of Ahasuerus' rejection of Vashti and his subsequent attachment to Esther. When the story begins she is a young orphan living under her guardian's protection, but soon she confronts an abrupt change. Mordecai transfers Esther from his home to the king's court, where she will live with other women as they are evaluated to replace Vashti, the disobedient queen. Wolkstein, unlike Gerstein, does not imply any justifiable streak of independence in Vashti; Mordecai simply tells Esther that Vashti refused the king's command and was banished. Given that Wolkstein does draw on what she refers to as "oral legends," it is significant that, like Gerstein, she refrains from offering any additional interpretations about Vashti's motives. Readers are left with the impression that the women are like two sides of a coin, different images who share the same fate of female dependence on men.

Esther and her fellow candidates for queen are not friends in a women's dormitory; they are young women being groomed for their sexual attractiveness to a powerful man, a normal situation in the ancient world. Wolkstein does not have Esther protest the injustice of this arrangement, avoiding historical anachronism. Instead, she focuses on the companionship of the girls, relating how they comfort one another, even as some "cry from homesickness." A group portrait of multi-ethnic women in their all-female environment envisions what is effectively a prison from a more promising perspective. When Mordecai visits, he brings traditional Jewish foods, as well as stories of the biblical patriarchs and matriarchs. Esther, believing that the king allows freedom of worship, does not understand the source of Mordecai's reminders to hide her background. Both her Jewishness and her gender have forced Esther into confinement. Her physical beauty is about to change her status, as Ahasuerus elevates her above the other women, but her Jewish self, like her real name, must remain hidden.

In *Queen Esther the Morning Star*, Ahasuerus is a dangerous buffoon. In *Esther's Story*, he is a majestic ruler, handsome, and sensitive to Esther's special qualities, calling her his "shining one." The power imbalance between them is minimized in a courtship scene, where Esther spontaneously picks up a rose and puts it in the king's hair. When he says to her appreciatively, "How beautiful you are!" she turns the phrase back toward him in a gesture of equality: "How beautiful *you* are!" Here the author has chosen to create a humane background to Esther's marriage, suggesting that mutual love separated it from the objectifying way in which Esther was chosen. Still, Esther is troubled by the rapid changes in her life: "Some days when I look in the mirror, I see the queen of Persia. Other days I see Esther, who was once Hadassah." The author does not attempt to easily resolve the two parts of Esther's life, as a woman who has been objectified and controlled by men, and one who becomes a symbol of valor and Jewish survival.

While in Gerstein's book Ahasuerus is consistently portrayed as an impulsive fool, it is more difficult to reconcile Wolkstein's romantic figure of the king with his blind acceptance of Haman's edict to destroy the Jews. Readers will share Esther's sense of panic, as she reads Mordecai's letter imploring her to save her people by risking her own life. He cites a prophecy by "a holy woman from Jerusalem" that Esther would become Persia's queen after Vashti's removal. The inconvenient truth of Vashti's harsh punishment is now identified as part of a higher purpose. Esther looks out the window at the morning star, source of her non-Jewish name, but returns to her original self for strength. Jewish literacy appears in Wijngaard's image as open volumes on the floor of her room. She remembers God's prophecy in Isaiah (46:4), "When your hair is white, I will be with you. I made you. I will care for you. I will sustain and rescue you," and decides, "If I am killed, then I will be killed" (a translation of Esther 4:16's "*vekhaasher avadeti, avadeti*").

While attending the banquet which Esther has requested, the king is reminded that Mordecai has saved his life and Esther knows she must act. Pointing the finger at Haman, and finally uncovering her true self, she declares, "Since I am a Jew, I too will die." Ahasuerus has his opportunity for heroism, sentencing Haman to die on his own gallows, although, without Esther's intervention, the king would have delegated to his minister the right to exterminate his innocent subjects. The Jewish people are empowered by the king to defeat their enemies, Esther and her husband live in harmony, and Mordecai's dignity is restored. But Wolkstein ends the book on an unusual note, inviting young readers to encounter the queen as an old woman. Over seventy, her white hair echoing the prophecy of Isaiah which had strengthened her resolve, Esther remembers her extraordinary heroism with characteristic modesty. As the festival of Purim is about to begin, she prepares to personally retell her story. Often the image of Queen Esther is frozen in children's books as one of an impossibly timeless beauty. Wolkstein allows her to grow old, and to "merit the respect which Jewish tradition demands for the aged."

Queen Esther is a symbol of selfless bravery, of Jewish female courage and beauty, but also of the constraints of gender. Mordicai Gerstein, in *Queen Esther the Morning Star*, frames the course of Esther's life as a chaotic adventure leading to success; the Jewish people survive and live on to eat *hamantaschen*. The Jewish girl of Diane Wolkstein and Juan Wijngaard's tale must survive oppression as a woman and the emotional hazards of a dual identity before she can rise to protect herself and her people. Children reading both books will note that the two Esthers embody some of the contradictions of the festival itself. Famously, the Book of Esther does not mention God, although it is full of imperfect humans acting according to their interpretation of God's will. Purim is a day of raucous celebration preceded by a day of fasting. Jews as near-victims are transformed into Jews as victors. Relating the story of Purim to children might also acknowledge the many dimensions, even difficult contradictions, of Esther's place in Jewish history. A woman forced to rely on her beauty, uprooted from her home, and deprived of her Jewish identity, becomes a revered symbol of Jewish strength in the face of adversity. The paradoxes of Queen Esther reflect those of Jewish history itself.

Esther in American Art

Dr. Samantha Baskind

T he Book of Esther, with its dramatic narrative and distinct character types, makes ripe material for artists. With rare exception, Western artists over the ages were not especially familiar with the nuances of the story or its vast commentary, from classical sources such as Flavius Josephus to rabbinic commentaries to more modern interpretations such as that by Louis Ginzberg. Rather, artists boiled down the Book of Esther to a parable of good versus evil and villain versus heroine. The tale's themes of beauty and exoticism, peril and menace, and festivity and bounty offered fertile visuals. As such, artists from both Europe and America were typically attracted to the multilayered saga less for its roots in sacred scripture and more for the opportunity to depict beautiful women, splendor, and histrionics. The diverse ways the Book of Esther has been conceived by a variety of American artists, Jewish and non-Jewish, and across media, offers a case study for examining the manifestations of one biblical story in the history of American art through a social, political, religious, and cultural lens.

Classical European artists gravitated to several aspects of the account of Esther's tale. Renaissance master Michelangelo painted three scenes from Esther on the Sistine Chapel ceiling, with the most prominent being Haman's punishment (1511). Rembrandt, the great-est artist of the Dutch Golden Age, painted a psychologically probing canvas of Haman's recognition of his fate (c. 1665, Hermitage) and his countryman Jan Steen portrayed Ahasuerus' wrath more than once (e.g., 1668, Cleveland Museum of Art). There are many paintings of a coura-geous Esther pleading before Ahasuerus, like that by the Italian artist Paolo Veronese (c. 1555, Kunsthistorisches Museum, Vienna). Artists were especially drawn to the melodrama of Esther fainting before Aha-suerus, an extratextual addition in the Septuagint, including the Italian artist Filippo Lippi (c. 1475–80, Musée Condé, Chantilly) and Antoine Coypel, from France (c. 1704, Louvre). The feast offered a chance to paint plenty and pomp, as seen in Flemish artist Frans Francken the Younger's unique and highly detailed copper painting (first half of the seventeenth century, National Gallery, Prague). There are scenes of Esther prettying for her meeting with the king (Jean-François de Troy, c. 1739, Louvre), Esther accusing Haman (Jan Victors, 1651, Bob Jones University, Greenville, South Carolina), the triumph of Mordecai (Paolo Veronese, 1556, Church of San Sebastiano), and occasionally a canvas of Vashti (Jacopo del Sellaio, c. 1490, Uffizi Gallery).

Esther found an especially wide audience in seventeenth-century Holland. Dozens of paintings and prints were made by prominent Dutch artists, many more than Rembrandt, Jan Victors, and Jan Steen, noted above. While attention to the story was initiated by its wide recognizabil-ity and spectacle, the Book of Esther's popularity in Holland may also be attributed to the Dutch people's identification with the Israelites of the Hebrew Bible. In their struggle for freedom from Spanish tyranny and religious oppression, the Dutch saw the Jewish oppression experienced in Persia as an appropriate metaphor. Although not in the realm of art, Americans too connected Esther and Purim to their revolutionary efforts in the late eighteenth century.[1] This lack, though, corresponds with the dearth of biblical art, and art in general, during the country's early decades.

The strain of Puritanism in America after the birth of the coun-try discouraged religious art, preferring the verbal as a means to com-municate ideas about God. As US vice-counsel to Italy and art collector

---

1. See Eran Shalev's chapter in this volume.

James Jackson Jarves perceived in 1864: "The popular faith [in America] is more rigidly puritanical in tone. This not only deprives art of the lofty stimulus of religious feeling, but subjects it to suspicion, as of doubtful morality."[2] In the nineteenth century, several American artists traveled to Europe, returning to their native land with a new appreciation of the grand manner of history painting – subjects encompassing historical, biblical, mythological, and literary themes. After visiting England, Samuel F. B. Morse hoped to make such painting viable on American soil. Morse's mother rebuked his religious and mythological paintings from a practical standpoint: "You must not expect to paint anything in this country, for which you will receive any money to support you, but portraits."[3] Morse, Thomas Cole, Washington Allston, and a few other prominent artists of that generation attempted biblical themes, but America's taste for history painting of any sort was somewhat rare.[4] Instead, the major subjects of artists became the unbridled land of the newly founded country, portraiture, and genre scenes depicting the lives of the people – if not out of interest in painting such topics then for the monetary reward.[5]

One of the earliest well-known American artists to portray Esther, William Rimmer (1816–79) painted a nineteenth-century traditional

2. James Jackson Jarves, *The Art-Idea*, ed. Benjamin Rowland, Jr. (1864; reprint Cambridge, 1960), 150–151.

3. Samuel F. B. Morse, *Samuel F. B. Morse: His Letters and Journals*, vol. 1, ed. Edward Lind Morse (Boston, 1914), 159.

4. The 1972–73 traveling exhibition, "The Hand and the Spirit: Religious Art in America 1700–1900," gathered notable works that explore religious matter, mostly from a Protestant perspective and primarily biblical imagery. For the catalog see Jane Dillenberger and Joshua C. Taylor, *The Hand and the Spirit: Religious Art in America 1700–1900* (Berkeley, 1972).

5. Recent scholarship illuminates the role of religion in American art, although most often Judaism plays a small part in these discussions. For some fairly current literature on American art with religious subjects, see Sally Promey's comprehensive article "The 'Return' of Religion in the Scholarship of American Art," *Art Bulletin* 85, no. 3 (September 2003): 581–603. Religion in its more spiritual dimensions has been addressed by scholars, including Joshua C. Taylor, "The Religious Impulse in American Art," in *Papers in American Art*, ed. John C. Milley (Mapleshade, 1976), 113–132. My contribution to this topic, *Jewish Artists and the Bible in Twentieth-Century America* (University Park, 2014), analyzes why and how American Jews so prominently created imagery prompted by the Bible in a much secularized twentieth century.

Dr. Samantha Baskind

rendering of her coronation (1847; fig. 1). Modeled after a vibrantly colored canvas by Frenchman Jean-François de Troy, one of his seven studies depicting episodes from the Book of Esther for the Gobelin Tapestries,
Rimmer's rendition stays faithful to the detailed, academic classicism
of its predecessor but in somewhat muted colors. Christian Schussele
(1824–79), who designed the American Medal of Honor, painted *Queen
Esther Denouncing Haman to Ahasuerus* (1866; fig. 2), another academic
work (art, in style and subject, advocated by traditional European art
academies), but this one smaller in size, highly horizontal, and in watercolor. Conceived as a populated theatrical performance, Esther histrioni-
cally extends her hands toward the king while beseeching for the redemption of her people, with an enthroned Ahasuerus leaning forward and
reaching his royal scepter toward his queen. The figures wear Bedouin
clothing and headdresses, and the palace has been conceived as a grand
and imagined exotic space, although not in ancient Persia. The Assyrian
and Babylonian statues denote the influence of Orientalism, a prevalent
nineteenth-century construct finding inspiration in theme and style from
an imagined exotic East, on Schussele's art. George Frederick Bensell
(1837–79) envisioned the same moment in an even more Orientalized,

Fig. 2. Christian Schussele, *Queen Esther Denouncing Haman to Ahasuerus*, 1866. Watercolor over
graphite on gray wove paper, 10 7/16 x 18 5/8 in. Pennsylvania Academy of the Fine Arts, Philadelphia. Courtesy of the Pennsylvania Academy of the Fine Arts, Philadelphia. Leo Asbell Fund Purchase

over five- by eight-foot canvas of *Esther Accusing Haman* (c. 1860, collection unknown). The luminous reds and golds, and decorative tapestries,
rugs, and sculptures in the court, connote the influence of European
Romantic painters and are stylistically meant to suggest an "authentic"
Middle Eastern atmosphere. Moses Jacob Ezekiel (1844–1917), the first
Jewish American artist to gain international repute, mentions a sculpted
torso of Esther in his memoirs (c. 1891, lost).[6]

A number of female artists, in this early period and later, were
attuned to the Book of Esther for its attention to a female figure.
M. Louise Stowell (1861–1930), a non-Jewish watercolorist, made many
works of a biblical nature including paintings featuring Moses, Noah,
and Elijah, along with Christian subjects. She pictured Queen Esther
and Vashti in precisely delineated individual images influenced by the
flat linearity of Japanese prints and Arts and Crafts design – both highly
fashionable at the time.[7] Her tiny watercolor, *Esther Sues and Saves the
Jews*, hung in the juried Pennsylvania Academy of the Fine Arts watercolor exhibition in 1905 (fig. 3). She offers a self-sacrificing Esther in
a Near Eastern court, on her knees in front of a towering Ahasuerus,
begging the king to subvert Haman's intended genocide of her people.
Another female artist, Minerva Teichert (1888–1976), also found Esther
appealing, although in this case her affinity for the subject came not just
because of the account's empowering female protagonist but also from
an allegiance to her observant Mormon background. Teichert's delicate painting, also an individual portrait of the queen, was made from
a live model in her Latter-Day Saint community (1939; Brigham Young
University Museum of Art, Provo, Utah). Aside from Teichert, drawn
to the subject for its religious nature, most other artists aspired to make
history paintings, the most prestigious category of art in the hierarchy of
genres as long-defined by the official academies in Europe. In America as
a whole, though, non-Jewish artists rarely portray Esther, and until the

---

6. Moses Jacob Ezekiel, *Moses Jacob Ezekiel: Memoirs from the Baths of Diocletian*, ed.
   Joseph Gutman and Stanley F. Chyet (Detroit, 1975), 296, 301.
7. Stowell wrote of this larger influence in an article published in a leading art journal.
   See M. Louise Stowell, "Japanese Color Prints and Some of their Makers," *Craftsman*
   5, no. 1 (1903): 52–67.

late twentieth century, Jewish artists only occasionally address Esther and other figures in her story, as well as related images of Purim.

As American Jewish artists began to make their mark in the twentieth century, some explored Esther's narrative. In the 1950s, Ruth Gikow (1915–82) and Abraham Rattner (1895–1978) depicted Esther, each in their own distinctive style. Ukrainian-born Gikow painted some biblical figures and especially stories in which women play a substantial role, in canvases such as *Queen Esther II* (1952, Saginaw Museum, Saginaw, Michigan) and *King Solomon and His Wives* (1961, private collection).[8] Perhaps partly influenced by her husband Jack Levine's focus on biblical matters, Gikow eschewed her characteristic images of social issues and then-contemporary existence, ranging from teenyboppers to civil rights demonstrators, to paint these subjects. Both conceptions take full advantage of Gikow's command of shimmering color application in her representation of the figures' Orientalized clothing, especially *Queen Esther II*. Gikow does not image a dramatic event but rather offers an encounter between Esther and a maidservant. Some male artists who paint Esther with her maidservants take a different tack. In nineteenth-century France, Théodore Chassériau (1841, Louvre) shows Esther as a sensual nude from the waist up being prettied for her meeting with the king by exotic maidservants.

With an estimated one-third of his works concerning religious or biblical themes, critics consistently note the important influence of Judaism on Rattner's expressionist art. As art historian John I. H. Baur observed in a 1959 exhibition catalog: "Art, for Rattner, is never primarily an esthetic activity. It is a means to an end, an expression of what he repeatedly calls 'livingness,' and a search for the divine in man. It is colored by his own deeply religious, if unorthodox, nature, by his immersion in the old testament and a sense of his rich Jewish heritage."[9] Rattner specifically felt that God's presence influenced his art: "A painting, if it

---

8. Unfortunately, the literature on Gikow is scarce. For a brief monograph with numerous plates, see Matthew Josephson, *Ruth Gikow* (New York, 1970). Also Diane Cochrane, "Ruth Gikow: Chronicler of our Times," *American Artist* 37, no. 366 (January 1973): 44–50, 73, with some thoughts from Gikow.

9. Lloyd Goodrich and John I. H. Baur, *Four American Expressionists: Doris Caesar, Chaim Gross, Karl Knaths, Abraham Rattner* (New York, 1959), 39. For a monograph on Rattner with excellent color plates, see Allen Leepa, *Abraham Rattner* (New York, 1974).

Fig. 1. William Rimmer. *The Coronation of Queen Esther*, 1847. Oil on panel, 19 ¾ x 26 ¼ in. Mead Art Museum, Amherst College. Gift of Herbert W. Plimpton: The Hollis W. Plimpton, Class of 1915, Memorial Collection. Bridgeman Images

Fig. 3. M. Louise Stowell, *Queen Esther Sues and Saves the Jews*, 1905. Watercolor and black ink on paper, 10 11/16 x 8 ¾ in. Memorial Art Gallery of the University of Rochester. Virginia Jeffrey Smith Fund, in honor of Grant Holcomb and Marie Vie

Fig. 4. Abraham Rattner, *Song of Esther*, 1958. Oil on composition board, 59 15/16 x 48 1/16 in. Whitney Museum of American Art, New York. Purchase, with funds from the Friends of the Whitney Museum of American Art. Inv.: 58:36. Digital image © Whitney Museum of American Art / Licensed by Scala / Art Resource, NY

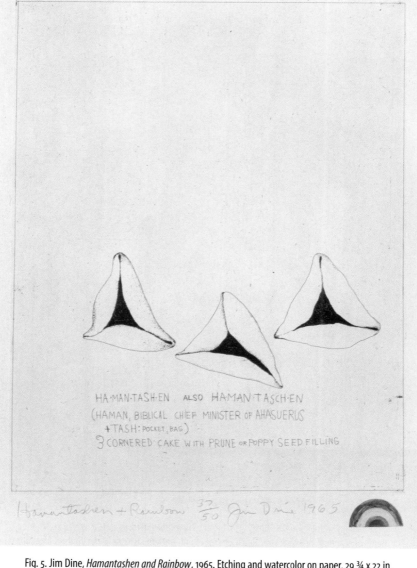

Fig. 5. Jim Dine, *Hamantashen and Rainbow*, 1965. Etching and watercolor on paper, 29 ¾ x 22 in. Jewish Museum, New York. JM 38-65. Photo credit: The Jewish Museum / Art Resource, NY
© 2020 Jim Dine / Artists Rights Society (ARS), New York

Fig. 6. Robert Indiana, *Purim: Four Facets of Esther*, 1967. Screen print on paper, 29 7/16 x 23 ½ in. Jewish Museum, New York. Commissioned by The Jewish Museum, JM 109-67. Photo by John Parnell. Photo credit: The Jewish Museum / Art Resource, NY © 2020 Morgan Art Foundation Ltd / Artists Rights Society (ARS), NY

Fig. 8. Arthur Szyk, *Mordechai and Esther*, 1950. From *The Book of Esther* (1974)

Fig. 12. Siona Benjamin, *Esther's Confrontation with Haman*, 2010. Gouache on parchment. Private collection

Fig. 13. Archie Rand, *Queen Esther*, 1992. Acrylic and marker on canvas, 18 x 24 in. Collection of the artist. Photo credit: Mary Faith O'Neill

is achieved at all, is made with the help of God.... I would recommend to those who desire to be initiated into the Temple to consider that art belongs to the spirit, and partakes of the nature of religion."[10] *Song of Esther* (1958; fig. 4), measuring five by four feet, is a characteristically color-infused, jewel-like canvas that veers toward abstraction. It takes close looking to make out what is going on and without a title, viewers would not be able to identify Esther as the painting's subject, a stark contrast to Gikow's Esther and especially narrative paintings by European academic artists and Rimmer's earlier conception. Taking up the majority of the composition, Esther materializes on a large canvas sitting on an easel, within which Esther herself sits on a throne. Surrounding the queen are a cacophony of jagged yellow shapes, perhaps signaling threats to her and the Jews. At the right, Rattner incorporates a self-portrait holding a palette and paintbrush, himself safe from the threats to the Jewish people in ancient times and more recently post-Holocaust. For Rattner, the subject matter of his work was surely important but so were his stylistic and color explorations.

During the '60s, Jim Dine (b. 1935) was associated with Pop art, but the cold impartiality of the movement went against the artist's desire to imbue his work with subjectivity. As he explained in a 1963 interview: "Pop art is only one facet of my work. More than popular images I'm interested in personal images."[11] Indeed, Dine explicitly allied himself with his art: "My work is like me, I think. Definitely it is me. I am it. I am the work. There is no question about that. I probably am as closely linked to my work as any artist I know. That is, if you know me, you know my work. I'm not closed off in that way."[12] To that end, he sporadically addressed Jewish themes, with two prints related to Purim: *Silver Star* (1966, Art Institute of Chicago) and *Hamantashen and Rainbow* (1965; fig. 5).

Dine often pictured everyday objects, and motifs are reiterated and reinterpreted in different media and styles. Rather than Esther herself, or

10. Abraham Rattner quoted in Allen Leepa, *The Challenge of Modern Art*, 1949 (reprint, New York, 1961), 195.
11. Jim Dine, "What is Pop Art? Part I," interview with G. R. Swenson in *ARTnews* 62, no. 7 (November 1963): 25. For a compendium of Dine's prints, see Elizabeth Carpenter, *Jim Dine Prints, 1985–2000: A Catalogue Raisonné* (Minneapolis, 2002).
12. Susie Hennessey, "A Conversation with Jim Dine," *Art Journal* 39 (Spring 1980): 17.

another figure from the eponymous book, *hamantaschen* – the three-cornered pastry approximating Haman's hat and a key signifier of the Purim holiday – serve as the object Dine assigned to best designate Purim in both prints. *Silver Star*, a black and white lithograph on paper, alludes to the holiday with a *hamantasch*, crown, and *grogger* floating among other objects in the flatly executed composition. *Hamantashen and Rainbow*, an etching and watercolor, more explicitly refers to the holiday. Three *hamantaschen* appear two-thirds of the way down the vertical composition, with the area above the pastries left empty for effect. Underneath the *hamantaschen*, within the print, Dine offers an explanation about the objects, not recognizable to many non-Jewish viewers. Carefully printed in all capital letters, Dine clarified:

HA-MAN-TASH-EN also HA-MAN-TASCH-EN (HAMAN, BIBLICAL CHIEF MINISTER OF AHASUERUS + TASH: POCKET, BAG) 3 CORNERED CAKE WITH PRUNE OR POPPY SEED FILLING

Dine titled the print at the bottom in cursive, along with the edition of the work, his signature, and date. In the far right corner, where artists typically sign, Dine instead rendered a brightly colored rainbow, a strong contrast to the black and white carefully etched print. By doing so, Dine emphasizes the survival of humanity amid evil – an apt and erudite reference to the Bible; the first rainbow was an assertion of God's presence after the Flood. The rainbow was a sign for Noah that life would continue, that God would never destroy the earth with a flood again (Gen. 9:11–15), and in this case the Jewish people would continue because of Esther's intercession against Haman's evil plan.

Two unique images of "Esther" are in the collection of the Jewish Museum in New York, both by non-Jews. For decades, the Jewish Museum has held an annual Purim Ball, one of the institution's major fundraisers. On the occasion of their 1967 ball, the museum commissioned a screenprint by Robert Indiana (1928–2018), then at the height of his career, titled *Purim: Four Facets of Esther* (fig. 6).[13] Acclaimed for

---

13. Indiana was no stranger to these types of commission; his bold style, influenced by the look of advertisements, made him a popular artist in this regard. For ex-

his Hard Edge paintings incorporating bold images, especially words and numbers, Indiana employs his iconic style for this screenprint, made in an edition of ninety. The four facets of Esther appear in the outlines of each concentric circle, within which are Stars of David and numbers indicating the four facets that Indiana highlights. Each facet, painted in flat orange, red, and blue, is an alliteration that delineates components of the book's plot: Fast, Faith, Feast, and Feat.

In 1992, African American artist Fred Wilson (b. 1954) gifted a recently completed ink print to the Jewish Museum, *Queen Esther/Harriet Tubman* (fig. 7), in honor of the ball.[14] Wilson's print features two strong women who fought for their people by amalgamating a sixteenth-century engraving of Esther with a well-known photograph of Harriet Tubman, born into slavery, who later escaped, and yet risked her life saving her people via the underground railroad. Wilson appropriates Esther from a print, part of a series about the Book of Esther, originally made by the Dutch engraver Maarten van Heemskerck. Dubbed the "Moses of her People," Tubman serves as a fitting connection to Esther, another woman who risks her life for her people. Tubman takes precedence, with Esther's shadowy figure behind her, the two women's bodies and faces, appropriately mask-like, fused into one. Not only do these brave women demonstrate leadership and sacrifice for their own, by linking them Wilson also draws connections between a larger, shared history of black and Jewish persecution.[15]

ample, MoMA commissioned Indiana to design their Christmas card (1965) and he received a poster commission from the Democratic National Committee, *Vote* (1976). Indiana is best known for his iconic *Love* sculpture. In 1977, Indiana installed an analogous twelve-foot-high Cor-Ten steel *AHAVA* sculpture (the Hebrew word for "love") at the Fifth Avenue and 60th Street entrance of New York's Central Park before sending it to the Israel Museum for permanent display. For a deeply engaged study of Indiana's art, see Allison Unruh, ed., *Robert Indiana: New Perspectives* (Ostfildern, 2012).

14. On Fred Wilson, see Doro Globus, ed., *Fred Wilson: A Critical Reader* (London/ Santa Monica, 2011).

15. See Hasia Diner, *In the Almost Promised Land: American Jews and Blacks, 1915–1935* (Baltimore, 1995), for a discussion of early Jewish support for racial equality. Jewish newspapers and magazines, in English and Yiddish, featured stories about black

Fig. 7. Fred Wilson, *Queen Esther/Harriet Tubman*, 1992. Ink on acetate, 14 3/8 x 10 ¾ in. Jewish Museum, New York. Gift of the artist, 1992-35. © The Jewish Museum. Photo credit: The Jewish Museum / Art Resource, NY

Four modern-day *megillot*, by Arthur Szyk, Leonard Baskin, Siona Benjamin, and JT Waldman, span seven decades and are vastly different in conception. Arthur Szyk (1894–1951), best recognized for his Passover Haggada, scathing war images denouncing Hitler, and fervent pro-Jewish material frequently touting Jewish strength and military prowess, also illustrated two versions of the Book of Esther as bound volumes. Both of these modern-day *megillot* are characterized by the artist's signature miniature detailing and strong color. Each stands in sharp contrast to traditional scrolls of Esther in that the pages are turned, not unfurled. The first, published as a limited edition in France as *Le Livre d'Esther* (1925), featured twenty paintings chronicling Esther's narrative with separate text. Relevant to this discussion of Esther in America is Szyk's second foray into the tale, completed the year before he died and published posthumously in Israel (1974).[16]

An excellent example of his mature style, Szyk's second *megilla* aptly tells the Esther saga in lavish color and detail, and the incorporation of text into image is comparable to medieval manuscript illumination. Many pages are unified by homogenous borders decorated with Jewish symbols such as a Star of David and the lions of Judah, only slightly differentiated by varying colors. Illustrations of Haman are particularly striking because he is always shown with a swastika, on either his clothes or hat. Szyk very purposefully created an analogy between the attempted genocide in ancient Persia and the recent destruction of six million Jews in Nazi Germany, only five years removed from the completion of the work.[17] The final full-page illustration does not present Esther swooning or timorous as per artistic convention. She dominates the page, resting grandly and assuredly on her throne in glorious

---

oppression. On art by Jews and African Americans that addresses correspondences between each group's shared oppression, see Milly Heyd, *Mutual Reflections: Jews and Blacks in American Art* (New Brunswick, 1999).

16. Arthur Szyk, *Le Livre d'Esther* (Paris, 1925), and Arthur Szyk, *The Book of Esther* (Israel, 1974). For the indispensable study on Szyk, see Joseph P. Ansell, *Arthur Szyk: Artist, Jew, Pole* (Portland, 2004). See also the chapter by Mishael Zion in this volume.

17. Szyk more neutrally presented Esther in a popular illustrated Bible published by the Jewish Publication Society of America. See Mortimer J. Cohen, *Pathways Through the Bible* (Philadelphia, 1946), full-page plate between pages 508 and 509.

splendor, having saved her people, with Mordecai standing behind her (fig. 8). A scribe sits at Esther's feet, writing on a slate, as per the book's text: "Then Esther the queen, the daughter of Abihail, and Mordecai the Jew, wrote down all the acts of power, to confirm this second letter of Purim" (Est. 9:29).

Leonard Baskin (1922–2000) tackled the Book of Esther several times. He made individual woodcuts of Esther (1952, collection unknown) and Haman (1955, Denver Art Museum), the latter of which is over four feet tall. Five years later, Baskin created a large, highly vertical woodcut of Esther's face in stark profile with a distorted Haman over her head (Museum of Modern Art, New York). To place the figures, who have no identifying narrative, Baskin wrote their names in Hebrew within the composition. Most prominently, Baskin's oversized volume *The Five Scrolls* (1984) contains illustrated versions of Ecclesiastes, Esther, Song of Songs, Ruth, and Lamentations, accompanied by text in Hebrew and English. *The Five Scrolls* is just one of many works prompted by Baskin's religio-cultural heritage, a formidable influence on his art and the outcome of his solid Jewish education. Until he was fifteen years old, Baskin, the son of an Orthodox rabbi, studied Talmud daily. The reverberations of that intensive education left their mark on his artistic production, as Baskin wrote in a short statement: "My brain is serried with an infinity of memory-traces that recall the sound and smell of *shul*, of home, of Yeshiva, of the nearly all-Jewish street."[18]

A large undertaking commissioned by the Central Conference of American Rabbis, *The Five Scrolls* was meant for worship and includes the service for the reading of the *megilla*. As the introduction explains: "This presentation of the Five Scrolls is intended to enrich festival worship and to contribute to the revitalization of festival observance among our people."[19] The book's editors, both Reform rabbis,

---

18. Leonard Baskin, "To Wear Bloodstain with Honor," *Judaism: A Quarterly Journal* 10, no. 4 (Fall 1961): 295.
19. Herbert N. Bronstein and Albert H. Friedlander, eds., *The Five Scrolls*, illustrated by Leonard Baskin (New York, 1984), xiii. For more on Baskin's Jewish identity vis-à-vis his art, see Matthew Baigell's chapter on the artist in *American Artists, Jewish Images* (Syracuse, 2006), 118–134.

clearly understood the volume's purpose to be one of "rejuvenation" and "recovery among liberal Jewry of festival observance." Even as they represent Reform Jewry, the editors lament the loss of tradition and idealistically hope such a beautiful volume will "raise the level of spirituality among an entire people."[20]

Simple in conception, Baskin's watercolor of Esther functions as a full-length "portrait" and he does not present her as a beautiful young woman or exotic in any way (fig. 9). Esther wears a drab gray dress and has mousy hair to her chin. She places her hand on heart, indicating the moment when Esther entreats the king for his intervention (7:3). Nor does Baskin include any distractions from the determined psychology of Esther's plight; she stands in an amorphous white space save for her name in large Hebrew letters near her head. The portrait of sorts is analogous to Baskin's plain presentation of the other chief players in the story, all with Hebrew labels indicating the name of the personage presented (there are twelve illustrations in total for the Book of Esther, culminating with the hanging of Haman's sons). In going against convention and eschewing narrative, Baskin's portrait of Esther stays true to his overriding concern with the human condition over and above offering a narrative account of the scroll. Years later, the multi-media artist David Wander (b. 1954), an admirer of Baskin, also illustrated all five scrolls; his fifty-five-foot *Megillat Esther* in accordion format comprises illuminated panels augmented by Hebrew text (2007).

Much less ambitious in scope and not as widely circulated, but by a prolific and versatile artist who worked as a watercolorist, draftsman, printmaker, textile designer, and primarily as a sculptor, is Chaim Gross' (1902–91) illustrated compilation *The Jewish Holidays, Customs, and Traditions* (1977). The volume features twenty-three watercolors based on a suite of lithographs published nine years earlier by Associated American Artists. Gross imaged ten major holidays in the Jewish lifecycle, from Rosh HaShana to Tisha B'av, and eleven critical customs, from circumcision to Havdala, with two title pages. The foreword to the edition exalts Gross for breathing life into what is for many a "vanished

---

20. Bronstein and Friedlander, viii.

Fig. 9. Leonard Baskin, *Esther*, 1984. Gouache. From *The Five Scrolls* (1984). © The Estate of Leonard Baskin

world" and the goal of the volume is just that: for Gross, an Eastern European immigrant and the son of hasidic Jews, to bring to the fore the festivals and customs of his childhood, of traditional Judaism, in art.[21] The watercolor for Purim, precisely titled *Feast of Lots* and dated 1967, depicts heads of key figures in the story (fig. 10). A serious Esther and King Ahasuerus occupy the center with what may be Mordecai in profile near the upper left corner, holding Haman's decree to slaughter the Jews. Other lightly delineated figures, in pencil and watercolor, pepper the composition, as does the word "Purim" in large Hebrew letters. The bottom right features the celebration of Purim, with figures dressed in carnivalesque costume as per the holiday's custom.

Fig. 10. Chaim Gross, *Feast of Lots*, 1967. From *The Jewish Holidays, Customs, and Traditions* (1977). Photo credit: Brittany Cassandra. © 2020 The Renee & Chaim Gross Foundation / Artists Rights Society (ARS), New York

---

21. Chaim Gross, *The Jewish Holidays, Customs and Traditions* (Hackensack, 1977), unpaged. Gross' four-story home in Greenwich Village has been transformed into a museum showcasing his work. For an informative interview with Gross, see Emery Grossman, *Art and Tradition* (New York, 1967).

In 2005, JT Waldman (b. 1977) published his acclaimed adaptation of the Book of Esther as a graphic novel.[22] A project seven years in the making, Waldman's contemporary *megilla*, over 150 pages in length, covers every verse in the book drawn in black-and-white with expressive lines, sometimes sparse and bold, and sometimes detailed and delicate. He adopts a variety of styles, ranging from Persian art to film noir, to convey Esther's story as well as his visual midrash on it. This heavily researched, scholarly work – which includes a glossary, bibliography, and endnotes with rabbinical citations that inform Waldman's visual interpretations – offers its own visual exegesis on the much-parsed tale, yet by virtue of the graphic novel format remains accessible to readers who understand his *megilla* on different levels. The text is written in Hebrew and English, with the Hebrew font bolder and more prominent, signifying it as the book's primary language. Splash pages and panels, purposefully inconsistent in shape and style, are deployed to suggest the whirlwind pace of the book and its twisty, chaotic nature. Waldman takes the pandemonium a step further when, close to the point in the narrative as Esther's plan to expose Haman takes shape, he throws his readers an unexpected curveball (Est. 6:1): the book abruptly appears "upside down" because it, in fact, is – readers must now turn the volume over and continue from right to left akin to Hebrew books.

Waldman divides his page illustrating Esther 2:17 into three panels with the Hebrew text interspersed in the gutters (fig. 11). As the verse reads in the *megilla*: "And the king loved Esther above all the women, and she obtained grace and favor in his sight more than all the virgins; so that he set the royal crown upon her head, and made her queen instead of Vashti." The top panel shows a content, reclining King Ahasuerus literally "above all the women" – here his two queens rendered as portraits below him. The royal crown he "set" on Esther's head sits in its own horizontal panel, atop the bottommost panel in which the portrait of Esther dominates. Close looking reveals a small number "8" in the

---

22. JT Waldman, *Megillat Esther* (Philadelphia, 2005). On Jewish graphic novels, see Samantha Baskind and Ranen Omer-Sherman, eds., *The Jewish Graphic Novel: Critical Approaches* (New Brunswick, 2008), and Derek Parker Royal, ed., *Visualizing Jewish Narrative: Jewish Comics and Graphic Novels* (London, 2016).

Esther in American Art

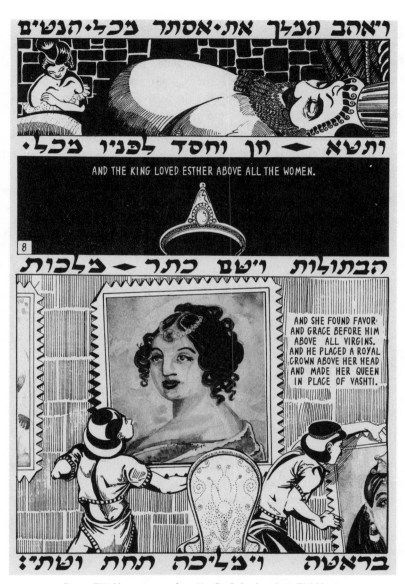

Fig. 11. JT Waldman, page 53 from *Megillat Esther* (2005). © JT Waldman

left corner of that dark panel, a reference to one of Waldman's endnotes, citing *Midrash Rabba*: "Until Esther was made Queen, Vashti's portrait remained hanging. Once Ahasuerus married Esther, however, he said: Take down Vashti's and put up Esther's."[23] Giving off the appearance of a fine watercolor, that portrait takes the form of an oversized postage stamp. To the right, removed from the finely hatched wall, a portrait of Vashti is being hauled away by a servant, already halfway off the page. The contrast of form and technique on this page serves as but one instance of Waldman's innovative and thought-provoking marriage of text and image.

A Bene Israel Jew born in Bombay and émigré to the United States in her twenties, Siona Benjamin (b. 1960) created a fifteen-foot-long, eleven-and-a-half-inch-wide illuminated *megilla* commissioned for a private patron (2010). The *megilla*, painted in gouache on parchment prepared in Israel, adopted a style approximating the tradition of Indian-Persian miniatures, with columns of meticulous Hebrew text. Seven full-page illustrations are embellished with ornate and lively borders replete with symbolism, along with smaller rectangular narrative components lining the bottom. The *megilla* features boldly hued blue-skinned figures in elegant Indian garb enacting the narrative components of the familiar tale. Blue holds several meanings for the artist – she sees blue as a universal color of the infinite (e.g., the ocean and sky are blue), and in the Hindu religion, the predominant faith of her native country, the god Krishna appears as blue. Equally germane is that this color serves as a commentary on her own Other identity as a woman and "Jew of color," as well as representing the tensions of the "spiritual borderlands formed by the 'displacements,'" as Benjamin puts it, of her hybrid American, Indian, and Jewish transcultural experiences.[24]

Benjamin's *megilla* does not feature a full-page treatment of the prevalent moment in art depicting Esther approaching the king to intercede on behalf of her people but does contain an unusual and

---

23. Waldman, 160.
24. Siona Benjamin, "Blue Like Me," in V. G. Julie Rajan and Sanja Bahun-Radunovic, eds., *From Word to Canvas: Appropriations of Myth in Women's Aesthetic Production* (Newcastle upon Tyne, 2009), 11.

violent depiction of Haman's sons hanging on the gallows. A particularly intriguing illumination shows *Esther's Confrontation with Haman*
(fig. 12). Set against the dominant orange and rich crimson background,
and surrounded by three ghostly figures on horseback swirling around
the two figures, an enraged Esther looms over a self-satisfied, smirking
Haman, clutching a knife he has procured to slaughter her people. The
most authentically "Oriental" image of Esther described in this essay,
as opposed to Schussele, Bensell, Stowell, and Gikow's appropriated
Orientalism, Benjamin's scroll stays true to a story that takes place in
the Persian diaspora by a Jewish artist who well-knows that diaspora.

A number of contemporary Jewish painters have tackled the Book of
Esther, among them Archie Rand (b. 1949). Rand made his first painting of
Esther in 1992, as part of his *Sixty Paintings from the Bible* series. Each canvas
in the series interprets an episode from the Hebrew Bible or the Apocrypha,
executed in colorful tones and with speech encased in comic book bubbles,
offering original, daring, and sometimes humorous interpretations of Judaism's foundational stories. At the forefront of Rand's richly hued Esther
painting, the queen kneels before Ahasuerus and reveals that Haman plans
to annihilate her people (fig. 13). At the center background of the painting,
the ultimate result of that revelation finds Haman hanging from the gallows.
The painting encapsulates several salient incidents from Esther 7:1–10, with
the relevant original text reading: "Then spoke the king Ahasuerus and said
unto Esther the queen: 'Who is he, and where is he, that durst in his heart
to do so?' And Esther said: 'An adversary and an enemy, even this wicked
Haman.'... And the king said, 'Hang him thereon.'" In Rand's interpretation
the king utters, in stream-of-consciousness, present-day vernacular, "Esther,
what's the matter, is somebody out to get you? Who? Who is it? Is it Haman?
Yes? Well then, hang him! Hang Haman on the gallows!"

Since *Sixty Paintings from the Bible*, Rand conceived a
four-canvas series about the four mitzvot of Purim: reading the *megilla*,
the giving of food, giving charity, and partaking in a festive meal (2015).
Four years later, Rand painted sixteen sequential canvases focusing solely on the Book of Esther, all in a high-key palette to convey
the "Mardi Gras setting of the ripping yarn," to use the artist's words

(2019).[25] Because of the extended nature of this project and the depth of Rand's Jewish knowledge, the small canvases cover aspects of the story culled from a variety of sources, few with Esther as the subject. These involve esoteric interpretations including Haman embroidering an idol onto his clothes (Est. 3:2 – *Pirkei DeRabbi Eliezer* ch. 50) and three angels assisting Esther to prepare for her meeting with the king (Est. 5:2 – R. Yoḥanan, Megilla 15b). Of the artists described in this essay, Waldman and Rand are especially attuned to the complexities of biblical stories and the sequential nature of their art allows each artist, in different media, to explore intricacies and nuance. Other recent Jewish American painters have made significant forays into the Esther saga, notably Richard McBee (b. 1949), Janet Shafner (1931–2011), and Ruth Weisberg (b. 1942).

The swell of Esther imagery described here, not exhaustive to say the least, relates to a previously uneasy yet now more present place of biblical themes in American art, and especially by Jewish artists. Historically, Jewish art, the stepchild of art history – in America and elsewhere – has been viewed as foreign, controversial, or even unseemly as it goes against the dominant Christian art historical narrative. That is to say, in America and the Western world the unmarked norm is taken as Christian and so, consequently, overt Jewish subjects stand out as marked, therefore culturally alien and strange. Likewise, Jewish concerns – ranging from the Bible to the Holocaust and in the specific case described here, the Book of Esther – simply do not adhere to the iconographic and nationalist bias inherent in the canon of American art. American art began as a field that endlessly debated its Americanness and tried to tease out its "native qualities," and Judaism and biblical art have not been considered indicative of the national character. History has shown that the so-called universal qualities comprising canonical American works are not going to be found in an Other ethnicity/religion's art.

Early artists such as Gikow, Baskin, and Gross' embrace of Jewish identity was made that much easier by the tenor of American society in

---

25. Archie Rand, conversation with the author, August 15, 2019. For all sixty paintings reproduced as full-page colorplates, see Samantha Baskind, *Sixty Paintings from the Bible*, exh. cat. (Cleveland, 2016).

the late 1960s and 1970s, when America was more amenable to ethnic diversity. This was a period of ethnic pride movements, in great part initiated by the new ethnic self-consciousness and esteem that pervaded black communities during and after the civil rights battles, and when groups like the Black Panther Party promoted black nationalism. With their rallying calls of "Black Power" and "Black is beautiful" (drawn from the Bible's Song of Songs), the Party brought esteem for one's heritage to the forefront of American society in an effort to change Jim Crow attitudes. The group's activism highlighted a desire to be appreciated for one's unique heritage, and that equality of power should be accorded every American citizen, regardless of race, religion, or creed. At the same time, the Immigration Act of 1965 reversed the national quotas instituted by the Immigration Acts of the 1920s, and the Bilingual Education Act was ratified in 1968 – motions that began to indicate the less restrictive mindset of America.

Over the past few decades, ethnic ambiguity has been considered boring, and Americans as a whole are more interested in tracing their lineage and returning to their roots. This wide resurgence of multicultural awareness and pride in one's Otherness has initiated a resurgence of Jewish pride and group cohesiveness as well. With a new appreciation and acceptance of difference in America, many Jews began to assert their ethnicity, which has impacted the visual arts. Jewishness is no longer perceived as a burden and being Jewish is not the elephant in the living room anymore. Indeed, artists have been much more open about their cultural, religious, and biblically inspired Jewishness, certainly a nod to the multicultural environment in which we now live and perhaps, as well, seeking to fulfill a need to connect with a rich, four-millennia-old but now dwindling tradition in the highly assimilated American diaspora.

Esther Goes to Hollywood: An American Midrash About a Wicked Antisemite, a Wise King, and Love Everlasting

Yosef Lindell

The pivotal moment is when Esther decides to come unbidden before the king.

She asks Hegai for a chariot, but he refuses her and warns her not to go. Undeterred, Esther runs to the palace through the driving rain alone. When she arrives, soaked, her gown clinging to her suggestively, King Xerxes has just appointed Haman his regent in a meeting with all of his trusted advisors, including Mordecai the scribe. The shot of Esther flinging open the great oak doors is shown from at least four different angles. As Esther approaches, one of the king's servants draws a sword to slay her. As she climbs the steps to the throne in slow motion, the sword reaches her neck. Mordecai looks toward heaven. But at the last moment, Xerxes pushes the sword away. He thrusts his royal scepter toward Esther as if he is exorcising a demon. Esther reaches the dais and faints in the king's arms.

This dramatic moment sounds like it's based on the biblical Book of Esther, but the details differ wildly. That's because I've actually just described a scene from the 2006 movie *One Night with the King*, directed by Michael Sajbel based on a novel by the Christian evangelical writer Tommy Tenney. The movie is only one of many American film adaptations of Esther, all of which depart from the storyline of the biblical book, and none of which can hold a candle to the original. Yet one important way of tracing how the story of Esther resonates in America is to examine how it's been treated, or mistreated, by Hollywood. Film portrayals of the biblical story, even if inaccurate, are a modern midrash that can shed light on the ways Esther's tale has taken root in American culture.

Film adaptations of Esther have been plentiful, albeit obscure. Five silent film versions were produced between 1910 and 1916.[1] *Queen Esther* (1948) directed by John T. Coyle was the first version with sound, but better known is *Esther and the King* (1960) directed by Raoul Walsh and starring Joan Collins as Esther.[2] Coming on the heels of a much more compelling biblical epic, *The Ten Commandments* (1956), *Esther and the King* "bears all the hallmarks of a B-list sword-and-sandals epic," with a huge cast, poor acting, and banal dialogue.[3] TV movies abounded too: *The Greatest Heroes of the Bible: the Story of Esther* (1978) is rather awful and only loosely follows the biblical story (similar to *Esther and the King*). On the other hand, Raffaele Mertes' *Esther* (1999), a European coproduction that originally aired on TNT as part of *The Bible Collection*, is a relatively faithful and compelling adaptation, although it adds Ezra and Nehemiah

---

1. Matt Page, "Films about Esther," *Bible Films Blog*, February 16, 2006, https://biblefilms.blogspot.com/2006/02/films-about-esther.html; Kevin M. McGeough, "Celluloid Esther: The Literary Carnivalesque as Transformed through the Lens of the Cinematic Epic," *Journal of the Bible and Its Reception* 4, no. 1 (2017): 120. Nearly all the movies noted in this survey are readily available on streaming sites, although a few, such as Amos Gitai's, are harder to find.
2. Page.
3. Carl S. Ehrlich, "Esther in Film," in Rhonda Burnette-Bletsch, ed., *The Bible in Motion: A Handbook of the Bible and Its Reception in Film* 1 (Berlin, 2015), 123.

to the story.[4] And while it's not an American version of the story, I ought to at least mention Israeli filmmaker Amos Gitai's 1986 *Esther* which, although a fairly faithful adaptation (the fact that it's mainly in Hebrew helps), was intended to reflect on the Israeli-Palestinian conflict.[5]

The new millennium brought more adaptations, but unlike their earlier counterparts, they were created by filmmakers with religious agendas. I've already noted *One Night with the King*, which was produced by the Christian company Gener8Xion Entertainment and distributed through FoxFaith, Fox's division aimed at evangelical Christians.[6] Although the plot is convoluted and the movie has pretensions – or maybe delusions – of being an epic on par with *The Lord of the Rings* (it actually shares two actors with Peter Jackson's *Rings* films), it's still a memorable watch if one is interested in how biblical stories are retold. (Be forewarned: I didn't say it was a good movie!) Another Christian adaptation, *The Book of Esther* (2013), directed by David A. R. White and produced by PureFlix Entertainment, is significantly worse.[7] In addition to featuring brief images of Jesus on the cross and the disembodied voice of God speaking aloud to Esther, the film arguably takes more license with the biblical story than any other, focusing primarily on an invented rivalry between Haman, who wants his daughter to become queen, and Mordecai, who supports Esther's candidacy. But worst of all is the super-low-budget *For Such a Time*, which actively pushes a Jews for Jesus agenda, and sadly, is readily available on Amazon Prime. The less said about that film the better.

---

4. Regarding Mertes' film, see ibid., 126. Another film, *The Thirteenth Day: The Story of Esther*, was aired on ABC in 1979 but never made commercially available. "Queen Esther's 13th Day (1979)," *Let There Be… FILM!* (March 20, 2012), http://letthere-befilm.blogspot.com/2012/03/queen-esthers-13th-day-1979.html.

5. The movie was filmed in an abandoned Arab neighborhood right outside of Haifa in a manner in which the modern world is consciously present: one sometimes hears cars, airplanes, or jackhammers in the background. At the end of the film, each of the lead actors – who are of different nationalities, including Israeli and Palestinian – comment on the actions of their characters. Through these comments, it becomes evident that Gitai is particularly concerned by the Jews' slaughter of their enemies at the close of the biblical story. Ehrlich, 124–126.

6. Ibid., 128; McGeough, 112.

7. As noted by Ehrlich, 133, the name PureFlix "says it all."

There have also been several adaptations made for children. "Queen Esther," a 1992 episode of the animated direct-to-video series *The Greatest Adventure: Stories from the Bible,* produced by Hanna-Barbera, revolves around three modern-day children who go back in time and witness the events of the Book of Esther. It's a short production and would be unremarkable except for the fact that it follows the biblical text quite closely despite its contemporary frame story. Better known is the *Veggie Tales* version, *Esther: The Girl Who Becomes Queen* (2000), which, featuring a sundry cast of animated vegetables, sanitizes the story by explaining that Haman wants to banish Mordecai's family to the "Island of Perpetual Tickling." For all its flaws – the Jews are not even mentioned – the *Veggie Tales* episode has a coherent story arc (not a given in these films) and a wholesome message about standing up for oneself and doing the right thing.[8] On the other hand, the live-action 2006 Mormon production *Esther and the King* is a much less compelling watch, with poor acting coupled with frequent musical numbers.[9]

Finally, two recent animated productions, both available on Amazon Prime, were made by and for Orthodox Jews. *Purim: The Lot* (2014) by Moshe Khusid is a psychedelic romp through various midrashic accounts that fails to tell the story of Esther in any recognizable way (for example, the movie spends several minutes graphically depicting an unrelated biblical episode in which Samson's eyes are gouged out and

8. But see Dan W. Clanton, Jr., *Daring, Disreputable, and Devout: Interpreting the Bible's Women in the Arts and Music* (New York, 2009), 128–129, who says that "in a post-Holocaust world," the film's "denigration of anti-Jewish persecution" is "irresponsible," and wonders aloud why the episode was produced, given how the story "has been so changed by the producers and so little of the original story is left."
9. For a spirited, but highly negative take on the Mormon version, see Arielle Kaplan, "I Watched This Mormon Purim Movie So You Don't Have To," *Alma* (March 15, 2019), https://www.heyalma.com/i-watched-this-mormon-purim-movie-so-you-dont-have-to/. The movie's frame story, which encourages children to fast, is based on the Mormon tradition of placing spiritual needs above physical ones, demonstrating real intent in supplications, and aiding in many ways those afflicted by poverty. See Sterling C. Hilton, "How can we teach the law of the fast to our children so that their fasts become a time of maximum spiritual growth and benefit?" *Ensign* (January 1997), https://www.churchofjesuschrist.org/study/ensign/1997/01/i-have-a-question/i-have-a-question.

he kills the Philistines in the Temple of Dagon). *Megillas Lester* (2014), on the other hand, does not aim for accuracy; its entire conceit is that a boy named Lester travels back in time and prevents Vashti's fall from grace, radically changing the story.

Perhaps not one of this motley crew of films makes for a great movie night, but their interpretations of the story of Esther are still worth examining. I will focus on how some of these adaptations address three issues. Why did Haman hate the Jews? What was the king like? And what was Esther's role in averting catastrophe?

I'll begin with Haman. In the biblical account, Haman seems to hate the Jews because Mordecai refuses to bow to him (Est. 3:5–6). Yet there is also an antisemitic undercurrent in Haman's speech to Ahasuerus, in which he calls the Jews "a people, scattered and dispersed among the other peoples" with its own laws who do not obey the king's laws (3:8). Further, by calling Mordecai a Benjaminite (2:5) and Haman an Agagite (3:1), the Bible may want readers to see the conflict between the two men as a rematch between the Jews and their age-old enemy Amalek. (In the Book of Samuel, King Saul, from the tribe of Benjamin, spared Amalek's king, Agag, even though he had been commanded to wipe out the entire nation.)

The movies play up both antisemitism and the rivalry between the Jews and Amalek. In Mertes' 1999 *Esther*, Haman is from Amalek, and Ezra (not Mordecai) refuses to bow to him because of the ancient feud between their peoples. Haman also peddles many antisemitic tropes throughout. He mentions that the Jews flaunt their wealth and tells Ahasuerus that they cheat on their taxes and are lazy, taking off from work one day out of seven. In *One Night with the King*, a film never content with subtlety, the conflict between the Jews and Amalek takes center stage. The movie opens several hundred years earlier with a depiction of Saul sparing Agag, and then cuts to the birth of Agag's child from whom Haman descended. Throughout the film, Haman, as an Amalekite heir, carries a talisman resembling a swastika entwined with a snake. Indeed, Haman's antisemitic pep rallies in the film are scarily reminiscent of Hitler's.[10] And at his rallies, Haman invokes classic antisemitic

---

10. McGeough, 119. Ehrlich, 131, points out that the film's production notes explicitly connect Haman to Hitler.

canards, saying that although he has individual Jewish friends, the Jews as a whole are trying to take over the world. Interestingly, Haman also claims that the Jews are Greek sympathizers who support democracy and the notion that all people are created equal, which he argues is contrary to the values of Persia.

White's 2013 *Book of Esther* presents the problem rather differently. Xerxes, obsessed with obedience, issues his decree against the Jews when he learns from Haman that Jewish scripture refers to God as a king sitting on a throne; Xerxes therefore assumes that the Jews must be disloyal to him. The film climaxes with a public hearing where Xerxes allows Haman and Mordecai to each present testimony, which (perhaps unwittingly) captures the flavor of medieval disputations where Christians used passages from Jewish texts to accuse the Jews of harboring anti-Christian sentiments. Mordecai consistently wears a large skullcap throughout the film, an anachronism that reinforces the notion of religious conflict. In sum, the movies tend to rely on familiar images of Jew-hatred, even though they don't all present Haman's animosity identically. By suffusing the story with themes of religious persecution – not to mention prayer – the films by and large attempt to make the story of Esther, famously known for its lack of explicit religiosity, a more pious tale that pits the God-fearing Jews against an antisemitic enemy.

The films are far more favorable to King Ahasuerus. In the Bible, Ahasuerus is a powerful ruler with an impressive bureaucracy at his command, but he's often inebriated and easily manipulated: quick to do away with Vashti, quick to sign away the fate of the Jews, and quick to have Haman hang. One can write him off as a fool, but many rabbinic interpreters saw a far more sinister character. The Talmud (Megilla 11a), for example, compares him to a hungry bear, accuses him of preventing the Jews from rebuilding the Temple, and notes that he "remained wicked from beginning to end."

The movies depict the king – usually Xerxes but sometimes Ahasuerus[11] – in different ways, but never as wicked. In *Veggie Tales*, where

---

11. Historians generally identify Ahasuerus with Xerxes. See Mitchell First, *Jewish History in Conflict: A Study of the Major Discrepancy Between Rabbinic and Conventional Chronology* (Northvale, 1997), 166–167 note 17.

he signs a tic-tac-toe board instead of a royal decree, he's an utter fool. In *One Night with the King*, he is a romantic. In Mertes' 1999 *Esther*, which is generally the most faithful to the biblical account of the entire bunch, Ahasuerus is unstable.[12] At first one sees him in silhouette only, drunkenly speaking to his advisors from behind a silk screen. The aura of mystery and instability surrounding the king from the get-go signals to the viewer that he is not to be trusted. Indeed, he's not in control of his emotions, and banishes Vashti from the kingdom while in a stupor. He is tender to Esther at times and gives her the cold shoulder at others. It's ultimately his paranoia that convinces him to wipe out a "small, insignificant clan" on Haman's recommendation without ever being told who they are.[13] And when Esther reveals what Haman has done, Ahasuerus seems unbalanced, not sure whom to believe or where to turn.

But many of the movies portray the king as a wise and heroic ruler instead. In Walsh's 1960 *Esther and the King*, Ahasuerus is a young, accomplished warrior often off fighting the Greeks.[14] Vashti, by contrast, is a schemer and adulterer, so he banishes her. Even though Ahasuerus prefers not to take another queen after that, he gathers the maidens anyway to abide by the laws of Persia. In White's 2013 *Book of Esther*, Xerxes has a strong sense of justice. Although hyper-concerned with obedience, both from his wives and from his subjects, he chooses Esther as his queen because he sees how kindly she treats her rival, Haman's daughter Zara. And at the end of the film, he hears out Haman's accusations of treason against Mordecai in a courtroom, because he believes Mordecai should not be condemned without trial. Even the heartthrob Xerxes in *One Night with a King* is physically fit, virtuous, respectful, and fair.[15]

The early films probably render the king a hero to contrast him with the traitorous Haman and encourage patriotic sentiment. In Walsh's 1960 epic, Haman is an unredeemed villain. He seeks to ally himself

---

12. Clanton, 122, 134, most clearly makes this point.
13. In fact, the Bible never explicitly indicates that Haman told Ahasuerus that he wanted to wipe out the Jews. When speaking to the king, Haman refers only to "a people, scattered and dispersed among the other peoples" (Est. 3:8).
14. See McGeough, 105, for further discussion of Ahasuerus' character in Walsh's movie.
15. Xerxes' presentation in this film may be meant to appeal to Christian women. Ibid., 116.

Yosef Lindell

with Alexander and the Greeks, plunders the royal treasury, sleeps with Vashti, and tries to sleep with Esther too, among other indiscretions. In the *Greatest Heroes of the Bible* adaptation from 1978, Haman is plotting rebellion and is behind an attempt on the king's life.[16] Undoubtedly, the conflict between the heroic monarch and the treasonous Haman in these films reflects American patriotic ideals and "fits well into a time that viewed the world in terms of binary opposites: black and white, cowboys and Indians, communism and freedom."[17] In the biblical account, however, it's harder to draw such lines. One does not fully know where Ahasuerus' wickedness ends and Haman's begins.

Yet there's another reason many films render a goodly King Ahasuerus: a wicked king cannot be one of the protagonists in a love story. And many of these movies, following Hollywood conventions, are romances. Perhaps the most telling line in Walsh's 1960 film is when Ahasuerus promises Esther up to half the kingdom, and she replies, "But I only want the kingdom of your heart." In fact, in the movie, Esther affirmatively chooses Ahasuerus over her Jewish fiancé Simon; she refuses to leave the palace with Simon when he comes to rescue her. The movie concludes with Ahasuerus returning from battle and Esther rushing into his arms. Well, whatever. What more can one expect from a film marketed with the tagline, "The Most Celebrated Love Adventure of All... From the Greatest Book of All"?[18] Similarly, the 1978 *Greatest Heroes of the Bible* version ends with the narrator's proclamation that Esther's "union with Xerxes was to become one of the great enduring love stories

---

16. The biblical account does suggest that Haman might be plotting treason; his idea of appropriate attire for the man whom the king desires to honor – which he believes is himself – involves the king's crown and other royal effects (Est. 6:8). This accusation is put in Esther's mouth at her second party by *Targum Rishon* (7:6): "The adversary is the wicked Haman who sought...to dress himself today in royal garments, to ride on your horse, and to lower the golden crown upon his neck, to rebel against you and to take away the kingdom from you." Bernard Grossfeld, trans., *The Aramaic Bible, Volume 18: The Two Targums of Esther* (Collegeville, 1991), 75.

17. Ehrlich, 124. See also Jo Carruthers, "Biblical Epic and the American State: The Traitor and Sanctified Violence in *Esther and the King* (1960)," in Eric Christianson and Christopher Partridge, eds., *Holy Terror: Understanding Religion and Violence in Popular Culture* (London, 2010), 42.

18. McGeough, 103.

of all time." And Sajbel's *One Night with the King* is a romance just like the novel on which it is based. Xerxes is played by Luke Goss, who was the drummer in a 1980s English boy band, and he spends much of the film shirtless.[19] Esther is something of a "Jewish Disney princess."[20] She's literate, conversant in multiple languages, and carries herself with a grace and innocence that impresses nearly everyone around her. She charms the king not just with her beauty, but with her daring: on a night when King Xerxes can't sleep, Hegai sends Esther from the harem to read to the king from the book of records. But quickly boring of the record tome, Esther instead tells Xerxes the biblical story of Jacob's love for Rachel. Enchanted, Xerxes soon chooses her to be the new queen. And nearly every movie contains some hint of romantic attachment between the pair: even in Mertes' more reasonable retelling, Ahasuerus declares his love for Esther at the end and she reciprocates.

And this takes us to the final issue I want to address: turning the book of Esther into a love story diminishes Esther's agency. In the biblical account, Esther saves the day. Although reticent at first to take up Mordecai's charge to appear before the king and plead for her people, she quickly has a change of heart (Est. 4:15–16). As Adele Berlin notes, Mordecai's instructions are vague, and it "was Esther alone who planned the parties and invited the guests. It was she who arranged exactly the right setting to expose the wickedness of Haman, much to the surprise of both the king and Haman."[21]

The more romantically inclined movies don't fully reflect Esther's daring and ingenuity. When Esther reveals her Jewishness to the king, it's usually the climax of the story, but not so in Walsh's 1960 film, where Esther's declaration does not sway Ahasuerus all that much. When she stands up to the king and speaks of her faith, he replies, "I do not believe your love," and only temporarily stays the execution of Mordecai and the Jews. As I noted, this Esther is not supposed to be clever or cunning, but

---

19. Ehrlich, 129, calls this version of Xerxes "the type of hunk most often found on the cover of Harlequin romances" and considers his bare-chestedness "seemingly an existential state for him in this movie."

20. Clanton, 131; McGeough, 114; Ehrlich, 131.

21. Adele Berlin, *The JPS Bible Commentary: Esther* (Philadelphia, 2001), 50.

seeking the kingdom of the heart. Rather, it's only after a co-conspirator of Haman's reveals to Ahasuerus Haman's plot against him and the king actually catches Haman trying to flee the city that the overwrought story ends at last. In the 1978 movie, Esther confronts Haman in private and tells him he can have his way with her if he convinces Xerxes to repeal the decree against the Jews. When Haman declines her offer and tries to rape her anyway, Esther cries out and Xerxes comes to the rescue. This film makes Esther's success more dependent on her being a woman and on the king's swift action to protect her than on her own intelligence and abilities.[22]

Although Esther in *One Night with the King* has greater agency than the Esther in older films, issues remain. The romance between Esther and Xerxes starts off swimmingly, but Xerxes begins to suspect Esther of adultery when he witnesses a clandestine meeting between her and Mordecai. Thus, when Esther reveals herself as a Jew at a candle-lit party held in a tent, the king, who already mistrusts her, is not inclined to believe her, particularly after Haman casts aspersions on her motives for making such a claim. Desperate, Esther dangles her necklace in front of Xerxes' eyes, which in the candlelight resembles a disco ball and reveals many whirling Stars of David (yes, a glaring anachronism).[23] Yet Haman yells that he sees nothing, and Xerxes exits confused. After a tense moment when Haman is at Esther's throat, we breathe a sigh of relief when Xerxes returns and disposes of Haman. Esther asks Xerxes why he came back, and he replies, "I saw them. I saw the stars." They kiss as the music soars. To be sure, Xerxes has realized that Esther was telling

---

22. Nonetheless, elements of this approach have been suggested by other interpreters. The Talmud (Megilla 15b) states that at her final party, Esther encouraged Ahasuerus' jealousy by falsely intimating that she and Haman were having an affair.

23. The Star of David was not a widely used Jewish symbol until the modern period. Although it was widespread by the eighteenth and nineteenth centuries, it was perhaps not until the twentieth century, when it was used both by the Nazis and on the Israeli flag, that it became Judaism's most recognizable marker. See Gershom Scholem, "The Curious History of the Six-Pointed Star: How the 'Magen David' Became the Jewish Symbol," *Commentary* (September 1949), https://www.commentarymagazine.com/articles/gershom-scholem/the-curious-history-of-the-six-pointed-starhow-the-magen-david-became-the-jewish-symbol. Yet it's likely that Sajbel used the Magen David in the film precisely because of its modern resonance and ubiquity.

the truth about being a Jew. But there is a subtext here as well: Esther's suspected infidelity is forgiven, and with the stars aligned, romance is rekindled. It is the hopeless way the pair look into each other's eyes – just as much as Esther's bravery – which ultimately makes the problems go away. Love conquers all.

There's simply no suggestion in the biblical text that Esther and the king were star-crossed lovers. When the Bible says that Ahasuerus loved Esther (2:17), it is difficult to know whether the term connotes "a deep emotional bond," a "passing fancy," or something in between.[24] Perhaps Ahasuerus quickly tired of Esther; indeed, after making her queen, he gathers virgins a second time (2:19). When Mordecai asks her to go to the king, she demurs initially, saying she has not been called for thirty days (4:11). And even at the end, it's hard to know whether Ahasuerus has Haman executed because of his great love for Esther or for some other reason: perhaps he feared scandal if word got out that he had had the queen's people eliminated.

Regardless, there is no indication that Esther loved the king. Mutual affection is rare in the Bible, and although men love women, we rarely hear if the woman reciprocates.[25] The Talmud (Sanhedrin 74b) states that Esther was "like the ground" (i.e., unmoving) in her sexual encounters with Ahasuerus. Suffice it to say, the Sages did not think she enjoyed herself much. The Septuagint's additions to the text make the same point, putting in Esther's mouth that she abhorred "the bed of the uncircumcised and of any alien" (Additions to Esther, C). Although interpreters always had religious reasons for keeping things cool between Esther and the king, it's hard to see that much romance in their union from a purely textual perspective either. Forcibly taken from her home, placed in a harem, and ultimately selected by monarchical whim, Esther finds herself in the right place at the right time to save her people. But there's little to suggest that she relishes the opportunity. The improbable and enduring love between Esther and the king in the movies says more about the expectations of American filmmakers and viewers than it does about the original story.

---

24. Berlin, 29.
25. The Song of Songs is an exception. Also, King Saul's daughter, Michal, loved David (I Sam. 18:20).

For each issue we've considered, filmmakers made interpretive choices that reflect an American milieu. Haman's antisemitism becomes more pronounced and recognizable to contemporary audiences. The king is either an American hero or a good American lover, which perhaps are one and the same. And Esther inevitably loses some of her agency, a victim of the conventions of a satisfying romance.

Yet perhaps we ought to cut the movies some slack. For all of their flights of fancy and questionable storytelling choices, the Esther films are following a long tradition: interpreters have never been satisfied just to leave the story of Esther as it is.

The Septuagint translation of Esther adds over one hundred verses not found in the Masoretic text and inserts prayers to God and other explicitly religious material.[26] Hints of the romance genre (or at least indications that the king treated Esther affectionately) are already present in the Septuagint's additions; Esther fainting in the king's arms in *One Night with the King* comes straight from there (Additions to Esther, D). Additionally, there are more midrashic collections on Esther than on any other biblical book, and they all embellish the story significantly.[27] Likewise, two Aramaic *targumim*, or translations, exist for Esther, and both are expansive retellings that function like midrash.[28] Finally, the Talmud in Megilla features a self-contained midrash on Esther. For seven pages, it elaborates on the story in sequence, which is highly unusual given the Talmud's typically discursive and scattered style.[29] Notably too, the Talmud is by no means literal in its reading of the story; in one well-known inventive reading, Queen Vashti grows a tail (Megilla 12b).

There seems to be something about Esther in particular that has drawn those within the Jewish tradition and without to recast it in ways that yield new stories and messages. A couple of points come

---

26. Berlin, l–li.
27. Aaron Koller, *Esther in Ancient Jewish Thought* (Cambridge, 2014), 164; see Berlin, lii–liv.
28. Berlin, liii.
29. In fact, the Esther midrash in Tractate Megilla may be the "only full midrashic exposition of an entire biblical book to have been incorporated into the Babylonian Talmud." Eliezer Segal, *The Babylonian Esther Midrash: A Critical Commentary* 1 (Atlanta, 1994), 1. See Koller, 163.

to mind. For one, the book troublingly fails to mention God and lacks other outwardly religious elements. Further, the Book of Esther's voice is not very biblical. The book is comical, even funny at times; full of hyperbole, repetition, caricatures, and surprising reversals.[30] It's likely that both Esther's irreligiosity and its irreverence led biblical interpreters to propose readings that made it more consistent with the rest of the biblical canon.[31] And it could also be that the humor in Esther makes it ripe for embellishment, signaling that the story is meant to be riffed on.[32] Perhaps there's less need for fidelity to a text that does not even take itself seriously.

One thing is for sure: there isn't just one way the story of Esther has been retold. And if, in some sense, midrash attempts to bring the Bible to life, film is a potent medium. Adapting the *megilla* for the silver screen, for better or worse, has become the midrashic method of modernity.

Now do yourself a favor and go and watch something else instead.

---

30. See Berlin, xvii–xxii.

31. Moshe Halbertal, in *People of the Book: Canon, Meaning, and Authority* (Cambridge, 1997), 23–26, suggests that exegetes must make biblical books "consistent with the rest of Scriptures" once they are canonized, and that with regard to Esther in particular, its canonization suppresses its comedic reading and addresses its lack of religiosity. See Koller, 170.

32. Some midrashim even focus on the book's humorous elements. For example, although Haman's complaint to Ahasuerus about the Jews seems more sinister than funny, *Targum Sheni* (3:8) makes light of it in a long, whimsical passage where Haman cycles through the Jewish year, spewing a litany of complaints about the Jews' odd holiday customs and alleged laziness and disloyalty. See Berlin, 39. I suppose Vashti's tail is kind of comical too.

Presidential Politics
and Purim

Esther in the White House: The Scroll of Esther and Surviving Palace Intrigue at 1600 Pennsylvania Avenue

Dr. Tevi Troy

T he story of Queen Esther has a tremendous cultural resonance. We can see this resonance even today, more than two thousand years after the events depicted in the Book of Esther, as the Queen Esther comparison is a frequent motif for political commentators assessing presidential politics.

These comparisons go across the political aisle and even across the gender divide. In the Donald Trump presidency, commentators debated Secretary of State Mike Pompeo's suggestion that Trump was a modern Queen Esther, sent to save today's Jewish people from destruction. As Secretary Pompeo mused, "Could it be that President Trump right now has been sort of raised for such a time as this, just like Queen Esther, to help save the Jewish people from the Iranian menace?"

Pompeo is far from the only one to make such a comparison to a modern political figure. A *New York* magazine profile reported that First Daughter Ivanka Trump was nicknamed "Queen Esther" at her synagogue for her ability to steer the ruler in directions helpful to the Jewish people. In an earlier administration, Israeli Prime Minister Benjamin Netanyahu invoked the Esther story by giving President Barack Obama a copy of the Book of Esther as a gift – and as an unsubtle reminder that a previous Persian empire had also tried to destroy the Jews. On the campaign trail in 2008, a voter told former First Lady and presidential aspirant Hillary Clinton that Queen Esther reminded him of Hillary, prompting Mrs. Clinton to share the tidbit that the Esther story was one of her favorite biblical stories. In 1999, when the Jewish intern Monica Lewinsky was revealed to have been having an affair with President Bill Clinton, the JTA reported that some referred to her as a "modern-day Queen Esther." Another interesting reaction to the Lewinsky scandal came from future Vice President Mike Pence, then a political pundit, who suggested that Clinton's activities reminded him that "in the Bible story of Esther we are told of a king who was charged to put right his own household because there would be 'no end of disrespect and discord' among the families of the kingdom if he failed to do so."

These comparisons are creative, and point to Esther's continuing hold on our imagination. Still, they do not capture the true essence of the Esther story. Esther was a young woman brought into the fractious environment of the Persian king who had to both survive and get her way with no legal authority beyond a marital relationship to the king. In this, the Esther story is the story of the modern First Lady. The First Lady has no independent power. She is there by virtue of her spouse's election as president. As Lady Bird Johnson observed of the role, "The First Lady is, and always has been, an unpaid public servant elected by one person, her husband." In order to be successful, the First Lady must navigate an often-treacherous White House environment with her wiles, her wisdom, and – she hopes – the help of one very powerful ally in the form of the president.

Esther managed to survive and succeed in the court of King Ahasuerus in an impressive way. She did so even though she was burdened by the additional handicap of being Jewish at a time when the regime, prompted by the king's top adviser Haman, was planning to annihilate the Jews. When her cousin and mentor Mordecai first notifies her that the Jews are threatened and she needs to intervene, she explains to him the very real danger she faces. In Esther 4:11, she tells Mordecai via an intermediary that "whosoever, whether man or woman, shall come unto the king into the inner court, who is not called, there is one law for him, that he be put to death, except such to whom the king shall hold out the golden scepter, that he may live; but I have not been called to come in unto the king these thirty days." Mordecai recognizes the danger, but does not accept her excuse, famously telling her in 4:14 that "who knoweth whether thou art not come to royal estate for such a time as this?"

Mordecai successfully convinces her that she must intervene, but his persuasiveness does not solve the problem of how to both save the Jews and at the same time not lose her head. For this, she is on her own, and resorts to a multi-step process. First, she calls on Mordecai and the whole Jewish community to fast and pray, knowing that she must have God on her side. But knowing that God helps those who help themselves, she also comes up with a multi-part strategy for navigating the treacherous politics of Ahasuerus' court, politics that have already vanquished her predecessor Vashti. She approaches Ahasuerus, but with a modest request – that the king and Haman should attend a party she has organized that day. At the party, in response to the king's offer that she can have whatever she wants, per 5:6, "even to the half of the kingdom," she requests that they again attend another party scheduled for the next day. This elaborate party scheduling was not purposeless. It was designed to make the king more favorably inclined toward her but also to allay any suspicions Haman might harbor. If Haman sees her as just an empty-headed party planner, then he could fall into the trap of underestimating her. Which is exactly what happens.

Esther reveals Haman's wickedness at the second party. Haman prostrates himself on her bed to beg for mercy. The king thinks that Haman is trying to seduce or, worse, rape her, and is enraged, saying in 7:8, "Will he even force the queen before me in the house?" Haman is taken away with his head covered. Royal aide Harbonah quickly steps in and informs the king that Haman has a gallows waiting for the purpose of hanging Mordecai. The king, in 7:9, says, "Hang him thereon," and they take Haman away to his deserved execution. His ten sons are hanged as well, forestalling the continuation of his wicked line. The Jews are saved, and Mordecai is elevated to Haman's old position. The story has a happy ending, but only because Esther successfully navigated the politics of Ahasuerus' court.

While no one is executed and whole peoples are generally not threatened in the modern White House, there is no doubt that politics in the modern White House are treacherous as well. Modern First Ladies often find themselves in the position of Esther: lacking statutory authority but having unmatched access to the most powerful person in the palace. To be successful, modern First Ladies must leverage that crucial relationship while not losing the support of the White House staff.

The role of the First Lady has also evolved over time, meaning that the definition of "success" has changed with it. While First Ladies used to be content with their role as chief social planner in the White House, more recent First Ladies have tried to have an issue that they make their own. This issue selection, however, comes with a tension. The more the First Lady's issues are in the purview of the White House policy staffers, the more difficulties the First Lady will face. When Lady Bird Johnson, for example, made the minor issue of highway beautification her focus, she faced few challengers. When Hillary Clinton tried to take over the Clinton health care reform, she faced more resistance, both internally and externally.

One First Lady who came up against internal challenges was Betty Ford. The Ford White House was a famously fractious White House, riven by rivalries from its outset. At the center of much of the tension was Robert Hartmann, a hard-drinking former journalist who served as Ford's speechwriter, political counselor, and vice-presidential chief of staff, who had the advantage of longstanding ties to Ford. Hartmann alienated nearly everyone on the White House staff except for Ford, so much so that his nickname in the White House was "SOB." Hartmann playfully suggested that it stood for "Sweet Old Bob," but he, and the rest of the staff, knew better.

Mrs. Ford also did not like Hartmann, recognizing that he was a poisonous influence in the White House and damaging to her husband.

Hartmann, for his part, was once again in denial – either legitimately or disingenuously – about how he was viewed by others, telling a reporter about the First Lady, "We are the best of friends." But once again Hartmann's closeness to Ford carried the day, and he would remain in the administration throughout Ford's term.

Hartmann's staying power does not mean that Betty was powerless, however. White House management was not her area, but she did manage to speak out on issues that were important to her. She was vocally pro-choice, and in favor of the controversial Equal Rights Amendment, to the consternation of Ford's political aides. Serving as chief of staff and deputy chief of staff to Ford were the young but formidable Donald Rumsfeld and Dick Cheney, who would go on to long careers in Republican politics. They wanted Ford to intervene and quiet Mrs. Ford down, but Ford would have none of it. "If you want Betty to tone it down," he told them, "then you tell her." The lesson was clear: Betty could not change the internal management of the White House, but neither could White House aides tell her what to do. Esther, for all her successes, would have marveled at Betty's ability to speak out on issues important to her that were contrary to administration policy.

Nancy Reagan was one First Lady who did try to get involved in internal White House management. Her heavy involvement in her husband's political career dated back to Ronald Reagan's period as governor. Savvy staffers were aware of the Sacramento rule: "A happy Nancy means happy governor." Her involvement continued during the presidential campaign of 1980. Aide Mike Deaver smartly developed a close, quasi-familial bond with both Reagan and Nancy, which would serve him well during his tenure with Reagan, something Haman would have been wise to do with Esther.

In the White House, Nancy got even more involved, especially when it came to managing second-term chief of staff Don Regan. Treasury secretary during the first Reagan term, he did not seem to understand the "Happy Nancy" rule. He also failed to extricate Reagan from the biggest misstep of his presidency, the Iran-Contra scandal. The administration stood accused of negotiating for the release of US hostages by selling arms to a hostile regime in Iran and using the proceeds from those sales to support the Nicaraguan contras, something that Congress had expressly prohibited.

Many believed the responsibility for the scandal rested with Regan. Relations deteriorated as Nancy started keeping a scorecard of Regan's various offenses. She did not like his November 1986 crack that he was running a "shovel brigade," responsible for cleaning up the president's messes. In January of 1987, she was angry that Regan insisted on Reagan giving the State of the Union Address only three weeks after he had undergone prostate surgery. They had multiple arguments about Iran-Contra over the phone, including several in which Regan hung up on Nancy. When Regan's predecessor Jim Baker heard about the hang-ups, he cracked – "That's not just a firing offense. That may be a hanging offense."

What finally finished Regan was not Iran-Contra, but a now mostly forgotten scandal. On February 15, 1987, the White House announced the hiring of a new communications director, John Koehler, who had an impressive record at the Associated Press and the United States Information Agency. Unfortunately, Koehler had something else on his record that was troubling and needed explaining: he participated in a Nazi youth group as a ten-year-old in his native Germany. The *Washington Post* reported this fact on February 20, and on February 21 Regan said that Koehler's name had come "directly from the East Wing." Everyone knew that "East Wing" meant Nancy, and in throwing Nancy under the bus, Regan had sealed his own fate. Reagan's diary entry the next day read, "That does it. Nancy had never met Koehler and had nothing to do with his appointment." Regan was gone within the week. Koehler was gone quickly as well. He started on March 1 and left on March 7, making his six-day tenure as White House communications director even shorter than Anthony Scaramucci's legendary eleven-day tenure under Trump in 2017.

Even with Regan gone, however, the rivalry did not come to an immediate end. At the Gridiron Dinner at the end of March of 1987, Reagan joked that "Nancy and Don tried to patch things up the other day. They met privately over lunch – just the two of them and their food tasters." But it was Regan who would have the last laugh. In his bitter memoir, he revealed to the world that Nancy used an astrologer to help determine the president's schedule, something that still shadows Nancy's reputation, even after her death. Of course, in the Purim story, it is Haman, not Esther, who is interested in divination, using lots to determine the best date for his evil scheme to destroy the Jews.

Regan's timebomb of a book had a lasting and harmful impact on Nancy's historical image. In the Purim story, Haman was executed after he left power, meaning he had no more cards left to play. He gets booed at every mention during the annual reading of the *megilla* by Jews on the holiday of Purim, and neither he nor any ancestors lived to tell their side of the story. Regan, in contrast, not only lived, but was able to get revenge via his revealing memoir.

Nancy got another comeuppance from a subsequent Esther in the form of successor First Lady Barbara Bush. Barbara had been Second Lady under Nancy when her husband George served as Reagan's vice president. Nancy sent messages through intermediaries that she wanted the Bushes – particularly Barbara – to stay out of the press, and actively kept the Bushes off the list for White House social events, such as the 1985 dinner for the Prince and Princess of Wales. It was so bad that Barbara would later remark that she did not even know what the White House residence looked like when she and George moved in as president and First Lady. Barbara mostly suffered in silence while Nancy ruled the roost, if acerbic entries in her private diary count as silence. But Barbara got small measures of revenge, such as the time when she read a book critical of Nancy, but changed the cover on the book so people around her wouldn't know what she was reading.

Once Barbara became First Lady, she got her payback in more prominent ways. First, she got much better press than Nancy and was generally better liked. Her aides referred to Barbara as "the national treasure," which was far better than the disparaging nicknames aides had called Nancy. Barbara also got in her digs, starting at the 1988 nominating convention where Bush looked forward to creating "a kinder and gentler nation." Nancy, resenting the implication about her husband's administration, asked, "Kinder and gentler than what?" But Barbara was also willing to be firm with Nancy. When Barbara learned that Nancy had falsely accused Barbara of keeping ex-president Reagan away from the White House, Barbara let her have it, telling Nancy over the phone,

"And we did have your wonderful husband to the White House and don't you ever call me again!" The two women never had anything more than a perfunctory conversation after that one. In this scenario, Nancy was Vashti to Barbara's Esther, and Barbara was making sure that everyone knew that Esther, and not Vashti, was now in charge.

As we get closer to the modern era, First Ladies are getting increasingly powerful. In the Obama White House, First Lady Michelle Obama was no nervous Esther, plotting in the background to advance her cause without losing her head. Women in general were more powerful in the Obama White House than in any previous White House, banding together as a group and working to advance each other's interests. The most powerful woman of this group was senior adviser Valerie Jarrett, powerful in large part because of her long-standing relationship with Michelle. Jarrett knew Barack and Michelle Obama longer than anyone, even before they were married; outlasted and even encouraged the exit of multiple chiefs of staff; and had access to the first couple that most White House aides could only dream of. By day she was a White House aide, attending meetings with the rest of the staff and calling Obama "Mr. President." At night, however, she would go to the White House residence with the first couple, hang out with them, and revert to calling the president "Barack." Her regular nocturnal opportunities to convey her policy views directly to the president outside the normal channels in this way earned her the nickname of "The Night Stalker."

Jarrett resented the implication that she took advantage of her closeness to the president and First Lady. When challenged on this, she denied violating the process, declaring, "If I have something to say, I don't hold back in meetings so I can have a private conversation with the president." She spoke in terms that would resonate with the Obama White House ethos, saying, "I respect the process." While she acknowledged spending time with the first couple in the residence, she claimed that the visits were for friendship, not policy reasons: they would talk about the kids and shows they liked such as *Downton Abbey*.

Other aides contradicted Jarrett's claim of innocuous evening visits. Given her importance in the White House and closeness to the president, they would not do so on the record. Anonymous aides felt that Jarrett kept her own counsel in official meetings during the day, only to make her case to the president in private. This alienated her colleagues, one of whom complained, "If you have a dissenting view, say it in the room. If you want to advocate for something, do it in the room, not later with the president." Aides who ran afoul of her, like Press Secretary Robert Gibbs, would find themselves short timers in an administration in which she served for all eight years. In this period, Michelle was akin to Esther, but Jarrett was like Harbonah, the key aide to Ahasuerus who brings in the crucial information that leads to the decision about Haman's fate after Haman angered the king.

Today, we are also getting closer to the era when the Esther in the White House might be not a woman but a man, something that almost happened with former President Bill Clinton in 2016. Regardless of gender, future First Ladies – and First Husbands – will continue to face challenges in the form of staff tensions for as long as the Republic lasts. Whatever those challenges, presidential spouses would be wise to look to the eternal lessons of Queen Esther for guidance on how to navigate the politics of being spouse to the most powerful person in the country.

The Purim Crisis of 1948: Harry S. Truman, Freda Kirchwey, and Chaim Weizmann

Philip Getz

On March 25, 1948, President Harry S. Truman released a statement regarding the situation in Palestine. It had been four months since the United Nations General Assembly had approved the plan to partition the territory into an Arab state and a Jewish state, and due to the violence that had proliferated, Truman stated that "unfortunately, it has become clear that the partition plan cannot be carried out at this time by peaceful means." He called for a temporary UN-administered trusteeship to maintain peace once the British Mandate was to end on May 15.[1]

---

1. Statement by President Truman, White House Press Release, March 25, 1948, David Niles Papers, Box 29, Harry S. Truman Library and Museum, https://www.truman-library.gov/library/public-papers/55/presidents-news-conference.

The day was Purim, and befitting a holiday about topsy-turvy events, Truman's statement appeared to be a reversal of the administration's earlier support for the partition plan, which the White House itself had secretly gone to lengths to ensure, persuading various countries to change their negative votes.[2] Eleanor Roosevelt was so appalled by Truman's ostensible backtracking on partition that she had to be persuaded not to resign from the US delegation to the United Nations on account of it.[3]

In fact, the apparent about-face was a form of damage control to roll back the impact of a speech America's ambassador to the UN, Warren Austin, had made five days earlier, the Friday of *Shabbat Zakhor*. In that speech Austin had intimated that the United States had reservations about partition, preferring to provide the warring Arabs and Jews "further opportunity to reach an agreement regarding the future government."[4] Austin's speech and Truman's damage-control statement, meant to obscure his administration's fumble, amounted to a concerning diplomatic and political crisis, "the Purim crisis," one might call it. Austin came off as out of touch with the realities of Jewish-Arab hostilities, and Truman, much like King Ahasuerus himself, appeared to lack genuine control and coherence regarding his own government's policy position.

In truth, Truman did lack control over his State Department on the topic of Palestine. Like FDR's State Department before him, Truman's had in fact been against partition from the start. Partition was only one of several plans that had been proposed for the future of Palestine, but it was the only formal proposal that provided for an independent Jewish state. Partition, therefore, became shorthand for Jewish statehood. The possibility alone was of deep concern to Truman's Secretary of State George R. Marshall, the decorated general, who feared that the existence of an independent Jewish state in Palestine would enflame

---

2. Allis Radosh and Ronald Radosh, *A Safe Haven: Harry S. Truman and the Founding of Israel* (New York, 2010), 272–276.

3. Ibid., 306.

4. Statement of Warren Austin before the Security Council of the UN, March 19, 1948; *Foreign Relations of the United States* (FRUS) 1944–1949 (Washington, DC), vol. 5, 742–744.

regional tensions and prevent access to Arab oil reserves, desperately needed in Marshall's plan to reconstruct a decimated Europe. Before the partition plan was passed by the UN, State Department experts had attempted to make "modifications" to the plan, modifications that Marshall himself described to be as "of a pro-Arab nature."[5] In addition, the State Department and diplomatic corps urged the government not to advocate for partition[6] and tried to halt its implementation once the plan was passed.[7] Austin's speech that set off the Purim crisis was an example of the last of these tactics.

The Purim crisis is emblematic of a deeper connection between Purim and Israel's independence. In Zionist circles, the state's founding is often referred to as a miracle in the literal sense of the term, and Religious Zionists perform various rituals to mark Israel's Independence Day as a religious holiday, most notably by reciting *Hallel*, which is only done on established religious holidays. The religious basis for doing so can be found in the *Ḥatam Sofer*, in the concluding words of what the author admits to be a rather verbose responsum:

> Establishing a holiday on the day a miracle was performed is a biblical obligation, as it is an *a fortiori* argument from the Torah. In my humble opinion, the day of Purim and the days of Ḥanukka are from the Torah! However, what to do on them – whether to send portions of food or to light candles or to commemorate them in some other way – is of rabbinic origin. Whoever does nothing to commemorate the days of Ḥanukka and Purim violates a biblical positive commandment.[8]

The *Ḥatam Sofer*'s specific references to both Ḥanukka and Purim point to two distinct but equally valid rabbinic conceptions or models of "the miraculous." Ḥanukka, which commemorates events in the second

---

5. Memorandum by Mr. Gordon Knox to Herschel Johnson, October 3, 1947, *FRUS*, vol. 5, 1173–1174.
6. Henderson to Marshall, September 22, 1947, "Certain Considerations Against Advocacy by the U.S. of the Majority Plan," *FRUS*, vol. 5, 1153–1159.
7. Memorandum Prepared by Department of State, April 2, 1948, *FRUS*, vol. 5, 778–796.
8. *Shut Ḥatam Sofer Yoreh Deʾah* 233.

century BCE, is representative of what is referred to as a *nes nigleh,* an exposed or explicit miracle. Such miracles involve a clear divergence of the natural order, a divine intervention that is inexplicable within the natural laws and logic of the universe. Many of the biblical miracles such as the splitting of the sea (Ex. 14:26–32) or the solar suspension in the battle at Gibeon (Josh. 10:13–14) would fall into this category. The Ḥanukka story itself exhibits at least two such explicit miracles: 1) The unlikely Macabbean victory over the mighty Seleucids; 2) The limited oil of the Menora lasting eight times as long as nature would allow.

The first of these miracles serves as the basis for the words of *Al HaNisim,* which praises God for having "delivered the strong into the hands of the weak, the many into the hands of the few." Only through God's direct intervention, it is traditionally held, would Matityahu and his five sons have been able to lead their forces to victory over the Seleucids.[9]

Purim, by contrast, is the quintessential example of a *nes nistar,* a hidden miracle. A *nes nistar,* as the tradition has it, assumes no such supernatural elements or explicit divine intervention. The conspicuous lack of God's name in the Book of Esther is widely considered to be a literary device illustrating that God is not always apparent in the process but evident in the outcome. As the Book of Esther recounts, "…when the king's command and decree were to be executed, the very day on which the enemies of the Jews had expected to get them in their power, the opposite happened, and the Jews got their enemies in their power" (Est. 9:1).[10] The miracle thus consists mainly in a dramatic reversal of fortune. Over the course of the thirteenth and fourteenth days of Adar, the Book of Esther tells us, the Jews felled 800 of their enemies in Shushan and 75,000 in the provinces of the kingdom. The text is markedly silent on how many Jews were engaged in the fighting but there is no indication that it was a case of "the many into the hands of the few." There is no explicit divine intervention in the balance of forces. Rather, it is a

9. Raymond P. Scheindlin, *A Short History of the Jewish People: From Legendary Times to Modern Statehood* (New York, 1998), 38.
10. All biblical translations are from *JPS Hebrew-English Tanakh: Second Edition* (Philadelphia, 1999).

dramatic shift in circumstance, brought about by twists and turns, and by the decisions and reactions of the story's characters: Esther, Haman, King Ahasuerus, and Mordecai, among others.

It has become customary among Religious Zionists to identify the founding of Israel, and therefore Yom HaAtzma'ut, with the Hanukka miracle model. Rabbi Chaim Druckman's essay "The Joy of Yom HaAtzma'ut" printed in *The Koren Mahzor for Yom HaAtzma'ut & Yom Yerushalayim* contains a section entitled "The Many into the Hands of the Few" that serves as a case in point:

> Is there a better example of "the many into the hands of the few"? On Hanukka, we repeatedly recite the *Al HaNissim* prayer in which we thank God for delivering "the many into the hands of the few." The Hanukka miracle took place more than two thousand years ago – but this wondrous event has happened also in our time! God delivered the many into the hands of the few, and thus saved us from certain death and gave us the gift of our own lives – is it not appropriate that we thank Him for this?[11]

Rabbi Druckman's emphasis on the Hanukka story reflects the conventional Israeli narrative of the 1948 Arab-Israeli war. In this narrative, Israel's fledgling military repelled the massive forces of seven Arab armies, a miraculous victory akin to that of the Maccabees over the Seleucids, a *nes nigleh*. The narrative was largely constructed by Israel's political elite and has endured as one of the country's most powerful founding myths. Chaim Herzog, son of Israel's Chief Rabbi Isaac Halevi Herzog, who fought in the 1948 war and later served as Israel's ambassador to the United Nations and as the country's sixth president, writes in his 1996 memoir, "The odds were definitely against us. We were able to mobilize a force of only 45,000, which included some 30,000 men and women whose functions were basically limited to local defense."[12]

---

11. *The Koren Mahzor for Yom HaAtzma'ut & Yom Yerushalayim: The Maidenbaum & Rothenberg Essays* (Jerusalem, 2015), 124.
12. Chaim Herzog, *Living History: A Memoir* (New York, 1996), 94.

Howard M. Sachar corroborates these numbers in his sweeping *A History of Israel: From the Rise of Zionism to Our Time*, but contextualizes them in a way that undermines the narrative completely. "The number itself was perhaps not much smaller than the total of Arab forces on the Palestine front, consisting of approximately 10,000 Egyptians, 4,500 Arab Legionnaires, 7,000 Syrians, 8,000 Iraqis, and 3,000 Lebanese."[13] A total of 32,500.

The opening in the 1980s of Israeli archival documents led some historians to revise these numbers, in favor of the Jews. According to Benny Morris:

> The Arab forces in Palestine consisted (until the end of May) of not more than 28,000 troops – some 5,500 Egyptians, 6,000–9,000 Arab Legionnaires, 6,000 from Syria, 4,500 from Iraq, a handful of Lebanese, and the remainder Palestinian irregulars and foreign volunteers.... By mid-July the IDF was fielding nearly 65,000 troops; by early spring 1949, 115,000. The Arab armies probably had about 40,000 troops in Palestine and Sinai by mid-July, and 55,000 in October, the number perhaps rising slightly by the spring of 1949.[14]

Avi Shlaim writes that although the Arab-Israeli War of 1948

> was persistently portrayed as a struggle of the few against the many... at each stage of the war, the IDF significantly outnumbered all the Arab forces arrayed against it, and by the final stage of the war its superiority ratio was nearly two to one. The final outcome of the war was therefore not a miracle but a reflection of the underlying Arab-Israeli military balance.[15]

In his final assessment, Shlaim, like Druckman, seems to uphold the Ḥanukka model of a miracle, "the many into the hands of a few." The

---

13. Howard M. Sachar, *A History of Israel: From the Rise of Zionism to Our Time* (New York, 1976), 317.
14. Benny Morris, *Righteous Victims: A History of the Zionist-Arab Conflict, 1881–2001* (New York, 2001), 217.
15. Avi Shlaim, *The Iron Wall: Israel and the Arab World* (New York, 2001), 35.

refutation of the conventional Israeli narrative, according to Shlaim, and presumably to Druckman as well, renders the application of the term "miracle" inaccurate.

Furthermore, Druckman's focus on the miraculousness of the war is peculiar for an additional reason. Israel's Independence Day is celebrated on the fifth of Iyar, which in 1948 corresponded to May 14, the day independence was declared. The war, however, went on for many more months, with the final armistice agreements not being signed until July 1949.[16] It would seem, therefore, that for the holiday to hold the religious significance accorded to it, per the view of the *Ḥatam Sofer*, the operative miracle of Yom HaAtzma'ut has to be something that occurred on that day. So what did occur on that day? And if it doesn't fit the Ḥanukka model of a miracle, does it fit the Purim model?

On May 14, 1948, the leaders of the Yishuv crammed inside the Tel Aviv Museum where David Ben-Gurion read aloud Israel's Declaration of Independence, to take effect at midnight. Noting the historical attachment of the Jews to the land, Ben-Gurion also acknowledged the destruction of European Jewry:

> The catastrophe which recently befell the Jewish people – the massacre of millions of Jews in Europe – was another clear demonstration of the urgency of solving the problem of its homelessness by re-establishing in Eretz-Israel the Jewish State, which would open the gates of the homeland wide to every Jew and confer upon the Jewish people the status of a fully privileged member of the comity of nations.
>
> Survivors of the Nazi holocaust in Europe, as well as Jews from other parts of the world, continued to migrate to Eretz-Israel, undaunted by difficulties, restrictions and dangers, and never ceased to assert their right to a life of dignity, freedom and honest toil in their national homeland.[17]

---

16. Morris, 251.
17. Declaration of the Establishment of the State of Israel, https://mfa.gov.il/mfa/ foreignpolicy/peace/guide/pages/declaration%20of%20establishment%20of%20

Eleven minutes after the declaration, President Harry S. Truman became the first world leader to recognize Israel's legitimacy.[18] The significance of this can hardly be overstated. Beyond the message it sent to other world leaders, Truman's recognition had immediate tangible benefits. While the state was functioning and reasonably prepared for the expected Arab invasion, recognition allowed it the ability to maneuver as an entity in international commerce. As the *New York Times* Jerusalem correspondent put it, "Would the ordinary commercial banks lend the Jewish state money without the approval of the US government?"[19]

So what of the Purim model? Of course, the major difference between Purim and Yom HaAtzma'ut is that while the Jews of fifth-century Persia averted their disaster, the Holocaust, in all of its horror, actually happened. But a closer look at the events between May 1945 and May 1948, from catastrophic destruction to recognized sovereignty, reveals its own cast of characters reminiscent of those in the Purim story, most notably, Ahasuerus (Truman), Esther (Freda Kirchwey), and Mordecai (Chaim Weizmann). It also displays many of the prevalent themes of the Book of Esther: desperate acts of lobbying, attempted subversion, and palace intrigue.

The story begins on May 8, 1945, when Chaim Herzog was serving as an intelligence officer in the British Army.

On 8 May, 1945, when Germany's final surrender took place, I was in the main street of Bremerhaven, the port north of Bremen. I thought of how privileged I was to be there – a soldier, placed among my sworn enemy, able to savor total and complete victory.

Bergen-Belsen had fallen to the British 8 Corps not long before. "I told some of the survivors that I was a Jewish officer from Palestine," writes Herzog. "They all burst into tears."[20] On that very day two years later,

---

state%20of%20israel.aspx.

18. Radosh and Radosh, *A Safe Haven*, 338.
19. Thomas J. Hamilton, "U.N. Morale Sagging Under Heavy Strains," *New York Times*, April 28, 1948, p. E4.
20. Herzog, 62–63.

"Moshe Shertok and David Ben-Gurion," representing the Jewish Agency at the United Nations Special Committee on Palestine (UNSCOP), "took their seats among the world's nations to make the first presentation before the United Nations of the Jewish case for a homeland in Palestine." [21] One can hardly imagine a more dramatic shift in circumstances for world Jewry than that which occurred between May 8, 1945, and May 8, 1947. After years of global inaction on behalf of Europe's Jews, Shertok and Ben-Gurion sat in the United Nations chamber to persuade the world to grant the Jews sovereignty and self-determination. But whereas in May 1945 the British had liberated the Jews from Bergen-Belsen, in May 1947 it was the British who insisted that the Arab Higher Committee of Palestine, the official Arab national movement in Palestine opposite the Jewish Agency, be included in the UNSCOP deliberations.[22]

The British proposal was at first glance as sensible and morally responsible as could be imagined. The Arabs constituted two-thirds of the population of Palestine and thus should have at least the same non-voting presence at UNSCOP as the Jews.[23] At the time, however, many involved in the international fact-finding missions and deliberations held the Arab Higher Committee in contempt for its intransigence and refusal to engage in negotiations. No individual was a more vocal opponent of the Arab Higher Committee than Freda Kirchwey, the staunchly leftist, antifascist, and pro-Soviet editor-in-chief of *The Nation*. Kirchwey, the undisputed Esther in this story, had visited Palestine the previous year, meeting with Chaim Weizmann at his home and at some point becoming devoted to the cause of Jewish statehood. Deeply committed to influencing public policy, Kirchwey had created a fundraising and policy-oriented organization called the Nation Associates, and in 1944 hired Lillie Schultz, a former assistant to Stephen Wise, "the leading American Zionist spokesman,"[24] as the organization's director. Indefatigable and of ferocious will, "Kirchwey and Schultz worked

21. Radosh and Radosh, *A Safe Haven*, 211.
22. Ibid.
23. Herbert G. Feis, *The Birth of Israel: The Tousled Diplomatic Bed* (New York, 1969), 13, 23.
24. Sachar, 220.

behind the scenes, coordinated activity with the Jewish Agency, and answered in programmatic detail every argument against the creation of a Jewish state offered by the State Department, the oil lobby, the British, and the Arabs."[25]

In Kirchwey's view, the Arab Higher Committee was nothing more than a puppet of Haj Amin al-Husseini, the Grand Mufti of Jerusalem. The Nation Associates produced an altogether indicting report of the Arab Higher Committee and the Mufti himself, providing clear (and classified) evidence of the Mufti's close affiliations with Hitler, Himmler, and Dino Alfieri; his coordination of the deadly riots of 1936; and the collaboration of his relative, Jamal al-Husseini, a member of the Arab Higher Committee's delegation to the UN, in fomenting the anti-British rebellion in Iraq during World War II. Kirchwey and the Nation Associates sent the report to Truman and to every UN delegation along with a 133-page report and a position paper in support of the partition of Palestine.[26]

Five months later and with the UN vote on partition just weeks away, the Nation Associates held a dinner at the Waldorf-Astoria devoted to "The Palestine Solution and Its Relationship to World Peace." As Allis and Ronald Radosh describe it,

> Pointing out suspected State Department plans to prevent the establishment of a Jewish state, *The Nation* publisher Freda Kirchwey wrote the invitation letter, signed by the Nation Associates, warning their constituency that "there is a gigantic double-cross in the offing at the United Nations." Not only was that an actual possibility, Kirchwey argued, but "President Truman is reported as capitulating to the Arabs," which meant that "there will be no hope for settling the Jews of Europe in Palestine."[27]

25. Ronald Radosh and Allis Radosh, "Righteous Among the Editors: When the Left Loved Israel," *World Affairs* 171, no. 1 (Summer 2008): 68–69.
26. Radosh and Radosh, *A Safe Haven*, 211–214.
27. Radosh and Radosh, *A Safe Haven*, 247.

One can scarcely read this passage without being reminded of Esther's dinner for Ahasuerus and Haman, Esther exclaiming to the king, "For we have been sold, my people and I, to be destroyed, massacred, and exterminated" (Est. 7:4).

The president would, the following year, recognize Israel's independence. But Truman was an improbable person to be the first world leader to do so. From his alleged early political flirtations with the Ku Klux Klan[28] to his unlikely displacement of Henry Wallace as Franklin Roosevelt's running mate in 1944, incidentally "much to the consternation of his wife, Bess, who wished to avoid the limelight,"[29] it was far from a foregone conclusion that Truman would find himself in a position to preside over the fate of Israel's independence and the salvation of Europe's Jewish refugees. John B. Judis is likely correct when he writes, "Far from being a Christian Zionist, Truman was deeply skeptical about the Zionist project of founding a Jewish state, as he repeatedly told Jewish leaders during his first year in office. He had personally overseen Henry Grady's work in developing the recommendations for a federated Palestine."[30] He was instinctually critical of Jewish exceptionalism, writing, "The Jews claim God Almighty picked 'em out for special privilege. Well I'm sure he had better judgment. Fact is, I never thought God picked any favorites."[31]

Truman thus, like Ahasuerus himself, needed to be turned to offer his proverbial signet ring. Thrust into the Palestine quagmire while trying to win World War II, Truman was at first "handicapped by his initial ignorance and confusion, and inclined to take a jaundiced view of the creation of a Jewish state," as Judis puts it. It seems clear that his primary goal from the end of the war until the declaration of statehood was always the resettlement of European refugees, not the creation of a Jewish state per se.[32] He eventually lost so much patience with the Zionist leadership that he refused

---

28. David McCullough, *Truman* (New York, 1992), 164.

29. Radosh and Radosh, *A Safe Haven*, 11.

30. John B. Judis, *Genesis: Truman, American Jews, and the Origins of the Arab/Israeli Conflict* (New York, 2014), 4.

31. Michael Joseph Cohen, *Truman and Israel* (Berkeley, 1990), 7.

32. Radosh and Radosh, *A Safe Haven*, 118.

to meet with them, exhibiting a particular dislike for Abba Hillel Silver, the Cleveland rabbi and chairman of the Jewish Agency's US division who was instrumental in building support for Jewish statehood within the Republican party.[33] Despite this and "in the face of sharp disagreements within his own administration and unrelenting pressure from Silver and American Zionists," Truman, between 1945 and 1948, became the most powerful and important supporter of Jewish statehood alive.[34] As Allis and Ronald Radosh explain in their brilliantly written and thoroughly researched book *Safe Haven: Harry S. Truman and the Founding of Israel*, this turn was the result of a complex combination of personal relationships, ethical callings, and political considerations. But, also like Ahasuerus, once he had turned, there was no going back. As Truman's advisor Clark Clifford told Secretary of Defense Robert Lovett, a staunch opponent of Jewish statehood, "Bob, there is no chance whatsoever that the president will change his attitude."[35]

After World War II, the United States and Britain grew further and further apart regarding their priorities in the Middle East, Britain being even more opposed to partition than the State Department. Foreign Secretary Ernst Bevin did not go through the same evolution of thought that Truman did, and though their positions drifted, two things they had agreed upon early on likely never changed. The first was that their countries "had given contradictory pledges to both sides," not unlike Ahasuerus' approval of both Haman's and Esther's requests. The second was that there was no question regarding who was "the most intelligent of all the Jewish leaders": the Belarussian-born organic chemist Chaim Weizmann.[36]

Truman's admiration for Weizmann, the Mordecai to Kirchwey's Esther, was well known to all of the Jewish and Zionist leaders. Reading through the history, one gets the impression that Truman almost never

---

33. Ibid., 249.
34. Judis, 188.
35. Radosh and Radosh, *A Safe Haven*, 335.
36. Minutes of meeting between Truman and Bevin at the White House, December 8, 1946, FO 371 61762/E221, PRO.

left a meeting with Weizmann without having committed to something. When the State Department tried to have the partition maps redrawn to exclude the Negev from the Jewish state – one of its self-described "pro-Arab" modifications – Eliahu Epstein, the Jewish Agency's representative in Washington, knew that Weizmann was the only person who could influence Truman to stop it. Appealing to Truman's farming childhood and the fact that Truman "had toiled for years to create regional development and flood controls in the Missouri Valley,"[37] Weizmann successfully explained how the Jews of Palestine had found success in cultivating supposedly arid land, and their desalination plans for the desert.[38]

In the months that followed that meeting, both Weizmann and Kirchwey were aware of the State Department's attempts to sabotage the partition plan and worked tirelessly to alert Truman and keep him in their sphere of influence. Kirchwey wrote to Truman stating that a senior State Department official was feeding the press indications of an "American effort to revise partition resolution," expressing her dismay to Truman that he "could conceivably be partner to such action." Revealing some potential coordination, Weizmann would later use very similar language, writing to Truman, incredulous "…that you would be a party to further disappointment of pathetic hopes, which you yourself have raised so high." Weizmann impressed upon Truman that the choice was "between Statehood and extermination. History and providence have placed this issue in your hands, and I am confident that you will decide it in the spirit of the moral law."[39]

By March of 1948, Weizmann no longer held an official leadership position in the Zionist movement, having two years earlier been denied reelection to the presidency of the Zionist Organization (largely due to Abba Hillel Silver).[40] Ironically, this made Weizmann the only Zionist personality Truman would agree to see, having by that point barred the Zionist leadership from the White House. At the pleading and shrewd behest of his former business partner, Eddie Jacobson, Truman agreed

---

37. Margaret Truman, "Palestine Was One of Truman's Most Difficult Dilemmas," *Sarasota Journal,* December 14, 1972.
38. Radosh and Radosh, *A Safe Haven,* 264.
39. Weizmann to Truman, April 9, 1948, Letter 138, *The Letters and Papers of Chaim Weizmann,* Series A, August 1947–1952, pp. 99–101.
40. Sachar, 274.

to meet with Weizmann – and only Weizmann – on the condition that he enter the White House (aptly) from the east lest he be seen by the press.[41] The meeting was both warm and productive on both sides but occurred the day before UN Ambassador Warren Austin's speech that set off the Purim crisis. Warren's speech not only suggested to the world that the United States was no longer supportive of partition, it contravened much of what Truman had told Weizmann the day before. Truman, reeling from the betrayal within his ranks, said to Clark Clifford, "How could this have happened? I assured Chaim Weizmann that we were for partition and would stick to it. He must think I'm a plain liar."[42] Truman noted the betrayal on his calendar, "The State Dept. pulled the rug from under me today."[43]

In an uncanny parallel to the Purim story, what happened seems to have been a possible case of a misappropriated "signet ring," a decree passed naively and without proper safeguards. The State Department had gotten Truman to sign a draft of Austin's statement "which included the proposal of trusteeship as an alternative" while the president was distracted "aboard his presidential yacht, somewhere between St. Croix and Key West."[44]

As in the Book of Esther, the situation on the ground needed to be handled by the Jews themselves, albeit sanctioned and made possible by the powers that be: the UN, the US, and the Soviet Union. Weizmann had noted this arrangement when securing the Balfour Declaration in 1917, saying, "Even if all the governments of the world gave us a country it would be a gift of words, but if the Jewish people will go and build Palestine, the Jewish state will become a reality and a fact."[45] In another bizarre reversal, the Soviet Union shocked the world with its early and explicit support for Jewish statehood, possibly to drive a wedge between their erstwhile Western allies Britain and the US.[46] Still, the Soviet Union's sup-

41. Radosh and Radosh, *A Safe Haven*, 301.
42. Ibid., 392, fn. 72; Judis, 404, fn. 53; McCullough, 611.
43. Entry on Truman's calendar, March 19, 1948, in Margaret Truman, *Harry S. Truman* (New York, 1972), 424–425.
44. Radosh and Radosh, *A Safe Haven*, 292.
45. Ibid., 353.
46. Laurent Rucker, "Moscow's Surprise: The Soviet-Israeli Alliance of 1947–1949,"

port proved instrumental in the Haganah's procurement of weapons from Czechoslovakia, which, in Avi Shlaim's estimation, "decisively tipped the scales in their favor."[47] As the Haganah's High Command had told UNSCOP, the Jews of Palestine were reasonably confident they could defeat the Arab onslaught militarily, the question was whether the world powers would "give the Jews a legal basis for arming and defending themselves."[48]

In the case of Ahasuerus, the legal basis is a decree permitting "the Jews of every city to assemble and fight for their lives; if any people or province attacks them, they may destroy, massacre, and exterminate its armed force together with women and children, and plunder their possessions" (Est. 8:11). While the text is at pains to tell us that that the Jews "did not lay hands on the spoil" (Est. 9:10, 15–16), the decree itself hints at a warrant for excessive violence. In the Palestine situation, as it happens, this is exactly what the State Department wanted to prevent. Sadly, and despite a US consul cable to Marshall stating that the Jews were not seeking to conquer territory outside of what had been allotted to them in partition – abstaining from laying their hands on the spoil, as it were – egregious acts of violence did occur, both before and after independence was declared.[49] In Lydda, a fitting example because like on Purim the violence occurred over the course of two days, three hundred Arab "women, children, old people," were killed in July 1948.[50]

Elliott Horowitz has written with great erudition on the historical relationship between Purim and Jewish violence, and in the examples he brings of Jews expressing discomfort and dismay over the violence recounted in the *megilla*, one sees remarkable foreshadowing of the intra-Jewish controversies over Zionism and the violence of 1948.[51] In advance of Purim sixty years earlier, in 1888, no less a figure than Claude

---

Working Paper 48, Woodrow Wilson International Center for Scholars, 20.
47. Shlaim, 35.
48. Jose Garcia Granados, *The Birth of Israel: The Drama as I Saw It* (New York, 1948), 173–182.
49. Wasson to Marshall, May 3, 1948, FRUS, vol. 5, pp. 898–901.
50. Ari Shavit, *My Promised Land: The Triumph and Tragedy of Israel* (New York, 2013), 107–108.
51. Elliott Horowitz, *Reckless Rites: Purim and the Legacy of Jewish Violence* (Princeton, 2006).

Goldsmid Montefiore, scion of proverbial Anglo-Jewish royalty, wrote in London's *Jewish Chronicle* that were Purim "gradually to lose its place in our religious calendar" he would not lament it. What bothered Montefiore about Purim was its accentuation "of the national element in Judaism."[52] In his *The Bible for Home Reading*, Montefiore wrote: "We can hardly dignify or extenuate the operations of the Jews by saying that they were done in self-defense...the slain apparently included both women and children."[53] The text also tells us of the deaths of Haman's sons, and while the Gemara unleashes harsh curses upon them,[54] the text itself tells us nothing of their guilt, only their association (Est. 9:7–10).

But while the graphic allowance of Ahasuerus' decree (at Esther's request) and the sheer number of casualties are enough to make us wince, that the Purim miracle plays a substantial role in rabbinic theology is beyond dispute. As Rava taught us, the Jews reaccepted the Torah during the days of Ahasuerus, without coercion, the implication being that it was on account of the Purim miracle that the covenant between God and the Jewish people remains valid today.[55] But perhaps the text of Esther is teaching us something about the sordid nature of hidden miracles, and of history itself. Truman, for his part, had a sense for the sordid. While supportive of Jewish statehood, he nursed an ever-present anxiety about the aggression that brewed within persecuted peoples, the dark side of new fortune. "Put an underdog on top and it makes no difference whether his name is Russian, Jewish, Negro, Management, Labor, Mormon, Baptist he goes haywire. I've found very, very [few] Jews who remember their past condition when prosperity comes."[56]

But dramatic reversal is indeed the miracle of Purim, and among all of those that occurred between 1945 and 1948, one of the most profound was what happened at the highest echelons of American government. Two months after Ambassador Austin had embroiled him in the Purim crisis, Truman returned the snub, not even alerting Austin of his

---

52. C. G. Montefiore, "Purim Difficulties," *Jewish Chronicle*, March 2, 1888, 8.
53. C. G. Montefiore, *The Bible for Home Reading*, vol. 2. (London, 1986), 403.
54. Megilla 16b.
55. Shabbat 88a.
56. Harry S. Truman, diary, July 21, 1947, President's Secretary's File, Box 232, HSTL.

plan to recognize Israel's independence. Instead he had Clark Clifford, for whom the State Department had particular disdain, tell the Department's Director of Special Political Affairs Dean Rusk. As the Radoshes describe the encounter:

> Clifford asked Rusk to tell the U.S. delegation. Rusk was aghast: "But this cuts across what our delegation has been trying to accomplish in the General Assembly," referring to its efforts to attain a truce and then trusteeship. "Nevertheless," Clifford instructed him, "this is what the President wishes you to do."[57]

In that moment of bringing the State Department low, Truman brought Weizmann high, reportedly saying after the announcement, "The old Doctor will believe me now."[58]

The following week Weizmann visited the White House in the first formal visit representing the new state and returned home with assurances from Truman that the United States would help with a loan for military and reconstruction purposes. As Vera Weizmann recounts, "When Truman told Chaim that he was the President of so many millions of Americans," Chaim retorted, "But I am the President of a million presidents."[59] As it says, "Mordecai left the king's presence in royal robes of blue and white" (Est. 8:15).

> King Ahasuerus imposed tribute on the mainland and the islands. All his mighty and powerful acts, and a full account of the greatness to which the king advanced Mordecai, are recorded in the Annals of the Kings of Media and Persia. For Mordecai the Jew ranked next to King Ahasuerus and was highly regarded by the Jews and popular with the multitude of his brethren; he sought the good of his people and interceded for the welfare of all his kindred. (Est. 10:1–3)

---

57. Radosh and Radosh, *A Safe Haven*, 338.
58. Vera Weizmann (as told to David Tutaev), *The Impossible Takes Longer: The Memoirs of Vera Weizmann* (New York, 1967), 234.
59. Ibid., 240.

The *Megilla* and
Modern Morality

Haman Redrawn: Remembering Esther and the Holocaust in America

Rabbi Mishael Zion

And the memory of these days shall not die out among their descendants. (Est. 9:28)

On the steps of the Lincoln Memorial in 1963, moments before Rev. Martin Luther King Jr. delivered his "I Have a Dream" speech, Rabbi Joachim Prinz addressed the March on Washington for Jobs and Freedom under the title "I speak to you as an American Jew." The sight of millions of Americans calling for justice reminded him of a different era in his personal history:

> When I was the rabbi of the Jewish community in Berlin under the Hitler regime, I learned many things. The most important thing that I learned under those tragic circumstances was that bigotry and hatred are not the most urgent problem. The most

urgent, the most disgraceful, the most shameful and the most tragic problem is silence.[1]

Prinz's resounding words have become a central text of American Jewish history, speaking to its own sense of calling as a community which must never again be silent. Prinz's words echo the crucial moment in the Book of Esther, where Mordecai warns his cousin: "If you shall remain silent at this time…" (Est. 4:14). Indeed, in his memoirs of Nazi-era Berlin, Prinz describes how reading the *megilla* became a seminal ritual for the Berlin Jewish community, as his synagogue became uncharacteristically filled to the brim on Purim: "People came by the thousands to the synagogue to listen to the story of Haman and Esther, [which] became the story of our own lives." The Scroll of Esther, read in Hebrew and then translated into German,

> suddenly made sense… [for] it was quite clear that Haman meant Hitler…. Never had I heard such applause in a synagogue when the names of the ten sons of Haman were read, describing their hanging from the gallows. Every time we read "Haman" the people heard Hitler, and the noise was deafening. The little noisemakers became more than toys. They were the instruments of a demonstration in the midst of frustration.[2]

For centuries, the *megilla* has been read by Jewish communities the world over twice annually. Yet during the years of the Nazi regime, and in the years immediately following the Holocaust, it received a special resonance. Commentators, artists, and rabbis read the scroll in a new light, even as adults and children used the holiday of Purim to respond to their anxieties and fears following the Holocaust. While the Jewish people have faced persecution and adversity over their history, there

1. March on Washington for Jobs and Freedom, August 28, 1963.
2. Joachim Prinz, "A Rabbi under the Hitler Regime," in *Gegenwart in Ruckblick*, ed. H. A. Strauss and K. R. Grossman (Heidelberg, 1970), 231–238. See also Elliott Horowitz, "The Rite to Be Reckless: On the Perpetration and Interpretation of Purim Violence," *Poetics Today* 15, no. 1, *Purim and the Cultural Poetics of Judaism* (Spring 1994): 9–54.

are only two moments in their collective memory in which they faced a governmental policy of outright destruction: Shushan and Wansee, Haman and Hitler. Thus the memories of these two moments are deeply entwined, even as one ended in a miraculous political salvation, while the other ended in tragedy and destruction for many Jewish communities.

Beyond the shared legacy of facing vicious antisemitism and the specter of complete annihilation, what ties these two events together is their focus on memory and retelling. From New York to Tel Aviv, and from Berlin to Casablanca, Jews responded to the Holocaust with a deep desire to memorialize and record, to retell and to enshrine. In this they echoed the sentiment reflected powerfully at the end of the *megilla*: again and again, Mordecai and Esther ask of the Jewish community to "never forget," to enshrine the days of Purim and the scrolls of Esther and Mordecai in Jewish collective memory, in the calendar, and in the canon. "Asked Esther of the Rabbis: Remember me for generations.... Write me for the generations," tells the Talmud (Megilla 7b), and in so doing they set a cultural structure for the creation of Jewish collective memory: tell the story, reinterpret ancient canon and tradition, and set a date of ritual memorialization in the annual calendar.

One such striking example of reinterpretation shines forth from one of the most rich and beloved artistic renditions of the *megilla* to be created in America: Arthur Szyk's 1950 Scroll of Esther.

Since the second-century paintings of the *megilla* adorning the walls of the synagogue at Dura Europos,[3] and through the Renaissance tradition of illuminated *megillot* by such artists as Salom Italia,[4] and all the way to the JT Waldman's graphic novel version of Esther, the artistic depiction of the *megilla* has been a prime arena of biblical reinterpretation.[5] Each artist reveals his own reading of the text in light of contemporary understandings, often allowing current events to be insinuated

---

3. Shalom Sabar, "Scroll of Esther, in Art," in *Encyclopedia Judaica*, Second Edition, vol. 18 (Detroit, 2007), 218–220.
4. Shalom Sabar, "A New Discovery: The Earliest Illustrated Esther Scroll by Shalom Italia," *Ars Judaica* 8 (2012): 119–136; Sharon Assaf and Emily D. Bilski, *Salom Italia's Esther Scrolls and the Dutch Golden Age* (Amsterdam, 2011).
5. See Samantha Baskind's chapter in this volume.

or echoed throughout the works of art. Choice of clothes, facial depictions, and contemporary regal paraphernalia are all brought into play as artists mix image and metaphor in their personal midrash of the traditional verses. Yet it is more rare for a single artist to create two vastly different versions of the same scroll.

This is the case for Arthur Szyk, the Polish born (Lodz, 1895) and renowned Jewish artist. In 1925 Szyk published an artistic illuminated edition of the Book of Esther.[6] Inspired by Orientalist art, the exhibition of medieval Persian miniatures, and ancient Achaemenid architecture, Szyk created rich and colorful images. Following the *megilla*'s obsession with thick description of cloth and architecture, his paintings are devoted to the intricate recreation of the "white and blue linen, fastened with cords of white linen and purple material to silver rings on marble pillars…" (Est. 1:7) with which Ahasuerus' palace is described. In this volume, Haman is described without much pathos, often hard to distinguish from the other characters in the *megilla*. The *megilla* becomes an opportunity to depict a chapter in Jewish history full of rich visual images and finery, with the historical and ethnic drama as mere background.

Szyk escaped Europe in 1940 and survived the Holocaust in New York, devoting many illustrations to protesting the Nazi regime and World War II.[7] Yet in the years after the Holocaust, he returned to the studio and created a new, second *megilla*. In this *megilla*, created on American soil during the years following the Holocaust[8] and completed in 1950, a year before his death, we encounter a strikingly different

---

6. Arthur Szyk, *Le Livre d'Esther* (Paris, 1925).
7. See Irvin Ungar, *Arthur Szyk: Soldier in Art* (Burlingame, 2017).
8. Immediately following the Holocaust, Szyk dedicated a 1946 volume of popular biblical illustrations to his mother and her maid, framing his artistic act as a modern Jewish ritual act – "an eternal Kaddish": "In March 1943 my beloved seventy-year-old mother, was taken from the ghetto of Lodz to the Nazi furnaces of Majdanek. With her, voluntarily went her faithful servant, the good Christian, Josefa, a Polish peasant. Together, hand in hand, they were burned alive. In memory of the two noble martyrs I dedicate my pictures of the Bible as an eternal Kaddish for these great souls"; Mortimer J. Cohen, *Pathways Through the Bible*, illustrated by Arthur Szyk (Philadelphia, 1946), quoted in Jonathan Sarna, *American Judaism: A History* (New Haven, 2004), 295.

Arthur Szyk, *Szyk with Haman on the Gallows*, from *The Book of Esther* (New Canaan, 1950). Watercolor and gouache, 7 x 5 in. Reproduced with the cooperation of Irvin Ungar

artistic interpretation.[9] This time, the romanticism of Oriental imagination becomes the backdrop, whereas the drama of an orphaned Esther
and her strikingly Jewish cousin Mordecai are pitted against a repulsive
and dangerous Haman. Significantly, Haman is adorned with Nazi swastikas and the SS Totenkopf (skulls and bones insignia). In the crowning scene of the scroll, atop the verse describing the hanging of Haman
(Est. 7:10), Szyk breaks the "fourth wall" and depicts himself, the modern artist, French beret on his head, writing a *megilla* in the traditional
fashion of *stam* writing. Above him hangs Haman, two swastikas prominently displayed on his clothes, hanging from the gallows. In one hand,
Szyk is writing out the traditional blessing recited at the end of the ritual
reading of the *megilla*, describing the Almighty as "He who gives His
people Israel repayment from all their opponents." In his other hand,
with a tongue-in-cheek anachronism, Szyk is holding a *hamantasch*.

This singular ars-poetica break from the artistic depictions of
the story of Esther, planting the artist-commentator in person into the
pages of the traditional scroll, is a deep statement about the role of the
commentator in all biblical writing, and especially in the *megilla*. Just
as the scroll itself refers to its authors with fervent self-awareness – "So
Queen Esther, daughter of Abihail, along with Mordecai the Jew, wrote
with full authority to confirm this second letter concerning Purim"
(Est. 9:29) – so Szyk makes a powerful statement about his own creation: by re-drawing the *megilla* after the Holocaust, he is gaining the
upper hand on the Nazi perpetrators of the Holocaust. The artistic act
in itself is the fulfillment of the aforementioned blessing, and perhaps
a modern reframing of it. Perhaps it is not the Almighty, but the artist
and commentator, who by depicting Haman as epitomizing the Nazis,
is giving, to quote the blessing recited after the reading of the *megilla*,
"His people Israel repayment from all their opponents."

9. The volume was published posthumously in Israel in 1974. More on Szyk, including
essays by Irvin Ungar, can be found at www.szyk.com.

When God Stopped Talking to His People: Rabbi Joseph Soloveitchik on the Book of Mordecai and Esther

Rabbi Shalom Carmy

Mrs. Tonya Soloveitchik, wife of Rabbi Joseph Soloveitchik, died on the fast of Esther (Purim eve) 1967 after a long illness. In subsequent years, Rabbi Soloveitchik, "the Rav," customarily dedicated a public lecture to her memory, delivered in English, around that time of year. The annual occasion gave the Rav the opportunity and the motivation to produce several substantial essays on the *megilla*. These essays, and others prepared in the same period, constitute chapters 1–4 of the posthumously published *Days of Deliverance*.[1] They are the subject of the following discussion.

---

1. Ed. Eli D. Clark, Joel B. Wolowelsky, and Reuven Ziegler (Jersey City, 2007). Page references in the text are to this book.

Rabbi Shalom Carmy

I.

The coincidence of the Rebbetzin's *yahrzeit* and Purim would not in itself have dictated an analysis of the biblical story of Mordecai and Esther. Not all of the memorial discourses were on the theme of Purim and the *megilla*; I recall lectures devoted to matters related to Passover and the Exodus which are equally suitable to the season. I also recall public lectures on the halakhic aspects of Purim and the reading of the *megilla* that were of a piece with the Rav's Talmud lectures. Even once the Rav decided to focus on theological or philosophical themes pertaining to Purim, rather than on halakhic ideas, he had ready alternatives that did not concentrate on the story of Mordecai and Esther and that are much explored in contemporary Orthodox Jewish thought. Had the Rav chosen, he could have spoken about significant themes in Jewish theology and consciousness that are attached to the story and celebration of Purim, in one way or another, but would not have required the kind of focus he brought to the narrative and psychological reality of the biblical story. These alternative themes play a role in the Esther lectures though they remain in the background.

One set of options he could have chosen would have highlighted ideas about the status of the Torah in the religious life of Israel. The Talmud (Shabbat 88a) says that the original acceptance of the Torah by Israel at Sinai was not whole-hearted but, in some sense, coerced; the fully free acceptance took place in the days of Ahasuerus. This statement, and its elaboration in medieval rabbinic literature, has important implications for the Rav's discussion of freedom and covenant. It is prominently featured in *Lonely Man of Faith*. In the Purim lectures the Rav mentions it as evidence of a re-commitment resulting from the Purim experience (14). As a major theological principle, however, it is not directly pertinent to the story of Esther and Mordecai or to the mortal threat to the Jewish people that turned into a victory.

The difference between the primal encounter at Sinai and the more fully consensual adoption of the Torah at the time of the *megilla* is also expressed by Jewish thinkers who define the former period as the age of the Written Torah and the latter, occurring during the time of the Second Temple, as the great flourishing of the Oral Law. This view is championed by the Netziv (Rabbi Naftali Berlin, d. 1892). In an appendix to his commentary on Exodus, the Netziv ties this development to the events of the *megilla*. Although the Rav valued Netziv's biblical commentary, he does not pick up on this idea. The Netziv's preoccupation with the distinctive contribution of the Oral Law and with the advances in rabbinic reasoning that are its hallmark encouraged him to trace a historical trajectory in which the methodological centrality of the Oral Law can be contrasted with an earlier First Temple model of Torah study that is less recognizably "rabbinic."[2] I suspect the Rav did not follow Netziv here because he was not interested in expounding a periodization of Torah study in these early generations. In *Lonely Man* his contrast between First Temple and Second Temple communities revolves around the transition from prophecy to prayer. This distinction indeed comes into play in the Esther discourses.

The Rav's lectures are largely devoted to the psychological-political struggle between the Jews and their enemies. But it is nonetheless different from other approaches to the *megilla* that likewise center on the threat of extermination to the Jews and its reversal. Eran Shalev, for example, shows early American readings of Esther that depict Ahasuerus as a tyrant-like George III and the Jews as prototypes of liberty comparable to the heroes of the American revolution.[3] The Rav is not attracted to this kind of anachronistic preaching. To begin with, although the *megilla* can be read convincingly as a satire of the great king and his royal court, it is not a critique of monarchy per se but of one particular king. Ahasuerus can be seen as the prototype of modern political authority, and the Rav is ready to hint in that direction, but neither the *megilla* nor the Rav's reading of it argue for an alternative form of government, be it republicanism or democracy. Secondly, the story of Purim is, in the

2. Rabbi Abraham Isaac Kook too has much to say about the difference between the spiritual life of the First Temple and later Judaism; see his classic essay *LeMahalakh HaIde'ot BeYisrael* in *Orot*. Where Netziv saw this development in Torah study as an advance, Rabbi Kook held that it reflected a retreat from earlier biblical spirituality. See Yaakov Blidstein, "Torah of the Land of Israel and Torah of Babylonia in the Thought of Netziv of Volozhin," in A. Ravitzky, ed., *Eretz Yisrael BaHagut HaYehudit HaḤadasha* (Jerusalem, 2005).

3. Eran Shalev, *American Zion: The Old Testament as a Political Text from the Revolution to the Civil War* (New Haven, 2013), 27–34. See also his chapter in this volume.

end, not a case study about universal political systems but rather a story about the Jewish people, their perilous history and singular relationship to God; it cannot be dissolved in universal categories.

At the same time, there is a danger of over-particularizing the story of the *megilla*. Faced with the Jewish reality of the story, and its echoes throughout Jewish history, one is tempted to treat animosity toward the Jew indiscriminately, as a brute fact about the world, a given that requires no further psychological investigation. From this perspective, there is no need to treat Ahasuerus and Haman as distinct individuals, acting out different motives: they, and their adherents, can all be subsumed under one rubric, as "them," the gentiles, from whom we must be saved. As we shall see, the Rav does not go down this simplistic path.[4]

A "Jewish-centered" commentary on the Book of Esther might also confront the question of revenge. Christians and enlightened, progressive people often condemn the book for approving Jewish bloodthirstiness toward their enemies. Martin Luther went so far as to advocate removing the book from the biblical canon for that reason. Hence Jewish writers are impelled to spend time defending Jewish standards. The Rav spoke about this matter in a 1949 Yiddish lecture in Boston that has survived in print. A digression within a lecture on charity refers to the Yiddish writer Chaim Zhitlovsky and to a number of assorted early twentieth-century pacifists who condemned violent reaction against evil.[5] The Rav submits that they have been refuted by history. It may be noted that this speech was offered to the Arbeiter-Ring

---

4. As far as I can tell, the lectures presented at Yeshiva University in *Days of Deliverance* do not use the term "antisemitism" to describe the Persians. Instead he speaks about hatred of the Jews. The term "antisemitism" appears in one discourse given in Boston. I cannot tell if this terminological variation is meant to avoid a potentially inflammatory "one size fits all" outlook on the persecutors of the Jews or whether it is random or intended to avoid anachronism. Likewise, the Purim lectures explicitly compare the Persian court to that of Stalin and his chief of police Lavrenty Beria, but he is sparing in explicit references to Hitler; one paragraph (38) describes the rise to power in Germany of a "tyrant and madman" who is not actually named; but in this section, neither, is Haman named, though he is clearly the personification of the Rav's "arrogant man." The Ḥanukka lectures in the second half of the book are freer in allusions to antisemitism and to the Nazis.
5. *Derashos un Kesavim* (Jersey City, 2009), 242.

in Boston, a Jewish group known for its secular orientation, a very short time after the Holocaust, and might be expected to touch on questions that concerned them.

Lastly, for many, both among the pious and the less observant, Purim – and the story that gave rise to it – is characterized as a day when ordinary restraints and inhibitions are thrown off, a day when the Jewish calendar's seriousness and sobriety are suspended, a day of merriment and the imbibing of adult beverages. This notion is reflected in the halakhot prescribing robust feasting on Purim and reflects relief and joy at catastrophe averted and redeemed. Hasidic and neo-hasidic discourse often meditate on this annual moment when everyday sobriety and rationality are "overturned." Academics discern here the colorful carnivalesque abandon that intrigues historians of medieval Europe and seems otherwise lacking in Jewish history and law.[6] The Rav vigorously resisted this intellectual and experiential tendency, which would impede sober analysis and meditation on the significance of Purim, its story and laws. Hence he stresses that the Fast of Esther preceding Purim is an essential complement to the festivities of Purim: "Purim is also a day of meditation, introspection, and serious self-examination" (3). The talmudic Sages offered two proof texts for the reading of the *megilla*, one deriving from Psalm 22 ("My God, why have You forsaken me?") which was attributed to the despairing Esther, and Psalm 30 ("Weeping may endure for the night, but joy in the morning").[7] All this is consistent with his ceaseless endeavor to rescue religious observance from unthinking shallowness. The Rav's Judaism was an adult religion, on Purim no less than the rest of the year.

II.

Perhaps the most striking feature of the Rav's essays on Esther and on Purim is the effort he makes to interpret the *megilla* within the larger framework of the human condition. A large portion of the first two

---

6. Elliott Horowitz, *Reckless Rites: The Legacy of Jewish Violence* (Princeton, 2006), combines this theme with a negative judgment on Jewish violence culminating in contemporary militant Zionism.
7. Chapter 5, "The Joy of Purim," proposes the Rav's conception of the joy appropriate to Purim.

chapters in *Days of Deliverance* speaks about what it means to be a human being before turning to the Book of Esther. These significant insights parallel ideas found elsewhere in his writing. One may helpfully list several significant themes in the Rav's analysis of the Purim story: first, his comments on the "normal" human condition; then his varied insights on the personality and ideology of Ahasuerus; then the evil personified by Haman, which perforce requires attention to the question of how Ahasuerus gave him great power and abdicated responsibility to him. Along with these matters, one wonders whether something similar could happen today in the democratic West; the Rav occasionally considers this, and we can also make inferences from his general analysis. The positive Esther and Mordecai side of the story leads the Rav to reflect on the typically different roles of men and women and their desirable interaction in times of crisis.

Let us review each lecture on its own, on the way to arriving at their cumulative import:

Vulnerability defines the human condition in "The Duality of Purim" (delivered 1974), which is the opening chapter of the compiled *Days of Deliverance*. Vulnerability can be physical: we can neither anticipate nor forestall the many potential threats that we face. It can also be spiritual, the Rav makes a point of noting: most sin can be traced back to human weakness and vulnerability, which is why atonement is possible. Humility is one primary ethical lesson. The Rav illustrates this critically by referring to Israeli overconfidence after the Six Day War, which, he insinuates, may have contributed to unpreparedness for the Yom Kippur War that followed. By contrast, in the story of the *megilla*, the Rav reminds us, Mordecai did not initially proclaim his connection with Queen Esther; had he succumbed to vanity and trumpeted this stroke of fortune, their effort to rescue their people would have become much more difficult.

"The Duality of Purim" continues with the Jewish discovery of Amalek. Earlier in the essay the Rav had offered an interpretation of sin as the result of human vulnerability, thus understanding moral and spiritual defectiveness from within, as it were. With respect to Amalek, who is a stand-in for Haman, he makes no such attempt. At times, he posits, human beings go berserk, beyond the limits of "ordinary" sinfulness. The

Rav is careful here to look at the phenomenon of Amalek in a universal human context, albeit one especially focused on the Jew, an approach that reflects the subsequent history of Jew hatred. He arrives at four conclusions about Amalek: Amalek incarnates total evil; Amalek's central preoccupation is to hate the Jew; that hatred aims at utter destruction; and it is all-inclusive (not distinguishing among Jews) (19).[8]

Where the 1974 lecture contemplates human vulnerability, "The Megillah and Human Destiny" (1970) defines the human predicament as that of finiteness. Both terms indicate the limited powers of man, but whereas the 1974 discourse began with the human fear of what can befall us, either physically or spiritually, the 1970 presentation introduces very early the moral paradox: in the very same Persian society that invited a huge variety of ethnic groups to prolonged feasting and celebration, one of those groups could easily be targeted for extermination and liberal-minded decent people could stand by.

The Rav explains all this by delineating two human strategies to overcome the crisis of finitude, the fear of nothingness. One is hedonistic. The desire for infinity and boundlessness can find expression in the pursuit of pleasure, as we see in the extravagant feasting that opens the Book of Esther, or in other forms of acquisitiveness. Western society, the Rav adds, "is a typical representative of the aesthetic society" (34). On this reading, Ahasuerus promises boundless freedom and pleasure-seeking, not an ideology of evil but of self-centered agnostic enjoyment.

The second project of escape from awareness of finiteness is here called "arrogance." Rather than dimming the I-exist awareness through sensuality and acquisition, man begins to think that he has liberated himself. Arrogant-tyrannical men are collectivists; typically they are disciplined, power-hungry, out to conquer the world. Arrogance is not self-indulgent but satanic, not agnostic but atheistic. "Amalek is the typical representative of the arrogant, tyrannical society, of irrational man

---

8. The Rav's most thorough discussion of "ordinary" human sin as distinct from demonic evil occurs in *The Emergence of Ethical Man*. See my "In Many Respects God Was Closer to Abraham than to Moses: Themes in *Emergence of Ethical Man*," in *Scholarly Man of Faith: Studies in the Thought and Writings of Rabbi Joseph B. Soloveitchik*, ed. Ephraim Kanarfogel and Dov Schwartz (Jerusalem, 2017), 11–26.

whose code is satanic, methods diabolical, and purpose destruction" (37). In effect, Amalek here stands for Haman in the *megilla*.

How, in "The Megillah and Human Destiny," does arrogant man gain power? It appears that he exploits a kind of "moral vacuum" (my term, not the Rav's). As the Rav puts it: "Only people who were pursuing pleasure – for whom values had no fixity, norms no ultimate validity – could tolerate man-Satan, irrational and destructive and cruel" (39). "The same may happen in the Western world" (38).

"The Days of Ahasuerus" (Boston, 1975) continues along these lines, but it contains interesting extensions and psychological insights derived from the biblical text. These include a variation on the pleasure-seeking theme we have already met and a new emphasis on the volatility of Ahasuerus' rulership.

Following rabbinic teaching, the Rav deems Ahasuerus a parvenu king, one who did not inherit his throne from his father. More than other kings, then, his authority is uneasy. Combining two rabbinic views as to whether Ahasuerus was a wise king or a foolish king, the Rav considers him both shrewd and irrational. The celebrations with which the book commences are more than a hedonistic orgy. Ahasuerus aims to boost his control by giving the people a good time. The Rav recognizes, however, that the Persian populace to whom the emperor must appeal is not homogeneous. He arranges one banquet for the aristocracy and a second one for the lower classes. All this is consistent with the psychology of the Rav's previous chapter: pleasure-seeking can simultaneously represent a distraction from human finitude and a tool for solidifying the popularity of the government providing the entertainment.

Ahasuerus' drunken command that Queen Vashti display herself to the male revelers testifies to the king's vulgarity. The Rav, however, points out that this summons did not occur during the first party of 180 days, the one for the upper echelons, but during the second week-long party. Ahasuerus was a self-seeking statesman: he knew that humiliating the queen would alienate the aristocrats; appraising the crowd, he became convinced that dragging the queen into the merriment would help cement his bond with the kind of people he had invited to the second feast. In this he miscalculated; he had forgotten that human beings and members of the royal family have dignity and resent disrespect.

If the reader of the previous lecture was told that pleasure-seeking creates a moral vacuum which can be exploited by the Hamans of this world, the Vashti incident teaches that the life of pleasure-seeking and the policy of procuring the applause of the multitude coarsens the personality and thus paves the way to the effacement of human dignity.

The other major psychological insight of this chapter is grounded in Ahasuerus' fickleness and erratic behavior. A royal edict attempts to establish the husband's dominion in the home, as if family relations can be dictated by fiat. Consequently, implies the Rav, he earns a reputation for instability. As a result, his subjects are liable to think twice before acting on his commands. Had Ahasuerus' style of ruling been more predictable and invariant, the Rav suggests, it is likely that the haters of the Jews would not have waited eleven months, until the time set for their destruction. Because Ahasuerus did not convey the impression of resoluteness and rationality they delayed and gave time for Mordecai and Esther to counter Haman's initiative.

The portrayal of Ahasuerus as a debauched and abusive person, particularly toward women, makes us wonder how Esther could please the king and later sway him. She had declined the cosmetic services of the court and did not blend into the court atmosphere as it is depicted. The Rav writes, using a phrase from the Talmud, that Esther may not have been conventionally beautiful, but possessed charm (*ḥen*) that fascinated Ahasuerus. This suggestion is not unrealistic: men who habitually exploit and degrade women may frequently make an exception for individual women. The Rav enriches the insight by adding that the mystery attaching to Esther, the fact that she did not divulge her background, would presumably deepen the sense of mystery and extract respect from the king.

"Mordecai and Esther" (New York, 1973) is the last chapter interpreting the Book of Esther. One focus of the chapter is the manner whereby Esther triumphed over Haman in the battle for the king's mind. The other is an assessment of the leadership provided by Mordecai and Esther together.

What is new in this lecture, with respect to the psychology of Ahasuerus, is the Rav's stress on the king's pathological insecurity – he does not shy away from calling him paranoid. The premise for this analysis emerges from the earlier lectures. Ahasuerus is insecure because he lacks the authority of an inherited position. Early in the *megilla* he is saved from the plot of Bigthan and Teresh by Mordecai's timely intelligence. Accordingly, even more than the average king, he must ever be vigilant against attempts to overturn his regime. His suspicions are easily aroused and the ascendant courtier is the one who can manipulate the king's fears at that moment. Until then that was Haman. Haman masterminds the plan of extermination by warning Ahasuerus that the Jews are a dispersed people whose loyalty to the king's ordinances is dubious. For the Rav, this insinuation is enough to obtain for Haman a *carte blanche* against his enemies.

Esther's defense succeeds by taking advantage of the king's fears. Inviting the king and Haman to dine, without explaining her actions, she creates room for Ahasuerus to wonder whether his indispensable minister and his queen might be in league. Ahasuerus' jealousy is provoked and by the time Esther accuses Haman of being the enemy of her people, he is prepared to believe the worst. Later in the evening, when Ahasuerus discovers Haman on the queen's bed, he leaps to the conclusion that Haman's ambitions are not merely treasonous but sexual as well.

By now we have been made privy to several ingredients of Ahasuerus' character. First is the pleasure-seeker and would-be crowd pleaser at the beginning of the biblical book and in the first two lectures in *Days of Deliverance*. "In the Days of Ahasuerus" presents a variation on this theme – the pleasure-seeker who is coarsened by his descent into lust and vulgarity. This lecture also reveals Ahasuerus' erratic behavior, which is important for the narrative of the *megilla* but is not explicitly linked to other features of his psychological profile. Lastly, we come to realize that Ahasuerus is highly suggestible to rumors or insinuations of betrayal.

Earlier in the compiled book the Rav warned that the moral-psychological phenomena he wrote about in connection with the *megilla* are rife in contemporary Western culture, so that "it can happen here." Such warnings do not appear in the third and fourth lectures. Perhaps that is because hedonism and the human degradation it brings are typical not only of individuals, but of groups. Furthermore, he implies that Ahasuerus humiliated Vashti precisely in order to share the values of

the crowd. Erratic behavior or "paranoid" fear of betrayal are characteristic of individuals, and it is powerful individuals who display them
conspicuously. The Rav did not minimize the impact of a toxic political
environment under autocratic rule and when he delivered his speeches,
it was impossible not to think of the self-destructive events in the Nixon
White House. He knew that demagogues inflame the populace against
unpopular minorities (see his comments in the Ḥanukka lectures in
Days of Deliverance), but scapegoating is not the same thing as craziness
and coups. The Rav apparently did not regard paranoia as a besetting
vice of democratic society. Pleasure-seeking can be a fatal plague in a
demotic culture; systematic paranoia is not pervasive in democracies
to the same degree.[9]

III.

"Mordecai and Esther" contains a sustained reflection on models of leadership. Three themes are central to the discussion. First, the Rav devotes
attention to the transition from the classical biblical age to the twilight
of biblical history. The *megilla* "marks the passing of a bright, beautiful
summer day, full of song, color and joy.... It ushers in a dark, dreary
autumnal night of silence and fear, a night in the course of which God
stopped talking to His people" (70). What this means is that prophecy
is coming to an end. What that means is that God's intervention in history is concealed. In the prophetic era (for example, the Exodus) God
speaks directly: "The communication is clear and understandable." After
prophecy, "the communications are laconic and enigmatic, consisting
of mysterious hints and signs, bright, dazzling flashes and intimations,
that mystify man, who is often lonely and feels forsaken" (71). Practically,
this means that human beings are forced to act on their own initiative,
without the advantage of precise divine instruction.

Consequently, the story of Mordecai and Esther requires an understanding of human leadership in an age of uncertainty. In the *megilla* the

---

9. A separate inquiry is whether the Rav is indebted to philosophical critiques of
democracy according to which demagogues appeal to popular desire for pleasure
and plenty and use it to subjugate the people. See, for example, Plato, *Republic*,
St. 561–576.

Rav discerns a dual conception of leadership, which he identifies with male and female roles respectively. "He initiates action, she finishes what he started. He is the theoretician, she the implementer. He thinks in the abstract, she in concrete terms. He is naïve at times; she is practical" (78). As a generalization about men and women, this flies in the face of many common stereotypes: Western culture often thinks of men doing the important executive things, while the spiritual and angelic woman, unfit for the challenges of action, cheers them on. I have often wondered whether the Rav is here drawing on prevalent gender roles among the rabbinic elite, where the husband dedicates himself to Torah study and ideas, the wife taking care of daily chores and making a living. One may adduce parallel cases in the Bible, for example Netziv's view of the idealistic Isaac who must be guided, in blessing his children, by Rebecca, who understands them better and knows what must be done.[10] And one cannot help asking whether the Rav is here indirectly expressing something about the nature of the partnership he had with Mrs. Soloveitchik, with whom he accomplished so much, educationally, intellectually, institutionally, and religiously.

How does this categorization explain the actions of Mordecai and Esther? On the Rav's understanding of the Book of Esther, Mordecai excels at diagnosing the danger: he grasped the import of disparate occurrences and he realized that Esther had been placed in her exalted and paradoxical position to fulfill a divinely assigned mission. Mordecai's intuition was right, yet had it been up to him, Esther would have gone directly to Ahasuerus to plead with him for her people. Esther does not concur; instead, she delays. She understood that a direct approach was too risky and liable to fail; Ahasuerus could not be taught or reasoned with. She sets in motion the series of private banquets, waiting and hoping for something to happen that would make her intervention effective.

The Mordecai-Esther partnership provides a window into the Rav's thinking about gender complementarity and offers insight on the dramatic unfolding of the story. It also outlines a model of leadership in an era when God's guidance is indirect and when creative human leadership, inspired by God, is necessary. On the one hand, this highlights the Rav's "activism," his belief that human beings must plan and execute

---

10. See *Haamek Davar* to Genesis 27.

God's mission. On the other hand, he is also emphasizing that the required action cannot be deduced formulaically. Mordecai must rely on his intuitive judgment and Esther on her practical wisdom; they cannot merely extract instructions for action as one follows a cookbook recipe.

I believe that the need to consider leadership in the post-prophecy world of apparent divine silence is why two of these lectures end with a discussion of prayer, the setting in which man speaks to God and seeks His guidance. The two discussions of prayer seem to overlap, yet they differ in their content. "The Megillah and Human Destiny" has much to say about the crisis of human finitude. Prayer enters the picture at the end in order to delineate the Jewish alternative to the projects of pleasure-seeking man and arrogant man. Prayer is rooted in the honest confession of human finitude and dependence on God. That is why Jewish prayer, in the Rav's view, centers on petition, the frank acknowledging of human need. The world outlook of prayer posits a life that is consecrated, courageous, and sacrificial. In the context of the *megilla* this entails undertaking to fulfill one's mission, willingness to defy Haman, and readiness to leave the stage once one's mission has been accomplished.

In "Mordecai and Esther" Esther is extolled for assembling the Jews for days of fasting and prayer (though the latter is not mentioned explicitly in the biblical text). Here the point is not only the awareness of finitude and crisis so much as the spiritual capacity to entreat God and what one might call the etiquette of petition. The Rav implies that this gift is one in which women are particularly suited to show the way. As exemplified by Esther, it means that implementation is not only a matter of political or social cunning and planning but is also manifested in the words one addresses to God, the emotional straightforwardness and hopeful innocence of the child.

At first blush, Rabbi Soloveitchik's discourses on the story of the *megilla* are a minor component in a huge body of teaching and writing embracing Jewish law and philosophy. Our brief survey demonstrates that his treatment of the Purim story provides both overlap and fresh perspectives on many of his most prominent themes regarding the human condition, the distortions, perturbations, and temptations to which we are subject, the confrontation with historical evil, the challenge of leadership in a lonely world where God is not directly present, the roles of men and women, and the life of prayer.

Esther and Self-Endangerment in American Medical Experimentation

Rabbi Dr. Jason Weiner

On the wall of the main auditorium in Cedars-Sinai Medical Center in Los Angeles is a mural titled "Jewish Contributions to Medicine." It depicts thirty-six of the most influential Jewish healers throughout history, beginning with Moses holding the "*naḥash haneḥoshet,*" the copper serpent described in Numbers 21, followed by Mar Shmuel, a leading second-century Babylonian rabbi and the most noted physician of the talmudic era, and Maimonides, before gradually making its way to the modern era. One of the American figures on the mural is not as well known as he should be, Dr. Jesse Lazear.

Dr. Lazear was born in Baltimore, Maryland, in 1866, earned his undergraduate degree at Johns Hopkins University before completing Medical School at the Columbia University College of Physicians and Surgeons, and then undertook specialization training in Paris at the Institut Pasteur. He was married in 1896 and had two children.[1] In 1898 the Spanish-American War broke out, in which the US Army lost 6,406 troops, 5,438 of whom died from yellow fever. This degree of loss due to contagion was obviously unsustainable for a military, and led to public outcries, prompting the US Surgeon General, George Miller Sternberg,[2] to take action.[3]

One of the most important actions was the formation of the Yellow Fever Board by the US Army in 1900 which was commanded by Walter Reed. The goal of this Board was to conduct research to determine how yellow fever is transmitted so that its spread might be prevented. Yellow fever epidemics during the late eighteenth and early nineteenth centuries had created a culture in which solo researchers tried to become heroes to solve the problem. At the beginning of the twentieth century, Lazear was determined to find the cure and become such a hero. At the time, there were numerous theories of how the disease spread, such as bacteria on clothing, insects, and more specifically, by mosquitos. Dr. Lazear was convinced that the best available evidence suggested a living host for yellow fever, and so he pursued the theory of mosquito transmission.

As a result of earlier research scandals, Sternberg had issued strict directives that nobody could be experimented on without consent, and that all consent had to be carefully documented. This gave rise to what was known as "the golden rule self-experimentation." This meant that researchers were expected not to try anything on others that they wouldn't be willing to try on themselves as well.[4]

---

1. *Wikipedia*, s.v. "Jesse William Lazear," https://en.wikipedia.org/wiki/Jesse_William_Lazear.
2. Although his name sounds Jewish, the story is told that Frank Heynick, author of *Jews and Medicine: An Epic Saga* (Hoboken, 2003), was disappointed when he came across the name of George Sternberg just as he was completing his manuscript. He had not mentioned Sternberg in his book and the idea of researching yet another life, editing and adding to the already 600-page book, was disheartening. After further research it turned out that Sternberg was not Jewish – "Thank heavens!" said the ecstatic Heynick (Max Gross, "Doctor Writes 'Epic Saga' of Jews in Medicine," *The Jewish Daily Forward*, August 15, 2003).
3. Robert Baker, *Before Bioethics* (New York, 2013), 255, 258.
4. Ibid., 255.

Dr. Lazear made significant progress on his theories, while researching in a hospital in Havana, Cuba. He ruled out a bacterium as the disease agent, and eventually confirmed his hypothesis that mosquitoes transmitted this disease by allowing mosquitoes to feed first on patients infected with yellow fever, followed by allowing study volunteers to be bitten by the mosquitoes, after which the study volunteers eventually fell ill with yellow fever. In the process his team determined that an infectious particle too small to be filtered with a standard bacterial filter was the source of the disease, thus discovering the first human virus.[5] He wrote to his wife in a letter dated September 8, 1900, "I rather think I am on the track of the real germ."[6]

Given the "golden rule self-experimentation" ethics of the time, Lazear decided to intentionally have himself, and two of his research assistants, be bitten by contaminated mosquitoes as part of his experiments. The two men Lazear exposed to yellow fever via these mosquitoes recovered. Lazear, however, was not so lucky. He contracted the disease and died two and a half weeks after writing that hopeful letter, just twelve days after being bitten, at the age of only thirty-four. The fact that this was a deliberate act, that his infection was the result of self-experimentation, was covered up at the time – for reasons unknown, but possibly connected with family insurance policies.[7] The researchers who recovered were awarded congressional medals of honor, and Lazear became known as "the martyr to science," even though the results of his particular self-inflicted bite unfortunately did not assist the research due to lack of documentation. As a result of this episode, Sternberg enacted strict research regulations and forbade any further self-experimentation, fearing that this practice could deplete medical personnel.[8]

Can Lazear's altruism be justified? What does Judaism say about putting oneself into such risk for the sake of the health and safety of the broader society? Though a Jew, there is little evidence to suggest Lazear

---

5. *History of Vaccines*, s.v. "Jesse Lazear," https://www.historyofvaccines.org/content/jesse-lazear.

6. *Wikipedia*, https://en.wikipedia.org/wiki/Jesse_William_Lazear#Career.

7. The truth was discovered in 1947 by Philip S. Hench from Lazear's own notebook, https://en.wikipedia.org/wiki/Jesse_William_Lazear.

8. Baker, 258.

was an observant Jew, and hence he was likely unfamiliar with most Jewish law. But he may have known of Purim, and it is in the Book of Esther where significant guidance on navigating this ethical dilemma may be found. Rabbi Joseph B. Soloveitchik, the Rav, argues that there is one verse in the *megilla* that is the central halakha of the entire Book of Esther: "And if I perish, I perish" (4:16). According to Rabbi Soloveitchik, this verse requires individuals to sacrifice their life if the destiny and future of the community are at stake.[9]

Rabbi Soloveitchik illustrates this principle with a profound episode from Jewish history that may have been forgotten had he not reminded the world of it.[10] It occurred one Hoshana Rabba in Vilna during the eighteenth century. An apostate Jew hid a stolen icon from the main cathedral inside the Old Synagogue and brought the archbishop to catch Jews pounding their *Hoshanot* at the church icon. Of course, the Jews in the synagogue that day had no idea the icon was even there; they had been set up. Nevertheless, thirty members of the Jewish Council (the "*parnasim*" of the community) were arrested for this "crime" and would certainly be put to death as a result.

Upon hearing of this impending tragedy, Rabbi Man ben Rabbi Man decided that he wanted to take the blame for this action in order to spare his community. Rabbi Man consulted with the rabbi, Shmuel Acharon, arguing that he was certain that if he told the authorities that he was the one who stole the icon, they would punish him with death but let the thirty Jews go. Rabbi Shmuel felt that he had to ask the Vilna Gaon this difficult question before giving Rabbi Man guidance. However, before Rabbi Shmuel could tell Rabbi Man what to do, Rabbi Man told him not to ask the Vilna Gaon because he had already realized what he must do based on the actions of Esther in the *megilla*.

That night, Shemini Atzeret, Rabbi Man turned himself in to the authorities, and indeed they allowed the other Jews to go free. They began to torture Rabbi Man and did so for many months until finally

---

9. *Mesorat HaRav Megillat Esther* (New York/Jerusalem, 2017), 93. Rabbi Zilberstein also quotes this verse to support self-endangerment for the sake of attempting to save the masses (*Shiurei Torah LeRofim* 6:396, p. 316, fn. 5).

10. Ibid., 90–93.

executing him publicly in front of the cathedral, on Shavuot. We know this story because Rabbi Soloveitchik, when visiting Vilna, heard the *El Malei Raḥamim* that was recited in Vilna for Rabbi Man every Hoshana Rabba and Shavuot. Since the destruction of European Jewry during the Holocaust, to the best of my knowledge, this *El Malei* is no longer recited anywhere. Yet another tradition lost because of the Holocaust. But thanks to Rabbi Soloveitchik, the story, and its vital lesson, remain.

Perhaps further support for Rabbi Man's actions can be found in the talmudic account of the "*Harugei Lod*," the brothers executed in the city of Lod during the time of the Roman occupation of the Land of Israel. The Roman emperor's daughter was found murdered and the Jewish community was blamed. The emperor threatened the Jews with mass execution unless they could produce the murderer. To save the Jewish people, two innocent brothers, Lilianus and Pappus, stepped forward and falsely confessed to the crime, and thus only the two of them were executed by the Roman official Turyanus, sparing the rest of the Jewish community.[11]

Some rabbinic authorities have permitted voluntary self-sacrifice in order to rescue the broader community, based on the Rabbis' praise for these righteous brothers.[12] On the other hand, Rabbi Kook disagreed, arguing that although saving the broader community is a very high value,[13] and one should engage in a small risk to attempt to do so,[14] these

---

11. Bava Batra 10b, Rashi, s.v. "*Harugei Lod*"; Taanit 18b, Rashi, s.v. "*BeLudkya*."

12. *Yeshuot Yaakov, Yoreh De'ah* 157:1 (available at https://hebrewbooks.org/pdfpager.aspx?req=9210&st=&pgnum=218&hilite=); see also *Tiferet Yisrael* on Mishna Berakhot 1:3 quoted in *Pitḥei Teshuva, Yoreh De'ah* 157(3), which states that one may enter a small risk in order to fulfill a mitzva, which may even be obligatory if it is for the sake of saving the masses (*hatzalat rabbim*), as quoted in *Mishpat Kohen* 143.

13. See detailed discussion on the importance of the entire community in Jewish thought and bioethics, in Avraham Steinberg, *HaRefuah KeHalakha*, vol. 5 (Jerusalem, 2017), 107–108.

14. *Mishpat Kohen* 143 argues, based on the *Sifrei* and Bava Metzia 112a, that when the danger is distant ("*safek raḥok*") or a standard level of risk that people generally enter into, then one should do so in order to attempt to save the many, and not worry about oneself, as many great Jews have done throughout history, as long as it is not a certain danger (in which case the obligation of "*veḥai bahem*" takes precedence). He argues in *Mishpat Kohen* 144 (9–10) that there is no obligation on an individual

stories do not prove that people who are not currently in any danger may opt to risk their life for the sake of the broader community, since the brothers in Lod and Queen Esther would have died along with their community anyway.[15]

In 2020, related questions arose once again, this time in the context of medical experimentation with regard to the coronavirus pandemic. As the death toll climbed, as well as the costs of shutting down entire countries to avoid the spread of the virus, there was a mad rush to develop a vaccine. But developing vaccines takes time. The reason is partially because of tragic stories such as that of Dr. Lazear; by the end of the twentieth century, very strict governmental protocols and regulations on vaccine testing were developed to try to prevent unnecessary deaths.

One such approach to testing potentially new vaccines is that researchers must randomize test subjects into two groups. Group A gets the vaccine, while Group B gets a placebo. Then the researchers simply wait and see if more people from Group B get sick than do those in Group A. If that happens, then that is a sign that the vaccine is effective. However, it can take many months before researchers get their answer because, in its simplest form, this kind of study depends upon waiting for people to get naturally exposed to the virus in their everyday lives. When, as part of social efforts to stem the spread of whatever is causing

---

to save the entire Jewish community since everyone must do their part. He thus suggests that at first Esther thought there were other ways to save the people without her risking her life, until she was convinced that she needed to do it herself. When one does so they get reward and credit for doing a mitzva, even if it is not obligatory. He concludes that there could be times when people could determine that they want to surrender their life for the higher value of the community when they calculate that the whole is more valuable than their own life (ibid., 15–17).

15. *Mishpat Kohen* 143. Rabbi Kook's claim that Esther would have died along with the Jewish community is based on Rashi to Esther 4:13, that Mordecai told her she would be included in the decree to kill all the Jews. Rabbi Kook claims that it was only once she found out that she would likely die along with everyone else that she realized she was obligated to take this risk. However, the suggestion that Esther would have been killed along with the Jewish community can be challenged and does not seem to be the opinion of Rabbi Soloveitchik or Rabbi Man, quoted above. Rabbi Meir Simha of Dvinsk, however, also seems to be of the opinion that one should never endanger oneself, even in order to save the entire nation (*Meshekh Ḥokhma*, Exodus 4:19; *Or Same'aḥ, Hilkhot Rotze'aḥ* 7:8).

an epidemic people are forced to stay apart, i.e., to engage in what is called "social distancing," it takes even longer to see if a proposed vaccine is effective.

To speed things up, an alternative protocol called a "challenge study" was suggested by some. A challenge study works very similarly to the traditional study described above – some people are given an experimental vaccine and some are not – but what differs is that in the challenge study, everyone in the study is then deliberately exposed to the disease for which the vaccine is being developed. Researchers then compare the two groups – the vaccine versus the control – knowing that everybody was exposed to the disease. Running a study in this manner could save several months (and thus thousands, if not millions of lives).[16] However, to expose people to a disease that is particularly dangerous, such as coronavirus, makes this a much riskier study. Some may get very sick, and a few may even die.

Based on the opinion of Rabbi Soloveitchik, drawing from the precedent of Queen Esther, I believe the lesson here is that with proper informed consent it would certainly be permitted for a Jew to serve as a participant in a "challenge study" associated with rapidly developing a vaccine for a disease such as the coronavirus, and even a very pious act.[17] Even according to the stricter opinion of Rabbi Kook, mentioned above, for a disease such as the coronavirus, the level of risk for those enrolling in such a study is relatively low (only young, healthy people are accepted for these studies and they receive careful medical oversight and attention), and because coronavirus put everyone in the world at risk, anyone who might volunteer to be a subject in such a study was already at some risk just by living in society. Entering the study simply

---

16. Nir Eyal, Marc Lipsitch, and Peter G. Smith, "Human challenge studies to accelerate coronavirus vaccine licensure," *The Journal of Infectious Diseases* 152 (March 2020), https://doi.org/10.1093/infdis/jiaa152; Andrea Cioffi, "COVID-19: Is Everything Appropriate to Create an Effective Vaccine?" *Journal of Infectious Diseases* (April 29, 2020), https://www.ncbi.nlm.nih.gov/pmc/articles/PMC7197522/; see also https://academic.oup.com/jid/advance-article-pdf/doi/10.1093/infdis/jiaa217/33283826/jiaa217.pdf.

17. See note 14 above and *Lev Avraham*, p. 284, and extensive discussion in Steinberg, *HaRefuah KeHalakha*, 53, on risk and entering experimental studies in Jewish law.

makes it happen in a controlled setting and can significantly benefit the entire society, so while not obligatory it could thus be seen as a mitzva.[18]

Similarly, although neither those entering a challenge study nor Dr. Lazear make their sacrifices only for the Jewish community, and while the various stories of risk that we have discussed in this chapter are certainly not identical, it seems that Dr. Lazear's actions can nonetheless also be justified and deserving of praise because he didn't definitely know that he would die, the results of his risky experiments could potentially save the masses, and he was personally at risk for yellow fever anyway along with everyone else in society.

May we never again face such dilemmas, but we can take comfort in knowing that from Persia to Vilna to the United States, as life-and-death communal challenges have inevitably arisen, our tradition has provided clear guidance, and in every generation heroic individuals have stepped up to the call of the hour.

---

18. Indeed, after nearing completion of this chapter, Rabbi Asher Weiss wrote a responsum to this author, published in *Minḥat Asher – Leket Shiurim UTeshuvot Iggerot UMaamarim HaNogim LeMagefat HaKorona*, 2nd ed. (Jerusalem, 2020), #5(2), in which he agreed that entering such a study is a *"mitzva gedola"* and *"pikuaḥ nefesh"* because there is a high chance that it could save an entire generation from illness and death. Rabbi Weiss argues that risk and self-endangerment are permissible when it is for essential public benefit, especially when it is young and healthy people acting on behalf of crucial communal needs. He also quotes Rabbi Shlomo Zalman Auerbach who notes that just like when there is a military threat to a community, leaders can endanger soldiers' lives by sending them to war for the good of the nation, so too the need to test medicines can be justified as a mitzva war of saving lives and protecting the community (*Minḥat Shlomo* 2:82 [12]); see also Rabbi Shaul Yisraeli in *Amud HaYemini* (Jerusalem 2000), 17.

The Lubavitcher Rebbe and the Messianic Potency of the American Purim

Rabbi Dr. Yosef Bronstein

INTRODUCTION

In the Lubavitcher Rebbe's first published remarks about Purim,[1] he alluded to the chasm that existed between the experiences of Jews in post-World War II America and those of the Purim story. While the latter lived under the shadow of a mortal threat from a diabolical antisemite, the former lived with peace and prosperity in the most comfortable host country since the exile from Jerusalem. Seemingly, one might suppose, the Book of Esther would have little relevance for American Jewry.

On many occasions,[2] though, Rabbi Menahem Mendel Schneerson (1902–1994), better known by his title, the Lubavitcher Rebbe, countered this perspective by citing a teaching of the Baal Shem Tov, the

---

1. *Likkutei Siḥot* 1, *Purim, se'if* 1.
2. For example, see *Likkutei Siḥot* 6, *Purim, se'if* 1; *Likkutei Siḥot* 16, *Hosafot – Purim*, 619–620; *Torat Menaḥem* 5720:2, 156; *Torat Menaḥem* 5742:2, 945–946. A video recording of the Rebbe articulating this idea is available at https://www.chabad.org/multimedia/video_cdo/aid/3953171/jewish/Stop-Living-in-the-Past.htm.

founder of Hasidism, regarding the Book of Esther. The Mishna teaches that one who reads the *megilla* out of sequence (*lemafre'a*) does not fulfill the mitzva.[3] The Baal Shem Tov employed a form of hasidic hermeneutics and offered an additional meaning to the Mishna: if a person reads the *megilla* and thinks that it is about the past (the literal meaning of *lemafre'a*) he has missed the purpose of the reading. The divine nature of the text combined with divine providence's hand in the wandering of the Jewish people means that each Jewish community, no matter the century or country, can plumb the depths of the Book of Esther and find crucially pertinent and applicable messages.

In this chapter I will sketch several of the Rebbe's primary themes regarding the relevance of the Book of Esther for American Jewry. This will be divided into two interrelated parts. The first section will outline several practical directives that the Rebbe drew from the *megilla* that he deemed uniquely germane for American Jewry, and to a lesser degree all Jews living in benevolent democracies. At first, these teachings might seem like an array of disconnected points, with their sole common denominator being that they are all sourced in the *megilla*. In the second section, however, we will take a deeper look at the Rebbe's kabbalistic-sociological conceptualization of the United States of America. Ultimately, as I argue, it was his understanding of America's role in the unfolding of ancient prophecies that served as the unifying background for the practical directives.

I. MESSAGES FROM THE *MEGILLA*

Integration and Influence

Against the backdrop of the general experience of Jews in the diaspora, the Rebbe noted that a unique feature of the American Jewish community was its level of integration and influence within broader society. This new reality generated a host of urgent questions: How should such a Jewish community self-conceptualize? How should it behave? What should be its mission?

In the Rebbe's view, the American Jewish community could find crucial guidance in the Book of Esther. On the whole, as the beginning

---

3. Mishna Megilla 2:1.

and the ending of the *megilla* make clear, the Jewish community of Shushan was well integrated into even the highest echelons of Persian society.[4] The story begins with Jews being invited to the king's private party and concludes with a Jewish queen and vizier. As such, one of the major themes of the Rebbe's Purim talks was using the *megilla* to delineate the parameters of integration and influence.

On the most basic level, the Rebbe argued that American Jewry must undergo a paradigm shift regarding the source of its unique position. Its privileged status in non-Jewish society should not be studied with the regular tools of sociology or construed as a natural fulfillment of the American dream. Rather, everything about the Jewish people's situation is directly attributable to God who orchestrates history in such a way that each Jewish community should be able to complete a specific task of their national, historical mission.

It was this realization of complete dependence on God that guided Mordecai and the Jews of Shushan when they heard the news of Haman's decree. Despite having well-placed friends in government, Mordecai's initial reaction was not to "organize a diplomatic mission to Ahasueverus"[5] and lobby him to rescind the decree. Rather, according to the traditional rabbinic interpretation of the story, his first act was to gather the community in fasting and prayer,[6] demonstrating that it was God who guided Persian society to accept or reject the Jewish community. Only after this religious response do Mordecai and Esther engage in their important, but secondary, efforts of political maneuvering to oust Haman.[7] Similarly, the Rebbe concluded,[8] the contemporary Jewish

---

4. *Likkutei Siḥot* 1, *Purim-Tzav, se'if* 1; *Likkutei Siḥot* 26, 437; *Torat Menaḥem* 5726:2, 155–156.

5. *Likkutei Siḥot* 1, *Purim, se'if* 2.

6. Even though prayer is not mentioned explicitly in the *megilla*, the Rebbe followed the midrashic interpretation (Esther Rabba 8:7) which asserts that Mordecai led the Jewish community in prayer.

7. *Torat Menaḥem* 5711:2, 319–320; *Torat Menaḥem* 5716:2, 139–140; *Torat Menaḥem* 5724:2, 138–139.

8. See *Likkutei Siḥot* 1, *Purim, se'if* 3, that this lesson is particularly relevant "in our time period," presumably referring to the Jewish community of America and of other Western benevolent countries.

community needed to internalize that its survival and success should
be attributed to God and God alone.[9]

The next stage of the Rebbe's interpretation takes this awareness
from the theoretical to the practical. How should an awareness of divine
providence practically impact the manner in which the Jewish community behaves? The Rebbe developed a two-pronged response. One of his
consistent themes was the importance of outwardly exhibiting Jewish
pride. It is natural for a minority group that has gained the acceptance
and respect of broader society to partially obscure its uniqueness in order
to further cement its status. The Rebbe saw this attitude and its behav-
ioral expressions as a rampant problem that plagued a defensive, and
self-conscious, American Jewish community.[10] In response, he emphasized that this was the precise mistake that caused the near-downfall of
an otherwise admirably observant Persian Jewish community.

The Talmud explains that the Jews of Persia deserved destruction due to their "enjoy[ment] of the wicked one's [Ahasuerus] feast."[11]
With his characteristic nuanced readings of Torah sources, the Rebbe
argued that the Talmud's emphasis on "enjoyment" is telling. There
is nothing wrong per se with the Jewish people's participation in the
party (the Rebbe assumed based on rabbinic sources that the food was
kosher),[12] or their rubbing shoulders with the high and mighty. Their
near-fatal mistake, though, was that they saw the king's court as being

---

9. It is surprising that despite the Rebbe's description of Mordecai's devout response
and the religious lesson for the contemporary Jewish community, God's name is
entirely absent from the text of the *megilla*. The Rebbe's understanding of this glaring
lacuna will be cited at the end of this chapter.

10. For sources and analysis, see Philip Wexler, Eli Rubin, and Michael Wexler, *Social
Vision: The Lubavitcher Rebbe's Transformative Paradigm for the World* (New York,
2019), 50–54; Judah Mischel, "Marching Orders: Considering the Lubavitcher
Rebbe's Impact Twenty-Five Years Since His Passing," *Jewish Action* (Fall 2019), who
considers the Rebbe's adoption of Jewish authenticity and pride (*Ge'on Yaakov*) as
transformative for American Jewry.

11. Megilla 12a.

12. See *Likkutei Siḥot* 31, Purim #1, *se'if* 1, that the Rebbe derived that the food was
kosher from Esther Rabba 2:13 and Megilla 12a. He admitted, though, that a simple
understanding of Song of Songs Rabba 7:8 is that the Jews ate non-kosher food at
the party.

independently important and as a standard for behavior. They felt that their success was dependent upon and defined by acting more Persian and socially acculturated to a point when Ahasuerus would no longer see them as radically distinct.[13]

According to the Rebbe, adopting this perspective removed them from God's protection and opened the door for Haman's persecution. Had they realized that their status in society was not due to Persian officials but to God, they would still have attended the party but would not have experienced an identity crisis regarding their Jewishness. On a practical level this means wearing distinctly Jewish attire, speaking publicly about God and His Torah, and openly declaring an unfailing fealty to the Jewish people even while being patriotic citizens.[14]

This approach is epitomized by Mordecai and Esther at the end of the *megilla*. After the danger passed, they did not abdicate their powerful positions and voluntarily move to the edges of Persian society. Rather, they kept their posts, which they perceived as God-given, and worked tirelessly for the betterment of the entire kingdom. But, crucially, they were internally and externally proudly Jewish. According to a midrash,[15] Mordecai wore his tefillin and tzitzit for all to see together with his crown, even as he walked in and out of the palace.[16]

The Rebbe noted that even as late as 1982 American Jewry "sadly"[17] still needed to learn this lesson. Even observant Jews were often concerned about appearing too Jewish or too "fanatical."[18] The message of the *megilla*, argued the Rebbe, is that American Jews need to inculcate within themselves the notion that their status was entirely dependent upon God and therefore being proudly and overtly Jewish, even, for example, in the halls of Congress,[19] would only help their cause.

---

13. *Likkutei Siḥot* 31, Purim #1, *se'if* 3–5. See also, *Likkutei Siḥot* 21, Purim #2, *se'if* 5, and particularly note 35.
14. *Torat Menaḥem* 5727:2, 217–220; *Torat Menaḥem* 5742:2, 954–958.
15. *Targum Esther* 8:15.
16. *Torat Menaḥem* 5728:2, 133–135.
17. *Torat Menaḥem* 5742:2, 950.
18. Ibid, 956.
19. *Torat Menaḥem* 5727:2, 218.

This point leads to the Rebbe's next message. Overt Jewish pride is not just a reflection of the Jewish community's internalization that its fate is in God's hands. It also brings a public awareness of God and His Torah to the broader community, thus infusing God and Torah values into the fabric of American society.

Starting in 1980, the Rebbe incessantly called for Jews to actively fulfill Maimonides' mandate[20] of bringing an awareness of God, the seven Noahide laws, and the moral/spiritual principles that they represent to the non-Jewish world. While in the past such religious activism would have been met with a wave of antisemitism, the openness and tolerance of America and other benevolent Western countries allowed for Maimonides' mandate to be fulfilled en masse for the first time in history.[21]

The Rebbe spoke of actualizing this vision in both the private and public spheres. In the private sphere, he noted that every Jew in America has a natural social network that includes non-Jewish neighbors, business associates, clients, or patients. The American norm is to develop friendly and cordial relationships with these social or professional contacts. This reality, he argued, must be seen as a God-given opportunity to actively bring these people closer to God through a stellar personal example and explicitly speaking about God and the Noahide commandments.[22]

---

20. *Mishneh Torah, Hilkhot Melakhim UMilḥamoteihem* 8:10. For a broader analysis, see Matityahu Broyde, "Ḥovatam Shel Yehudim LeOded Shemirat Mitzvot Benei No'aḥ Al Yedei Nokhrim," *Dinei Yisrael* 19 (5757–5758). For an analysis of the Rebbe's activism regarding the Noahide mitzvot, see Yizhak Krauss, *HaShevi'i: Meshiḥiyut BaDor HaShevi'i Shel Ḥabad* (Tel Aviv, 2007), 224–249; Alon Dahan, *Go'el Aharon: Mishnato HaMeshiḥit Shel Rebbi Menaḥem Mendel Schneerson HaRebbi MiLubavitch* (Tel Aviv, 2014), 535–585; Chaim Miller, *Turning Judaism Outward: A Biography of Rabbi Menachem Mendel Schneerson the Seventh Lubavitcher Rebbe* (New York, 2014), 319–337; Yosef Bronstein, *Engaging the Essence: The Philosophy of the Lubavitcher Rebbe* (forthcoming), ch. 16. For an analysis of the Rebbe's theoretical writings where he affirms the existence of a divine spark within non-Jews while still retaining the ontological superiority of Jews, see Elliot Wolfson, *Open Secret: Postmessianic Messianism and the Mystical Revision of Menahem Mendel Schneerson* (New York, 2009), 224–264.

21. *Torat Menaḥem* 5743:3, 1333; *Torat Menaḥem* 5747:2, 616.

22. *Torat Menaḥem* 5743:2, 636; *Torat Menaḥem* 5745:2, 849–851.

In the public sphere, the Rebbe called upon Jews to partake in the American political process to promote policies that carried the spirit of biblical values. These endeavors included a wide range of policy proposals, including injecting spiritual and moral values into the public educational system, criminal justice reform, and even transitioning from fossil fuels to solar energy.[23] The Rebbe's decades of efforts bore fruit and at the end of his life he was awarded a Congressional Gold Medal (the highest civilian award bestowed by Congress) for being a national voice for values, ethics, and social change.[24]

The Rebbe considered Purim to be a particularly auspicious time for these efforts. At the end of the *megilla* we read that "many of the peoples of the land became Jews" (Est. 8:17). Assuming that even the narrative sections of Torah are fundamentally normative, the Rebbe often spoke of this verse as implicitly commanding Jews to positively influence the non-Jewish society in which they lived. On several occasions he dedicated sections of his Purim talk to these endeavors,[25] including a notable impassioned critique of the American criminal justice system on Purim 1976.[26]

---

23. For sources and analysis see Wexler and Rubin, *Social Vision*, 147–217; Jan Feldman, *Lubavitchers as Citizens: A Paradox of Liberal Democracy* (Ithica, 2003), 38–59.
24. https://www.gpo.gov/fdsys/pkg/BILLS-103hr4497rds/html/BILLS-103hr4497rds.htm.
25. See, for example, *Torat Menahem* 5721:1, 136; *Torat Menahem* 5727:2, 216–219; *Torat Menahem* 5747:2, 611–612.
26. *Sihot Kodesh* 5736:1, 616–617. Audio recording is available at https://www.chabad.org/therebbe/livingtorah/player_cdo/aid/3403355/jewish/Prisoners-are-People.htm. Briefly, the Rebbe argued that incarceration, the standard American response to a crime, is used in exceedingly rare circumstances in the halakhic system as it dehumanizes the criminal and effaces his *tzelem Elokim* (having been created in the image of God). Instead of rampant incarceration, the Torah's system focuses on punishments that are primarily educational and corrective in nature. In the 1976 Purim talk, the Rebbe focused on the need to change prisons from places of confinement and constriction to facilities of rehabilitation and education. The Aleph Institute (https://aleph-institute.org/wp/about/), which is dedicated to the "religious, educational, and spiritual needs" of the incarcerated and their families in addition to "criminal justice reform and recidivism reduction through preventive-education and faith-based rehabilitation programs, re-entry assistance, alternative sentencing guidance and counsel, and policy research and recommendations," was

Rabbi Dr. Yosef Bronstein

Female Activists
The Rebbe felt that another highly relevant aspect of the Book of Esther was its heroine. On the one hand, he affirmed the traditional sources' perspective that the primary job of a Jewish woman was to be the *akeret habayit* (pillar of the home). However, he also laid the halakhic and philosophical groundwork for expanding women's roles which reached practical expression in his carving out of an independent space for women in Chabad, prioritizing female education, and actively encouraging capable women to leave their homes and positively impact others.[27]

The Rebbe pointed to Esther as a model for such innovative activities. As he noted in a 1954 letter to the Lubavitch Women's Organization,[28] Esther's heroic actions took place far from the safe confines of a Jewish home. She understood that God placed her in the epicenter of Persian life for a purpose and she took advantage of her setting to save the Jewish people, even risking her own life in the process. Similarly, Jewish women today need to answer God's calling and positively represent Him and His people no matter where they find themselves – be it inside their homes or out in the street.[29]

II. THE KABBALA OF THE AMERICAN PURIM
Thus far, we have seen the Rebbe as an innovative teacher and creative communal leader through his reading of the *megilla* as a contemporary text intended for American Jewry. But seeing the sum of the Rebbe's teachings on the Book of Esther as a compendium of practical lessons is akin to seeing the tip of an iceberg without realizing the giant glacier that lies beneath the surface.

founded in 1981 by Rabbi Sholom Lipskar at the express direction of the Rebbe. For more on the Rebbe's vision of criminal justice reform and the work of the Aleph Institute, see Wexler and Rubin, *Social Vision*, 188–201.

27. For a general analysis of this issue, see Ada Rapoport-Albert, "From Women as Hasid to Women as 'Tsadik' in the Teachings of the Last Two Lubavitcher Rebbes," in *Hasidic Studies: Essays in History and Gender* (Liverpool, 2018), 427–470; "The Emergence of a Female Constituency in Habad," in ibid., 369–426.
28. *Iggerot Kodesh* 8, letter 2,520.
29. See also, *Torat Menaḥem* 5742:2, 1065–1066; *Torat Menaḥem* 5744:2, 1203–1209.

322

As a hasidic master, the Rebbe viewed all of reality through the lens of Jewish mysticism. The American experience was no exception. Throughout his forty-plus years of leadership, the Rebbe rigorously applied his understanding of Torah and Jewish mysticism to analyzing the United States of America and emerged with a kabbalistic conceptualization of the country's history, societal structure, and purpose. In his view, America and its Jewish community had a crucial role to play in advancing the world toward the utopian, messianic era.[30] The practical directives that the Rebbe drew from the Book of Esther were all expressions of a single, central theme that he saw as threading through his conception of America, Purim, and preparing the world for *Mashiaḥ*.

The Nature of the Cosmos

Like all hasidic thought, Chabad literature, from its earliest iteration in *Tanya*,[31] describes the spiritual cosmos as a multi-layered edifice. God figuratively sits at the top of the system with an infinite number of "worlds" that emanate from Him. The "worlds" that are closer to God are more spiritual in nature and the beings that occupy those realms can palpably and powerfully experience divine intimacy. As one moves along the continuum to greater and greater distances, God's presence becomes increasingly hidden. The final and "lowest" plane of existence is our material world which almost entirely conceals God's presence.[32]

Based on this description, it is not surprising that Chabad literature has many negative things to say about the physical world. The absence of revealed divinity in it creates a vacuum in which evil and impure forces thrive, making our world a treacherous place to navigate.[33] Life on Earth, from this perspective, is an unceasing struggle between the spark of divinity within us and these forces of evil.[34] Birth into this

---

30. For a recent analysis of this issue, see Phillip Wexler and Eli Rubin, "'The Lower Half of the Globe': Kabbalah and Social Analysis in the Lubavitcher Rebbe's Vision for Judaism's American Era," in *Kabbalah in America: Ancient Lore in the New World*, ed. Brian Ogren (Leiden, 2020), 292–315.

31. Published in 1796 by Rabbi Shneur Zalman of Liady, the founder of Chabad Hasidism.

32. See, for example, *Tanya, Shaar HaYiḥud VeHaEmuna*, chs. 1–2.

33. *Tanya, Likkutei Amarim*, chs. 6–7.

34. *Tanya, Likkutei Amarim*, chs. 12–13.

world is considered a form of death for the soul as it is forced to descend from its spiritual abode up high and be trapped in a sea of materiality.[35]

However, despite this pessimistic baseline, the Chabad masters paradoxically developed a positive perspective of our world. In truth, nothing is "far" from God or bereft of divinity. In the hasidic worldview, God's oneness means that He is the only true substance of reality. Accordingly, even (and perhaps especially) the banal materiality of our world is permeated with divinity – we just have to work to reveal it.[36]

With this background, we can turn to a passage from *Tanya* that became central in the Rebbe's talks and worldview. Chapter 36 of the *Likkutei Amarim* section describes the purpose of creation and the nature of the Messianic Era:

> It is a well-known Rabbinic statement that the purpose of the creation of this world is that the Holy One, blessed be He, desired to have an abode in the lower worlds (*Dira BeTaḥtonim*)…the ultimate purpose [of creation] is this lowest world, for such was His blessed will that He shall have satisfaction when the evil force is subdued and the darkness is turned to light…[37]

God created the cosmos for the purpose of the *taḥtonim* – the lowest plane. It is specifically here that God wants His light to shine, a divine desire that will be fulfilled in messianic times. Through its fulfillment of mitzvot, the Jewish people incrementally bring God's light closer and closer to the lowest realm until God's wish of a *Dira BeTaḥtonim* becomes a reality.[38]

A *Dira BeTaḥtonim*

Moving forward approximately 150 years from the publication of *Tanya*, the Rebbe made this theme central to his teachings. For a litany of

---

35. *Likkutei Siḥot* 38, *Ḥukkat*, *se'if* 3.
36. See, for example, *Tanya, Shaar HaYiḥud VeHaEmuna*, ibid.; *Tanya, Iggeret HaKodesh*, letter 6.
37. Translation is adapted from https://www.chabad.org/library/tanya/tanya_cdo/aid/1029041/jewish/Chapter-36.htm.
38. See the continuation of this topic in chapter 37.

reasons that lie beyond the present forum[39] the Rebbe declared the post-World War II generation as the "last generation of exile."[40] As such, it had the unique mandate of completing the historical mission of creating a *Dira BeTaḥtonim*.

Already in his first speech as leader of Chabad, the Rebbe declared that this mission necessitated a shift in religious orientation.[41] Previous generations of Jews might have tended toward a more spiritualized service characterized by intense Torah study and heartfelt prayer. These Jews of yesteryears might have eyed the material world and non-Jewish society around them with great suspicion. However, as the world approaches the days of *Mashiaḥ*, the focus of contemporary Jews must shift from the heavens to revealing the divine nature of even the "*taḥtonim* or all people, places, and things that seem far from God."

For the Rebbe, this meant developing a renewed focus on the elements of this world that traditional religion placed on the periphery. If earlier generations of Jews prioritized cognition, emotions, and experiences, the last generation needed to underscore the importance of physical actions – *maase*. If traditional Judaism encouraged yeshiva students to stay within the safe confines of the *beit midrash* far from the dangers of the outside world, the final generation needed to engage the outside world directly and reveal it as the true home for God. The combination of a focus on actions and the world outside the *beit midrash* was the fuel for modern Chabad's activism. Similarly, if traditional religion perceived the male-female relationship as hierarchical, the final generation needed to vigorously develop a theory and practice of new leadership vistas for women.

It was within this framework that the Rebbe contextualized the existence of America and its Jewish community. From a certain perspective, America was the ultimate *taḥtonim*, often described by the Rebbe as "the farthest" point on the periphery from the traditional centers of

---

39. For a fuller discussion, see Bronstein, ch. 20.
40. *Torat Menaḥem* 5747:2, 353; *Torat Menaḥem* 5748:1, 543; *Torat Menaḥem* 5748:2, 295; *Iggerot Kodesh* 15, letter 5467; *Iggerot Kodesh* 19, letter 7438.
41. *Torat Menaḥem* 5711:1, 192–203.

spirituality.[42] According to Chabad tradition, America was so spiritually barren that it did not even overtly feel the effects of the Sinaitic revelation which reverberated around the world.[43] In this vein, Rabbi Yitzhak Yosef, the Rebbe's father-in-law and sixth leader of Chabad, said that even as he fled to America to escape the Nazis, he prayed that he would not become mired in American materialism.[44]

However, it is specifically this identity as the "lowest" of the lands that indicates America's potential. America was not just another non-Jewish country, but one that was explicitly founded upon biblical values and embraced freedom, justice, and charity.[45] Its standing on the global scene as an influential superpower meant that the time was ripe for the entire world to shift toward creating societies that were based on a shared belief in God and His core values.[46] Having America live up to its potential was a key element in engendering this global shift in consciousness and social structure.

This divine mission for America placed an acute level of responsibility on its Jewish community. First, when thinking about the totality of the Jewish people, American Jews needed to awaken from their slumber and realize that God wanted them to transform America from a Torah wasteland to the center of the global Torah community. America must be converted from the *tahtonim* to the greatest exporter of Torah and Hasidism that the world has ever seen.[47] Second, and more broadly, the American Jewish community had the sacred task of motivating American society as a whole to achieve its potential as a model, God-infused country.[48]

---

42. *Likkutei Sihot* 33, *Hosafot* 28th of Sivan, *se'if* 1; *Torat Menahem* 5713:3, 125; *Torat Menahem* 5718:2, 147–150.

43. *Iggerot Kodesh Admor Moharayatz* 2, letter 617.

44. *Sefer HaSihot* 5703, 41–42.

45. See, for example, *Torat Menahem* 5743:2, 906–908; *Torat Menahem* 5744:3, 1432–1435; *Torat Menahem* 5747:2, 54–57; *Torat Menahem* 5750:2, 70–71; *Torat Menahem* 5751:2, 94.

46. See, for example, *Torat Menahem* 5751:3, 188–189.

47. *Torat Menahem* 5751:3, 376–385, and particularly 380–383.

48. *Torat Menahem* 5745:4, 2464.

As with all the events of history, the Rebbe perceived the Jewish people's migration to America as divinely guided. In the generation before *Mashiaḥ*, he felt, the Jewish people must focus on the lowest elements of our world in the "lowest" country. It would have to engage the outside world (non-observant Jews and the broader American public) with an activist orientation (physical activity), using all segments of the Jewish community, including women. By doing so, the final generation would successfully reveal that every aspect of this world is, actually, an ideal home for God, a *Dira BeTaḥtonim*.

The Nature of Purim

In Chabad literature, Purim is the day that represents this paradoxical and topsy-turvy dismantling of hierarchies, a day when masks abound and nothing is at it seems – "*venahafokh hu*" (Est. 9:1). On Purim, Jews revel in physicality – eating, drinking, and drunken partying – to an extent that is forbidden throughout the year.[49] The Talmud declares that we are to drink to the point of deconstructing the usual conceptions of good and evil (to a degree) and declare that we do not know the difference between cursed is Haman and blessed is Mordecai.[50] The Book of Esther can potentially be read as a secular story as it does not contain God's name or overt miracles.[51] And yet, kabbalistic literature teaches that Purim is the holiest day of the year, surpassing even Yom Kippur. The meaning of this, according to the Rebbe, is that on Purim a messianic light shines upon our world and we can see the base materiality and seeming secularity as the ultimate home for God.[52]

We can now return to the lessons the Rebbe derived from Purim and the Book of Esther. His teachings highlighted two basic themes: 1) The integrated and influential American Jewish community must remain

---

49. *Torat Menaḥem 5748:2, 404–406.*
50. *Likkutei Siḥot 7, Vayikra #3; Torat Menaḥem 5752:2, 356 note 166.*
51. *Likkutei Siḥot 16, Purim.* In this talk the Rebbe tied together the following three themes: 1) the Purim miracle occurring through natural channels, 2) the key role of Esther as a woman in the story, and 3) the nature of the ultimate divine revelation.
52. For more sources and an analysis of the Rebbe's perspective on the messianic nature of Purim, see Yoel Kahn, "Yemei HaPurim Einam Beteilim LeOlam," *Maayanotekha* 43 (Adar 5775): 2–10; Wolfson, 56–57, 147.

engaged in society while proudly bearing the name of God in public and actively changing society for the better; 2) Inspired by Esther, women too must enter the public sphere to engage with, and better, society as a whole. In addition to being independently important endeavors, these activities serve as unique callings for American Jewry – the leaders of what the Rebbe called "the final generation." These are ways of using the messianic power of Purim to reveal the divinity of every aspect of our world and create a *Dira BeTaḥtonim.*

Rabbi Norman Lamm on Purim's Call for Moral Responsibility

Rabbi Dr. Ari Lamm

T he Six Day War was over. The echoes of Commander Motta Gur's famous declaration, "The Temple Mount is in our hands," still reverberated throughout the Jewish world. Several months later, the Chief Rabbinate of Israel prescribed a day of gratitude for the liberated Jerusalem. The Israeli government followed suit shortly thereafter, establishing the first official Yom Yerushalayim on the twenty-eighth day of Iyar in 1968. On that very morning, a warm Sunday in May, Rabbi Norman Lamm ascended the podium of his synagogue, Manhattan's Jewish Center, to address an assembled crowd of college students belonging to America's leading Zionist youth movements.

Yom Yerushalayim was a brand-new holiday, with as yet no established traditions, liturgy, or associated scripture. Rabbi Lamm had free rein to draw upon any resource from within the Jewish canon to mark the occasion. Astoundingly, of the plethora of options available to him, he chose to frame his remarks around the Book of Esther, and the story of

Purim. Of all possible texts and traditions to celebrate the ancient capital of the Jewish homeland, why would he draw upon the quintessential Jewish diaspora narrative? To be sure, by the end of the century, some Israeli scholars had begun to interpret Esther's well-known satirical elements as comprising a covert argument against the possibility of Jewish life in exile.[1] Rabbi Lamm, however, did not adopt such a reading, so we are left to wonder why he marked the first Yom Yerushalayim with a reflection upon the Bible's best-known diasporic text.

The key to understanding Rabbi Lamm's choice lies in appreciating his interpretive approach to the Book of Esther. Rabbi Lamm stood in a long line of commentators who perceived hidden meanings in the biblical work. Within this tradition, he adopted a consistent method for reading Esther that he applied throughout his intellectual career. Drawing upon the early Religious Zionist educator and thinker Zvi Zinger Yaron, Rabbi Lamm argued that the book speaks in two registers: *shalom* (peace) and *emet* (truth).[2] *Shalom* refers to Esther's politically correct meaning, which rendered it fit to circulate within elite Persian circles. *Emet* constitutes the book's true morality, which Jewish readers could divine only through carefully analyzing its text. In essence, Rabbi Lamm understood the Book of Esther as a Straussian document.[3] In his sermon for *Parashat Zakhor* in 1962, he explained that Esther was "written on two levels: revealed and concealed, open and hidden, an outer and an inner story.... In other words, the Megilla is an unusually splendid example of a diplomatic document which tries to accommodate the competing demands of *shalom* and *emet*." In this way, of course, Esther best expresses the precarity of the Jewish condition in the diaspora.

But how do the *shalom* and *emet* readings combine to communicate the work's intended message? Rabbi Lamm pointed out that on

---

1. See, for example, Jonathan Grossman, *Esther: The Outer Narrative and the Hidden Reading*, Siphrut 6 (Winona Lake, 2011).
2. A reference to the Book of Esther's apparent self-description as "words of peace and truth" (Est. 9:30).
3. The German-American philosopher Leo Strauss (1899–1973) argued that philosophers fearing persecution did not always present their thoughts openly and explicitly. Their true intent could often only be discerned through a close reading in-between the lines of their writing.

the level of *shalom*, the Book of Esther is a tale typical of antiquity in which the king is the story's main protagonist. The Hebrew word for king, *melekh*, appears more than any other in the entire book. The king is at the center of every scene in the text and dominates the narrative from beginning to end. The *emet* reading, however, reveals that King Ahasuerus is an easily manipulated fool, whose ubiquity in the story cleverly disguises his impotence. At every turn, someone else is telling the king what to do, whether his advisors, his vizier, his spouse, or his servants. As a whole, the book therefore only *appears* to laud human actors as supreme, independent moral agents. In reality, the Book of Esther argues above all that we are all subject to God's judgment and ultimate plan. There is no king in Esther but the King of Kings.

The careful reader will discern that, in Rabbi Lamm's reading, Esther's lesson is not, in fact, unique to the celebration of Purim. At all times, not only on Purim, we must each account for our own place in the divine drama of history. Unlike other occasions in the Jewish calendar, the point of Purim is not to commemorate a specific event, but to shape regular human behavior. In this respect, Rabbi Lamm partook of an important stream of modern Jewish thought that sees Purim and the Book of Esther as guides to discerning the spiritual amidst the humdrum realities of daily life. It can be found, for example, in Rabbi Abraham Isaac Kook's emphasis on Purim as revealing the "true I."[4] In Rabbi Kook's view, humankind's highest task is to discover its natural, indigenous thirst for God, and Purim is the spiritual fulcrum of this constant endeavor. In a similar vein, Rabbi Isaac Hutner described Purim as emblematic of the search for God that humans conduct under normal, non-miraculous circumstances.[5]

Among these modern thinkers, Rabbi Lamm developed a distinctive answer to the question of what specific insight we should draw from the Book of Esther and the holiday of Purim about everyday morality.

He began to address the question of the true meaning of the Purim story in the following year, in a sermon titled "The Royal

---

4. See, for instance, "Iggeret HaPurim," in *Maamarei HaRe'iyah*, 153–154, and *Mo'adei HaRe'iyah*, 258.
5. See, e.g., *Paḥad Yitzḥak*, Purim 10 and 34.

Insomnia." He began by noting that traditional commentators widely agree that Esther's narrative turning point is at the outset of chapter 6, in which the king experiences a sleepless night. The Talmud embellished this moment with a description of Ahasuerus' internal dialogue.[6] The king first began to toss and turn due to his anxiety that Esther and Haman were plotting to kill him. Despairing that none of his loved ones, advisors, or servants showed any faithfulness toward him, Ahasuerus began to wonder if perhaps he, himself, were the problem. Did his familiars' disloyalty stem from his own ingratitude for their fellowship or service? He therefore ordered his gentleman-in-waiting to search the royal records to determine whether he had neglected to thank any of his subjects for rendering aid to the throne. Sure enough, the king discovered that he had yet to acknowledge Mordecai's heroic foiling of the assassination plot detailed earlier in the Esther story (Est. 2:19–23).

Rabbi Lamm identified this chain of thought as the moral linchpin of the Esther story. Ahasuerus transforms from a paranoid despot, blaming everyone else for his problems, into a man convinced of his own moral agency, who sought to hold himself accountable. For Rabbi Lamm, this represented the central theme of Esther and Purim: the importance of assuming responsibility. As he described it, "On Purim an otherwise undistinguished Persian potentate points the way to spiritual progress... from fear of what others may do to me, to a fear of what I may have failed to do for others."

Over the course of decades' worth of public addresses and writings on Purim, he would continually re-affirm and develop this view. Just under a decade later, for example, Rabbi Lamm delivered a sermon called "Rising Expectations." In this 1972 address, he tackled the problem of how to adjudicate clashing preferences in society. What happens, say, when one group within the American body politic believes that it has been wronged, but its preferred remedies seem to come at some other group's expense? In the wake of the late '60s, Rabbi Lamm, in part, had in mind tensions between black and Jewish communal activists. While he believed it was almost certainly impossible for everyone to get what they want, he was also convinced that each

6. Megilla 15b.

party could genuinely claim justice for its position. In order to address this conundrum, the best we can do is to direct our high expectations not at others, but at ourselves. In a characteristic passage, Rabbi Lamm argued that "Immature Man imposes his rising expectations on others: his wife, his family, his society." By contrast, he continued, "Mature Man subjects not others but himself to the critique of rising expectations: what more can I give to the world, to family, to children, to my people, to humanity and God and Torah? In what way, he constantly asks himself, have I made the world a better place to live in than the state in which I found it when I entered it?"

Rabbi Lamm anchored this point in a careful analysis of the differences between Haman and Mordecai. In particular, he noted that Haman's career was characterized by constant demands of others. Haman had everything his heart could possibly desire – a loving family and high political office with all its attendant prestige. But still, he could not abide one lonely Jew who failed to show the proper obsequiousness. It is for this reason that the Talmud compared Haman to Adam.[7] In Rabbi Lamm's interpretation, Adam too had everything, and yet could not resist eating from the one tree from which God had forbidden him to eat. By contrast to Haman and Adam, Mordecai dedicated his life not to fulfilling his personal desires and achieving his own political advancement, but to defending his people and uplifting society. This is why the characteristic commandments of Purim are *mishlo'aḥ manot* and *matanot le'evyonim*, giving material sustenance and financial support to others.

For Rabbi Lamm, Purim was not only a call to pay greater attention to individual morality. He believed that Purim's ethic of personal responsibility should also serve as a guiding principle for Jewish engagement in the debates over American social politics. Recall that he composed "Rising Expectations" during the heyday of Jewish liberal politics in the 1970s, when many leading American Jewish activists were deeply concerned to promote a radical separation between church and state. In the course of his intellectual career, Rabbi Lamm frequently expressed his frustration that such efforts appeared unaccompanied by a commitment to the Jewish traditions they were supposed to protect. In this

7.   Ḥullin 139b.

particular sermon, Rabbi Lamm gave stern voice this concern. Instead of agitating against Sunday Blue Laws and sectarian practices in public schools, he stressed, we should ask ourselves whether or not we, in our own conduct, demonstrate sufficient care for the spiritual values that such policies purportedly threaten. Do we keep the Sabbath as we should? Do we observe the Jewish holidays as we should? If we wish for our values to be taken seriously in the public discourse, we Jews must be sure consistently to set the highest expectations for our own adherence to those values.

But Rabbi Lamm was not content to cast Purim only as a time for individuals or communities to expect more from themselves. He also believed that the events narrated in the Book of Esther licensed others – especially God – to demand more *from* us. To make this point, Rabbi Lamm introduced into his theory of Esther the Talmud's discussion of the Sinai theophany and its relation to Purim.[8] The Rabbis relate that as the Israelites gathered around Mount Sinai, preparing to receive the Torah, God lifted the mountain over their heads. He gave them a choice: either accept the Torah, or I will cast this mountain down upon you. In the Sages' view, such a threat constituted a *modaa rabba le'oraita*, a reasonable argument that our covenant with the Almighty should be non-binding. It was, after all, coerced. To resolve this problem, the Rabbis argued that the situation was remedied on Purim. At that time, in the Talmud's interpretation, the Jews voluntarily "established and imposed" (Est. 9:27) the Torah upon themselves anew.

On Purim of 1968, just over a month before his Yom Yerushalayim address, Rabbi Lamm invoked this text as the key to Purim's spiritual logic. According to his reading in a sermon titled "Neither Here Nor There," the Talmud's point is that both God's manifest goodness – the joy of the Sinai revelation – and His threats – dangling the mountain over the Israelites' heads – are so coercive as to render any moral decisions made under those circumstances null and void. In his words, "God's promises and His threats, the blessing of His presence and the threat of His wrath, are both coercive and force me to do His will under duress, without making a free choice of my own. Only a demon in human form

---

8. Shabbat 88a.

would have done otherwise." The biblical story of Sinai, and events like it, are certainly inspiring, but are removed from the mundane realities of everyday living. Most of us do not face such extremes on a normal basis.

The events of Purim, however, stand in stark contrast to the rabbinic interpretation of Sinai. To return to the interplay between *shalom* and *emet*, the Esther narrative *could* be read in a secular, even atheistic manner. It could merely be a story about how the Jews of Persia gained salvation through some happy coincidence of political maneuvering and happenstance. One can easily imagine the "enlightened" atheists like the Richard Dawkinses or Steven Pinkers of the day berating the benighted masses for attributing the events of Esther to the hand of providence. But for the spiritually attuned person, the story clearly lends itself to an exalted reading. God's presence may not have been as obvious as His intervention at Sinai, but it was no less real for that. For the moral purposes of entering into a covenant with God, then, Purim is much more similar to everyday life in that it is "neither here nor there." It is just ambiguous enough to allow humans to make considered judgments about it, and thus for God to expect that we assume responsibility for our moral and spiritual choices. Rabbi Lamm therefore dissented from Rabbi Samson Raphael Hirsch's piquant aphorism that "the Jewish calendar is the catechism of the Jew." In fact, asserted Rabbi Lamm, Purim teaches us to seek spiritual fulfillment not in the emotional extremes of the Jewish festivals; rather, we are to find it in the "Purims of life" – in the everyday moments that are "neither here nor there."

A month later, Rabbi Lamm would deploy this very logic – a reading of Esther and Purim he had been developing for years – to explain the significance of the very first Yom Yerushalayim. He began by reiterating that extreme experiences do not allow people to make sustained moral commitments. In some cases, radical happiness can even block a person from meaningfully assuming responsibility for himself. The ecstasy accompanying the revelation at Sinai was such that our acceptance of the Torah at that time could not be truly binding. Extending this point, he pointed out that extreme tragedy could have the same effect: "We cannot really blame the victim of the concentration camp who called upon God out of his misery and received no answer, who was himself witness to the ultimate debasement of man created in the image of God.

We cannot condemn him for abandoning religion, much as we would
prefer that he emulate those few hardy souls who were able to survive
the Holocaust with their faith intact." Both the Sinai theophany and the
Holocaust, then, could constitute a *modaa rabba le'oraita*.

But in contrast to the highs of Sinai or the lows of the Holocaust, the Six Day War struck Rabbi Lamm as much more reminiscent
of Purim. Jewish fortune had been restored, but it was still possible –
in fact, a common occurrence to this day – for commentators to offer
secular, naturalistic explanations for Israel's victory and the liberation of
Jerusalem. Specifically in this environment, Jews could actually *choose*
to believe in God and return to Him without their choice being marred
by psychological or spiritual coercion. As he concluded:

> Hence, for the first time in living memory we have complete reli-
> gious options. We can claim the excuse neither of God's forcible
> presence, nor of His tragic absence. And therefore our *shemirat
> hamitzvot* (observance of the commandments) is a more genu-
> inely free decision. Therefore too, we have more opportunity to
> reach out to others, we have something to tell them about. And
> most important, we have a greater moral responsibility for our
> own faith, our own *emuna*. So that Yom Yerushalayim presents
> a revelation of *Shalem* [the earliest biblical name for Jerusalem] –
> not only the wholeness of the Holy City, but our own individual
> *shelemut,* our spiritual wholeness and perfection as believing Jews.

In the end, Rabbi Lamm's understanding of Purim positioned the Book
of Esther as the perfect text for Yom Yerushalayim. Esther is not merely
a rumination on diaspora Jewish life, nor is it simply an esoteric call for
aliya. It is, rather, nothing less than a guide to making virtuous choices
in the course of everyday life, at the personal level, the political level,
and the national-historical level.

We are just over half a century since Rabbi Lamm's Yom Yerushalayim address, and just months removed from my beloved grandfather's
passing. The Jewish people, and all of society, face new challenges in
emotionally and psychologically ambiguous times. Humanity is in the
grips of a global pandemic, and American civic discourse has become

dangerously frayed. On a daily basis we are deluged by righteous claims and counterclaims by one or another political, social, or cultural group. Now, more than ever, it is not clear where is here and where is there. At a time like this, Rabbi Lamm's interpretation of Purim as a manual for regular decision-making is as essential as ever. As he taught us, ambiguous times are our best opportunities to make morally meaningful choices. We must resolve to assume personal responsibility – whether as individuals, a community, or a nation – for acting virtuously. And we must direct our highest spiritual expectations squarely at ourselves.

America's Hamanite Moment

Dr. Liel Leibovitz

R*ambo: First Blood Part II* came out in Israel when I was ten, and ever since I saw it I wanted two things and two things only: a cool, red headband, and a big, shiny gun. Neither struck my parents as particularly reasonable, and so I waited a few months until Purim drew near and then, ever so casually, told my mother that this year, I'll be dressing up as my hero, the world's most pectorally impeccable Green Beret.

When the big day came, I smeared some shoe polish under my eyes for effect, tied the coveted band around my head – doing my best to ignore the fact that it was really just a silk sash my mother had removed from one of her dresses, a misfortune that would have never befallen the real Rambo – grabbed the toy gun, and went to school.

Purim, in Nof Yam elementary, was a festival as sweet as it was predictable. You'd spend two hours pretending like it was a normal school day, doing your best to listen while furtively eyeing the small pile of *mishlo'aḥ manot* that each kid had brought from home. As the teacher carried on, you'd try to figure out which of the cellophane-wrapped treasures will end up yours, and prayed softly that you'd receive one of the nicer baskets prepared by one of the more attentive girls rather than some chaotic platter thrown together by an inattentive boy and containing little more than a pair of *hamantaschen* and, if you were lucky, a small bag of Bamba.

I was still looking at the goods when the teacher embarked on another one of the day's customs, the reading of the *megilla*. I had heard it so many times before, and so tapped my desk impatiently, wishing that Queen Esther had conducted her business in one nightly feast for the king and Haman rather than two. And then, out of the trill of the familiar, popping out of the *megilla* like the tip of an iceberg out of a dark ocean, came the following words:

> And the rest of the Jews who were in the king's provinces assembled and protected themselves and had rest from their enemies and slew their foes, seventy-five thousand, but upon the spoil they did not lay their hands on the thirteenth of the month of Adar, and they rested on the fourteenth thereof, and made it a day of feasting and joy. (Est. 9:16–17)

Pretending to be John Rambo was one thing; munching on poppy-filled pastry while nodding contently to a story about the joyous massacre of scores of civilians over not one but two days was another. I put my gun down. All of a sudden, my favorite holiday felt a lot less kid friendly.

Over the next few decades, I continued to be haunted by the specter of Purim. And, the more I read, the less lonely I felt. That bit about the slaughter, I learned, had troubled Jews since at least Victorian times: Ellis Abraham Davidson, a prominent educator and writer, was entrusted with publishing a version of the Hebrew Bible that would introduce its riches to the gentiles from a Jewish perspective, and ended up cutting most of the stuff about the slaughter. His contemporary, Claude Goldsmid Montefiore, a darling of Balliol College, Oxford, was equally as repulsed by Purim and, in his own version of the Hebrew Bible, apologized to his readers for that messy business of bloodletting. "We can hardly dignify or extenuate the operations of the Jews by saying that they were done in self defense," he wrote. "For we are told that all the officials helped the Jews, and that none durst withstand them. Moreover, the slain apparently included both women and children. There is no fighting, but just as there was to have been a massacre of unresisting Jews, so now there is a massacre of unresisting gentiles."[1] In his *landsmen's* defense, Montefiore simply argued that he very much doubted that any Jew celebrating Purim really understood what it was he or she were celebrating. And, ever the gentleman, he expressed his wish that the odious holiday "were to lose its place in our religious calendar."[2]

Purim, thankfully, persisted, and with it the discomfort of many enlightened Jews eager to explain away its hard kernel. Shulem Deen, a gifted writer and former Hasid, has credited the holiday for accelerating his decision to leave Orthodoxy's fold; "I wanted a world," he wrote, "in which *seventy-five thousand dead* makes one shudder, if ever so slightly, before enjoying *hamantaschen* and whiskey."[3] And Rabbi Dr. Haim Burgansky, a Bar Ilan University professor, gave his own midrash on Purim, suggesting that the *real* reason we fast on Taanit Esther was merely to mourn for all those innocent souls plucked by Mordecai's murderous minions.[4]

These exegeses ought to have moved me. They strummed on the very same tender string in me that shuddered at the song of slaughter. Instead, these apologias merely drove me back to the text itself, back to chapter 9 of the *megilla*, aching to understand just why my heroes took so gleefully to carnage.

Read the story as pure *peshat*, and you'll be left with a sour aftertaste, cringing at the cruel symmetry between Haman's genocidal plan and the Jews' eventual retribution. You may not mind much the suspension of the Agagite and his boys – these baddies had it coming – but you'll probably wonder why the famous Jewish quality of mercy failed to materialize and spare the pitiful Persians their lives. At the very least, you'll ask, like Montefiore, why we enlightened moderns continue to

1. C. G. Montefiore, *The Bible for Home Reading*, 2:403; quoted in Elliott Horowitz, *Reckless Rites: Purim and the Legacy of Jewish Violence* (Princeton, 2008), 29.
2. C. G. Montefiore, "Purim Difficulties," *Jewish Chronicle*, March 2, 1888, 8; quoted in Horowitz, 30.
3. Shulem Deen, "How Purim, Judaism's Boozy Rejoinder to Halloween, Shook My Faith," *The New Republic*, March 5, 2015.
4. See Thamar F. Gindin, *The Book of Esther Unmasked* (Israel, 2016), 236.

celebrate this bloody holiday with such vigor, a question, sadly, not too frequently or eloquently addressed.

Of course, the answer is right there in the *megilla*, rewarding, as Jewish texts always do, a patient and layered reading. Go back to chapter 3, and you'll see Haman as a menace in full. Slighted by Mordecai, he could easily have applied his might as the viceroy of a great empire and crushed his foe. Had he done that, Haman would've been a familiar figure to readers of ancient tales, a prideful hothead who lets his hubris have the best of him.

But the Agagite isn't a hothead. He waits until his wrath is distilled into potent fuel, and then carefully constructs his operatic bloodshed. He draws lots and makes plans. And it's not just Mordecai he seeks to annihilate but all Jews everywhere.

Why? The *megilla* (3:6) simply states that it was "contemptible to him to lay hands on Mordecai alone," which may be the key to unlocking Haman's terrifying theology. Exterminating the Jews isn't just a way to sate his lowly appetites; it's an affirmation of his warped worldview, in which power may rest solely with one source, and all who question or oppose or complicate it in any way must die.

> And Haman said to King Ahasuerus, "There is a certain people scattered and separate among the peoples throughout all the provinces of your kingdom, and their laws differ from [those of] every people, and they do not keep the king's laws; it is [therefore] of no use for the king to let them be." (3:8)

They have different laws, therefore it is of no use to let them be: the same words might've been spoken by Hitler's goons or Stalin's thugs, but they continue to resonate today with America's young and educated and self-assured who brook no dissent and tolerate no divergence from dogma. In newsrooms and classrooms and boardrooms, many view the world just as Haman once had, a perennial struggle between the blamelessly good and the irredeemably evil, a struggle that can only conclude if the good achieve absolute power and use it to wipe evil out.

This, hallelujah, is not the Jewish idea of justice. We've no foes that call out for an a priori pogrom. Not even Amalek. As the Israeli scholar Rabbi David Levy wisely reminds us,[5] what makes the Bible's commandment in Deuteronomy 25:19 to wipe out Amalek's memory difficult is that it's rooted in the duty of memory. We are obligated to wipe out the Amalekites not because they're an abstraction, a convenient catch-all for all that we find distasteful and challenging, but because they are the perpetrators of a specific act against a specific people under specific circumstances. It's their actions that make them odious, not their essence. The same is true with the Persians felled by the Jews on these two days in Adar so long ago: they died not because they were a faceless Other, but because they had prepared to join Haman, an Amalekite by descent and deed, in his vicious plot.

Still, why murder? No crime, after all, had been committed; none of the mob that would have annihilated the Jews did as much as pick up a pitchfork. Why kill so many, and then ask for an additional day to kill yet more?

To begin to answer this question, Rabbi Levy reminds us of an apparently paradoxical condition during ancient times: the more murders plagued the Jews during mishnaic times, the less inclined the Sanhedrin was to judge the murderers. This, he writes, is because God's law isn't and should never be a mere deterrent, a blunt instrument of justice; instead, it's a path for the righteous to follow, and if so many people choose to abandon it, there's little anyone can do to make things right. But if you witness an aberration so shocking as Haman's – his plot, we're told in Esther 3:15, was so heinous and so out of the ordinary as to dumbfound his fellow Shushanites – you're commanded to act forcefully so as to make sure that it doesn't take hold and become the new normal. Seen in this light, revenge, Rabbi Levy writes, "expresses the people's healthy existence; it's a saying that the people will not tolerate any attempt to harm their own." This is why we should always remember the villainy of Amalek: to forget it is to say, however implicitly, that killing Jews is permissible, forgivable, and recurrent.

Here, then, is the moment that the Purim story transcends from a gritty tale of revenge to a benevolent if bloody expression of morality.

5. David Levy, "Miḥyat Amalek BeYameinu: HaOmnam?" *Tzarikh Iyyun* (13 Adar, 5779), https://iyun.org.il/sedersheni/amalek/.

Unlike Haman, Mordecai and Esther insist that guilt isn't transitive but personal; it applies only to those who have transgressed, not to all members of a group, race, nation, or class. Unlike Haman, Mordecai and Esther are interested neither in power nor in riches but in justice – again and again we are reminded that the Jews refused to partake in the spoils, leaving the property of their vanquished foes unclaimed. And unlike Haman, Mordecai and Esther do not take the killing lightly: their campaign is motivated not by personal considerations or calculations but by the desire to uphold what ought to be the foundation of every legal system anywhere – the principle that actions have consequences. To let the Persian plotters go unpunished, then, would've meant not only dismissing an attempt against the Jews as pardonable, but would have also dismantled the foundations of lawfulness and righteousness throughout the empire by showing that one may very well try one's hand at genocide and walk away unscathed.

And here, too, is where Mordecai and Esther's story shakes off the dust of antiquity and breathes new life into our tortured American moment. You needn't be a particularly astute political observer to notice that the Land of the Free is having its Hamanite Moment: cadres of powerful men and women – professors and journalists, pundits and CEOs, lawmakers and tastemakers – are rising to advocate that we abandon America's great promise of regarding all as equal and demanding instead that we regard our fellow citizens not as pieces of one cohesive and gorgeous mosaic but as stratified tribes perennially at war, some inherently privileged and sinful and others eternally virtuous and oppressed. And while these vicious viceroys, thankfully, don't cast lots and sign death sentences, they are busy feeding anyone and everyone who dares defy their logic to Cancel Culture, that punishing machine that robs the innocent of their hard-earned possessions, from income to companionship. These joyless Jacobins are everywhere busy toppling statues of America's founders, denouncing its myths and symbols as monuments to oppression and greed, and accusing opponents of thought crimes. They are assembled under the banner of social justice, but are neither particularly social nor especially just. Instead, they dream, like the Agagite, of having the power to suppress those who refuse to bow before them. Their ultimate goal is power, and their theology is one of division and replacement:

for their truth to burn bright, all others must be extinguished. Succumb to their demands, and America will be America no more, just as Persia would've surely perished had Haman had his way. A great empire, as America proved in its own ferocious civil war, isn't one in which human beings can be doomed for no other reason than belonging to the wrong race, caste, religion, or class. A great empire is one that sets clear laws and exacts a price of anyone who blatantly subverts them. And anyone who feels particularly gloomy about America's future odds should recall that Mordecai and Esther, too, rose from lowly and marginal subjects to viceroy and queen, remaking the kingdom for the better and undoing the dark legacy of the murderous and divisive Haman.

You could end your reading of the *megilla* there and still feel confident that Purim is far from the primordial celebration of unchecked retribution it is so often and so wrongly understood to be. But the *megilla* offers us one more layer of meaning, this one pertaining not to the collective, national drama but to our own personal responsibility. To ask what we must do to hasten a brighter American future and dispel the darkness of our current political moment, we must once again look at Esther and Mordecai, and read their story again, this time as a mystical parable about redemption that urges all of us – Americans, Jews and non-Jews alike – to have the courage of our convictions as Mordecai did when he harshly assured Esther that if she failed to play her part, "relief and rescue will arise for the Jews from elsewhere" (4:14).

To illustrate this point – the story of the *megilla* as a parable, urging us to always remain vigilant, reject the black bile that too often threatens to drown out hope and good cheer, and work tirelessly toward redemption, our own and the world's – we have a strange yet compelling story about the Purim tale's two leading men. Haman and Mordecai, the midrashic collection *Aggadat Esther* (5:9) tells us, weren't random passers-by who bumped into each other on the streets of Shushan; they were ancient acquaintances whose feud traced back to the building of the Second Temple, with Mordecai having been an industrious builder and Haman a wicked disrupter determined to postpone the work and hamper the Jewish people's spiritual well-being. And not the Jewish people's alone: The Temple, Isaiah reminds those who have forgotten, was built as a house of prayer for the whole world, a place where the word of God would flow forth as the water covers the sea (Is. 11:9). It was the earthly embodiment of the divine presence, a reassurance that there's more to life than the pursuits of the flesh and that God's law is more intricate and merciful than the naked power that mortal rulers so desperately seek. By disrupting the Temple's building, then, Haman was getting in the way of mankind's spiritual well-being, jeopardizing, in pure Amalekite fashion, the tenets of universal justice and the possibility of human flourishing for his own perverse purposes.

The struggle between Mordecai and Haman, then, neither begins nor ends in Shushan. It's an eternal struggle between those whose faith leads them to see others with dignity and compassion, and those whose resentments drive them to all forms of tyranny. It's the struggle between those who wish to uphold the legacy of Washington and Jefferson, Frederick Douglass and Martin Luther King Jr., and those who want to replace it with fifty shades of censorship. And it's the struggle between those who see it as their duty to personally strive to repair the world by adhering to the timeless tenets of justice and those who lazily expect the work of redemption to be done immediately and by the power of their social media demands.

The Jews, Tractate Megilla (12a) reminds us, were subjected to the schemes of Haman because they had partaken in Ahasuerus' feast; instead of exercising their spiritual destiny and returning to help rebuild Zion, they warmed up to foreign customs, abandoning their own sense of destiny and purpose. Mordecai's mission, then, was to awaken their spirit, to win the battle not only against Agagite-led enemies of flesh-and-blood but also against complacency, against lazy lack of belief in the power of personal commitment. Our mission, here and now in America, is not that different: we've gotten comfortable in the decades-long feast of the twentieth century, letting go of our distinctions and loosening our observances. Now that the nation is thick with Agagites, however, it again needs the Jews, forever the moral minders of sclerotic empires, to shake off the cobwebs of complacency, reread the ancient stories, and remind us of the enduring relevance of foundational values.

We must remember, as Rabbi Levy urges us, that there will always be those – like Haman, like Amalek – who will prey on us in our moment of weakness, when we're tired or numb or just eager to enjoy a drink and forget all about the turbulence of fate. When that happens, we have but one obligation: Fight, not only against the would-be oppressors but against oppression itself, against the idea that we're powerless to chart our own course and demand our own rights. Fight against those who deny America's godly promise. Fight against those who deny the Jews their safety and security. Fight against those who see the world as an everlasting war between two immovable camps. Fight against the cynics and the cowardly. Fight against those who wish to replace a cohesive community with warring tribes. Fight against those who urge you to remain silent because only other members of other tribes have the moral right to speak. They are all one and the same, a million little Hamans; we must reject them all.

In the very opening of his majestic interpretation of the *megilla*, the Vilna Gaon sets the tone for what's to follow by insisting that the story we're about to read "hints at the trials of mankind, its war against the Evil Inclination, and the eventual downfall of the Devil."[6] Forget Milton, or, for that matter, Rambo: for a tale of wrestling with evildoers and evil itself, for a confirmation of will and wonder, for a call to personal responsibility and communal solidarity, look no further than Purim, the greatest Jewish story ever told.

---

6. *Megillat Esther Im Peirush HaGra*, https://beta.hebrewbooks.org/pdfpager.aspx?re q=14232&st=&pgnum=1&hilite=.

A Letter in a Scroll: Textual Ethics and the Esther Exception

Rabbi Dov Lerner

After one of the more dazzling, daring, and serendipitous heists in American history, Benjamin Franklin Gates stands on the cusp of applying lemon juice and heat to the back of the original copy of the American Declaration of Independence. In a tense moment, an archivist and eventual co-conspirator, Abigail Chase, clasps his hand and stops him with the words: "Someone who is trained to handle antique documents is going to do it." What follows is the discovery, or rather revival, of an invisible cipher hidden by the Founding Fathers that leads, eventually, to an unimaginable collection of historic treasures and confirms the presence of a secret order of modern Knights Templar.

Of course, this scene and this scheme are fictional – depicted in the Disney blockbuster *National Treasure* (2004) – but the premise and the execution of the plot crystallize a sentiment that pulses at the very heart of an institution that supervises and adjudicates how Americans live their lives. The film's investiture of history with mystery and force, the characters' handling of a manuscript with reverence and awe, the suspense and tension and the painstaking attention paid to exhuming truths embedded in old texts – all inhere in the constitutional theory of "originalism"; a theory which, as we shall explore, sits in stark opposition to the spirit of rabbinic textual ethics – with the exception of their attitude toward the Book of Esther.

* * *

A loaded term, "originalism" covers a complex web of conceptual subsets,[1] but writ large it bespeaks an attachment to the principle that in applying the legal meaning of the American Constitution, judges and justices need to seek the meaning of its words at the time that they were written – as they were intended by those who wrote them. To do this with integrity intact, an arbiter is required to develop a competency in the English spoken in the 1780s by the authors of the Constitution and the broader public. They ought also to make recourse to any published or personal letters of the authors that might insinuate any sense of the intended meaning of the original articles and ensuing amendments, while also attending to the texts and intentions of contemporaneous legislative documents from the States that existed at the time.

A view that resides on the other side of the theoretical spectrum makes a claim for what is called the "Living Constitution," a term first employed with this sense by Howard Lee McBain in his 1927 book of the same name. In this view – which, like Originalism, encompasses a broad array of perspectives[2] – the legal meaning of the text is open to interpretation. Antonin Scalia, of Supreme Court fame, somewhat disdainfully branded this constellation of views as seeing the Constitution as "a 'morphing' document that means, from age to age, what it ought

---

1. For a helpful survey of a variety of constitutional theories, see Larry Alexander, "Constitutional Theories: A Taxonomy and (Implicit) Critique," *San Diego Law Review* vol. 51, issue 3 (2014). For one example of distinction between different originalisms, see Stephen F. Hayward, "Two Kinds of Originalism," *National Affairs* (Winter 2017), https://www.nationalaffairs.com/publications/detail/two-kinds-of-originalism.
2. See Larry Alexander's article referenced in previous note.

to mean."[3] And those who see themselves as defenders of the framers' intentions suggest that their originalism is superior to this living constitutionalism for one primary reason – it is the lesser evil.

In a talk entitled exactly that – "Originalism: The Lesser Evil" – delivered at the University of Cincinnati, Scalia acknowledged the near impossibility of knowing the precise intentions of the framers at the time of the Constitution's adoption. And yet, for him, the alternative encompassed so many practical defects and theoretical flaws that he preferred the imprecise to the amorphous.[4] This sentiment, shared by his former colleague Justice Clarence Thomas, was expressed during a 2008 lecture to the Manhattan Institute as follows:

> Let me put it this way; there are really only two ways to interpret the Constitution – try to discern as best we can what the framers intended or make it up. No matter how ingenious, imaginative or artfully put, unless interpretive methodologies are tied to the original intent of the framers, they have no more basis in the Constitution than the latest football scores. To be sure, even the most conscientious effort to adhere to the original intent of the framers of our Constitution is flawed, as all methodologies and human institutions are; but at least originalism has the advantage of being legitimate and, I might add, impartial.[5]

And though Scalia admitted that originalism has never been the sole method of constitutional exegesis, he asserted that, in the past, those who employed a more flexible hermeneutic "had the decency to lie, or at least to dissemble, about what they were doing."[6] Only in the last few years, he suggested, have those who embrace, what he calls, "nonoriginalist exegesis" taken pride in explicitly declaring the intellectual legitimacy

---

3. Antonin Scalia and Amy Gutmann, *A Matter of Interpretation: Federal Courts and the Law* (new edition, Princeton/Oxfordshire, 2018), 47.
4. Antonin Scalia, "Originalism: The Lesser Evil," *University of Cincinnati Law Review* 57, issue 849 (1989): 7.
5. See https://www.manhattan-institute.org/html/2008-wriston-lecture-judging-government-consent-8895.html.
6. Scalia, "Originalism: The Lesser Evil," 3.

of their interpretive allegiances. And this incremental surfacing of closet judicial-activists just happens to overlap with the rise of interest within the American academy not in rabbinic history but in rabbinic hermeneutics. It seems therefore not implausible to see this overlap as a result of the connection between originalism and living-constitutionalism on the one hand, and two ancient, fundamentally divergent, views of text and the universe – one Greek and the other Hebrew.

* * *

In his *Golden Doves with Silver Dots*, José Faur, a scholar of law and hermeneutics, traces the major differences between, what he calls, the Greek metaphysical perspective and the Hebrew semiological one. As a central hinge of his larger argument, Faur depicts an emerging divergence between the Greek and Hebrew minds in relation to the written word, based on the work of Socrates and the rabbinic Sages.[7]

 In Plato's *Phaedrus*, a dialogue which references an Egyptian myth of the creation of script – in which the god Theuth invents, among other things, arithmetic, astronomy, dice, and letters – Socrates contends that text is infested with peril.[8] On one level, he argues, the written word enfeebles memory – for while it ostensibly aids with the preservation of information, it does so in a state that is detached from the minds of men, who will, due to a mixture of lethargy and opportunity, rely on inscriptions rather than recall. Worse than the production of forgetfulness for Socrates, however, is that text fosters hubris and deceit. Texts "tell" rather than "teach," to use his turn of phrase, in that they present themselves as self-evident projections of truths but allow for no cross-examination or interrogation or debate; if you ask for clarification, written texts simply "go on telling just the same thing forever." The "majestic silence" emanating from reticent texts both fails to educate its readers and endows them with a sense of false achievement – a critique eloquently staged in Gus Van Sant's *Good Will Hunting*, when an autodidactic Matt Damon

7. José Faur, *Golden Doves with Silver Dots: Semiotics and Textuality in Rabbinic Tradition* (Bloomington, 1986), Introduction, and chs. 1 and 5.
8. *Phaedrus* 14, 274c–275b.

assails a well-read but stunningly shallow post-graduate for ignorance and vanity. In a sentence, the written word, for Socrates, is a "pharmakon," a poison toxic to true edification and discovery, which in turn can only arise in "living, breathing discourse … of which the written one can be fairly called an image."[9]

Through the prism of Socrates' lens, texts are but traces of speech petrified in time – diminished by their inscription, dangerous in their deception, and valuable only to the extent that we can comprehend the author's original intention. Naturally, judicial originalism appears to share this perspective, through which the Constitution was written as a mere concession to the ravages of time and the need for proof to make contracts binding – leaving the means of practical conservation lying in ink rather than memory.

On the other hand, Faur's depiction of the Hebrew mind could barely be more different. Hebrews are the "People of the Book," with text at the very center of their culture and identity. In a passage that is evocative of this conception, Rabbi Jonathan Sacks describes the place of sacred text in Jewish life:

> I wonder if any people has ever loved a book as we love the *Torah*. We stand when it passes as if it were a king. We dance with it as if it were a bride. If it is desecrated or destroyed we bury it as if it were a relative or a friend. We study it endlessly as if in it were hidden all the secrets of our being.[10]

There is nothing more vital, more pivotal, and more fundamental to the Hebrew mind than the Hebrew Bible – and, for Faur, it was written not as a concession to the limits of memory but as a testament to the power of script. Through the prism of a midrashic reading of Song of Songs 1:11 – "We will make you golden doves with silver dots" – he articulates the rabbinic Sages' notion of Scripture as a polysemic text, rippling with divinity and an infinity of semantic possibilities, far more

---

9. Ibid. 14, 276a.
10. Jonathan Sacks, *A Letter in the Scroll: Understanding Our Jewish Identity and Exploring the Legacy of the World's Oldest Religion* (New York, 2001), 39.

edifying and engaging than a torrent of shallow speech. He cites well-known illustrations of such a claim – such as the Sages' interpretation of Jeremiah 23:29 ("My word is like…a hammer that shatters a rock") and the relatively familiar rabbinic refrain, "These and those are the words of the Living God"[11] – to demonstrate that for the Hebrew "the ultimate object of reading is not to discover the mind of the author but to generate meaning."[12]

This claim on Faur's part is not particularly exceptional; modern scholars tend to agree on an affinity between the Sages' exegetical imagination and the tenets of textual polysemy.[13] His paleographic argument, however – that these exegetical tendencies on the part of Hebrews and Greeks connect to their respective preferences for scrolls as opposed to codices – is striking.[14] The codex, which came to replace scrolls across the ancient world,[15] was seen by Jews as an unacceptable vessel for the text of Scripture – at least for liturgical and ritual purposes. So, besides the break between metaphysical and semiological minds and the consequences for their respective perspectives on script, Greeks and Jews held and read physically different textual objects.

In Faur's description, a Torah scroll is written solely on the parchment's recto (inside), and thus rolls closed, leaving the text itself always

---

11. Faur, xiii, xiv.

12. Ibid., xxvii.

13. See Michael A. Fishbane, *The Exegetical Imagination: On Jewish Thought and Theology* (Cambridge, 1998); Daniel Boyarin, *Intertextuality and the Reading of Midrash* (Bloomington, 1994); Azzan Yadin-Israel, *Scripture and Tradition: Rabbi Akiva and the Triumph of Midrash* (Philadephia, 2015); Azzan Yadin, *Scripture as Logos: Rabbi Ishmael and the Origins of Midrash* (Philadelphia, 2013); David Stern, *Midrash and Theory: Ancient Jewish Exegesis and Contemporary Literary Studies* (Evanston, 1996); Susan A. Handelman, *The Slayers of Moses: The Emergence of Rabbinic Interpretation in Modern Literary Theory* (Albany, 2012); Eugene B. Borowitz, *The Talmud's Theological Language-Game: A Philosophical Discourse Analysis* (Albany, 2012); Alexander Samely, *Forms of Rabbinic Literature and Thought: An Introduction* (Oxford, 2007); among others.

14. Faur is not alone is seeing the Hebrew preference for scrolls as determinative for their cultural consciousness. Frank Kermode, in his *The Genesis of Secrecy*, suggests that the Jewish-Christian divide between scrolls and codices had an influence on their respective eschatologies; see Frank Kermode, *The Genesis of Secrecy: On the Interpretation of Narrative* (London, 1979), 88–89.

15. Colin H. Roberts and T. C. Skeat, *The Birth of the Codex* (London, 1987).

bounded by its own verso (outside) – a fact that he sees as testament to the exegetical tendency of the Sages to conceive of Scripture as self-contained, unique, and intertextual. The book or codex, on the other hand, utilizes both the inner and outer sides of the textual platform, and thus cannot be rolled and self-contained. On this basis, Faur projects a fundamental rift in textual ethics – with Hebrews venerating text as a sacred vessel of celestial infinity, and Greeks identifying script with a less animated and inferior form of speech. For Socrates, the application of interpretive pressure to a text is a form of futile violence; for the rabbinic Sages, it unveils divinity.

This rift between Western and Jewish textual ethics, in Faur's telling, first began to collapse with the rise of twentieth-century critical theory. In the so-called age of reason, starting at the turn of the eighteenth century, Enlightenment scholars of the Bible assumed a Greek textual ethic in the realm of Scripture – and in their search for solely what they saw as the plain sense of Scripture, the vilification of rabbinic interpretive proclivities became especially pronounced.[16] Gotthold Ephraim Lessing, friend of Moses Mendelssohn, says it most succinctly:

> Every Primer is only for a certain age. To delay the child, that has outgrown it, longer in it than it was intended for, is hurtful. For to be able to do this in a way in any sort profitable, you must insert into it more than there is really in it, and extract from it more than it can contain. You must look for and make too much of allusions and hints; squeeze allegories too closely; interpret examples too circumstantially; *press too much upon words.* This gives the child a petty, crooked, hair splitting understanding; it makes him full of mysteries, superstitions; full of contempt for all that is comprehensible and easy. *The very way in which the Rabbis handled their sacred books!* The very character which they thereby imparted to the character of their people! A Better

---

16. See Edward Breuer, *The Limits of Enlightenment: Jews, Germans, and the Eighteenth-century Study of Scripture* (Cambridge, 1996), chs. 77–108.

Instructor must come and tear the exhausted Primer from the child's hands. (emphasis added)[17]

Aside from the glaring cultural prejudices, Lessing's representation of the biblical text as quite simple to read and quite simply misread by the rabbinic Sages exhibits precisely the gaping division between Greek and Jewish textual ethics that Faur sketches. Is a text meant to be read as a speech is heard – i.e., as a particular message from a specific author to a designated audience – only being less effective than the spoken word due to the reader's inability to press the author for clarity? Or is a written text an artefact of an entirely different order – a repository of multifarious meanings submerged for the attentive reader to hermeneutically disinter?

Western literary critics first began to earnestly contend with the possibility of a written text's distinct polysemy in the twentieth century. First there were figures, like Yuri Lotman, a Russian semiotician, who suggested that not all texts are equal – that there are species of script which are no more than petrified speech, while others convey far more meaning. Lotman labels these latter texts as "artistic," and plots an algorithm which identifies their hermeneutic "entropy" and measures what he calls their "semantic saturation."[18] Beyond the textual computations of Lotman, however, figures like Jacques Derrida, Roland Barthes, and Paul Ricoeur argued that texts do not divide into intrinsic species – polysemic and plain – but that all texts can be seen as "artistic" under exegetical pressure, and at their most powerful are read as swelling with multiple layers of meaning.[19] Faur argues that it was precisely in the wake of this shift in the literary academy that the broader attitude toward the rabbinic principles of exegesis went from ostracization and indifference to curiosity and interest, and

---

17. Gotthold Ephraim Lessing, *The Education of the Human Race* (London, 1858), 44–46.
18. See Jurij Lotman, *The Structure of the Artistic Text* (Ann Arbor, 1977), ch. 1.
19. See Jacques Derrida, *The Gift of Death & Literature in Secret* (Chicago, 2008), second part; Roland Barthes, *Image-Music-Text* (New York, 1977), 142; Paul Ricoeur, "What is a text?" in *Hermeneutics and the Human Sciences*: Essays on Language, Action, and Interpretation (New York, 1981).

works such as Geoffrey Hartman's *Midrash and Literature*[20] appear to buttress his claim.

For our purposes, it so happens that this shift in the literary sphere correlates chronologically with the beginnings of the explicit embrace of living constitutionalism. And perhaps it is no coincidence that this swing toward the Hebraic textual ethic was launched, in the eyes of many, by the Jewish Associate Justice, Louis Brandeis.[21] One point of irony is that in his defense of living constitutionalism, asking jurists to see the words penned by James Madison as vested with interpretive flexibility – much as the Sages saw Scripture – Howard Lee McBain wrote, "The Constitution of the United States was not handed down on Mount Sinai by the Lord God of Hosts. It is not revealed law."[22] Though McBain appears to have imbibed a Hebraic textual ethic – insisting on script's hermeneutic distinction from speech – he seems to have inherited a Socratic view of Scripture, freezing its meaning for all time. For the Sages, Scripture is not an exception to the ethics of exegetical flexibility; it is the exemplar.

However, the rabbinic Sages themselves do appear to make an exception of their own – as we shall see – in the context of the reading of the Book of Esther.[23]

* * *

The text of Esther itself appears conflicted in respect to its own character, and the rabbinic Sages latch onto the ambiguity. In the ninth chapter, it declares itself to be both a letter – an *iggeret*, and a scroll – a *sefer* (Est. 9:26, 29, 32), which even if on their face were on the verge of

---

20. Geoffrey H. Hartman and Sanford Budick, *Midrash and Literature* (New Haven, 1986).
21. See Edward A. Purcell Jr., "The Judicial Legacy of Louis Brandeis and the Nature of American Constitutionalism," *Touro Law Review*, vol. 33, no. 1 (2017): article 4.
22. Howard Lee McBain, *The Living Constitution: A Consideration of the Realities and Legends of Our Fundamental Law* (New York, 1927), 272.
23. I say "reading" of the book of Esther specifically. The Sages did engage in extensive exegesis of the text, filling pages of Talmud and Midrash with a range of readings. However, the choreography of the ritual public reading of Esther exhibits an entirely different sensibility, as we shall see.

synonymity, appear in such proximity as to be exegetically provocative. Hence, in the name of a sage who bridged the mishnaic and talmudic eras, the script of Esther is deemed a hybrid text with legal consequences:

> **Rabbi Ḥelbo said** that **Rav Ḥama bar Gurya said** that **Rav said**: The **Megilla is referred to as a "book"** (Est. 9:32), **and it is also referred to as a "letter"** (Est. 9:29). **It is called a "book,"** to teach **that if one sewed** its parchment sheets together **with flax threads it's unfit; and it is called a "letter"** to teach **that if one stitched** it **with** only **three threads of sinew it's fit.**[24]

Two nouns that may not sound particularly distinct lead, in their confluence, in this case, to a synthetic textual identity – where the requisite comprehensive seams of a canonical scroll are deemed excessive, but the provisional stitches of a missive are considered insufficient; the text of Esther cannot be bound with flax but need not be stitched from top to bottom. For the most well-known medieval commentator, Rashi, this compromise appears to result from the lowering of scriptural standards – in his words, "It is called a 'letter,' i.e., it is not as stringent as a scroll."[25] But the consequences of the text's elemental conglomeration go beyond the seams and into the script itself, perhaps insinuating less a mere concession or difference in degree than a qualitatively novel difference in kind.

There are a pair of views that appear to see the Book of Esther's ritual chirography as symptomatic of a schismatic textual object – part letter, part scroll – wrestling for its core identity. The fourteenth-century Rabbi Vidal of Tolosa, Maimonidean commentator par excellence, sees Esther's text as majority "letter," exhibiting hints of a scriptural character only in instances explicitly depicted in Talmud, such as the requisite

---

24. Megilla 19a (translation based on Steinsaltz; unbolded text interpolated for elucidation and clarity).
25. Rashi, ad loc., s.v. *"Venikraat Iggeret."*

writing materials and implements.[26] Mordecai ben Hillel HaKohen, thirteenth-century German halakhist, on the other hand conceives of Esther's textual disposition as majority "scroll" with specific epistolic elements catalogued by the Sages of the Talmud.[27]

Nahmanides, however, appears not to see Esther's text as compositionally schismatic, but as bearing a coherent character of a unique kind; his view insinuates that the previous two mongrelize a sacred text, suppressing its distinctive integrity. For Nahmanides, the Book of Esther is not a text at odds with itself; it is neither chiefly scroll nor principally letter, it is straightforwardly *a letter in a scroll*. All the elements of the text connected to its material production and inscription exhibit the character of a formal "scroll" – it must be written in proper ink and on proper parchment. And those elements marginally related to the text's production and inscription bear the imprint of this character – the script sits on scored lines called *sirtut*, and, as described, the seams must be stitched to a minimal degree. On the other hand, all the elements of the text that pertain not to its material production or inscription, but its ritual performative transmission, exhibit the character of a "letter." While the ceremonial chanting of Scripture typically entails the reader standing on their feet, the ritual obligation to read the Book of Esther can be fulfilled fully seated, but can also be fulfilled standing; while scriptural cantillation is determined by sentential punctuation, necessitating a pause between verses, the reader of the Book of Esther breathes in the middle of sentences; and, most crucially, in the context of Faur's contention, the text of Esther is not rolled like a scroll but folded like a letter when read.[28]

For Nahmanides, when ritually read each year the Book of Esther exhibits this essential hybridity that ensconces a Socratic presentation of text within the trappings of a polysemous scripture. In this one instance, a rabbinic textual ethic that vests the canon with divinity and exegetical infinitude shifts, and the words of Esther are read as if they had a singular unequivocal message. While the material

---

26. *Maggid Mishneh*, Laws of Megilla and Ḥanukka, ch. 2, s.v. "*Ve'ein Ha'or Shelah*."
27. *Mordecai*, Megilla, #795.
28. *Ḥiddushei HaRamban*, Megilla 17a.

implies eternity, the delivery conveys urgency; while the script and the score and the stitches exude perpetuity, the dissemination projects the power of a now.

* * *

Each week in synagogue Scripture speaks in a neutral voice, read from a rolled scroll that invites the reader and listener to apply exegetical pressures and unleash layers of unseen meaning – to engage numerological, phonetic, homiletic, acronymic, syntactic, associative, and symbolic tools to engender heretofore unimagined semantics. Ordinarily, the Sages adopt an ethic that treats a text, not as an object but a subject that responds to creativity with invention. The text of Esther, however, is an exception.

When Esther is read each year on Purim, the Sages ask us to adopt a Socratic posture and invite us all to become originalists, to treat the text not as a puzzle to be probed but a speech to be heard. We are invited, through the avenues of history and empathy, to imagine Esther's existence and resist the interpretive impulse to burrow for celestial transcendence. Esther's message of faith in the wake of uncertainty and responsibility in the face of calamity – her tale of audacity and daring – is too precious and too urgent, too pertinent and eternal, to risk being lost in the sacred haze of the exegetical imagination.

Our Sages ask us to imagine that in the Book of Esther we have an ancient artefact in our hands and were we to apply heat and lemon juice to its surface it would reveal the imprint of Esther's touch. We are asked to muffle our exegetical energies and embark on a journey of active empathy, listening to Esther's words and attending to her intention – to see, in the text of Esther, a letter in a scroll.

Contributors

Dr. Samantha Baskind is the author of five books, most recently *The Warsaw Ghetto in American Art and Culture* (University Park, 2018), and co-editor of *The Jewish Graphic Novel: Critical Approaches* (New Brunswick, 2008), the foundational volume in the field. She has also published over one hundred articles and reviews in encyclopedias, academic journals, edited volumes, museum catalogs, and the popular press. She served as editor for US art for the twenty-two-volume revised edition of the *Encyclopaedia Judaica* and is currently series editor of "Dimyonot: Jews and the Cultural Imagination," published by Penn State University Press. She is a Professor of Art History at Cleveland State University.

Israel Ben-Porat is a PhD student in early American history at The Graduate Center, CUNY, and he teaches at the City College of New York, CUNY. He received his bachelor's degree *summa cum laude* from Yeshiva University in 2018 and his en-route master's degree from The Graduate Center in 2020. His research interests range broadly in religious, intellectual, and legal history. His dissertation, under the advisement of David Waldstreicher, will focus on the reception of biblical law in transatlantic Puritanism.

Rabbi Dr. Yosef Bronstein received rabbinic ordination from Rabbi Isaac Elchanan Theological Seminary and a PhD in Talmudic Studies from YU's Bernard Revel Graduate School of Jewish Studies. He currently teaches Halakha and Jewish Philosophy at Michlelet Mevaseret Yerushalayim and online for Yeshiva University's Isaac Breuer College. His books, *Engaging the Essence: The Philosophy of the Lubavitcher Rebbe* and *Reshimot Shiurim shel Maran HaRav Yosef Dov Soloveitchik al Masekhet Kiddushin*, are forthcoming.

Dr. Erica Brown is the Director of the Mayberg Center for Jewish Education and Leadership and an Associate Professor of Curriculum and Pedagogy at The George Washington University. Erica was a Jerusalem Fellow, is a faculty member of the Wexner Foundation, an Avi Chai Fellow, and the recipient of the 2009 Covenant Award for her work in education. She is the author of twelve books on leadership, the Hebrew Bible, and spirituality; her most recent book is *The Book of Esther: Power, Fate, and Fragility in Exile* (New Milford/Jerusalem, 2020).

Dr. Emily Colbert Cairns is an Associate Professor of Spanish at Salve Regina University in Newport, Rhode Island. She specializes in gender, *converso*, and crypto-Jewish identity in the early modern period and has published with *eHumanista, Chasqui, Cervantes Journal*, and *Hispanófila*. She is the co-editor (with Brian M. Phillips) of *Confined Women: The Walls of Female Space in Early Modern Spain* (Hispanic Issues Online, 2020) and is the author of *Esther in Early Modern Iberia and the Sephardic Diaspora: Queen of the Conversas* (Basingstoke, 2017). Currently she is guest editing a critical cluster for *La Córonica*. She has held research fellowships at the Bancroft Library (UC California, Berkeley) and the Biblioteca Nacional in Madrid. She spent the fall of 2019 conducting research in the Archivo de la Diputación de Sevilla in support of her current book project on breastfeeding practices in the early modern period.

Rabbi Shalom Carmy teaches Jewish Studies and Philosophy at Yeshiva University. He served as the editor of *Tradition* from 2004 to 2019 and writes the "Litvak at Large" feature in *First Things*.

Rabbi Dr. Zev Eleff is Chief Academic Officer of Hebrew Theological College and an Associate Professor of Jewish History at Touro College. He graduated from the Jay and Jeanie Schottenstein Honors Program at Yeshiva College (2009) and was ordained at the Rabbi Isaac Elchanan Theological Seminary (2011). His most recent book is *Authentically Orthodox: A Tradition-Bound Faith in American Life* (Detroit, 2020).

Malka Fleischmann is a writer and educator living in Manhattan. Malka served as the Director of Knowledge and Ideas at the Jewish Education Project, a Hebrew school Director (Tribeca Torah), Head of Camp (Stone), Director of Faith-Based Programming (Touro College and University System), Judaic Studies educator (SAR and Ramaz Middle Schools), and speechwriter. Formerly a Wexner Fellow-Davidson Scholar and M2 Fellow, Malka is a graduate of the University of Pennsylvania and Harvard Divinity School and has roots firmly planted in Camp Stone. Her writing has been published in the *New York Times, Jewish Week,* and *Tablet Magazine.*

Philip Getz is Senior Editor for Philosophy and Religion at Palgrave Macmillan.

Rabbi Shmuel Hain is the Rabbi of Young Israel Ohab Zedek of North Riverdale/Yonkers and *Rosh Beit Midrash* at SAR High School, where he directs the graduate Beit Midrash Fellowship, teaches advanced Judaic Studies classes, and oversees after-school and alumni learning programs. He is also Co-Director of Machon Siach at SAR High School, a research institute for high school educators. He previously served from 2005 to 2011 as *Rosh Beit Midrash* of the Graduate Program for Women in Advanced Talmudic Studies at Yeshiva University. He graduated with honors from Yeshiva College with a bachelor's degree in Psychology and received a master's degree in Medieval Jewish History from YU's Bernard Revel Graduate School of Jewish Studies. He was an inaugural fellow of the Bella and Harry Wexner Kollel Elyon at Rabbi Isaac Elchanan Theological Seminary, where he was ordained in 2001 and where he taught advanced Talmud classes to *semikha* students and undergraduates from 1999 to 2012. He has authored and edited several volumes of Torah and academic scholarship, including a volume in "The Orthodox Forum Series" entitled *The Next Generation of Modern Orthodoxy* (New York, 2012). Rabbi Hain was awarded the Daniel Jeremy Silver Fellowship at Harvard University for the 2020–2021 academic year to support his research and writing integrating academic, pastoral, and halakhic perspectives on Jewish laws of mourning.

Rabbi Dr. Stuart W. Halpern is Senior Advisor to the Provost and Senior Program Officer of the Straus Center for Torah and Western Thought at Yeshiva University. Dr. Halpern received his bachelor's degree from the University of Pennsylvania, a master's degree in Psychology in Education from Teachers College at Columbia University, a master's degree in Bible from YU's Bernard Revel Graduate School of Jewish Studies, an MBA in Nonprofit Management from Touro University, a doctorate in Education from YU's Azrieli Graduate School of Education and Administration, and rabbinic ordination from Rabbi Chaim Brovender. He has edited or co-edited seventeen books, including most recently *Proclaim Liberty Throughout the Land: The Hebrew Bible in the United States* (New Milford/London, 2019) and *Gleanings: Reflections on Ruth* (New Milford/Jerusalem, 2019). His writing has appeared in *Tablet Magazine, Jewish Review of Books, Tradition, The Lehrhaus,* and the *Jewish Journal.* He teaches in Yeshiva University, synagogues, Hillels, and adult educational settings across the US, Europe, and Israel.

Dr. Dara Horn is the award-winning author of five novels: *In the Image* (New York, 2002), *The World to Come* (New York, 2006), *All Other Nights* (New York, 2009), *A Guide for the Perplexed* (New York, 2013), and *Eternal Life* (New York, 2018). She has received many honors for her books, including selection as one of Granta's Best Young American Novelists, inclusion in the *New York Times* Book Review's and the *San Francisco Chronicle*'s Best Books of the Year and Booklist's Best Books of the Decade, and two National Jewish Book Awards; her books have been translated into twelve languages. Her nonfiction work has appeared in the *New York Times, Wall Street Journal, Washington Post, Atlantic, Jewish Review of Books, Smithsonian,* and many other publications, and she is a regular columnist for *Tablet Magazine*. Horn received her doctorate in Comparative Literature from Harvard University, specializing in Hebrew and Yiddish. She has taught these subjects at Sarah Lawrence College, City University of New York, Harvard University, and most recently YU's Stern College for Women. She lives in New Jersey with her husband and four children.

Rabbi Dr. Ari Lamm is the Chief Executive Officer of the Bnai Zion Foundation and a historian of religion. Prior to his tenure at Bnai Zion, Rabbi Lamm served as Special Advisor to the President of Yeshiva University. He is also formerly the William Fischman Resident Scholar at the Jewish Center in Manhattan. A graduate of Yeshiva University, Rabbi Lamm earned his master's degree, as a US-UK Fulbright Scholar, in Jewish Studies and Eastern Christianity from University College London, a master's degree from Princeton University in Religion, and *semikha* from the Rabbi Isaac Elchanan Theological Seminary. He earned his PhD in Ancient Judaism and Christianity from Princeton University. He is a founding editor and contributor at *The Lehrhaus*, a premier online publication for contemporary Jewish thought (www.thelehrhaus.com), and an alumnus of the Wexner Graduate Fellowship in Jewish Studies. His writing has appeared in the *Wall Street Journal, Jerusalem Post, Tablet Magazine,* and *First Things*.

Dr. Liel Leibovitz is Editor at Large at *Tablet Magazine*, host of its *daf yomi* podcast "Take One," and co-host of its podcasts "Unorthodox" and "Hebrew School." He is the author or co-author of several books, including, most recently, *The Newish Jewish Encyclopedia: From Abraham to Zabar's and Everything in Between* (New York, 2019) and *Stan Lee: A Life in Comics* (New Haven, 2020). He holds a PhD in Communications from Columbia University.

Rabbi Dov Lerner serves as the Rabbi of the Young Israel of Jamaica Estates and is a Resident Scholar at Yeshiva University's Straus Center for Torah and Western Thought, where he has taught courses on "Milton and Midrash" and "Malbim and Modernity" and has led seminars on the confluence of C. S. Lewis and Jewish thought. He is a currently a doctoral candidate at the University of Chicago's Divinity School, where his dissertation focuses on Malbim's exegetical response to the threats of modernity.

Yosef Lindell is a lawyer, writer, and lecturer living in Silver Spring, MD. He has a master's degree in Jewish History from YU's Bernard Revel Graduate School of Jewish Studies. His work has appeared in the *Atlantic, Forward, Jewish Action,* and also at *The Lehrhaus,* where he is an editor.

Rabbi Alex Maged is a JD candidate at Harvard Law School and the Community Scholar for the Young Israel of Brookline. He received rabbinic ordination and a master's degree in Biblical Studies from YU's Bernard Revel Graduate School of Jewish Studies and has served as a scholar-in-residence in communities across North America on Jewish and comparative law and literature. His original interpretations of biblical texts can also be found widely in print, and at WhatsPshat.org, a blog he founded in 2013 which has attracted a community of 1,300 subscribers. He has visited Israel as part of the International Chidon HaTanach and the Bronfman Fellowship, and lived there for a year while studying at Yeshivat Lev HaTorah.

Dr. Emily Schneider writes about children's literature and reviews books at the Jewish Book Council, as well as on *Tablet Magazine, The Horn Book,* the *Intellectual Freedom* blog of the American Library Association, and other publications, and on her blog, *Imaginary Elevators.* She holds a doctorate in Romance Languages and Literatures from Harvard University.

Dr. Eran Shalev is an Associate Professor of History at the University of Haifa. He is the author of *American Zion: The Bible as a Political Text from the Revolution to the Civil War* (New Haven, 2012) and *Rome Reborn on Western Shores: Historical Imagination and the Creation of the American Republic* (Charlottesville, 2009). He is currently writing a book titled *The Star Spangled Republic: The American Constellation in the Political Cosmos.*

Dr. Ariel Clark Silver is the author of *The Book of Esther and the Typology of Female Transfiguration in American Literature* (Lanham, 2018). She has presented and published internationally on topics related to literature, women, and religion in the nineteenth century.

Rabbi Tzvi Sinensky is *Rosh Yeshiva* of Gur Aryeh, a classical school emphasizing the integration of joyful, rigorous Torah learning with the best of the Western canon. He directs the newly redesigned Lamm Heritage Archives, serves as editor of *The Lehrhaus*, and is a research analyst at the Burning Glass Institute. A highly sought-after lecturer and widely published author, his forthcoming dissertation explores the intersection between halakha, gender studies, and theories of masculinity.

Rabbi Dr. Meir Y. Soloveichik is Director of the Zahava and Moshael Straus Center for Torah and Western Thought at Yeshiva University and Rabbi at Congregation Shearith Israel in Manhattan. He graduated *summa cum laude* from Yeshiva College, received his *semikha* from Rabbi Isaac Elchanan Theological Seminary, and was a member of its Beren Kollel Elyon. In 2010, he received his doctorate in Religion from Princeton University. Rabbi Soloveichik has lectured throughout the United States, in Europe, and in Israel to both Jewish and non-Jewish audiences on topics relating to Jewish theology, bioethics, wartime ethics, and Jewish-Christian relations. His essays on these subjects have appeared in the *Wall Street Journal, New York Times, Commentary, First Things, Azure, Tradition,* and *Torah u-Madda Journal.*

Dr. Shaina Trapedo teaches English at YU's Stern College for Women and Manhattan High School for Girls. She received her PhD from the University of California, Irvine, where she specialized in Renaissance Literature with specific interests in performance studies, biblical studies, and cultural rhetoric. Her current book project, *From Scripture to Script: David, Daniel, Esther and the Performance of Early Modern Identity,* considers the affordances and risks of hermeneutic engagements on the Renaissance stage. In her teaching and scholarship, she continues to explore the connections between literacy, cultural identity, and social engagement.

Dr. Tevi Troy is a best-selling presidential historian and former White House aide. From 2007 to 2009, Dr. Troy was the Deputy Secretary of the US Department of Health and Human Service – the second in command and chief operating officer of the largest civilian department in the federal government. Before arriving at HHS, Dr. Troy served at the White House as Deputy Assistant to the President for Domestic Policy. Dr. Troy was also the White House Jewish liaison, acting as President Bush's main adviser on Jewish issues and the administration's point person with the Jewish community. Dr. Troy is the author of four books, including *Fight House: Rivalries in the White House from Truman to Trump* (Washington, DC, 2020). His previous books were *Intellectuals and the American Presidency; Shall We Wake the President? Two Centuries of Disaster Management from the Oval Office* (Guilford, 2016) and the bestseller *What Jefferson Read, Ike Watched, and Obama Tweeted: 200 Years of Popular Culture in the White House* (Washington, DC, 2013). He has also written over 250 published articles, for the *New York Times, Wall Street Journal, Washington Post, Politico, Commentary, JTA, Tablet Magazine, Forward, Times of Israel, Jerusalem Post,* and other publications. Dr. Troy's many other affiliations include serving as an Adjunct Fellow at Hudson Institute, a member of the Board of Fellows of the Jewish Policy Center, and a board member of the Louis D. Brandeis Center for Human Rights. Dr. Troy has a bachelor's degree from Cornell University and a PhD in American Civilization from the University of Texas Dr. Troy lives in Kemp Mill, Maryland, with his wife, Kami, and four children. He is originally from Queens, New York.

Rabbi Dr. Jason Weiner, BCC, serves as the Senior Rabbi and Director of the Spiritual Care Department at Cedars-Sinai in Los Angeles, where he is responsible for the chaplaincy team and all aspects of spiritual care. Rabbi Weiner previously served as the Assistant Rabbi at Young Israel of Century City. Rabbi Weiner is also the Rabbi of Knesset Israel Synagogue of Beverlywood. He has earned two rabbinic ordinations, as well as a doctorate in Clinical Bioethics from Loyola University (Chicago), where he also earned a master's degree in Bioethics and Health policy, in addition to a master's degree in Jewish History from YU's Bernard Revel Graduate School of Jewish Studies. He is the author of *Jewish Guide to*

Practical Medical Decision-Making (Jerusalem, 2017) and *Guide to Observance of Jewish Law in a Hospital* (New York, 2014), and has published more than two dozen scholarly articles and book chapters, as well as several "popular" pieces. Rabbi Weiner frequently serves as a scholar-in-residence at conferences and synagogues throughout the nation on topics related to Jewish medical ethics, pastoral care, and health and wellness, and teaches hands-on Jewish medical ethics in the hospital to numerous Jewish high schools in Los Angeles.

Rabbi Mishael Zion is the author of *Esther: A New Israeli Commentary*, a Hebrew cultural commentary on the Book of Esther, edited by Prof. Avigdor Shinan (Rishon LeZion, 2019). Together with his father, Noam Zion, he is the author of *Halaila Hazeh: An Israeli Haggadah* (Israel, 2004) and *A Night to Remember: The Haggadah of Contemporary Voices* (Israel, 2007). Mishael serves as Director of the Mandel Program for Leadership in Jewish Culture and Co-Founder of the Klausner Minyan. Previously, he was the Co-Director and Rabbi of the Bronfman Fellowships. Mishael holds a bachelor's degree in Sociology and Jewish Thought from the Hebrew University of Jerusalem, and rabbinic ordination from Yeshivat Chovevei Torah Rabbinical School in New York.

Megillat Esther

א **וַיְהִי בִּימֵי אֲחַשְׁוֵרוֹשׁ הוּא אֲחַשְׁוֵרוֹשׁ הַמֹּלֵךְ מֵהֹדּוּ וְעַד־כּוּשׁ שֶׁבַע א**

ב וְעֶשְׂרִים וּמֵאָה מְדִינָה: בַּיָּמִים הָהֵם כְּשֶׁבֶת ׀ הַמֶּלֶךְ אֲחַשְׁוֵרוֹשׁ

ג עַל כִּסֵּא מַלְכוּתוֹ אֲשֶׁר בְּשׁוּשַׁן הַבִּירָה: בִּשְׁנַת שָׁלוֹשׁ לְמָלְכוֹ עָשָׂה מִשְׁתֶּה לְכָל־שָׂרָיו וַעֲבָדָיו חֵיל ׀ פָּרַס וּמָדַי הַפַּרְתְּמִים וְשָׂרֵי

ד הַמְּדִינוֹת לְפָנָיו: בְּהַרְאֹתוֹ אֶת־עֹשֶׁר כְּבוֹד מַלְכוּתוֹ וְאֶת־יְקָר

ה תִּפְאֶרֶת גְּדוּלָּתוֹ יָמִים רַבִּים שְׁמוֹנִים וּמְאַת יוֹם: וּבִמְלוֹאת ׀ הַיָּמִים הָאֵלֶּה עָשָׂה הַמֶּלֶךְ לְכָל־הָעָם הַנִּמְצְאִים בְּשׁוּשַׁן הַבִּירָה לְמִגָּדוֹל

ו וְעַד־קָטָן מִשְׁתֶּה שִׁבְעַת יָמִים בַּחֲצַר גִּנַּת בִּיתַן הַמֶּלֶךְ: חוּר ׀ כַּרְפַּס וּתְכֵלֶת אָחוּז בְּחַבְלֵי־בוּץ וְאַרְגָּמָן עַל־גְּלִילֵי כֶסֶף וְעַמּוּדֵי שֵׁשׁ מִטּוֹת ׀ זָהָב וָכֶסֶף עַל רִצְפַת בַּהַט־וָשֵׁשׁ וְדַר וְסֹחָרֶת:

ז וְהַשְׁקוֹת בִּכְלֵי זָהָב וְכֵלִים מִכֵּלִים שׁוֹנִים וְיֵין מַלְכוּת רָב כְּיַד

ח הַמֶּלֶךְ: וְהַשְּׁתִיָּה כַדָּת אֵין אֹנֵס כִּי־כֵן ׀ יִסַּד הַמֶּלֶךְ עַל כָּל־רַב

ט בֵּיתוֹ לַעֲשׂוֹת כִּרְצוֹן אִישׁ־וָאִישׁ: גַּם וַשְׁתִּי הַמַּלְכָּה

י עָשְׂתָה מִשְׁתֵּה נָשִׁים בֵּית הַמַּלְכוּת אֲשֶׁר לַמֶּלֶךְ אֲחַשְׁוֵרוֹשׁ: בַּיּוֹם הַשְּׁבִיעִי כְּטוֹב לֵב־הַמֶּלֶךְ בַּיָּיִן אָמַר לִמְהוּמָן בִּזְּתָא חַרְבוֹנָא בִּגְתָא וַאֲבַגְתָא זֵתַר וְכַרְכַּס שִׁבְעַת הַסָּרִיסִים הַמְשָׁרְתִים אֶת־פְּנֵי

יא הַמֶּלֶךְ אֲחַשְׁוֵרוֹשׁ: לְהָבִיא אֶת־וַשְׁתִּי הַמַּלְכָּה לִפְנֵי הַמֶּלֶךְ בְּכֶתֶר מַלְכוּת לְהַרְאוֹת הָעַמִּים וְהַשָּׂרִים אֶת־יָפְיָהּ כִּי־טוֹבַת מַרְאֶה

יב הִיא: וַתְּמָאֵן הַמַּלְכָּה וַשְׁתִּי לָבוֹא בִּדְבַר הַמֶּלֶךְ אֲשֶׁר בְּיַד הַסָּרִיסִים

יג וַיִּקְצֹף הַמֶּלֶךְ מְאֹד וַחֲמָתוֹ בָּעֲרָה בוֹ: וַיֹּאמֶר הַמֶּלֶךְ לַחֲכָמִים יֹדְעֵי הָעִתִּים כִּי־כֵן דְּבַר הַמֶּלֶךְ לִפְנֵי כָּל־יֹדְעֵי דָּת וָדִין:

יד וְהַקָּרֹב אֵלָיו כַּרְשְׁנָא שֵׁתָר אַדְמָתָא תַרְשִׁישׁ מֶרֶס מַרְסְנָא מְמוּכָן שִׁבְעַת שָׂרֵי ׀ פָּרַס וּמָדַי רֹאֵי פְּנֵי הַמֶּלֶךְ הַיֹּשְׁבִים רִאשֹׁנָה בַּמַּלְכוּת:

טו כְּדָת מַה־לַּעֲשׂוֹת בַּמַּלְכָּה וַשְׁתִּי עַל ׀ אֲשֶׁר לֹא־עָשְׂתָה אֶת־

1 1 It happened in the days of Aḥashverosh – Aḥashverosh who ruled 127
2 provinces from Hodu to Kush. At that time, when King Aḥashverosh
3 sat upon his royal throne in the imperial city of Shushan in the third
year of his rule, he made a feast for his ministers and courtiers, the elite
of Persia and Media, all his noblemen and the ministers of his provinces.
4 There, for many days – 180 days in all – he displayed all the wealth of
5 his noble reign and the dazzling glory of his greatness. When that time
had passed, the king held a feast for all the people of the imperial city
of Shushan, from the greatest to the lowliest, in the courtyard of the
6 king's palace garden. There, swaths of fine fabric – of precious white
cotton and sky-blue wool – were caught up with cords of the finest
linen and purple and draped over silver bars and columns of marble;
and couches of gold and silver were arranged on a terrace paved with
7 alabaster and marble, with mother of pearl and black onyx. And the
guests were served drinks in vessels of gold, vessels unlike any
8 other – royal wine, abundant as the king's largesse. And the drinking
followed a rule of no duress, for the king had thus instructed all the
overseers of his home: honor the wishes of each and every
9 man.   Meanwhile Vashti the queen made a feast of her own, a
10 women's feast in King Aḥashverosh's royal palace. And on the seventh
day, when the king had grown merry with wine, he instructed
Mehuman, Bizta, Ḥarvona, Bigta and Avagta, Zetar and Karkas – the
11 seven eunuchs who attended King Aḥashverosh – to bring Vashti the
queen before the king in her royal crown, to show the peoples and the
12 ministers her charms, for she was beautiful indeed. But Queen Vashti
refused to come at the king's word, conveyed through the eunuchs. So
13 fury engulfed the king, and his rage blazed inside him.   Now
the king addressed the wise men, those well versed in procedure – for
it was the king's practice to consult with those who knew the law and
14 the statutes; and those closest to him were Karshena, Shetar, Admata,
Tarshish, Meres, Marsena, and Memukhan, the seven ministers of
Persia and Media who came freely into the king's presence and
15 occupied the highest positions in the realm. What, he asked, would the
law have them do with Queen Vashti for refusing to obey the word of

טו מַאֲמַר הַמֶּלֶךְ אֲחַשְׁוֵרוֹשׁ בְּיַד הַסָּרִיסִים: וַיֹּאמֶר מוֹמֻכָן מְמוּכָן
לִפְנֵי הַמֶּלֶךְ וְהַשָּׂרִים לֹא עַל־הַמֶּלֶךְ לְבַדּוֹ עָוְתָה וַשְׁתִּי הַמַּלְכָּה
כִּי עַל־כָּל־הַשָּׂרִים וְעַל־כָּל־הָעַמִּים אֲשֶׁר בְּכָל־מְדִינוֹת הַמֶּלֶךְ
טז אֲחַשְׁוֵרוֹשׁ: כִּי־יֵצֵא דְבַר־הַמַּלְכָּה עַל־כָּל־הַנָּשִׁים לְהַבְזוֹת
בַּעְלֵיהֶן בְּעֵינֵיהֶן בְּאָמְרָם הַמֶּלֶךְ אֲחַשְׁוֵרוֹשׁ אָמַר לְהָבִיא אֶת־
יז וַשְׁתִּי הַמַּלְכָּה לְפָנָיו וְלֹא־בָאָה: וְהַיּוֹם הַזֶּה תֹּאמַרְנָה ׀ שָׂרוֹת
פָּרַס־וּמָדַי אֲשֶׁר שָׁמְעוּ אֶת־דְּבַר הַמַּלְכָּה לְכֹל שָׂרֵי הַמֶּלֶךְ וּכְדַי
יח בִּזָּיוֹן וָקָצֶף: אִם־עַל־הַמֶּלֶךְ טוֹב יֵצֵא דְבַר־מַלְכוּת מִלְּפָנָיו וְיִכָּתֵב
בְּדָתֵי פָרַס־וּמָדַי וְלֹא יַעֲבוֹר אֲשֶׁר לֹא־תָבוֹא וַשְׁתִּי לִפְנֵי הַמֶּלֶךְ
יט אֲחַשְׁוֵרוֹשׁ וּמַלְכוּתָהּ יִתֵּן הַמֶּלֶךְ לִרְעוּתָהּ הַטּוֹבָה מִמֶּנָּה: וְנִשְׁמַע
פִּתְגָם הַמֶּלֶךְ אֲשֶׁר־יַעֲשֶׂה בְּכָל־מַלְכוּתוֹ כִּי רַבָּה הִיא וְכָל־הַנָּשִׁים
כ יִתְּנוּ יְקָר לְבַעְלֵיהֶן לְמִגָּדוֹל וְעַד־קָטָן: וַיִּיטַב הַדָּבָר בְּעֵינֵי הַמֶּלֶךְ
כא וְהַשָּׂרִים וַיַּעַשׂ הַמֶּלֶךְ כִּדְבַר מְמוּכָן: וַיִּשְׁלַח סְפָרִים אֶל־כָּל־
מְדִינוֹת הַמֶּלֶךְ אֶל־מְדִינָה וּמְדִינָה כִּכְתָבָהּ וְאֶל־עַם וָעָם כִּלְשׁוֹנוֹ
כב לִהְיוֹת כָּל־אִישׁ שֹׂרֵר בְּבֵיתוֹ וּמְדַבֵּר כִּלְשׁוֹן עַמּוֹ: אַחַר
ב הַדְּבָרִים הָאֵלֶּה כְּשֹׁךְ חֲמַת הַמֶּלֶךְ אֲחַשְׁוֵרוֹשׁ זָכַר אֶת־וַשְׁתִּי וְאֵת
ב אֲשֶׁר־עָשָׂתָה וְאֵת אֲשֶׁר־נִגְזַר עָלֶיהָ: וַיֹּאמְרוּ נַעֲרֵי־הַמֶּלֶךְ מְשָׁרְתָיו
ג יְבַקְשׁוּ לַמֶּלֶךְ נְעָרוֹת בְּתוּלוֹת טוֹבוֹת מַרְאֶה: וְיַפְקֵד הַמֶּלֶךְ
פְּקִידִים בְּכָל־מְדִינוֹת מַלְכוּתוֹ וְיִקְבְּצוּ אֶת־כָּל־נַעֲרָה־בְתוּלָה
טוֹבַת מַרְאֶה אֶל־שׁוּשַׁן הַבִּירָה אֶל־בֵּית הַנָּשִׁים אֶל־יַד הֵגֶא
ד סְרִיס הַמֶּלֶךְ שֹׁמֵר הַנָּשִׁים וְנָתוֹן תַּמְרֻקֵיהֶן: וְהַנַּעֲרָה אֲשֶׁר תִּיטַב
בְּעֵינֵי הַמֶּלֶךְ תִּמְלֹךְ תַּחַת וַשְׁתִּי וַיִּיטַב הַדָּבָר בְּעֵינֵי הַמֶּלֶךְ וַיַּעַשׂ
ה כֵּן: • אִישׁ יְהוּדִי הָיָה בְּשׁוּשַׁן הַבִּירָה וּשְׁמוֹ מָרְדֳּכַי בֶּן
ו יָאִיר בֶּן־שִׁמְעִי בֶּן־קִישׁ אִישׁ יְמִינִי: • אֲשֶׁר הָגְלָה מִירוּשָׁלַיִם
עִם־הַגֹּלָה אֲשֶׁר הָגְלְתָה עִם יְכָנְיָה מֶלֶךְ־יְהוּדָה אֲשֶׁר הֶגְלָה

374

16 King Aḥashverosh as conveyed to her by the eunuchs?   And
Memukhan replied before the king and the ministers: "It is not only
the king that Vashti the queen has wronged, but all the ministers and
17 all the peoples in all the provinces of King Aḥashverosh. For this tale
of the queen will go out to all the women, who will cast their husbands
into their contempt when they say, 'King Aḥashverosh commanded
18 Vashti the queen to be brought before him, but she did not come!' Yes,
this very day, all the ministers' wives of Persia and Media, who have
heard what the queen did, will tell all the king's ministers, and there
19 will be no end to the contempt and the fury. If, then, it so please the
king, let a royal declaration be sent out from him and be written among
the laws of Persia and Media, never to be contravened – that Vashti
shall come no more before King Aḥashverosh and that the king shall
20 give her royal position to a woman who is better than she. And the royal
decree that the king will issue shall be heard in all his empire, vast as it
is: that all women must honor their husbands, from the greatest of
21 them to the least." The proposal pleased the king and the ministers, and
22 the king accepted Memukhan's word. He sent scrolls to all the king's
provinces – province by province, each in its script, and people by
people, each in its language – ruling that every man must be master in
2 1 his home, speaking the language of his own people.   Some
time later, when King Aḥashverosh's rage had subsided, he remembered
Vashti, and what she had done, and what had been decreed against her.
2 The king's attendants, those who served him closely, said, "Let beautiful
3 young virgins be sought for the king; let the king appoint officers in all
the provinces of his realm to gather every beautiful young virgin to the
imperial city of Shushan, to the harem, into the charge of Hegeh, the
king's eunuch, the keeper of the maidens, to be given their ointments
4 there. Whichever young woman the king likes best – let her become
queen in Vashti's place!" The suggestion pleased the king, and that is
5 what he did.   Now there was a Jewish man in the imperial city
of Shushan, and his name was Mordekhai son of Yair son of Shimi son
6 of Kish of the tribe of Binyamin. He had been exiled from Jerusalem
among the exiles expelled with Yekhonya, king of Yehuda – exiled by

ז נְבוּכַדְנֶצַּר מֶלֶךְ בָּבֶל: וַיְהִי אֹמֵן אֶת־הֲדַסָּה הִיא אֶסְתֵּר בַּת־דֹּדוֹ
כִּי אֵין לָהּ אָב וָאֵם וְהַנַּעֲרָה יְפַת־תֹּאַר וְטוֹבַת מַרְאֶה וּבְמוֹת אָבִיהָ

ח וְאִמָּהּ לְקָחָהּ מָרְדֳּכַי לוֹ לְבַת: וַיְהִי בְּהִשָּׁמַע דְּבַר־הַמֶּלֶךְ וְדָתוֹ
וּבְהִקָּבֵץ נְעָרוֹת רַבּוֹת אֶל־שׁוּשַׁן הַבִּירָה אֶל־יַד הֵגַי וַתִּלָּקַח אֶסְתֵּר

ט אֶל־בֵּית הַמֶּלֶךְ אֶל־יַד הֵגַי שֹׁמֵר הַנָּשִׁים: וַתִּיטַב הַנַּעֲרָה בְעֵינָיו
וַתִּשָּׂא חֶסֶד לְפָנָיו וַיְבַהֵל אֶת־תַּמְרוּקֶיהָ וְאֶת־מָנוֹתֶהָ לָתֵת לָהּ
וְאֵת שֶׁבַע הַנְּעָרוֹת הָרְאֻיוֹת לָתֶת־לָהּ מִבֵּית הַמֶּלֶךְ וַיְשַׁנֶּהָ וְאֶת־

י נַעֲרוֹתֶיהָ לְטוֹב בֵּית הַנָּשִׁים: לֹא־הִגִּידָה אֶסְתֵּר אֶת־עַמָּהּ וְאֶת־
מוֹלַדְתָּהּ כִּי מָרְדֳּכַי צִוָּה עָלֶיהָ אֲשֶׁר לֹא־תַגִּיד: וּבְכָל־יוֹם וָיוֹם

יא מָרְדֳּכַי מִתְהַלֵּךְ לִפְנֵי חֲצַר בֵּית־הַנָּשִׁים לָדַעַת אֶת־שְׁלוֹם אֶסְתֵּר

יב וּמַה־יֵּעָשֶׂה בָּהּ: וּבְהַגִּיעַ תֹּר נַעֲרָה וְנַעֲרָה לָבוֹא ׀ אֶל־הַמֶּלֶךְ
אֲחַשְׁוֵרוֹשׁ מִקֵּץ הֱיוֹת לָהּ כְּדָת הַנָּשִׁים שְׁנֵים עָשָׂר חֹדֶשׁ כִּי כֵּן
יִמְלְאוּ יְמֵי מְרוּקֵיהֶן שִׁשָּׁה חֳדָשִׁים בְּשֶׁמֶן הַמֹּר וְשִׁשָּׁה חֳדָשִׁים

יג בַּבְּשָׂמִים וּבְתַמְרוּקֵי הַנָּשִׁים: וּבָזֶה הַנַּעֲרָה בָּאָה אֶל־הַמֶּלֶךְ אֵת
כָּל־אֲשֶׁר תֹּאמַר יִנָּתֵן לָהּ לָבוֹא עִמָּהּ מִבֵּית הַנָּשִׁים עַד־בֵּית

יד הַמֶּלֶךְ: בָּעֶרֶב ׀ הִיא בָאָה וּבַבֹּקֶר הִיא שָׁבָה אֶל־בֵּית הַנָּשִׁים שֵׁנִי
אֶל־יַד שַׁעַשְׁגַּז סְרִיס הַמֶּלֶךְ שֹׁמֵר הַפִּילַגְשִׁים לֹא־תָבוֹא עוֹד אֶל־

טו הַמֶּלֶךְ כִּי אִם־חָפֵץ בָּהּ הַמֶּלֶךְ וְנִקְרְאָה בְשֵׁם: וּבְהַגִּיעַ תֹּר־אֶסְתֵּר
בַּת־אֲבִיחַיִל ׀ דֹּד מָרְדֳּכַי אֲשֶׁר לָקַח־לוֹ לְבַת לָבוֹא אֶל־הַמֶּלֶךְ
לֹא בִקְשָׁה דָּבָר כִּי אִם אֶת־אֲשֶׁר יֹאמַר הֵגַי סְרִיס־הַמֶּלֶךְ שֹׁמֵר

טז הַנָּשִׁים וַתְּהִי אֶסְתֵּר נֹשֵׂאת חֵן בְּעֵינֵי כָּל־רֹאֶיהָ: וַתִּלָּקַח אֶסְתֵּר
אֶל־הַמֶּלֶךְ אֲחַשְׁוֵרוֹשׁ אֶל־בֵּית מַלְכוּתוֹ בַּחֹדֶשׁ הָעֲשִׂירִי הוּא־

יז חֹדֶשׁ טֵבֵת בִּשְׁנַת־שֶׁבַע לְמַלְכוּתוֹ: וַיֶּאֱהַב הַמֶּלֶךְ אֶת־אֶסְתֵּר
מִכָּל־הַנָּשִׁים וַתִּשָּׂא־חֵן וָחֶסֶד לְפָנָיו מִכָּל־הַבְּתוּלוֹת וַיָּשֶׂם כֶּתֶר־

יח מַלְכוּת בְּרֹאשָׁהּ וַיַּמְלִיכֶהָ תַּחַת וַשְׁתִּי: וַיַּעַשׂ הַמֶּלֶךְ מִשְׁתֶּה גָדוֹל

376

7 Nevukhadnetzar, king of Babylon. And Mordekhai was guardian to
Hadasa – Esther – his uncle's daughter, for she had no father or mother.
The girl was lovely and beautiful, and when her father and mother had
8 died, Mordekhai had adopted her as his own child. When the king's
word and his law were heard, and vast numbers of young women were
gathered in the imperial city of Shushan into the charge of Hegai,
Esther too was taken to the king's palace into the charge of Hegai, the
9 keeper of the women. The young woman pleased him, and she carried
kindness with her, and he hastened to give her all her ointments and
meals and the seven young maids from the king's palace to whom she
was entitled; and he moved her and her maids to the best quarters in
10 the royal maidens' quarters. And Esther made no mention of her
people or her birth, for Mordekhai had instructed her strictly not to
11 reveal them. But every single day Mordekhai would walk around before
the harem courtyard to find out whether Esther was well and what was
12 being done with her. As each young woman would reach her turn to
come before King Aḥashverosh – after twelve months following her
beauty regime (for that was how many the days of their ointments
were: six months in myrrh oil and six months in perfumes and the
13 women's ointments) – the young woman would come before the king.
All that she asked for would be given her to bring with her from the
14 royal harem to the palace of the king. She would enter in the evening,
and in the morning she would return to the royal harem, passing into
the charge of Shaashgaz, the king's eunuch, keeper of the concubines.
Then she would come no more before the king unless he desired her
15 and she was called for by name. When the time came for Esther
daughter of Aviḥayil – Mordekhai's uncle – whom Mordekhai had
adopted as his own child, to come before the king, she did not ask for
anything except for what Hegai, the king's eunuch, keeper of the
women, told her to bring. Yet Esther carried grace in the eyes of all who
16 saw her. Esther was taken to King Aḥashverosh, to his royal palace, in
the tenth month, the month of Tevet, in the seventh year of his reign.
17 And the king loved Esther more than all the other women, and she
pleased him and carried grace and kindness with her, more so than all
the other virgins; and he placed a royal crown upon her head and made
18 her queen in Vashti's place. And the king made a great feast for all his

לְכָל־שָׂרָיו֙ וַעֲבָדָ֔יו אֵ֚ת מִשְׁתֵּ֣ה אֶסְתֵּ֔ר וַהֲנָחָ֥ה לַמְּדִינוֹת֙ עָשָׂ֔ה וַיִּתֵּ֥ן

יט מַשְׂאֵ֖ת כְּיַ֥ד הַמֶּֽלֶךְ׃ וּבְהִקָּבֵ֥ץ בְּתוּל֖וֹת שֵׁנִ֑ית וּמָרְדֳּכַ֖י יֹשֵׁ֥ב בְּשַֽׁעַר־

כ הַמֶּֽלֶךְ׃ אֵ֣ין אֶסְתֵּ֗ר מַגֶּ֤דֶת מֽוֹלַדְתָּהּ֙ וְאֶת־עַמָּ֔הּ כַּאֲשֶׁ֛ר צִוָּ֥ה עָלֶ֖יהָ

מָרְדֳּכָ֑י וְאֶת־מַאֲמַ֤ר מָרְדֳּכַי֙ אֶסְתֵּ֣ר עֹשָׂ֔ה כַּאֲשֶׁ֛ר הָיְתָ֥ה בְאׇמְנָ֖ה

כא אִתּֽוֹ׃   בַּיָּמִ֣ים הָהֵ֔ם וּמׇרְדֳּכַ֖י יֹשֵׁ֣ב בְּשַֽׁעַר־הַמֶּ֑לֶךְ קָצַ֣ף

בִּגְתָ֣ן וָתֶ֗רֶשׁ שְׁנֵֽי־סָרִיסֵ֤י הַמֶּ֙לֶךְ֙ מִשֹּׁמְרֵ֣י הַסַּ֔ף וַיְבַקְשׁוּ֙ לִשְׁלֹ֣חַ יָ֔ד

כב בַּמֶּ֖לֶךְ אֲחַשְׁוֵרֽוֹשׁ׃ וַיִּוָּדַ֤ע הַדָּבָר֙ לְמׇרְדֳּכַ֔י וַיַּגֵּ֖ד לְאֶסְתֵּ֣ר הַמַּלְכָּ֑ה

כג וַתֹּ֧אמֶר אֶסְתֵּ֛ר לַמֶּ֖לֶךְ בְּשֵׁ֥ם מׇרְדֳּכָֽי׃ וַיְבֻקַּ֤שׁ הַדָּבָר֙ וַיִּמָּצֵ֔א וַיִּתָּל֛וּ

שְׁנֵיהֶ֖ם עַל־עֵ֑ץ וַיִּכָּתֵ֗ב בְּסֵ֛פֶר דִּבְרֵ֥י הַיָּמִ֖ים לִפְנֵ֥י

ג א הַמֶּֽלֶךְ׃   אַחַ֣ר ׀ הַדְּבָרִ֣ים הָאֵ֗לֶּה גִּדַּל֩ הַמֶּ֨לֶךְ אֲחַשְׁוֵר֜וֹשׁ

אֶת־הָמָ֧ן בֶּֽן־הַמְּדָ֛תָא הָאֲגָגִ֖י וַֽיְנַשְּׂאֵ֑הוּ וַיָּ֙שֶׂם֙ אֶת־כִּסְא֔וֹ מֵעַ֖ל כׇּל־

ב הַשָּׂרִ֖ים אֲשֶׁ֥ר אִתּֽוֹ׃ וְכׇל־עַבְדֵ֨י הַמֶּ֜לֶךְ אֲשֶׁר־בְּשַׁ֣עַר הַמֶּ֗לֶךְ כֹּרְעִ֤ים

וּמִֽשְׁתַּחֲוִים֙ לְהָמָ֔ן כִּי־כֵ֖ן צִוָּה־ל֣וֹ הַמֶּ֑לֶךְ וּמׇ֨רְדֳּכַ֔י לֹ֥א יִכְרַ֖ע וְלֹ֥א

ג יִֽשְׁתַּחֲוֶֽה׃ וַיֹּ֨אמְר֜וּ עַבְדֵ֤י הַמֶּ֙לֶךְ֙ אֲשֶׁר־בְּשַׁ֣עַר הַמֶּ֔לֶךְ לְמׇרְדֳּכָ֑י

ד מַדּ֙וּעַ֙ אַתָּ֣ה עוֹבֵ֔ר אֵ֖ת מִצְוַ֣ת הַמֶּ֑לֶךְ׃ וַ֠יְהִ֠י (באמרם) [בְּאׇמְרָ֨ם] אֵלָ֜יו י֤וֹם וָיוֹם֙ כְּאׇמְרָ֔ם

וְלֹ֥א שָׁמַ֖ע אֲלֵיהֶ֑ם וַיַּגִּ֣ידוּ לְהָמָ֗ן לִרְאוֹת֙ הֲיַֽעַמְדוּ֙ דִּבְרֵ֣י מׇרְדֳּכַ֔י כִּֽי־

ה הִגִּ֥יד לָהֶ֖ם אֲשֶׁר־ה֥וּא יְהוּדִֽי׃ וַיַּ֣רְא הָמָ֔ן כִּי־אֵ֣ין מׇרְדֳּכַ֔י כֹּרֵ֥עַ

ו וּמִֽשְׁתַּחֲוֶ֖ה ל֑וֹ וַיִּמָּלֵ֥א הָמָ֖ן חֵמָֽה׃ וַיִּ֣בֶז בְּעֵינָ֗יו לִשְׁלֹ֤חַ יָד֙ בְּמׇרְדֳּכַ֣י

לְבַדּ֔וֹ כִּֽי־הִגִּ֥ידוּ ל֖וֹ אֶת־עַ֣ם מׇרְדֳּכָ֑י וַיְבַקֵּ֣שׁ הָמָ֗ן לְהַשְׁמִ֧יד אֶת־כׇּל־

הַיְּהוּדִ֛ים אֲשֶׁ֛ר בְּכׇל־מַלְכ֥וּת אֲחַשְׁוֵר֖וֹשׁ עַ֥ם מׇרְדֳּכָֽי׃

ז בַּחֹ֤דֶשׁ הָרִאשׁוֹן֙ הוּא־חֹ֣דֶשׁ נִיסָ֔ן בִּשְׁנַת֙ שְׁתֵּ֣ים עֶשְׂרֵ֔ה לַמֶּ֖לֶךְ

אֲחַשְׁוֵר֑וֹשׁ הִפִּ֣יל פּוּר֩ ה֨וּא הַגּוֹרָ֜ל לִפְנֵ֣י הָמָ֗ן מִיּ֧וֹם ׀ לְי֛וֹם וּמֵחֹ֖דֶשׁ

ח לְחֹ֛דֶשׁ שְׁנֵים־עָשָׂ֖ר הוּא־חֹ֥דֶשׁ אֲדָֽר׃   וַיֹּ֤אמֶר הָמָן֙ ג

לַמֶּ֣לֶךְ אֲחַשְׁוֵר֔וֹשׁ יֶשְׁנ֣וֹ עַם־אֶחָ֗ד מְפֻזָּ֤ר וּמְפֹרָד֙ בֵּ֣ין הָֽעַמִּ֔ים בְּכֹ֖ל

מְדִינ֣וֹת מַלְכוּתֶ֑ךָ וְדָתֵיהֶ֞ם שֹׁנ֣וֹת מִכׇּל־עָ֗ם וְאֶת־דָּתֵ֤י הַמֶּ֙לֶךְ֙ אֵינָ֣ם

ministers and courtiers: the feast of Esther. And he granted the provinces both a remission of their dues and gifts as vast as the king's 19 largesse. As the virgins were gathered in for a second time, Mordekhai 20 was sitting at the King's Gate. Esther had not told of her birth or of her people, just as Mordekhai had instructed her; for Esther still heeded Mordekhai's words, just as she had when she had lived under his 21 care.　　　As Mordekhai sat at the King's Gate at that time, fury engulfed Bigtan and Teresh, two of the king's eunuchs, guards of the threshold, and they plotted to lay their hands on King Ahashverosh. 22 But Mordekhai learned of the plot and conveyed the knowledge to 23 Queen Esther, and Esther told the king in Mordekhai's name. The matter was investigated and found to be true, and the two men were hung from a post; and the story was written down before the king in

3 1 the scroll of the chronicles.　　　Some time after this, King Ahashverosh promoted Haman son of Hamedata the Agagite, raising 2 him to a seat above those of all his fellow ministers. And all the king's courtiers serving at the King's Gate would kneel and bow before Haman, for so had the king instructed, but Mordekhai would neither 3 kneel nor bow down. So the king's courtiers serving at the King's Gate would ask Mordekhai, "Why do you not obey the king's command?" 4 When, day after day, they said this to him and he paid no attention, they reported the matter to Haman, interested to see whether Mordekhai's word would stand – for he had explained that he was a 5 Jew. And Haman noticed that Mordekhai, indeed, did not kneel or bow 6 down before him, and it filled Haman with rage. The thought of laying his hands only on Mordekhai filled him with contempt, for they had told him who Mordekhai's people were. No, Haman sought to destroy all of the Jews, all of Mordekhai's people, all across the empire of 7 Ahashverosh. And so in the first month, the month of Nisan, of the twelfth year of King Ahashverosh's reign, a *pur* – lots, in other words – was cast before Haman, day for day and month for month, and 8 it fell to the twelfth month, the month of Adar.　　　Haman then spoke to King Ahashverosh: "There is one people, scattered and dispersed among the peoples across all the provinces of your realm, whose laws are different from those of all the other peoples, and who do not obey the king's own laws, and it really is not worth the king's

עֹשִׂים וְלַמֶּלֶךְ אֵין־שֹׁוֶה לְהַנִּיחָם: אִם־עַל־הַמֶּלֶךְ טוֹב יִכָּתֵב ט

לְאַבְּדָם וַעֲשֶׂרֶת אֲלָפִים כִּכַּר־כֶּסֶף אֶשְׁקוֹל עַל־יְדֵי עֹשֵׂי הַמְּלָאכָה

לְהָבִיא אֶל־גִּנְזֵי הַמֶּלֶךְ: וַיָּסַר הַמֶּלֶךְ אֶת־טַבַּעְתּוֹ מֵעַל יָדוֹ וַיִּתְּנָהּ י

לְהָמָן בֶּן־הַמְּדָתָא הָאֲגָגִי צֹרֵר הַיְּהוּדִים: וַיֹּאמֶר הַמֶּלֶךְ לְהָמָן יא

הַכֶּסֶף נָתוּן לָךְ וְהָעָם לַעֲשׂוֹת בּוֹ כַּטּוֹב בְּעֵינֶיךָ: וַיִּקָּרְאוּ סֹפְרֵי יב

הַמֶּלֶךְ בַּחֹדֶשׁ הָרִאשׁוֹן בִּשְׁלוֹשָׁה עָשָׂר יוֹם בּוֹ וַיִּכָּתֵב כְּכָל־אֲשֶׁר־

צִוָּה הָמָן אֶל אֲחַשְׁדַּרְפְּנֵי־הַמֶּלֶךְ וְאֶל־הַפַּחוֹת אֲשֶׁר ׀ עַל־מְדִינָה

וּמְדִינָה וְאֶל־שָׂרֵי עַם וָעָם מְדִינָה וּמְדִינָה כִּכְתָבָהּ וְעַם וָעָם כִּלְשׁוֹנוֹ

בְּשֵׁם הַמֶּלֶךְ אֲחַשְׁוֵרֹשׁ נִכְתָּב וְנֶחְתָּם בְּטַבַּעַת הַמֶּלֶךְ: וְנִשְׁלוֹחַ יג

סְפָרִים בְּיַד הָרָצִים אֶל־כָּל־מְדִינוֹת הַמֶּלֶךְ לְהַשְׁמִיד לַהֲרֹג וּלְאַבֵּד

אֶת־כָּל־הַיְּהוּדִים מִנַּעַר וְעַד־זָקֵן טַף וְנָשִׁים בְּיוֹם אֶחָד בִּשְׁלוֹשָׁה

עָשָׂר לְחֹדֶשׁ שְׁנֵים־עָשָׂר הוּא־חֹדֶשׁ אֲדָר וּשְׁלָלָם לָבוֹז: פַּתְשֶׁגֶן יד

הַכְּתָב לְהִנָּתֵן דָּת בְּכָל־מְדִינָה וּמְדִינָה גָּלוּי לְכָל־הָעַמִּים לִהְיוֹת

עֲתִדִים לַיּוֹם הַזֶּה: הָרָצִים יָצְאוּ דְחוּפִים בִּדְבַר הַמֶּלֶךְ וְהַדָּת נִתְּנָה טו

בְּשׁוּשַׁן הַבִּירָה וְהַמֶּלֶךְ וְהָמָן יָשְׁבוּ לִשְׁתּוֹת וְהָעִיר שׁוּשַׁן

נָבוֹכָה: וּמָרְדֳּכַי יָדַע אֶת־כָּל־אֲשֶׁר נַעֲשָׂה וַיִּקְרַע מָרְדֳּכַי א ד

אֶת־בְּגָדָיו וַיִּלְבַּשׁ שַׂק וָאֵפֶר וַיֵּצֵא בְּתוֹךְ הָעִיר וַיִּזְעַק זְעָקָה גְדוֹלָה

וּמָרָה: וַיָּבוֹא עַד לִפְנֵי שַׁעַר־הַמֶּלֶךְ כִּי אֵין לָבוֹא אֶל־שַׁעַר הַמֶּלֶךְ ב

בִּלְבוּשׁ שָׂק: וּבְכָל־מְדִינָה וּמְדִינָה מְקוֹם אֲשֶׁר דְּבַר־הַמֶּלֶךְ וְדָתוֹ ג

מַגִּיעַ אֵבֶל גָּדוֹל לַיְּהוּדִים וְצוֹם וּבְכִי וּמִסְפֵּד שַׂק וָאֵפֶר יֻצַּע לָרַבִּים:

וַתָּבוֹאינה נַעֲרוֹת אֶסְתֵּר וְסָרִיסֶיהָ וַיַּגִּידוּ לָהּ וַתִּתְחַלְחַל הַמַּלְכָּה ד

מְאֹד וַתִּשְׁלַח בְּגָדִים לְהַלְבִּישׁ אֶת־מָרְדֳּכַי וּלְהָסִיר שַׂקּוֹ מֵעָלָיו

וְלֹא קִבֵּל: וַתִּקְרָא אֶסְתֵּר לַהֲתָךְ מִסָּרִיסֵי הַמֶּלֶךְ אֲשֶׁר הֶעֱמִיד ה

לְפָנֶיהָ וַתְּצַוֵּהוּ עַל־מָרְדֳּכָי לָדַעַת מַה־זֶּה וְעַל־מַה־זֶּה: וַיֵּצֵא הֲתָךְ ו

אֶל־מָרְדֳּכָי אֶל־רְחוֹב הָעִיר אֲשֶׁר לִפְנֵי שַׁעַר־הַמֶּלֶךְ: וַיַּגֶּד־לוֹ ז

וַתְּבוֹאנָה

380

9 while to leave them so. If it so please the king, let it be decreed in writing to destroy them, and I shall weigh out ten thousand talents of silver into the hands of the administrators, to be delivered to the king's
10 treasury." The king removed the ring from his finger and gave it to
11 Haman son of Hamedata the Agagite, enemy of the Jews. And the king said to Haman, "The silver is yours, and so is the people: do with them
12 as you will." The king's scribes were called on the thirteenth day of the first month, and all that Haman commanded the king's viceroys, the administrators of every single province and the ministers of every single people, was written to province by province, each in its script, to people by people, each in its language – written in the name of King
13 Ahashverosh and sealed with the king's ring. Scrolls were sent out with the runners to all the provinces of the king ruling that they kill, destroy, and annihilate all the Jews, young and old, children and women alike, all in one day – the thirteenth day of the twelfth month, which is the
14 month of Adar – and seize the plunder. The text of that letter was to be laid down as law in each and every province, displayed for every people
15 to see, to make them ready for that day. The runners rushed out at the king's word, and the law was laid down in the imperial city of Shushan. The king and Haman sat down to drink – and the town of Shushan
4 1 stood aghast.   Mordekhai understood all that had happened, and he tore his clothes and dressed himself in sackcloth and ashes; and he walked out to the middle of the town, crying out, a loud and bitter
2 cry. He came as far as the entrance to the King's Gate, for no one may
3 enter the King's Gate dressed in sackcloth. And in every single province, wherever the king's word and law extended, deep mourning prevailed among the Jews, fasting and weeping and grief; the multitudes lay
4 down upon sackcloth and ashes. Esther's young maids and her eunuchs came and told her of this, and the queen's whole body shook. She sent clothes for Mordekhai to put on, to lay aside the sackcloth he was
5 wearing, but he would not accept them. So Esther called Hatakh, one of the king's eunuchs assigned to her, and instructed him to go and
6 speak to Mordekhai to find out what all this was and why. Hatakh went
7 out to Mordekhai, to the town square before the King's Gate, and

מָרְדֳּכַי אֵת כָּל־אֲשֶׁר קָרָהוּ וְאֵת ׀ פָּרָשַׁת הַכֶּסֶף אֲשֶׁר אָמַר הָמָן
ח לִשְׁקוֹל עַל־גִּנְזֵי הַמֶּלֶךְ בַּיְּהוּדִיִּים לְאַבְּדָם: וְאֶת־פַּתְשֶׁגֶן כְּתָב־ בַּיְּהוּדִים
הַדָּת אֲשֶׁר־נִתַּן בְּשׁוּשָׁן לְהַשְׁמִידָם נָתַן לוֹ לְהַרְאוֹת אֶת־אֶסְתֵּר
וּלְהַגִּיד לָהּ וּלְצַוּוֹת עָלֶיהָ לָבוֹא אֶל־הַמֶּלֶךְ לְהִתְחַנֶּן־לוֹ וּלְבַקֵּשׁ
ט מִלְּפָנָיו עַל־עַמָּהּ: וַיָּבוֹא הֲתָךְ וַיַּגֵּד לְאֶסְתֵּר אֵת דִּבְרֵי מָרְדֳּכָי:
יא וַתֹּאמֶר אֶסְתֵּר לַהֲתָךְ וַתְּצַוֵּהוּ אֶל־מָרְדֳּכָי: כָּל־עַבְדֵי הַמֶּלֶךְ וְעַם
מְדִינוֹת הַמֶּלֶךְ יֹדְעִים אֲשֶׁר כָּל־אִישׁ וְאִשָּׁה אֲשֶׁר יָבוֹא אֶל־הַמֶּלֶךְ
אֶל־הֶחָצֵר הַפְּנִימִית אֲשֶׁר לֹא־יִקָּרֵא אַחַת דָּתוֹ לְהָמִית לְבַד
מֵאֲשֶׁר יוֹשִׁיט־לוֹ הַמֶּלֶךְ אֶת־שַׁרְבִיט הַזָּהָב וְחָיָה וַאֲנִי לֹא נִקְרֵאתִי
יב לָבוֹא אֶל־הַמֶּלֶךְ זֶה שְׁלוֹשִׁים יוֹם: וַיַּגִּידוּ לְמָרְדֳּכָי אֵת דִּבְרֵי
יג אֶסְתֵּר: וַיֹּאמֶר מָרְדֳּכַי לְהָשִׁיב אֶל־אֶסְתֵּר אַל־תְּדַמִּי בְנַפְשֵׁךְ
יד לְהִמָּלֵט בֵּית־הַמֶּלֶךְ מִכָּל־הַיְּהוּדִים: כִּי אִם־הַחֲרֵשׁ תַּחֲרִישִׁי
בָּעֵת הַזֹּאת רֶוַח וְהַצָּלָה יַעֲמוֹד לַיְּהוּדִים מִמָּקוֹם אַחֵר וְאַתְּ וּבֵית־
טו אָבִיךְ תֹּאבֵדוּ וּמִי יוֹדֵעַ אִם־לְעֵת כָּזֹאת הִגַּעַתְּ לַמַּלְכוּת: וַתֹּאמֶר
טז אֶסְתֵּר לְהָשִׁיב אֶל־מָרְדֳּכָי: לֵךְ כְּנוֹס אֶת־כָּל־הַיְּהוּדִים הַנִּמְצְאִים
בְּשׁוּשָׁן וְצוּמוּ עָלַי וְאַל־תֹּאכְלוּ וְאַל־תִּשְׁתּוּ שְׁלֹשֶׁת יָמִים לַיְלָה
וָיוֹם גַּם־אֲנִי וְנַעֲרֹתַי אָצוּם כֵּן וּבְכֵן אָבוֹא אֶל־הַמֶּלֶךְ אֲשֶׁר לֹא־
יז כַדָּת וְכַאֲשֶׁר אָבַדְתִּי אָבָדְתִּי: וַיַּעֲבֹר מָרְדֳּכָי וַיַּעַשׂ כְּכֹל אֲשֶׁר צִוְּתָה
ה א עָלָיו אֶסְתֵּר: וַיְהִי ׀ בַּיּוֹם הַשְּׁלִישִׁי וַתִּלְבַּשׁ אֶסְתֵּר מַלְכוּת וַתַּעֲמֹד
בַּחֲצַר בֵּית־הַמֶּלֶךְ הַפְּנִימִית נֹכַח בֵּית הַמֶּלֶךְ וְהַמֶּלֶךְ יוֹשֵׁב עַל־
ב כִּסֵּא מַלְכוּתוֹ בְּבֵית הַמַּלְכוּת נֹכַח פֶּתַח הַבָּיִת: וַיְהִי כִרְאוֹת הַמֶּלֶךְ
אֶת־אֶסְתֵּר הַמַּלְכָּה עֹמֶדֶת בֶּחָצֵר נָשְׂאָה חֵן בְּעֵינָיו וַיּוֹשֶׁט הַמֶּלֶךְ
לְאֶסְתֵּר אֶת־שַׁרְבִיט הַזָּהָב אֲשֶׁר בְּיָדוֹ וַתִּקְרַב אֶסְתֵּר וַתִּגַּע בְּרֹאשׁ
ג הַשַּׁרְבִיט: וַיֹּאמֶר לָהּ הַמֶּלֶךְ מַה־לָּךְ אֶסְתֵּר הַמַּלְכָּה וּמַה־בַּקָּשָׁתֵךְ
ד עַד־חֲצִי הַמַּלְכוּת וְיִנָּתֵן לָךְ: וַתֹּאמֶר אֶסְתֵּר אִם־עַל־הַמֶּלֶךְ טוֹב

Mordekhai told him all that had happened to him, and all about the silver that Haman had promised to have weighed out to the king's
8 treasury in return for the right to destroy the Jews. And he gave him the text of the decree that had been issued in Shushan to annihilate them, telling him to show it to Esther and to speak to her, instructing her strictly to go to the king and plead with him, to implore him to help
9 her people. Hatakh came and told Esther what Mordekhai had said.
10 And Esther told Hatakh, instructing him to repeat her words to
11 Mordekhai: "All the king's courtiers and all the people of his provinces know that there is only one law for any man or woman who comes before the king, into the inner courtyard, without being called: to be killed. Unless, that is, the king extends the golden scepter toward him so that he may live on. As for me – I have not been called to come
12 before the king these thirty days past." And they told Mordekhai what
13 Esther had said. Mordekhai sent back his reply to Esther: "Do not imagine that you can escape to the king's palace from the fate of all the
14 Jews. For if you keep your silence at this time, relief and salvation will come forth for the Jews from some other place, but you and your father's house will be lost forever. And who can say; could it not be for
15 just such a time as this that you came into royalty?" Esther sent back
16 word to Mordekhai: "Go – gather all the Jews in Shushan and fast for me: do not eat and do not drink for three whole days, day or night; I and my maids will fast also. So shall I come before the king in defiance
17 of the law – and if I am lost, I am lost." Mordekhai walked away; and
5 1 he did all that Esther had instructed him to do. On the third day, Esther dressed herself in royalty and came to stand in the inner courtyard of the king's palace, facing the king's palace, while the king sat upon his
2 royal throne in the great hall, facing the palace entrance. When the king noticed Queen Esther standing in the courtyard, she carried grace in his eyes, so the king extended the golden scepter in his hand toward
3 Esther, and Esther came forward and touched the scepter's end. And the king said to her, "What brings you, Esther, my queen? And what
4 would you ask? Be it even half my kingdom, it shall be yours." Esther said, "If it so please the king, may the king and Haman come today to

ה יָבוֹא הַמֶּלֶךְ וְהָמָן הַיּוֹם אֶל־הַמִּשְׁתֶּה אֲשֶׁר־עָשִׂיתִי לוֹ: וַיֹּאמֶר
הַמֶּלֶךְ מַהֲרוּ אֶת־הָמָן לַעֲשׂוֹת אֶת־דְּבַר אֶסְתֵּר וַיָּבֹא הַמֶּלֶךְ וְהָמָן
ו אֶל־הַמִּשְׁתֶּה אֲשֶׁר־עָשְׂתָה אֶסְתֵּר: וַיֹּאמֶר הַמֶּלֶךְ לְאֶסְתֵּר
בְּמִשְׁתֵּה הַיַּיִן מַה־שְּׁאֵלָתֵךְ וְיִנָּתֵן לָךְ וּמַה־בַּקָּשָׁתֵךְ עַד־חֲצִי
ז הַמַּלְכוּת וְתֵעָשׂ: וַתַּעַן אֶסְתֵּר וַתֹּאמַר שְׁאֵלָתִי וּבַקָּשָׁתִי: אִם־
מָצָאתִי חֵן בְּעֵינֵי הַמֶּלֶךְ וְאִם־עַל־הַמֶּלֶךְ טוֹב לָתֵת אֶת־שְׁאֵלָתִי
וְלַעֲשׂוֹת אֶת־בַּקָּשָׁתִי יָבוֹא הַמֶּלֶךְ וְהָמָן אֶל־הַמִּשְׁתֶּה אֲשֶׁר
ח אֶעֱשֶׂה לָהֶם וּמָחָר אֶעֱשֶׂה כִּדְבַר הַמֶּלֶךְ: וַיֵּצֵא הָמָן בַּיּוֹם הַהוּא
שָׂמֵחַ וְטוֹב לֵב וְכִרְאוֹת הָמָן אֶת־מָרְדֳּכַי בְּשַׁעַר הַמֶּלֶךְ וְלֹא־קָם
י וְלֹא־זָע מִמֶּנּוּ וַיִּמָּלֵא הָמָן עַל־מָרְדֳּכַי חֵמָה: וַיִּתְאַפַּק הָמָן וַיָּבוֹא
יא אֶל־בֵּיתוֹ וַיִּשְׁלַח וַיָּבֵא אֶת־אֹהֲבָיו וְאֶת־זֶרֶשׁ אִשְׁתּוֹ: וַיְסַפֵּר לָהֶם
הָמָן אֶת־כְּבוֹד עָשְׁרוֹ וְרֹב בָּנָיו וְאֵת כָּל־אֲשֶׁר גִּדְּלוֹ הַמֶּלֶךְ וְאֵת
יב אֲשֶׁר נִשְּׂאוֹ עַל־הַשָּׂרִים וְעַבְדֵי הַמֶּלֶךְ: וַיֹּאמֶר הָמָן אַף לֹא־הֵבִיאָה
אֶסְתֵּר הַמַּלְכָּה עִם־הַמֶּלֶךְ אֶל־הַמִּשְׁתֶּה אֲשֶׁר־עָשָׂתָה כִּי אִם־
יג אוֹתִי וְגַם־לְמָחָר אֲנִי קָרוּא־לָהּ עִם־הַמֶּלֶךְ: וְכָל־זֶה אֵינֶנּוּ שֹׁוֶה
לִי בְּכָל־עֵת אֲשֶׁר אֲנִי רֹאֶה אֶת־מָרְדֳּכַי הַיְּהוּדִי יוֹשֵׁב בְּשַׁעַר
יד הַמֶּלֶךְ: וַתֹּאמֶר לוֹ זֶרֶשׁ אִשְׁתּוֹ וְכָל־אֹהֲבָיו יַעֲשׂוּ־עֵץ גָּבֹהַּ חֲמִשִּׁים
אַמָּה וּבַבֹּקֶר ׀ אֱמֹר לַמֶּלֶךְ וְיִתְלוּ אֶת־מָרְדֳּכַי עָלָיו וּבֹא עִם־הַמֶּלֶךְ
אֶל־הַמִּשְׁתֶּה שָׂמֵחַ וַיִּיטַב הַדָּבָר לִפְנֵי הָמָן וַיַּעַשׂ
הָעֵץ:
ו א בַּלַּיְלָה הַהוּא נָדְדָה שְׁנַת הַמֶּלֶךְ וַיֹּאמֶר
לְהָבִיא אֶת־סֵפֶר הַזִּכְרֹנוֹת דִּבְרֵי הַיָּמִים וַיִּהְיוּ נִקְרָאִים לִפְנֵי הַמֶּלֶךְ:
ב וַיִּמָּצֵא כָתוּב אֲשֶׁר הִגִּיד מָרְדֳּכַי עַל־בִּגְתָנָא וָתֶרֶשׁ שְׁנֵי סָרִיסֵי
הַמֶּלֶךְ מִשֹּׁמְרֵי הַסַּף אֲשֶׁר בִּקְשׁוּ לִשְׁלֹחַ יָד בַּמֶּלֶךְ אֲחַשְׁוֵרוֹשׁ:
ג וַיֹּאמֶר הַמֶּלֶךְ מַה־נַּעֲשָׂה יְקָר וּגְדוּלָּה לְמָרְדֳּכַי עַל־זֶה וַיֹּאמְרוּ
ד נַעֲרֵי הַמֶּלֶךְ מְשָׁרְתָיו לֹא־נַעֲשָׂה עִמּוֹ דָּבָר: וַיֹּאמֶר הַמֶּלֶךְ מִי בֶחָצֵר

5 the feast that I have prepared for him." And the king called out, "Make Haman hurry to carry out Esther's word!" And the king and Haman
6 came to the feast that Esther had prepared. At that drinking feast, the king said to Esther, "What is your desire, then? It shall be yours. What
7 would you ask? Be it even half my kingdom, it shall be done." And
8 Esther answered: "This is my desire and my request," she said. "If I have the king's favor, and if it so please the king to grant what I desire, to honor my request – let the king and Haman come again to the feast that I shall prepare for them. And tomorrow I shall do as the king asks."
9 Haman went out on that day, happy and buoyant of heart. But when he saw Mordekhai at the King's Gate, and when Mordekhai did not stand up and did not tremble in his presence, Haman was filled with
10 rage against him. Yet Haman restrained himself until he reached his
11 home, and then he sent for all his friends and for his wife, Zeresh. And Haman told them of his glorious wealth and the great number of his sons and all the ways the king had elevated him and raised him above
12 all the other ministers and courtiers of the king. Finally Haman said, "And Esther brought no one else but me with the king to the feast that she made, and tomorrow too I am invited to her along with the king.
13 Yet all this is worth nothing to me whenever I see that Jew Mordekhai
14 sitting there at the King's Gate." Zeresh his wife replied, along with all his friends: "Let a post be erected full fifty cubits high. In the morning, say the word to the king, and Mordekhai shall be hung up from it. Then you will go happy to the feast with the king." The idea pleased Haman,
6 1 and he erected the post.   The king slept fitfully that night. He called for the scroll of the records, the chronicles, to be brought to him,
2 and they were read aloud before him. There it was found written that Mordekhai had reported Bigtan and Teresh, two of the king's eunuchs, guards of the threshold, who had planned to lay hands upon King
3 Ahashverosh. The king said, "What honor or greatness has been granted Mordekhai for doing this?" and the king's pages, those who
4 were attending him, said, "Nothing at all has been done for him." "Who

וְהָמָן בָּא לַחֲצַר בֵּית־הַמֶּלֶךְ הַחִיצוֹנָה לֵאמֹר לַמֶּלֶךְ לִתְלוֹת אֶת־

ה מָרְדֳּכַי עַל־הָעֵץ אֲשֶׁר־הֵכִין לוֹ: וַיֹּאמְרוּ נַעֲרֵי הַמֶּלֶךְ אֵלָיו הִנֵּה

י הָמָן עֹמֵד בֶּחָצֵר וַיֹּאמֶר הַמֶּלֶךְ יָבוֹא: וַיָּבוֹא הָמָן וַיֹּאמֶר לוֹ הַמֶּלֶךְ

מַה־לַעֲשׂוֹת בָּאִישׁ אֲשֶׁר הַמֶּלֶךְ חָפֵץ בִּיקָרוֹ וַיֹּאמֶר הָמָן בְּלִבּוֹ

ז לְמִי יַחְפֹּץ הַמֶּלֶךְ לַעֲשׂוֹת יְקָר יוֹתֵר מִמֶּנִּי: וַיֹּאמֶר הָמָן אֶל־הַמֶּלֶךְ

ח אִישׁ אֲשֶׁר הַמֶּלֶךְ חָפֵץ בִּיקָרוֹ: יָבִיאוּ לְבוּשׁ מַלְכוּת אֲשֶׁר לָבַשׁ־בּוֹ

הַמֶּלֶךְ וְסוּס אֲשֶׁר רָכַב עָלָיו הַמֶּלֶךְ וַאֲשֶׁר נִתַּן כֶּתֶר מַלְכוּת

ט בְּרֹאשׁוֹ: וְנָתוֹן הַלְּבוּשׁ וְהַסּוּס עַל־יַד־אִישׁ מִשָּׂרֵי הַמֶּלֶךְ הַפַּרְתְּמִים

וְהִלְבִּישׁוּ אֶת־הָאִישׁ אֲשֶׁר הַמֶּלֶךְ חָפֵץ בִּיקָרוֹ וְהִרְכִּיבֻהוּ עַל־

הַסּוּס בִּרְחוֹב הָעִיר וְקָרְאוּ לְפָנָיו כָּכָה יֵעָשֶׂה לָאִישׁ אֲשֶׁר הַמֶּלֶךְ

י חָפֵץ בִּיקָרוֹ: וַיֹּאמֶר הַמֶּלֶךְ לְהָמָן מַהֵר קַח אֶת־הַלְּבוּשׁ וְאֶת־

הַסּוּס כַּאֲשֶׁר דִּבַּרְתָּ וַעֲשֵׂה־כֵן לְמָרְדֳּכַי הַיְּהוּדִי הַיּוֹשֵׁב בְּשַׁעַר

יא הַמֶּלֶךְ אַל־תַּפֵּל דָּבָר מִכֹּל אֲשֶׁר דִּבַּרְתָּ: וַיִּקַּח הָמָן אֶת־הַלְּבוּשׁ ד

וְאֶת־הַסּוּס וַיַּלְבֵּשׁ אֶת־מָרְדֳּכָי וַיַּרְכִּיבֵהוּ בִּרְחוֹב הָעִיר וַיִּקְרָא

יב לְפָנָיו כָּכָה יֵעָשֶׂה לָאִישׁ אֲשֶׁר הַמֶּלֶךְ חָפֵץ בִּיקָרוֹ: וַיָּשָׁב מָרְדֳּכַי

יג אֶל־שַׁעַר הַמֶּלֶךְ וְהָמָן נִדְחַף אֶל־בֵּיתוֹ אָבֵל וַחֲפוּי רֹאשׁ: וַיְסַפֵּר

הָמָן לְזֶרֶשׁ אִשְׁתּוֹ וּלְכָל־אֹהֲבָיו אֵת כָּל־אֲשֶׁר קָרָהוּ וַיֹּאמְרוּ לוֹ

חֲכָמָיו וְזֶרֶשׁ אִשְׁתּוֹ אִם מִזֶּרַע הַיְּהוּדִים מָרְדֳּכַי אֲשֶׁר הַחִלּוֹתָ לִנְפֹּל

יד לְפָנָיו לֹא־תוּכַל לוֹ כִּי־נָפוֹל תִּפּוֹל לְפָנָיו: עוֹדָם מְדַבְּרִים עִמּוֹ

וְסָרִיסֵי הַמֶּלֶךְ הִגִּיעוּ וַיַּבְהִלוּ לְהָבִיא אֶת־הָמָן אֶל־הַמִּשְׁתֶּה אֲשֶׁר־

א עָשְׂתָה אֶסְתֵּר: וַיָּבֹא הַמֶּלֶךְ וְהָמָן לִשְׁתּוֹת עִם־אֶסְתֵּר הַמַּלְכָּה: ז

ב וַיֹּאמֶר הַמֶּלֶךְ לְאֶסְתֵּר גַּם בַּיּוֹם הַשֵּׁנִי בְּמִשְׁתֵּה הַיַּיִן מַה־שְּׁאֵלָתֵךְ

אֶסְתֵּר הַמַּלְכָּה וְתִנָּתֵן לָךְ וּמַה־בַּקָּשָׁתֵךְ עַד־חֲצִי הַמַּלְכוּת וְתֵעָשׂ:

ג וַתַּעַן אֶסְתֵּר הַמַּלְכָּה וַתֹּאמַר אִם־מָצָאתִי חֵן בְּעֵינֶיךָ הַמֶּלֶךְ וְאִם־

ד עַל־הַמֶּלֶךְ טוֹב תִּנָּתֶן־לִי נַפְשִׁי בִּשְׁאֵלָתִי וְעַמִּי בְּבַקָּשָׁתִי: כִּי

נִמְכַּרְנוּ אֲנִי וְעַמִּי לְהַשְׁמִיד לַהֲרוֹג וּלְאַבֵּד וְאִלּוּ לַעֲבָדִים וְלִשְׁפָחוֹת

is in the courtyard?" asked the king. Haman had come to the outer courtyard of the king's palace to speak to the king about hanging
5 Mordekhai on the post he had prepared for him. The king's pages said to him, "Ah, there is Haman standing in the courtyard," and the king
6 said, "Show him in!" In Haman came, and the king asked him, "What should be done for a man the king wishes to honor?" Said Haman to
7 himself, "Whom could the king wish to honor more than me?" So
8 Haman told the king: "The man the king wishes to honor – let the clothes of royalty be brought forth, clothes that the king himself has worn, and a horse on which the king has ridden, on its head a royal
9 crown; and let these clothes and this horse be entrusted to one of the king's noble ministers to dress the man the king wishes to honor. And let him lead that man, riding on the horse, across the town square, crying out before him as they go, 'This is what is done for the man
10 whom the king wishes to honor!'" "Hurry!" said the king to Haman. "Take the clothes and the horse as you have said, and do just that for Mordekhai the Jew, who sits at the King's Gate – let no detail fall short
11 of what you have described!" So Haman took the clothes and the horse and dressed Mordekhai and led him across the town square, crying out before him as they went, "This is what is done for the man whom the
12 king wishes to honor!" Then Mordekhai returned to the King's Gate, and Haman rushed back to his house grief stricken, covering his face.
13 Haman told his wife Zeresh and all his friends all that had happened to him, and his wise men with his wife Zeresh said, "If this Mordekhai before whom you have begun to fall is of Jewish blood, you will not
14 overcome him; you will fall, you must fall before him –" they were still speaking when the king's eunuchs arrived to fetch Haman, with fearful
7 1 haste, to the feast that Esther had prepared. So the king and Haman
2 arrived to drink with Queen Esther. On that second day also, at the drinking feast, the king said to Esther, "What is your desire, Esther, my queen? It shall be yours. What would you ask? Be it even half my
3 kingdom, it shall be done." And Queen Esther answered: "If I have your favor, my king," she said, "and if it so please the king – let me have my
4 life as my desire, my people as my request. For we have been sold, my people and I, to be killed, destroyed, and annihilated. Had we but been

ה נִמְכַּרְנוּ הֶחֱרַשְׁתִּי כִּי אֵין הַצָּר שֹׁוֶה בְּנֵזֶק הַמֶּלֶךְ: וַיֹּאמֶר
הַמֶּלֶךְ אֲחַשְׁוֵרוֹשׁ וַיֹּאמֶר לְאֶסְתֵּר הַמַּלְכָּה מִי הוּא זֶה וְאֵי־זֶה הוּא
י אֲשֶׁר־מְלָאוֹ לִבּוֹ לַעֲשׂוֹת כֵּן: וַתֹּאמֶר אֶסְתֵּר אִישׁ צַר וְאוֹיֵב הָמָן
הָרָע הַזֶּה וְהָמָן נִבְעַת מִלִּפְנֵי הַמֶּלֶךְ וְהַמַּלְכָּה: וְהַמֶּלֶךְ קָם בַּחֲמָתוֹ
מִמִּשְׁתֵּה הַיַּיִן אֶל־גִּנַּת הַבִּיתָן וְהָמָן עָמַד לְבַקֵּשׁ עַל־נַפְשׁוֹ
מֵאֶסְתֵּר הַמַּלְכָּה כִּי רָאָה כִּי־כָלְתָה אֵלָיו הָרָעָה מֵאֵת הַמֶּלֶךְ:
ח וְהַמֶּלֶךְ שָׁב מִגִּנַּת הַבִּיתָן אֶל־בֵּית ׀ מִשְׁתֵּה הַיַּיִן וְהָמָן נֹפֵל עַל־
הַמִּטָּה אֲשֶׁר אֶסְתֵּר עָלֶיהָ וַיֹּאמֶר הַמֶּלֶךְ הֲגַם לִכְבּוֹשׁ אֶת־הַמַּלְכָּה
ט עִמִּי בַּבָּיִת הַדָּבָר יָצָא מִפִּי הַמֶּלֶךְ וּפְנֵי הָמָן חָפוּ: וַיֹּאמֶר חַרְבוֹנָה
אֶחָד מִן־הַסָּרִיסִים לִפְנֵי הַמֶּלֶךְ גַּם הִנֵּה־הָעֵץ אֲשֶׁר־עָשָׂה הָמָן
לְמָרְדֳּכַי אֲשֶׁר דִּבֶּר־טוֹב עַל־הַמֶּלֶךְ עֹמֵד בְּבֵית הָמָן גָּבֹהַּ חֲמִשִּׁים
י אַמָּה וַיֹּאמֶר הַמֶּלֶךְ תְּלֻהוּ עָלָיו: וַיִּתְלוּ אֶת־הָמָן עַל־הָעֵץ אֲשֶׁר־
ח א הֵכִין לְמָרְדֳּכָי וַחֲמַת הַמֶּלֶךְ שָׁכָכָה: בַּיּוֹם הַהוּא נָתַן
הַמֶּלֶךְ אֲחַשְׁוֵרוֹשׁ לְאֶסְתֵּר הַמַּלְכָּה אֶת־בֵּית הָמָן צֹרֵר הַיְּהוּדִיִּים הַיְּהוּדִים
ב וּמָרְדֳּכַי בָּא לִפְנֵי הַמֶּלֶךְ כִּי־הִגִּידָה אֶסְתֵּר מָה הוּא־לָהּ: וַיָּסַר
הַמֶּלֶךְ אֶת־טַבַּעְתּוֹ אֲשֶׁר הֶעֱבִיר מֵהָמָן וַיִּתְּנָהּ לְמָרְדֳּכָי וַתָּשֶׂם
ג אֶסְתֵּר אֶת־מָרְדֳּכַי עַל־בֵּית הָמָן: וַתּוֹסֶף אֶסְתֵּר וַתְּדַבֵּר
לִפְנֵי הַמֶּלֶךְ וַתִּפֹּל לִפְנֵי רַגְלָיו וַתֵּבְךְּ וַתִּתְחַנֶּן־לוֹ לְהַעֲבִיר אֶת־
ד רָעַת הָמָן הָאֲגָגִי וְאֵת מַחֲשַׁבְתּוֹ אֲשֶׁר חָשַׁב עַל־הַיְּהוּדִים: וַיּוֹשֶׁט
הַמֶּלֶךְ לְאֶסְתֵּר אֵת שַׁרְבִט הַזָּהָב וַתָּקָם אֶסְתֵּר וַתַּעֲמֹד לִפְנֵי
ה הַמֶּלֶךְ: וַתֹּאמֶר אִם־עַל־הַמֶּלֶךְ טוֹב וְאִם־מָצָאתִי חֵן לְפָנָיו וְכָשֵׁר
הַדָּבָר לִפְנֵי הַמֶּלֶךְ וְטוֹבָה אֲנִי בְּעֵינָיו יִכָּתֵב לְהָשִׁיב אֶת־
הַסְּפָרִים מַחֲשֶׁבֶת הָמָן בֶּן־הַמְּדָתָא הָאֲגָגִי אֲשֶׁר כָּתַב לְאַבֵּד
י אֶת־הַיְּהוּדִים אֲשֶׁר בְּכָל־מְדִינוֹת הַמֶּלֶךְ: כִּי אֵיכָכָה אוּכַל וְרָאִיתִי
בָּרָעָה אֲשֶׁר־יִמְצָא אֶת־עַמִּי וְאֵיכָכָה אוּכַל וְרָאִיתִי בְּאָבְדַן
ז מוֹלַדְתִּי: וַיֹּאמֶר הַמֶּלֶךְ אֲחַשְׁוֵרֹשׁ לְאֶסְתֵּר הַמַּלְכָּה

sold as slaves and bondwomen, I would have kept my silence, for that
5 anguish is not worth any loss to the king." King Ahashverosh
spoke; he said to Esther the queen: "Who is it – which one – who put
6 it into his heart to do such a thing?!" "It is a foe, an enemy," said Esther,
"this vicious man: Haman!" And Haman was suddenly terrified before
7 the king and the queen. The king rose up in his rage and left the wine
feast for the palace garden as Haman stood up to entreat for his life with
Esther the queen, for he saw that the king was already set upon his
8 downfall. By the time the king came back from the palace garden to the
feasting chamber, Haman had thrown himself onto Esther's
couch – "What!" said the king. "Would you take the queen too, and
with me in the palace?!" The words came forth from the king's mouth,
9 and Haman's face was covered over. One of the eunuchs, Harvona, said
to the king, "You know, the post Haman prepared for Mordekhai, who
spoke up so well for the king, is standing now in Haman's house, fifty
10 cubits high." And the king said, "Hang him from it!" Thus was Haman
hung up from the very post he had prepared for Mordekhai – and the
8 1 king's rage subsided. On that day, King Ahashverosh granted
Queen Esther the entire estate of Haman, enemy of the Jews, and
Mordekhai came before the king, for Esther had finally revealed what
2 he was to her. The king took off the very ring that he had once given to
Haman and gave it instead to Mordekhai, and Esther appointed
3 Mordekhai to govern Haman's estate. But then Esther spoke
to the king again, falling down at his feet, weeping and pleading with
him to overturn the wickedness of Haman the Agagite and the plot
4 that he had thought up against the Jews. The king extended his golden
scepter to Esther, and Esther raised herself up and stood before the
5 king. She said, "If it so please the king, and if I have his favor, and if it
seems right to the king and I am pleasing in his eyes – let the decree be
written to revoke the scrolls that were the plot of Haman son of
Hamedata the Agagite, who wrote to destroy all the Jews in all the
6 king's provinces. For how can I live to see the evil that will come upon
my people; how can I live to see the loss of those I am born
7 of?" King Ahashverosh said to Queen Esther and to
Mordekhai the Jew, "Look, I have given Esther Haman's estate, and he

וּלְמָרְדֳּכַי הַיְּהוּדִי הִנֵּה בֵית־הָמָן נָתַתִּי לְאֶסְתֵּר וְאֹתוֹ תָּלוּ עַל־

ח הָעֵץ עַל אֲשֶׁר־שָׁלַח יָדוֹ בַּיְּהוּדִיים: וְאַתֶּם כִּתְבוּ עַל־הַיְּהוּדִים בַּיְּהוּדִים
כַּטּוֹב בְּעֵינֵיכֶם בְּשֵׁם הַמֶּלֶךְ וְחִתְמוּ בְּטַבַּעַת הַמֶּלֶךְ כִּי־כְתָב
אֲשֶׁר־נִכְתָּב בְּשֵׁם־הַמֶּלֶךְ וְנַחְתּוֹם בְּטַבַּעַת הַמֶּלֶךְ אֵין לְהָשִׁיב:

ט וַיִּקָּרְאוּ סֹפְרֵי־הַמֶּלֶךְ בָּעֵת־הַהִיא בַּחֹדֶשׁ הַשְּׁלִישִׁי הוּא־חֹדֶשׁ
סִיוָן בִּשְׁלוֹשָׁה וְעֶשְׂרִים בּוֹ וַיִּכָּתֵב כְּכָל־אֲשֶׁר־צִוָּה מָרְדֳּכַי אֶל־
הַיְּהוּדִים וְאֶל הָאֲחַשְׁדַּרְפְּנִים־וְהַפַּחוֹת וְשָׂרֵי הַמְּדִינוֹת אֲשֶׁר ׀
מֵהֹדּוּ וְעַד־כּוּשׁ שֶׁבַע וְעֶשְׂרִים וּמֵאָה מְדִינָה מְדִינָה וּמְדִינָה

י כִּכְתָבָהּ וְעַם וָעָם כִּלְשֹׁנוֹ וְאֶל־הַיְּהוּדִים כִּכְתָבָם וְכִלְשׁוֹנָם: וַיִּכְתֹּב
בְּשֵׁם הַמֶּלֶךְ אֲחַשְׁוֵרֹשׁ וַיַּחְתֹּם בְּטַבַּעַת הַמֶּלֶךְ וַיִּשְׁלַח סְפָרִים בְּיַד

יא הָרָצִים בַּסּוּסִים רֹכְבֵי הָרֶכֶשׁ הָאֲחַשְׁתְּרָנִים בְּנֵי הָרַמָּכִים: אֲשֶׁר
נָתַן הַמֶּלֶךְ לַיְּהוּדִים ׀ אֲשֶׁר ׀ בְּכָל־עִיר וָעִיר לְהִקָּהֵל וְלַעֲמֹד עַל־
נַפְשָׁם לְהַשְׁמִיד וְלַהֲרֹג וּלְאַבֵּד אֶת־כָּל־חֵיל עַם וּמְדִינָה הַצָּרִים

יב אֹתָם טַף וְנָשִׁים וּשְׁלָלָם לָבוֹז: בְּיוֹם אֶחָד בְּכָל־מְדִינוֹת הַמֶּלֶךְ
אֲחַשְׁוֵרֹשׁ בִּשְׁלוֹשָׁה עָשָׂר לְחֹדֶשׁ שְׁנֵים־עָשָׂר הוּא־חֹדֶשׁ אֲדָר:

יג פַּתְשֶׁגֶן הַכְּתָב לְהִנָּתֵן דָּת בְּכָל־מְדִינָה וּמְדִינָה גָּלוּי לְכָל־הָעַמִּים
יד וְלִהְיוֹת הַיְּהוּדִיים עֲתוּדִים לַיּוֹם הַזֶּה לְהִנָּקֵם מֵאֹיְבֵיהֶם: הָרָצִים הַיְּהוּדִים
רֹכְבֵי הָרֶכֶשׁ הָאֲחַשְׁתְּרָנִים יָצְאוּ מְבֹהָלִים וּדְחוּפִים בִּדְבַר הַמֶּלֶךְ עֲתוּדִים

טו וְהַדָּת נִתְּנָה בְּשׁוּשַׁן הַבִּירָה: ◂ וּמָרְדֳּכַי יָצָא ׀ מִלִּפְנֵי
הַמֶּלֶךְ בִּלְבוּשׁ מַלְכוּת תְּכֵלֶת וָחוּר וַעֲטֶרֶת זָהָב גְּדוֹלָה וְתַכְרִיךְ

טז בּוּץ וְאַרְגָּמָן וְהָעִיר שׁוּשָׁן צָהֲלָה וְשָׂמֵחָה: ◂ לַיְּהוּדִים הָיְתָה ה

יז אוֹרָה וְשִׂמְחָה וְשָׂשֹׂן וִיקָר: ◂ וּבְכָל־מְדִינָה וּמְדִינָה וּבְכָל־עִיר
וָעִיר מְקוֹם אֲשֶׁר דְּבַר־הַמֶּלֶךְ וְדָתוֹ מַגִּיעַ שִׂמְחָה וְשָׂשׂוֹן
לַיְּהוּדִים מִשְׁתֶּה וְיוֹם טוֹב וְרַבִּים מֵעַמֵּי הָאָרֶץ מִתְיַהֲדִים כִּי־

ט א נָפַל פַּחַד־הַיְּהוּדִים עֲלֵיהֶם: וּבִשְׁנֵים עָשָׂר חֹדֶשׁ הוּא־חֹדֶשׁ

8 has been hung from the post for laying hands upon the Jews. Now, write whatever you like about the Jews in the king's name and seal it with the king's ring – but no writing that has been written in the name of the
9 king and sealed with the king's ring can ever be revoked." So at that time, the king's scribes were called – on the twenty-third day of the third month, the month of Sivan – and they wrote down all that Mordekhai dictated, to the Jews and to the viceroys, the administrators, and the ministers of all the provinces from Hodu to Kush, 127 provinces, to province by province, each in its script, to people by people, each in
10 its language, and to the Jews in their script and in their language. It was written in the name of King Aḥashverosh and sealed with the king's ring, and the scrolls were sent with the horseback runners, riding the
11 swift horses of the royal stable, the offspring of the royal mares, to convey that the king had granted the Jews in every single town the right to come together to stand up and defend their lives, to kill, destroy, and annihilate all the armed hordes of the peoples and provinces who threatened them, even the children and women, and to loot plunder,
12 all on one day, the thirteenth day of the twelfth month – the month of
13 Adar – in all the provinces of King Aḥashverosh. The text of that decree was to lay down the law in every single province, displayed for every people to see, that the Jews should make themselves ready for that day
14 to wreak vengeance on their enemies. The runners, riding the swift horses of the royal service, galloped out at great speed, spurred on at the king's word, and the law was laid down in the imperial city of
15 Shushan.   So Mordekhai left the king's presence in royal clothes of sky-blue wool and fine white fabric, wearing a great coronet of gold and a mantle of finest linen and purple, and the town of Shushan
16 was filled with jubilation and happiness. And the Jews basked in light
17 and happiness, joy and great honor. And in each and every province, in each and every town, as far as the king's word and law reached, happiness and joy touched the Jews, with feasting and a holiday; and many of the local people joined the Jews, for awe of the Jews had
9 1 overwhelmed them. On the thirteenth day of the twelfth month, the month of Adar, when the king's word and his law were to come into

אֲדָר בִּשְׁלוֹשָׁה עָשָׂר יוֹם בּוֹ אֲשֶׁר הִגִּיעַ דְּבַר־הַמֶּלֶךְ וְדָתוֹ
לְהֵעָשׂוֹת בַּיּוֹם אֲשֶׁר שִׂבְּרוּ אֹיְבֵי הַיְּהוּדִים לִשְׁלוֹט בָּהֶם וְנַהֲפוֹךְ
ג הוּא אֲשֶׁר יִשְׁלְטוּ הַיְּהוּדִים הֵמָּה בְּשֹׂנְאֵיהֶם: נִקְהֲלוּ הַיְּהוּדִים
בְּעָרֵיהֶם בְּכָל־מְדִינוֹת הַמֶּלֶךְ אֲחַשְׁוֵרוֹשׁ לִשְׁלֹחַ יָד בִּמְבַקְשֵׁי
רָעָתָם וְאִישׁ לֹא־עָמַד לִפְנֵיהֶם כִּי־נָפַל פַּחְדָּם עַל־כָּל־הָעַמִּים:
ג וְכָל־שָׂרֵי הַמְּדִינוֹת וְהָאֲחַשְׁדַּרְפְּנִים וְהַפַּחוֹת וְעֹשֵׂי הַמְּלָאכָה
אֲשֶׁר לַמֶּלֶךְ מְנַשְּׂאִים אֶת־הַיְּהוּדִים כִּי־נָפַל פַּחַד־מָרְדֳּכַי
ד עֲלֵיהֶם: כִּי־גָדוֹל מָרְדֳּכַי בְּבֵית הַמֶּלֶךְ וְשָׁמְעוֹ הוֹלֵךְ בְּכָל־
ה הַמְּדִינוֹת כִּי־הָאִישׁ מָרְדֳּכַי הוֹלֵךְ וְגָדוֹל: וַיַּכּוּ הַיְּהוּדִים
בְּכָל־אֹיְבֵיהֶם מַכַּת־חֶרֶב וְהֶרֶג וְאַבְדָן וַיַּעֲשׂוּ בְשֹׂנְאֵיהֶם
ו כִּרְצוֹנָם: וּבְשׁוּשַׁן הַבִּירָה הָרְגוּ הַיְּהוּדִים וְאַבֵּד ⟩ חֲמֵשׁ מֵאוֹת

וְאֵת ו	אִישׁ:
וְאֵת ו	ז פַּרְשַׁנְדָּתָא
וְאֵת ו	דַּלְפוֹן
וְאֵת ו	ח אַסְפָּתָא:
וְאֵת ו	פּוֹרָתָא
וְאֵת ו	אֲדַלְיָא
וְאֵת ו	ט אֲרִידָתָא:
וְאֵת ו	פַּרְמַשְׁתָּא
וְאֵת ו	אֲרִיסַי
וְאֵת ו	אֲרִידַי
עֲשֶׂרֶת ⟨	י וַיְזָתָא:

בְּנֵי הָמָן בֶּן־הַמְּדָתָא צֹרֵר הַיְּהוּדִים הָרָגוּ וּבַבִּזָּה לֹא שָׁלְחוּ אֶת־
יא יָדָם: בַּיּוֹם הַהוּא בָּא מִסְפַּר הַהֲרוּגִים בְּשׁוּשַׁן הַבִּירָה לִפְנֵי הַמֶּלֶךְ:
יב וַיֹּאמֶר הַמֶּלֶךְ לְאֶסְתֵּר הַמַּלְכָּה בְּשׁוּשַׁן הַבִּירָה הָרְגוּ הַיְּהוּדִים

effect, on the day when the Jews' enemies had hoped to overcome them – it all was turned around, as the Jews themselves overcame

2 those who hated them. The Jews came together in their cities throughout the provinces of King Aḥashverosh to lay hands upon those who sought their harm, and no man could stand before them,

3 for fear of them had fallen upon all nations. And the ministers of the provinces, the viceroys and the governors, and the administrators of the king's court, all promoted the Jews, for fear of Mordekhai had fallen

4 on them. For Mordekhai was great now in the king's palace, and word of him was spreading to all the provinces: this man, this Mordekhai,

5 was becoming ever greater. The Jews dealt all their enemies a terrible blow, of sword and slaughter and destruction; they did whatever

6 they pleased to those who hated them. In the imperial city of Shushan

7 the Jews killed and destroyed five hundred men, and they killed

Parshandata	and
Dalfon	and
8 Aspata	and
Porata	and
Adalya	and
9 Aridata	and
Parmashta	and
Arisai	and
Aridai	and
10 Vayzata,	the ten

sons of Haman son of Hamedata, enemy of the Jews – but they did not

11 touch the plunder. On that same day, the number of those killed in the

12 imperial city of Shushan was brought to the king, and the king said to Queen Esther, "The Jews have killed five hundred men in the imperial

וְאַבֵּד חֲמֵשׁ מֵאוֹת אִישׁ וְאֵת עֲשֶׂרֶת בְּנֵי־הָמָן בִּשְׁאָר מְדִינוֹת
הַמֶּלֶךְ מֶה עָשׂוּ וּמַה־שְּׁאֵלָתֵךְ וְיִנָּתֵן לָךְ וּמַה־בַּקָּשָׁתֵךְ עוֹד וְתֵעָשׂ:

יג וַתֹּאמֶר אֶסְתֵּר אִם־עַל־הַמֶּלֶךְ טוֹב יִנָּתֵן גַּם־מָחָר לַיְּהוּדִים אֲשֶׁר
בְּשׁוּשָׁן לַעֲשׂוֹת כְּדָת הַיּוֹם וְאֵת עֲשֶׂרֶת בְּנֵי־הָמָן יִתְלוּ עַל־הָעֵץ:

יד וַיֹּאמֶר הַמֶּלֶךְ לְהֵעָשׂוֹת כֵּן וַתִּנָּתֵן דָּת בְּשׁוּשָׁן וְאֵת עֲשֶׂרֶת בְּנֵי־

טו הָמָן תָּלוּ: וַיִּקָּהֲלוּ הַיְּהוּדִים אֲשֶׁר־בְּשׁוּשָׁן גַּם בְּיוֹם אַרְבָּעָה עָשָׂר הַיְּהוּדִים
לְחֹדֶשׁ אֲדָר וַיַּהַרְגוּ בְּשׁוּשָׁן שְׁלֹשׁ מֵאוֹת אִישׁ וּבַבִּזָּה לֹא שָׁלְחוּ

טז אֶת־יָדָם: וּשְׁאָר הַיְּהוּדִים אֲשֶׁר בִּמְדִינוֹת הַמֶּלֶךְ נִקְהֲלוּ ׀ וְעָמֹד
עַל־נַפְשָׁם וְנוֹחַ מֵאֹיְבֵיהֶם וְהָרֹג בְּשֹׂנְאֵיהֶם חֲמִשָּׁה וְשִׁבְעִים אָלֶף

יז וּבַבִּזָּה לֹא שָׁלְחוּ אֶת־יָדָם: בְּיוֹם־שְׁלוֹשָׁה עָשָׂר לְחֹדֶשׁ אֲדָר וְנוֹחַ

יח בְּאַרְבָּעָה עָשָׂר בּוֹ וְעָשֹׂה אֹתוֹ יוֹם מִשְׁתֶּה וְשִׂמְחָה: וְהַיְּהוּדִיים וְהַיְּהוּדִים
אֲשֶׁר־בְּשׁוּשָׁן נִקְהֲלוּ בִּשְׁלוֹשָׁה עָשָׂר בּוֹ וּבְאַרְבָּעָה עָשָׂר בּוֹ וְנוֹחַ

יט בַּחֲמִשָּׁה עָשָׂר בּוֹ וְעָשֹׂה אֹתוֹ יוֹם מִשְׁתֶּה וְשִׂמְחָה: עַל־כֵּן הַיְּהוּדִים
הַפְּרוֹזִים הַיֹּשְׁבִים בְּעָרֵי הַפְּרָזוֹת עֹשִׂים אֵת יוֹם אַרְבָּעָה עָשָׂר הַפְּרָזִים
לְחֹדֶשׁ אֲדָר שִׂמְחָה וּמִשְׁתֶּה וְיוֹם טוֹב וּמִשְׁלֹחַ מָנוֹת אִישׁ לְרֵעֵהוּ:

כ וַיִּכְתֹּב מָרְדֳּכַי אֶת־הַדְּבָרִים הָאֵלֶּה וַיִּשְׁלַח סְפָרִים אֶל־כָּל־
הַיְּהוּדִים אֲשֶׁר בְּכָל־מְדִינוֹת הַמֶּלֶךְ אֲחַשְׁוֵרוֹשׁ הַקְּרוֹבִים

כא וְהָרְחוֹקִים: לְקַיֵּם עֲלֵיהֶם לִהְיוֹת עֹשִׂים אֵת יוֹם אַרְבָּעָה עָשָׂר

כב לְחֹדֶשׁ אֲדָר וְאֵת יוֹם־חֲמִשָּׁה עָשָׂר בּוֹ בְּכָל־שָׁנָה וְשָׁנָה: כַּיָּמִים
אֲשֶׁר־נָחוּ בָהֶם הַיְּהוּדִים מֵאֹיְבֵיהֶם וְהַחֹדֶשׁ אֲשֶׁר נֶהְפַּךְ לָהֶם
מִיָּגוֹן לְשִׂמְחָה וּמֵאֵבֶל לְיוֹם טוֹב לַעֲשׂוֹת אוֹתָם יְמֵי מִשְׁתֶּה
וְשִׂמְחָה וּמִשְׁלֹחַ מָנוֹת אִישׁ לְרֵעֵהוּ וּמַתָּנוֹת לָאֶבְיֹנִים:

כג וַיְקַבֵּל הַיְּהוּדִים אֵת אֲשֶׁר־הֵחֵלּוּ לַעֲשׂוֹת וְאֵת אֲשֶׁר־כָּתַב מָרְדֳּכַי

כד אֲלֵיהֶם: כִּי הָמָן בֶּן־הַמְּדָתָא הָאֲגָגִי צֹרֵר כָּל־הַיְּהוּדִים חָשַׁב עַל־

כה הַיְּהוּדִים לְאַבְּדָם וְהִפִּל פּוּר הוּא הַגּוֹרָל לְהֻמָּם וּלְאַבְּדָם: וּבְבֹאָהּ
לִפְנֵי הַמֶּלֶךְ אָמַר עִם־הַסֵּפֶר יָשׁוּב מַחֲשַׁבְתּוֹ הָרָעָה אֲשֶׁר־חָשַׁב

394

city of Shushan alone, as well as Haman's ten sons – what must they have done in the rest of the king's provinces? And now, what is your desire? It shall be yours. What would you ask further? It shall be done."

13 Esther said, "If it so please the king, may the Jews of Shushan be granted tomorrow also to do as they did today, and let Haman's ten sons be

14 hung from the post." Thus the king commanded; the law was laid down

15 in Shushan, and Haman's ten sons were hung up. And the Jews of Shushan gathered on the fourteenth day of Adar also and killed three

16 hundred men in Shushan, never once touching the plunder. Meanwhile, the rest of the Jews in the king's provinces, having come together and stood up to defend their lives, found rest from their enemies, killing seventy-five thousand of those who hated them, though they did not

17 touch the plunder. That was on the thirteenth day of the month of Adar. On the fourteenth day they rested, and they made it a day of feasting

18 and happiness. The Jews who were in Shushan came together both on the thirteenth and on the fourteenth, and rested on the fifteenth, and

19 made that a day of feasting and happiness. Thus it came about that provincial Jews living in unwalled towns make the fourteenth day of the month of Adar a day of happiness, of feasting and festivity, and of

20 sending one another good things to eat. Mordekhai wrote all this down and sent scrolls to all the Jews in all the provinces of King Aḥashverosh,

21 near and far, to establish among them that they should mark the

22 fourteenth and fifteenth days of Adar every single year: the days when the Jews rested from their enemies and the month that was turned for them from sorrow to happiness, from mourning to celebration – to make them days of feasting, happiness, sending one another good

23 things to eat, and giving gifts to the poor. And so the Jews accepted upon themselves what they had already begun to perform and all that

24 Mordekhai had written to them. For Haman son of Hamedata the Agagite, enemy of all the Jews, had plotted against the Jews to destroy them, and had drawn the *pur* – lots – to consume and to destroy them.

25 When this came before the king, he declared by the scroll that the evil plot Haman had hatched against the Jews must come down upon his

כב עַל־הַיְּהוּדִים עַל־רֹאשׁוֹ וְתָלוּ אֹתוֹ וְאֶת־בָּנָיו עַל־הָעֵץ: עַל־כֵּן
קָרְאוּ לַיָּמִים הָאֵלֶּה פוּרִים עַל־שֵׁם הַפּוּר עַל־כֵּן עַל־כָּל־דִּבְרֵי

כג הָאִגֶּרֶת הַזֹּאת וּמָה־רָאוּ עַל־כָּכָה וּמָה הִגִּיעַ אֲלֵיהֶם: קִיְּמוּ וְקִבְּל
הַיְּהוּדִים ׀ עֲלֵיהֶם ׀ וְעַל־זַרְעָם וְעַל כָּל־הַנִּלְוִים עֲלֵיהֶם וְלֹא יַעֲבוֹר
לִהְיוֹת עֹשִׂים אֵת שְׁנֵי הַיָּמִים הָאֵלֶּה כִּכְתָבָם וְכִזְמַנָּם בְּכָל־שָׁנָה

כד וְשָׁנָה: וְהַיָּמִים הָאֵלֶּה נִזְכָּרִים וְנַעֲשִׂים בְּכָל־דּוֹר וָדוֹר מִשְׁפָּחָה
וּמִשְׁפָּחָה מְדִינָה וּמְדִינָה וְעִיר וָעִיר וִימֵי הַפּוּרִים הָאֵלֶּה לֹא יַעַבְרוּ

כה מִתּוֹךְ הַיְּהוּדִים וְזִכְרָם לֹא־יָסוּף מִזַּרְעָם: וַתִּכְתֹּב
אֶסְתֵּר הַמַּלְכָּה בַת־אֲבִיחַיִל וּמָרְדֳּכַי הַיְּהוּדִי אֶת־כָּל־תֹּקֶף לְקַיֵּם

ל אֵת אִגֶּרֶת הַפֻּרִים הַזֹּאת הַשֵּׁנִית: וַיִּשְׁלַח סְפָרִים אֶל־כָּל־הַיְּהוּדִים
אֶל־שֶׁבַע וְעֶשְׂרִים וּמֵאָה מְדִינָה מַלְכוּת אֲחַשְׁוֵרוֹשׁ דִּבְרֵי שָׁלוֹם

לא וֶאֱמֶת: לְקַיֵּם אֶת־יְמֵי הַפֻּרִים הָאֵלֶּה בִּזְמַנֵּיהֶם כַּאֲשֶׁר קִיַּם עֲלֵיהֶם
מָרְדֳּכַי הַיְּהוּדִי וְאֶסְתֵּר הַמַּלְכָּה וְכַאֲשֶׁר קִיְּמוּ עַל־נַפְשָׁם וְעַל־

לב זַרְעָם דִּבְרֵי הַצּוֹמוֹת וְזַעֲקָתָם: וּמַאֲמַר אֶסְתֵּר קִיַּם דִּבְרֵי הַפֻּרִים
הָאֵלֶּה וְנִכְתָּב בַּסֵּפֶר: וַיָּשֶׂם הַמֶּלֶךְ ׀ אֲחַשְׁרֹשׁ ׀ מַס אֲחַשְׁוֵרוֹשׁ י א

ב עַל־הָאָרֶץ וְאִיֵּי הַיָּם: וְכָל־מַעֲשֵׂה תָקְפּוֹ וּגְבוּרָתוֹ וּפָרָשַׁת גְּדֻלַּת
מָרְדֳּכַי אֲשֶׁר גִּדְּלוֹ הַמֶּלֶךְ הֲלוֹא־הֵם כְּתוּבִים עַל־סֵפֶר דִּבְרֵי הַיָּמִים

ג לְמַלְכֵי מָדַי וּפָרָס: > כִּי ׀ מָרְדֳּכַי הַיְּהוּדִי מִשְׁנֶה לַמֶּלֶךְ אֲחַשְׁוֵרוֹשׁ
וְגָדוֹל לַיְּהוּדִים וְרָצוּי לְרֹב אֶחָיו דֹּרֵשׁ טוֹב לְעַמּוֹ וְדֹבֵר שָׁלוֹם
לְכָל־זַרְעוֹ: *

26 own head, and that he and his sons must be hung from the post. So these days were named Purim after the *pur*. So, following the words of
27 the letter and what they had seen and what had befallen them, they established and accepted, for themselves and for their children, and for all who would ever come to join their ranks, that they would keep these two days, never to be neglected, as they are prescribed and at the right
28 times, every single year. Indeed, these days are remembered and marked in every single generation, family by family, province upon province, town upon town; and these days of Purim will never be neglected by the Jews, nor will their memory ever cease to be among
29 their children.   And Queen Esther daughter of Aviḥayil, together with Mordekhai the Jew, wrote with all their authority to
30 confirm this second letter of Purim. They sent out scrolls to all the Jews across 127 provinces – all of Aḥashverosh's realm – words of peace and
31 truth. The scrolls were to confirm these days of Purim in their times just as Mordekhai the Jew and Esther the queen had fixed them, and indeed as they had all fixed their fast days and entreaties, for themselves
32 and for their children. Esther's words confirmed this practice of Purim,
10 1 and it was written down in the scroll.   As for King Aḥashverosh, he levied a tribute from the people of all the land and of the islands of
2 the sea. And the full account of his authority and might, and all the greatness of Mordekhai, whom the king exalted – are they not already written in the scroll of the chronicles of the kings of Media and Persia?
3 For Mordekhai the Jew was second in command to King Aḥashverosh and revered too among the Jews – beloved of all the multitudes of his brothers, working for the good of his people, and speaking words of peace for all his children.

The fonts used in this book are from the Arno family